The Internet in Indonesia's New Democracy

The Internet in Indonesia's New Democracy is a detailed study of the political and cultural practices surrounding the provision and consumption of the Internet in Indonesia at the turn of the twenty-first century. Hill and Sen detail the emergence of the Internet into Indonesia in the mid-1990s, and cover its growth through the dramatic economic and political crises of 1997–98 and the subsequent transition to democracy.

Conceptually, the Internet is seen as a global phenomenon, with global implications; however, this book develops a way of thinking about the Internet within the limits of geo-political categories of nations and provinces. The political turmoil in Indonesia provides a unique context in which to understand the specific local and national consequences of a global and universal technology.

David T. Hill is Professor of Southeast Asian Studies and Fellow of the Asia Research Centre at Murdoch University, Western Australia.

Krishna Sen is Professor of Asian Media and Director of the Media Asia Research Group at Curtin University of Technology, Perth, Western Australia.

Asia's Transformations

Edited by Mark Selden

Binghamton and Cornell Universities, USA

The books in this series explore the political, social, economic and cultural consequences of Asia's transformations in the twentieth and twenty-first centuries. The series emphasises the tumultuous interplay of local, national, regional and global forces as Asia bids to become the hub of the world economy. While focussing on the contemporary, it also looks back to analyse the antecedents of Asia's contested rise. This series comprises several strands:

Asia's Transformations aims to address the needs of students and teachers, and the titles will be published in hardback and paperback. Titles include:

China in War and Revolution, 1895–1949
Peter Zarrow

Confronting the Bush Doctrine
Critical views from the Asia-Pacific
Edited by Mel Gurtov and Peter Van Ness

Japan's Quiet Transformation
Social Change and Civil Society in the twenty-first century
Jeff Kingston

State and Society in Twenty-first-century China
Edited by Peter Hays Gries and Stanley Rosen

The Battle for Asia
From decolonization to globalization
Mark T. Berger

Ethnicity in Asia
Edited by Colin Mackerras

Chinese Society, second edition
Change, conflict and resistance
Edited by Elizabeth J. Perry and Mark Selden

The Resurgence of East Asia
500, 150 and 50 year perspectives
Edited by Giovanni Arrighi, Takeshi Hamashita and Mark Selden

The Making of Modern Korea
Adrian Buzo

Korean Society
Civil society, democracy and the state
Edited by Charles K. Armstrong

Remaking the Chinese State
Strategies, society and security
Edited by Chien-min Chao and Bruce J. Dickson

Mao's Children in the New China
Voices from the Red Guard generation
Yarong Jiang and David Ashley

Chinese Society
Change, conflict and resistance
Edited by Elizabeth J. Perry and Mark Selden

Opium, Empire and the Global Political Economy
Carl A. Trocki

Japan's Comfort Women
Sexual slavery and prostitution during World War II and the US occupation
Yuki Tanaka

Debating Human Rights
Critical essays from the United States and Asia
Edited by Peter Van Ness

Hong Kong's History
State and society under colonial rule
Edited by Tak-Wing Ngo

Asia's Great Cities
Each volume aims to capture the heartbeat of the contemporary city from multiple perspectives emblematic of the authors' own deep familiarity with the distinctive faces of the city, its history, society, culture, politics and economics, and its evolving position in national, regional and global frameworks. While most volumes emphasise urban developments since the Second World War, some pay close attention to the legacy of the longue durée in shaping the contemporary. Thematic and comparative volumes address such themes as urbanisation, economic and financial linkages, architecture and space, wealth and power, gendered relationships, planning and anarchy, and ethnographies in national and regional perspective. Titles include:

Singapore
Wealth, power and the culure of control
Carl A. Trocki

Representing Calcutta
Modernity, nationalism and the colonial uncanny
Swati Chattopadhyay

Hong Kong
Global city
Stephen Chiu and Tai-Lok Lui

Shanghai
Global city
Jeff Wasserstrom

Beijing in the Modern World
David Strand and Madeline Yue Dong

Bangkok
Place, practice and representation
Marc Askew

Asia.com is a series which focusses on the ways in which new information and communication technologies are influencing politics, society and culture in Asia. Titles include:

The Internet in Indonesia's New Democracy
David T. Hill and Krishna Sen

Asia.com
Asia encounters the Internet
Edited by K. C. Ho, Randolph Kluver and Kenneth C. C. Yang

Japanese Cybercultures
Edited by Mark McLelland and Nanette Gottlieb

Literature and Society is a series that seeks to demonstrate the ways in which Asian literature is influenced by the politics, society and culture in which it is produced. Titles include:

Chinese Women Writers and the Feminist Imagination (1905–1945)
Haiping Yan

The Body in Postwar Japanese Fiction
Edited by Douglas N. Slaymaker

Routledge Studies in Asia's Transformations is a forum for innovative new research intended for a high-level specialist readership, and the titles will be available in hardback only. Titles include:

1. **Fertility, Family Planning and Population Control in China**
Edited by Dudley L. Poston, Che-fu Lee, Chiung-Fang Chang, Sherry L. McKibben and Carol S. Walther

2. **Genders, Transgenders and Sexualities in Japan**
Edited by Mark McLelland and Romit Dasgupta

3. **Developmental Dilemmas**
Land reform and institutional change in China
Edited by Peter Ho

4. **Japanese Industrial Governance**
Protectionism and the licensing state
Yul Sohn

5. **Remaking Citizenship in Hong Kong**
Community, nation and the global city
Edited by Agnes S. Ku and Ngai Pun

6. **Chinese Media, Global Contexts**
Edited by Chin-Chuan Lee

7. **Imperialism in South East Asia**
'A fleeting, passing phase'
Nicholas Tarling

8. **Internationalizing the Pacific**
The United States, Japan and the Institute of Pacific Relations in war and peace, 1919–1945
Tomoko Akami

9. **Koreans in Japan**
Critical voices from the margin
Edited by Sonia Ryang

10. **The American Occupation of Japan and Okinawa***
Literature and memory
Michael Molasky

* Now available in paperback

Critical Asian Scholarship is a series intended to showcase the most important individual contributions to scholarship in Asian Studies. Each of the volumes presents a leading Asian scholar addressing themes that are central to his or her most significant and lasting contribution to Asian studies. The series is committed to the rich variety of research and writing on Asia, and is not restricted to any particular discipline, theoretical approach or geographical expertise.

China's Past, China's Future
Energy, food, environment
Vaclav Smil

China Unbound
Evolving perspectives on the Chinese past
Paul A. Cohen

Women and the Family in Chinese History
Patricia Buckley Ebrey

Southeast Asia
A testament
George McT. Kahin

The Internet in Indonesia's New Democracy

David T. Hill and Krishna Sen

Routledge
Taylor & Francis Group
LONDON AND NEW YORK

First published 2005
by Routledge
2 Park Square, Milton Park, Abingdon, Oxon OX14 4RN

Simultaneously published in the USA and Canada
by Routledge
270 Madison Ave, New York, NY 10016

Routledge is an imprint of the Taylor & Francis Group

Transferred to Digital Printing 2005

Typeset in Times New Roman by Bookcraft Ltd, Stroud, Gloucestershire

British Library Cataloguing in Publication Data
A catalogue record for this book is available from the British Library

Library of Congress Cataloging in Publication Data
Hill, David T.
The Internet in Indonesia's new democracy / David T. Hill, Krishna Sen. – 1st ed.
p. cm. – (Asia's transformations)
Includes bibliographical references and index.
1. Political participation – Technological innovations – Indonesia.
2. Internet–Political aspects – Indonesia. 3. Democratization – Indonesia.
I. Sen, Krishna, 1954– II. Title. III. Series.
JQ776.H56 2005
303.48'33'09598–dc22 2004023614

ISBN 0–415–28564–X

Contents

List of tables

Acknowledgements

No book of this kind is the product simply of the authors. Our ability to compile this work is the result of the help of countless colleagues and friends, going back to our initial interest in the Internet in Indonesia, stimulated by a period living in Yogyakarta in 1996. For enabling us to spend this period in Indonesia, and for welcoming us on several occasions since, our thanks go to Professor Ichlasul Amal and the staff of Gadjah Mada University.

We depended heavily on explanations and guidance from many friends and acquaintances, in Indonesia and Australia, to help us understand the technology and how it worked. Often this help came in electronic form from individuals we have never met: responses from Internet café owners across Indonesia to e-mailed questions; postings on the 'Indonesian_internet' Yahoo! list from a community of researchers with shared interests; responses to queries we put to individual posters on local government websites.

There are some to whom particular debts are acknowledged. Our work in this book and our understanding of the Internet in Indonesia more generally rely on the pioneering work of Onno W. Purbo, who over several years has generously shared his own research and writings with us. Onno participated in a conference convened by Krishna at Curtin University of Technology, Western Australia, in February 2002, and kindly left with us a stack of CDs filled with his voluminous writings, all of which he makes publicly available on the net as part of his commitment to the concept of open-source 'copy-left', not copyright, materials! As an acknowledgement of the inspiration he has been to so many and of the tireless work he has done to promote affordable and equitable Internet access in Indonesia, this book is dedicated to Onno W. Purbo and the cyberactivists of Indonesia.

This research would have been impossible had it not been for funding support from the Australian Research Council. At a time when research funding for Australian universities is increasingly scarce, we appreciate the support of the ARC – virtually the only substantial source of research funding for Humanities and Social Sciences in Australia – for our work over many years.

Our work has gained enormously from the presence of the Asia Research Centre at Murdoch University, under both the previous director, Richard Robison, and the current head, Garry Rodan. For more than a decade, the Centre has contributed significantly to research on contemporary Asia and has provided much of the intellectual environment within which the book has been composed. For snippets of material and his stimulating collegial discussions – and disagreements – about the Internet in Indonesia while he was engaged in writing his own book at the Centre, our thanks go also to Max Lane.

Harry and Melanie Bhaskara and Bwee Wisuda have provided us with a depth of friendship that has made our time in Indonesia a delight. We have imposed upon their generous hospitality and benefited from their insights over countless meals together.

At various times during this project, we have benefited from the research assistance of Wendy Sahanaya and Penny Coutas. Wendy's attention to fine detail and Penny's painstaking explanation of the mysteries of high technology have been much appreciated.

As the Jakarta Regional Officer of the National Library of Australia, Oliver Mann has demonstrated yet again the tremendous benefit of having a devoted and highly skilled librarian in Jakarta overseeing the collection of materials for Australian libraries. Beyond that, we were constantly amazed to receive clippings in the post, or an e-mail note, drawing our attention to some item Oliver had come across in the course of his work. That he went so far beyond the definition of his job, ever conscious of our particular research interests, amazed us.

Rene L. Pattiradjawane and the staff at the *Kompas* newspaper (following the paper's tradition of supporting researchers) gave us very helpful advice very early in our project on both sources and Internet applications generally. More generally, our many friends in the Indonesian media – too many to mention individually – over more than two decades, have always supported our endeavours with encouragement and ideas. These include friends in the Alliance of Independent Journalists (AJI), the Institute for the Free Flow of Information (ISAI) and the Institute for the Study of Press and Development (LSPP), but there were many others also.

We make particular mention of the help given by Charles Scheiner, who provided extensive assistance with the chapter on East Timor, reading early drafts, and clarifying and correcting our misunderstandings.

We also acknowledge the permission to use some material previously published, in earlier versions, as articles in the following journals: *Indonesia*, *The Pacific Review*, *Asian Studies Review* and *South East Asia Research*.

When academics take time away from teaching responsibilities to undertake research, they necessarily impose upon over-worked colleagues to take over some of their duties. For colleagues to pick up such extra tasks is a major imposition. For this, David would like to thank his colleagues in Asian Studies at Murdoch University (particularly the Head of Programme, Radha Krishnan, and Irianto Tedja, who took on extensive teaching duties during the writing of this book), as well as David Armstrong and David Reeve, for their good-humoured preparedness to take on extra administrative tasks in the Australian Consortium for 'In-Country' Indonesian Studies (ACICIS).

Similarly, Krishna would like to thank her colleagues in the Department of Media and Information at Curtin University of Technology. She would also like to thank Professor Tom Stannage for his constant support throughout her time at Curtin.

Writing a book is hard work. Writing a book with another person, while it lightens some of the load, is a constant – often tense – process of negotiation and compromise. Attempting this while living with your co-author can be fraught with problems. But even more stressful is living with two people who are writing a book together! Our daughter Su-mita has endured two such books and spent most of her life listening to her parents discuss their projects over the communal table. For the past four years, this book has dominated the life of our family and was factored into virtually all scheduling of activities. It has been an unfair imposition and Su-mita has foregone more than could reasonably have been expected of her, while continuing to delight her parents as they watch her grow from a child (who went on her first 'field trip' at three months!) to a teenager with her own autonomous view of the world.

Abbreviations and Indonesian terms

AAAS	American Association for the Advancement of Science
ABRI	Indonesian Armed Forces
AJI	Alliance of Independent Journalists (Alliansi Jurnalis Independen)
AM	amplitude modulation (radio)
apakabar	mailing list
APC	Association for Progressive Communications
APJII	Association of Indonesian Internet Service Providers
ASAP	Action in Solidarity with Asia and the Pacific
ASEAN	Association of Southeast Asian Nations
ASIET	Action in Solidarity with Indonesia and East Timor
AWARI	Indonesian Internet Kiosk Association
AWAYO	Yogyakarta Internet Kiosk Association
BakuBae	reconciliation movement in Ambon
BBS	bulletin board system
BNI	Indonesian State Bank
BPIS	Strategic Industries Agency
BPPT	Bureau for the Assessment and Application of Technology
BPS	Central Bureau of Statistics
bps	bytes per second
BRI	Indonesian People's Bank
BSF/LSF	Board (later Institute) of Film Censorship
bupati	district heads
CCDA	Crisis Centre of the Diocese of Ambon
ccTLD	Country Code Top Level Domain (for example, '.id' for 'Indonesia')
CERN	European Laboratory for Particle Physics
CIDA	Canadian International Development Agency
CIET	Campaign for an Independent East Timor
CNRM	National Council of the Maubere Resistance
CNRT	National Council of Timorese Resistance
Deparpostel	Department of Tourism, Post and Telecommunications
Deppen	Department of Information

DPD	House of Regional Representatives
DPR	People's Representative Council
E-LAW	Environmental Law Alliance Worldwide
ETAN(/US)	East Timor Action Network
ETTA	East Timor Transitional Administration
FICA	Federation of Indonesian Christians in America
FKAWJ	Communication Forum of the Followers of the *Sunnah* and the Community of the Prophet
FKKI	Indonesian Christian Communication Forum
FKM	Moluccan Sovereignty Front
FKSMI	Jakarta Student Senate Communication Forum
FM	frequency modulation (radio)
Forkot	City Forum (Forum Komunitas Mahasiswa se-Jabotabek) students' organisation
golkar	functional groups (political party)
HMI	Islamic Students' Association
HPMA	American–Moluccan Friendship Association
HTML	hyper-text markup language
HTTP	hyper-text transfer protocol
Hukum Acara Pidana	Criminal Code
I2BC	Indonesia Internet Business Community
IANA	Internet Assigned Number Authority
ICMI	Indonesian Muslim Intellectuals' Association
ICT	information and communication technology
IFES	International Foundation for Election Systems
IFET	International Federation for East Timor
IGC	Institute for Global Communications
IID	Initiatives for International Dialogue (Philippines-based NGO)
IIX	Indonesia Internet eXchange
IMF	International Monetary Fund
IMT	Indonesia Media Technologies
INFID	International NGO Forum for Indonesian Development
Infight	Indonesian Front for the Defence of Human Rights
InterFET	International Force for East Timor
IPB	Bogor Agricultural Institute
ISAI	Institute for the Free Flow of Information
ISP	Internet Service Provider
ITB	Bandung Institute of Technology
ITS	Surabaya Institute of Technology
ITU	International Telecommunications Union
JAKER	People's Art Network
JCDET	Joint Committee for the Defence of the East Timorese
JOMC	Joint Operations and Media Centre (in the 1999 elections)
kabupaten	administrative district (residency)

Kbps	Kilobytes per second
KdP	*News from PIJAR* periodical
kecamatan	sub-district
KIPP	Independent Election Monitoring Committee
KKN	corruption, collusion and nepotism
KMNRT	Office of the Minister of State for Research and Technology
Komnas HAM	National Commission on Human Rights
Kopkamtib	Command for the Restoration of Security and Order
Koti	Supreme Operations Command
KPU	General Election Commission
KTP	citizen's identity card
LAPAN	Indonesian Aeronautics and Space Institute
Laskar Jihad	Holy War Brigade
LBH	Legal Aid Institute
LPHAM	Institute to Uphold Human Rights
LPU	General Election Board
LSPP	Institute for the Study of Press and Development
MMC	Maluku Media Centre
MPR	People's Consultative Assembly
Mbps	Megabytes per second
MSF	Médecins Sans Frontières
NAMFREL	National Citizens' Movement for Free Elections
NDI	National Democratic Institute for International Affairs
NGO	non-governmental organisation
PAN	National Mandate Party
P3TIE	Centre for the Study and Application of Information Technology and Electronics
PBB	Moon and Star Party
PC	personal computer
PDI	Indonesian Democratic Party
PDI-P	Indonesian Democratic Party of Struggle
pemuda	(revolutionary) youth
PGI	Federation of Indonesian Churches
PGP	Pretty Good Privacy (encryption programme)
PIJAR	Centre for Information and Reform Action Network
PKB	National Awakening Party
PKI	Indonesian Communist Party
PPBI	Indonesian Centre for Labour Struggle
PPI	Indonesian Election Committee
PPP	Development Unity Party
PRD	Democratic People's Party
preman	hoodlums, petty criminals
PRSSNI	Indonesian Commercial Radio Broadcasters' Association
PWI	Association of Indonesian Journalists
RENETIL	National Resistance of East Timorese Students

RMS	Republic of South Moluccas
RRI	Radio of the Republic of Indonesia
SARA	ethnic (*Suku*), religious (*Agama*), racial (*Ras*) or inter-class (*Antar golongan*) tensions
SIC	printing permit
SISFONAS	National Information System
Siskohat	Integrated Pilgrimage Computerisation System
SIT	publication permit
SIUPP	permit for a press publication enterprise
SME	small and medium enterprises
SMID	Students in Solidarity with Democracy in Indonesia
SMS	Short Message Service (mobile phone text message)
SOMET	Safety Office for Media in East Timor
SPRED	SMS Programme for Retrieving Electronic Data
SPRIM	Indonesian People's Solidarity Struggle with the Maubere People
SRD	Jakata People's Union
SRS	Solo People's Union
STN	National Peasants' Union
Syari'ah	Islamic Law
TAPOL	Indonesia Human Rights Campaign
TCP/IP	transmission control protocol/Internet protocol
TNI	Indonesian National Army
TVRI	Television of the Republic of Indonesia
UGM	Gadjah Mada University, Yogyakarta
UHF	ultra high frequency (television)
UKM	small and medium enterprises
ummat	religious community
UNAMET	United Nations Mission in East Timor
UNDP	United Nations Development Programme
UNESCO	United Nations Education, Scientific and Cultural Organisation
UNFREL	University Network for a Free and Fair Election
URL	uniform resource locator (website address)
VoIP	voice-over Internet protocol, using Internet connections to make telephone calls
WALHI	Indonesian Environmental Forum
warintek	technology and information kiosk
warnet	Internet café or kiosk
wartel	telephone kiosk
wartelnet	Internet telecommunication kiosk
WWW	World Wide Web
YLBHI	Indonesian Legal Aid Foundation

Explanatory notes

Indonesian names: Indonesians may be known by single (for example, Sukarno) or multiple names (for example, Onno W. Purbo). The final (or sole) common name has been used for bibliographical purposes (although the individual may not ordinarily be known by that name in Indonesia).

Indonesian spelling: The Indonesian language has used various spelling systems, with the remnants of former systems still reflected in some common names. We have generally used the post-1972 system (known as 'EYD') for common names: for example, using 'Suharto' rather than 'Soeharto'. We have made occasional exceptions where individuals appear to have indicated strong preference for alternative (pre-1972) spellings.

Internet measurements: Internet content is measured in binary digits (0 or 1) called 'bits', with eight bits equal to one byte, 1,000 bytes in a 'kilobyte' (Kb), 1,000 Kb in a megabyte (Mb), and so on. Speed is measured in units per second (for example, Kbps).

Internet sites: There is no guarantee that Internet sites listed in this book remain in existence. One method of tracking defunct sites is via the Web Archive, <www.archive.org/web/web.php> (accessed 7 June 2004).

1 The global information highway in a national context

It is difficult to talk about the Indonesian Internet or the Indonesian 'World Wide Web' (WWW) as one talks about other national media. The Indonesian limits we are trying to impose here on our study of the Internet and WWW, which are by definition global, are much less self-evident than notions of other national media such as Indonesian cinema or the Indonesian press or television.[1] Even our attempt to talk about the Internet *in* Indonesia is imprecise as some of the groups and individuals who enter the bit of cyberspace on which we are focussed are not necessarily *in* Indonesia or *Indonesian* by any legal or ethnic criteria. We have therefore set boundaries for this study not by defining what is 'Indonesian' on the net, but in identifying online activities that are overtly connected to street demonstrations, parliamentary debates and other material sites of Indonesian political life. Such analysis is necessarily based on assumptions emerging out of Indonesian studies about the fall of Suharto and its aftermath on the one hand and theories of the connections between media and politics on the other. The rest of this chapter is an attempt to lay bare those assumptions.

At its most concrete this book charts the growth and specific political uses of the Internet across the Indonesian archipelago since the early 1990s. At its broadest it is about the relation between democratisation and new computer-mediated communication systems, the Internet and the World Wide Web. These concerns are linked by events in the 1990s. Indonesia's rush to join the information superhighway of the Internet began in earnest in 1996. Two years later, Asia's oldest authoritarian government, led for over thirty years by General Suharto, collapsed. Our research was driven by the need to investigate the much-vaunted democratic potential of the Internet and related technologies (e-mail, WWW) and to understand how (if at all) the medium could be (and was being) mobilised against an authoritarian regime and the political legacy it left behind.

For quite different reasons, both amongst scholars of the Internet and amongst those of Indonesia, the euphoria about impending freedom and equality has now given way to more precise, more guarded and empirical questions about types of governance, their processes and their institutions. In Internet studies, more and more empirical work is suggesting that the impact of this technology (like those that have gone before it) is likely to be determined in large measure by the specificities of social and political contexts both in the capitalist west[2] and in the various authoritarian and transitional nations around the globe.[3] The naïve faith in the Internet's capacity to evade surveillance has been eroded in the face of governments' demonstrated capacity to prosecute and imprison people on the basis of their online activities.[4] In Indonesia, the end of authoritarianism has been marked by a free media and an elected parliament (important signifiers of democracy) and at the same time by continuing corruption and militarism (legacies of Suharto's New Order), and ethnic and religious violence has intensified, leading to fears of national disintegration. Our work on the Internet and democracy in Indonesia is broadly aligned to these post-euphoric, though not necessarily pessimistic, readings of the Internet's capacity to facilitate Indonesia's journey towards a pluralist democracy.

Political transition in Indonesia

Major-General Suharto, the strongman who dominated Indonesian politics for more than three decades, began his ascendancy to power on 1 October 1965.[5] On 16 October, President Sukarno reluctantly installed him as Commander of the Army and Chief of Staff of the Supreme Operations Command (Koti).[6] Gradually entrenching his grip on power and effectively placing Sukarno under house arrest, Suharto became Acting President in March 1967 and was invested as full President in March the following year. On 21 May 1998, 31 years after assuming the presidency, Suharto read out his brief resignation, broadcast live around the world, handing over the presidential office to his deputy, a civilian engineer with no independent power base, B.J. Habibie.[7]

Suharto's self-proclaimed 'New Order' presided over substantial economic growth, a growing middle class and expansion of the education system on the one hand, and corruption, nepotism and systematic repression of dissent on the other. For most political analysts the New Order's demise began with widespread Jakarta riots following the regime-backed attack on the headquarters of the opposition Indonesian Democratic Party (Partai Demokrasi Indonesia, PDI) on 27 July 1996. The government had earlier intervened in the activities of the PDI, one of two notionally 'opposition' parties, ousting the elected leader, Megawati Sukarnoputri (daughter of first president Sukarno), and replacing her with a government-backed appointee. On 27 July, after months of stalemate as the government attempted to isolate and neutralise Megawati, hoodlums (*preman*) mobilised by military officers attacked the PDI's Jakarta headquarters to wrest it from Megawati's supporters. The attack resulted in at least two deaths with more than 180 injured, and unleashed a public outpouring of anger and resentment at the New Order on a scale unseen since 1974.[8] The resulting vandalism, havoc and looting spilled down the main boulevards of the capital, and was graphically captured by both domestic and international media.

Many economists mark the decline in the New Order from the beginning of the Asian financial crisis, triggered by the collapse of the Thai financial sector and the floating of the Thai *baht* in July 1997, which rapidly wiped out years of growth when its reverberations struck Indonesia. Others stress deeper roots of problems in crony capitalism, corruption and nepotism. The rupiah plummeted against the US dollar (from about 2,500 rupiah in August 1997 to 17,000 rupiah in January 1998), leaving few companies able to service foreign debts, particularly on short-term loans.[9] The domestic financial system was unable to cope, and public confidence was severely undermined by the forced closure of 16 banks on 1 November 1997. In effect, 'every modern enterprise in the nation was bankrupt, the savings of the middle class were wiped out and labourers were thrown out of work by the millions'.[10] Suharto agreed to several bailout packages with the International Monetary Fund (IMF), then reneged, as the economy continued into free fall.[11]

The opening months of 1998 brought worsening riots over rising food prices. Despite this, and despite his failure to identify policies to cope with the worst economic crisis since his accession to power, Suharto nonetheless succeeded in March 1998 in engineering his re-election for a seventh presidential term by the 'upper house' (People's Consultative Assembly, Majelis Permusyawaratan Rakyat, MPR), which had done little apart from ritually re-anoint Suharto every five years. Suharto's re-election and his newly selected cabinet (stacked with his daughter, cronies and protégé B.J. Habibie as Vice-President) failed to placate international markets or Indonesian dissidents.[12] Demonstrations erupted on 'almost all Indonesian universities and other institutions of higher education, throughout the length and breadth of the archipelago', as popular support for the protests intensified and their frequency increased.[13] Clashes between demonstrators and security forces led to deaths around the country, including most dramatically the sniper killing of four students at Trisakti University in Jakarta on 12 May, which triggered Indonesia's most extensive riots ever around Jakarta in the days after 14 May. Unrest followed in Surabaya, Solo and elsewhere.[14]

Most studies suggest that on the one hand Suharto's elaborate and corrupt power structure collapsed from within; and that on the other hand the movement for democracy (more than just the resignation of a particular ruler) was, in the main, an urban one, led by students and the professional middle classes.[15] In an early study of the fall of Suharto, Aspinall posits four key political actors whose actions were crucial in the political transition: Suharto himself, the urban poor, the middle class, and the ruling political elite, particularly the military.[16] Aspinall demonstrates the growing isolation of the aging ruler in the last few months, most evident in his final cabinet, which contained 'the narrowest representation of elite opinion of any New Order cabinet'.[17] The desertion of the embattled president by Jakarta's political elite was sudden, and needs to be seen against the backdrop of massive street protests, which went on day after day both before and after Suharto's resignation, constantly replaying the messages and images of anti-NewOrder *reformasi* and 'people power'.

The Indonesian student movement has a long, proud tradition as the moral conscience of the nation. Student brigades fought against the Dutch during the struggle for independence. Students were mobilised again in support of Suharto's ousting of President Sukarno in 1965. The New Order had dramatically enhanced educational opportunities, increasing the years of compulsory education and expanding the number of tertiary colleges and universities around the archipelago, so that university student numbers more than trebled in the decade to 1993.[18] They were largely contained on campuses after anti-government protests in 1974 and 1978 by a series of policies aimed at the 'normalisation' (read 'depoliticisation') of campus life.

Sections of the depoliticised student population redirected their energies to an array of NGOs (non-governmental organisations), coalescing around broader social-justice and human-rights issues. Non-governmental organisations mushroomed around the country, active in public education and legal advocacy, organising ad hoc around single issues, or into more permanent national coalitions.[19] For many students, their participation in such civil-society groups continued long after leaving university, as middle-class graduates in the non-governmental sector became a primary force of organised opposition to the New Order, having 'a significant public impact, reaching out to farmers, landless, industrial labour, women, minorities and other marginalised groups'.[20]

By the early 1990s, campuses were again becoming the sites of political activism, as some students – albeit initially hesitantly and in modest numbers – became involved in more direct political organising, such as setting up radical political organisations that formed the nuclei of a left-wing political party, the Democratic People's Party (Partai Rakyat Demokrasi, PRD). Such student (and university-graduate) activists were drawn to Megawati and her independent faction of the PDI because of its seemingly defiant stand against government intervention in the months preceding the attack on the PDI headquarters in July 1996.

As protests swelled against Suharto in early 1998, shadowy military intelligence units attempted to crush the movement by abducting at least a dozen student leaders from Jakarta, Yogyakarta and Bandar Lampung.[21] Among them was student activist Pius Lustrilanang, who had been abducted from outside the central Jakarta offices of Indonesia's most influential NGO, the Legal Aid Institute, on 2 February to be held, interrogated and tortured. Such kidnappings had frequently been employed in the earlier years of the New Order to eliminate critics, 'but in 1998 the disappearances received unprecedented media attention in Indonesia, and led to much concern from the international community'.[22] When released, Pius braved threats to his life to describe his detention and torture before the National Commission for Human Rights (*Komnas HAM*) on 27 April 1998. His dramatic testimony, immediately prior to seeking safety abroad, sparked media coverage and galvanised middle-class concerns over the illegal detention of critics of the government, demonstrating the vulnerability of the New Order regime and its incapacity to prevent either the testimony or the escape.

Each attired in the insignia and distinctively coloured jackets of his or her respective Alma Mater, the students rallied en masse in Jakarta and other cities in the final weeks of Suharto's rule – the range of colours indicating the multiplicity of universities from which they came, and hence the geographical spread of their support in this alliance against Suharto. In the midst of the worst economic downturn in 30 years, the demonstrators' cry of opposition to 'KKN' – corruption, collusion and nepotism – resonated widely amongst the middle classes and even big business who resented Suharto putting the interests of his own family and cronies above those of the economy generally by refusing to cancel ostentatious 'mega-projects' associated with First Family members against the sound advice of his finance minister, Mar'ie Muhammad.[23] When Muhammad had attempted to reform the shaky banking sector by closing 16 of the country's 200+ banks in November 1997, including several associated with the First Family, the President's son Tommy was able simply to transfer his bank's assets and re-open under a different name, effectively demonstrating his immunity from government control.[24] That the middle class had lost faith in Suharto's preparedness to back the tough policies necessary to stabilise the economy was nowhere more evident than when, on 19 May, hundreds of entrepreneurs, bankers and financial managers from the Jakarta Stock Exchange took to the streets alongside the students calling for Suharto to resign for 'paralysing' the economy.[25]

The government's failure to demonstrate responsible economic management following the 1997 Asian financial crisis had alienated even those economic interests whose very emergence the New Order has fostered since the 1980s. Between 1990 and 1997, the Indonesian economy had boomed, with the financial services sector creating 'a burgeoning class of Indonesian *nouveau riche*, local stockbrokers and domestic investors'.[26] As the value of their assets dropped with the rupiah, a panic set in. Evans observed that, on 8 January 1998, when the rupiah dropped below 10,000 to the US dollar, even the wealthy 'flocked to supermarkets to empty the shelves of life's essentials' and 'yuppies (foreign and local) wandered around the stock exchange in a state of barely disguised shock. If proof was needed that the Soeharto era was coming to an imminent end, that was it'.[27]

Suharto's announcement that he would restructure his cabinet, implement reform, and call elections in which he would no longer be a candidate, failed to garner public confidence or stem the loss of support from previously faithful quarters. The 9 a.m. televising of Suharto's resignation in favour of B.J. Habibie on 21 May was greeted with euphoria, most evidently by the students occupying the parliament. Habibie, who only a few months earlier had been appointed Vice-President in a corrupt and in many ways ineffectual government, was sworn in as President and charged with the responsibility of moving Indonesia towards a democracy. He was not a credible successor, either for the supporters of the anti-NewOrder *reformasi* movement (as the loose coalition of the very diverse opposition against Suharto had come to be called) or the international money market (the rupiah dipped to its lowest point three days after his appointment). The economy was in tatters. Movements seeking independence or autonomy for territories such as East Timor, Aceh and West Papua threatened to fracture the nation. Violence, including inter-religious and communal clashes, increased in frequency and degree, most notably in Maluku and West Kalimantan, where world headlines were captured by bloody internecine massacres.[28]

Yet the Habibie interregnum set in motion a process that led to the independence of East Timor and the withdrawal of Indonesian occupation forces in 2000, after a quarter of a century of New Order's colonisation – quite literally changing the political map of Indonesia. Hundreds of political prisoners all around Indonesia were released. A long history of centralised control from Jakarta, going back (many would argue) to the colonial era, began to be reversed as radical new laws in 1999 transferred a wide range of legislative and executive authority over political and economic life to elected governments at city and regency (*kabupaten*) levels.[29]

The removal of a host of inoperable and repressive censorship and licensing laws transformed Indonesia's print and broadcast media into one of the freest in the region. The first post-Suharto Information Minister, Mohamad Yunus Yosfiah, began to review and reform media laws, consulting both UNESCO and the international anti-censorship organisation Article 19 in the process.[30] The print media boomed, with hundreds of new, and often stridently political, publications appearing within months. The strict regulation of private TV and radio stations was largely abandoned, leaving broadcast media open to further commercialisation. A special sitting of the MPR in November 1998 scheduled general elections for mid-1999 and, for the first time since 1973 when Suharto had restricted the number of political parties to three, new political parties were freely permitted, with hundreds mushrooming over the next year. But violent clashes between pro-reform demonstrators and the security forces (or their hoodlum militia surrogates) continued. The newly unfettered media meant that television, both domestic and international, now broadcast live from bloody street battles.[31]

The General Elections of 7 June 1999 were fought out between 48 registered parties. The electorate embraced the opportunities to campaign with boisterous parades and rallies; policy debates and electioneering were carried by an upbeat mass media. The poll was regarded by most observers as largely free and fair. Megawati Sukarnoputri's PDI-P (Partai Demokrasi Indonesia–Perjuangan, Indonesian Democratic Party of Struggle) – the ideological continuation of the PDI, whose party headquarters had been so brutally attacked by military-backed hoods in July 1996 – polled best with 33.7 per cent. Following with 22.4 per cent was Suharto's former political vehicle Golkar, which claimed to have been rehabilitated as a democratic and reform-minded party. After a complex and sometimes sordid parliamentary process of negotiations, Abdurrahman Wahid became the first democratically (if indirectly)[32] elected Indonesian president. The first democratically elected parliament since 1955 flexed its muscle against the president in ways that no previous Indonesian parliament had, and, after months of instability and a stalled process of reform, effectively sacked him on 23 July 2001. Megawati Sukarnoputri, daughter of Indonesia's first head of state, became the fifth Indonesian president.[33]

Under a series of constitutional amendments passed between 2001 and 2003 the election of the president and the structure of the MPR have substantially altered, taking effect from the 2004 elections. The president and vice-president are now elected by direct popular vote, on the basis of a ticket proposed by parties or coalitions.[34] There are no longer any presidential appointees to the MPR, nor any reservation of parliamentary seats for the armed forces. The MPR now consists entirely of two popularly elected bodies: the 550-member People's Representative Council (Dewan Perwakilan Rakyat, DPR) plus a newly constituted House of Regional Representatives (Dewan Perwakilan Daerah, DPD) with four members from each province, who participate in 'legislation affecting various regional issues, … the budget and, … questions of tax, education and religion'.[35]

In terms of formal institutions, Indonesia now has a democratic government. But in 2004, as we finish this book, six years after the collapse of authoritarian rule, Indonesianists are hotly debating the nature of power and degree of popular participation that lie behind the democratic electoral façade. The conviction that the end of the New Order would usher in peaceful, liberal pluralist democracy with substantial popular participation was never widely held amongst academic observers of Indonesia and did not last long within Indonesia's own democratic movement. Communal conflict, the increasing visibility of militant Islam, and separatist movements in Aceh and West Papua inherited from the New Order, and intensifying in its aftermath, revived anxiety about national disintegration and in some quarters dampened the enthusiasm for popular democracy. These anxieties have long histories in Indonesia, and had been part of the rhetoric of both Suharto, and Sukarno in the legitimation of their centralising and authoritarian rule.

There appear to be two broad directions in the academic assessments of the nature of the post-authoritarian state in Indonesia. At the more optimistic end (and this is particularly in writings in the first two or three years after the fall of Suharto) there is a relatively straightforward assumption that 'freed of many of the restrictions of the New Order, a poorly prepared but highly motivated political process returned to the challenge of negotiating a democratic political consensus through parliamentary means'.[36] But there is an increasingly dominant and more pessimistic view that the functionaries of the state are unwilling and unable to pursue a seriously reformist political agenda to make the government and the bureaucracy truly accountable to the citizens. Harold Crouch suggests that '[t]he state has been penetrated by interests that are opposed to reform.'[37] In the same volume Vedi Hadiz, on the basis of his research on Sumatra, concludes that '*Reformasi* has not meant a political defeat for the array of interests nurtured and incubated under the New Order's vast network of patronage' but that the new democratic institutions have instead been captured by the old elites.[38] Golkar's success in the parliamentary elections of 2004 and the victory in presidential elections of a former general, Susilo Bambang Yudhoyono, adds obvious credibility to the pessimistic view.[39]

To many who observed the dramatic end of the New Order, urban student rebels and professionals in the media, acting on behalf of the discontented middle class, seemed to be the heroes not just of the end of authoritarianism, but of a reform agenda embedded in their *reformasi* movement. But as John Sidel has suggested, there may be serious limitations to the role of the middle-class intelligentsia with its faith in liberal democracy, civic spiritedness and tolerance 'against a backdrop of dangerously illiberal, uncivil, and sectarian mass politics'.[40] Similarly, Antlöv argues: 'Many civil society groups that made up this movement during the 1990s were not particularly politically savvy … . Their … role was to act as intermediaries (some would say gatekeepers) for oppressed farmers and workers. Relations between them and the grassroots were anything but democratic.'[41]

Two key issues seem to be at stake in Indonesia, as elsewhere in the struggle for democracy: making the state accountable, and creating the conditions for a public sphere with meaningful, popular participation in the political process. On the other side of the equation, the greatest threat embedded within the process of democratisation seems to be the rise of separatist and communal conflicts. Our purpose is to place the Internet among these struggles.

Media and democracy

Any attempt to map the tessellations of the Internet into these political processes is embedded not just in the recent discussions about the net, but also in a long-standing and common assumption of media and cultural studies that the media are both produced by and reflect and reproduce political systems and processes. The precise nature of this connection, and how to analyse it, is indeed the central problematic of Media Studies and (at least since the translation into English of Habermas' *Structural Transformation of the Public Sphere*, perhaps ever since the work of the Frankfurt School) also in studies of politics (in the English language).

The main lines of the debate over digital media and democracy are not new. Media Studies, born from the analyses of 'old' print and broadcast media, has always been divided, 'with one side (Benjamin, Enzensberger, McLuhan) arguing for potential democratisation and the other side (Adorno, Habermas and Jameson) seeing the dangers to liberty as predominant'.[42] While 'historically the threat to individual expression has been seen to come from an arbitrary state',[43] work on the political economy of the media in the west has increasingly focussed on the large corporations whose control over the media is seen to erode the rights of the average citizen and his or her capacity to play a role in political decision-making. There is a substantial body of research that demonstrates the growth of monopolistic control of vast corporations over print and broadcast media and the capacity of this corporatised media to set the political agenda of nations.[44] These works demonstrate the massive inequities between the producers and consumers of media products, which raises serious questions about the western capitalist 'free' media's role in production and reproduction of democratic processes, summarised in the title of McChesney's much cited book *Rich Media, Poor Democracy.* From an explicitly left political position, unusual in contemporary American Media Studies, McChesney demonstrates the increasing concentration of media in the hands of a few powerful businesses in the USA in particular (Chapters 1 and 2), which, he argues, supports a capitalist system 'where elites make most fundamental decisions and the bulk of the population is depoliticised'.[45]

Habermas' work on the public sphere provides a way of thinking about the media not just as an extension of either the state or the corporate sphere, and certainly not as the idealised fourth estate, but as a political force in its own right. For Habermas the 'bourgeois public sphere' is a space (physical or ideational) where 'private people come together as a public'.[46] This public sphere, he argues, was made up of equals or at least with a disregard for status, engaged in discourse and debates which could be won or lost on the basis of the value of the argument. It emerged outside of the hierarchic institutions of the state (the courts in Habermas' description of seventeenth-century Europe[47]) and its main function was political and literary debate and discussion informed in large measure by the early print media's facilitation of distribution of information. In Chapter 6 of his seminal book, Habermas elaborates on how the structure and function of newspapers changed in the late nineteenth century. 'Nevertheless the degree of economic concentration and technological–organisational coordination in the newspaper publishing industry seems small in comparison to the new media of the twentieth century – film, radio and television'.[48] The capital requirement and their 'publicist power' was 'so gigantic' that in some nations the 'establishment of these media was from the start under government direction or ... control .... Whereas formerly the press was able to limit itself to the transmission of and amplification of rational–critical debate of private people assembled into the public, now conversely the debate gets *shaped by the mass media itself.*'[49]

Habermas goes on to describe the ways in which the corporatised and state-controlled media then produce a 'staged public opinion',[50] which 'does not seriously have much in common with the final unanimity wrought by the time consuming process of mutual enlightenment', such as that which, in the logic of Habermas' argument, happened in the pre-media public sphere. Habermas calls this the 'refeudalization' of the public sphere.

Critics of Habermas have drawn attention to the fact that, both theoretically and in terms of the eighteenth-century social practices he was seeking to describe, his notion of public sphere was inherently meritocratic, bourgeois, male and intellectual, and thus necessarily excluded large sections of the society.[51] Such critique notwithstanding, Habermas' theorisation has become an indispensable point of departure in discussions of media and democracy and a constant point of reference in discussion of the Internet, to which we will return shortly.

In studies located in Asia, however, questions about media and politics continue to be centrally about arbitrary powers of governments.[52] Scholars working on Asia have replicated questions about media ownership mainly in relation to crony capitalist media owners who have collaborated with authoritarian regimes to restrict democratic freedoms of speech and information. Privatised crony-owned media survive, thrive in and actively support repressive regimes. A very large portion of the literature on Asian media is devoted to documenting censorship, propaganda and restrictions on media ownership, all undoubtedly characteristics of authoritarian states.

The second problematic that pervades the discussion of media in Asia is the ambiguous role of the western media in the context of authoritarian regimes. Western media coverage of events, such as the Tiananmen demonstration in China, the fall of military dictators such as Marcos in the Philippines and Suharto in Indonesia, even the vitriol which the western media draw from former Prime Ministers Mahathir of Malaysia and Lee Kuan Yew of Singapore, is often taken as evidence of western media working against authoritarianism and by extension in favour of democratisation in Asia. On the other hand, the research on news media and even more on entertainment media suggests that western media gives scant and erratic coverage to events in Asia[53], and the cheap news and entertainment products from the west fill up Asian air-space with foreign products encouraging spectators to escape local politics rather than engage with it.

From the 1980s onwards, as satellite technologies enabled major western television stations to go global, both ends of the debate over the western media's role in

Asia were re-invigorated. Global television networks boosted even further the powers of the multinational media's centralised system of distributing information, images and ideas. But at the same time, in certain circumstances, global media had a liberationary aspect in so far as they breached the capacity of national governments to control what their citizens could see and hear. Sometimes, as in the days before Suharto's resignation, or in the aftermath of the elections in East Timor, global media were also the vehicle for distributing stories that might otherwise be suppressed by a national government. There is, therefore, no single trajectory along which to measure the role of the global media in the process of democratisation. While on the right the notion of the western 'free' media's liberationist role in authoritarian states persists to some extent (more often in political speeches than in serious academic analysis), on the left there is no longer a unified notion of the cultural imperialism of the western media.

Internet and democracy

Alongside satellite television, the Internet was the other new medium that began to make its presence felt in the west in the late 1980s and in Asia (including Indonesia) in the 1990s. A 'multi-nodal horizontal network', the Internet was seen as the polar opposite of the 'old' 'centrally despatched multi-media system'[54] into whose architecture satellite television was being absorbed.

The Internet shifted the terms of the media-democracy debate in a number of ways. The new medium of communication had obliterated the distinction between producers and consumers, a dichotomy that was at the heart of the leftist and political-economy critique of the old media's anti-democratic design. If every individual consumer could also produce and distribute information, ideas and later images, then the question of 'who owned what' mattered little or not at all. In much of the theoretical and popular writing, the Internet was seen simultaneously as the answer to the democratic conundrum in the developed west and the solution to the democratic aspirations of peoples living under authoritarian regimes, in spite of the common knowledge that about four-fifths of the world's population did not (and at the time of finishing this book still do not) have access to the Internet (we return to the implications of this fundamental inequity many times through the book).

Internet versus the authoritarian state

Censorship of print and broadcast media is often seen as both a marker and a tool of authoritarian regimes. 'The Net interprets censorship as damage and routs around it' (repeatedly cited quotation from John Gilmore) has been something of a mantra for net activists working within authoritarian regimes. There is plenty of documentation of the two ways in which activists have used this new mode of communication. Firstly, e-mail facilitates underground contact outside of state surveillance, nationally and internationally. Secondly and more importantly, e-mail newsgroups and websites operate as alternative news sources outside of the censored national media, thus weakening the control of the state not only over images and messages consumed within the nation, but also over the nature of the national image that is projected globally.

Kalathil and Boas have argued that accounts of 'e-mail use in Russia during the 1991 coup attempt, … Internet use by the supporters of the 1994 Zapatista uprising in Mexico, or … the use of e-mail by students coordinating the protests that contributed to the fall of Suharto' (referring in part to our own earlier work) offer only 'anecdotal evidence of the Internet's threat to authoritarian regimes' as 'analysts have had difficulty drawing direct causal link between Internet use and eventual political change'.[55] Causality of major political events is rarely conclusive, particularly not in the kind of empirical studies to which Kalathil and Boas are referring. We have documented both 'clandestine' and 'alternative media' usage of the Internet in relation to East Timor in Chapter 6 and political activism prior to the fall of Suharto in Chapter 3. And while conclusive causal links between particular media technology and the independence of Timor and the fall of Suharto are indeed hard to make, it is our contention that these processes are nonetheless impossible to imagine without some reference to the Internet.

More specifically from our point of view, the net was socially imagined as a tool of opposition to authoritarianism, adding thus to the confidence of 'netizens' in Suharto's Indonesia (see Chapters 2 and 3). Our analysis of the role of the Internet in the fall of Suharto and the independence of Timor proceeds not from a technologically determinist view, but from the ethnographic and historically specific evidence of the social construction of this technology in a particular way. This is one sense in which we see the Internet as imbricated into these political processes.

The vast majority of the literature (mostly activist or descriptive academic work) reporting on the use of the Internet against repressive regimes is premised on the assumption that the conventional media are entirely under the control of the state and therefore entirely articulated into a coherent policy of censorship and propaganda. Audience studies of television and film, and in particular Stuart Hall's 1980 seminal essay 'Coding and decoding in the television discourse',[56] have provided theoretical insights and empirical evidence to suggest that audiences do not necessarily understand the texts in the same way as the creators of those texts – be they the media owners or content-producing professionals (directors, journalists and so on) or a state intent on censorship. Some of this research valorising the process of individual 'decoding' of media messages has been criticised for its 'neglect of the social macrocosm embedding reception and necessarily determining some of its conditions'.[57] Despite legitimate questions about the limits of audience autonomy, ethnographic research nonetheless demonstrates over and over again that neither the state nor any other single agency can control entirely the meaning that is generated at every point of consumption of media messages. Following this general position, we have shown elsewhere[58] that fractures within the Indonesian state and diverse cultural and social decoding practices of Indonesian audiences gave the New Order a less than perfect capacity to control what the citizens received from the media. But neither does the state require complete control over the meaning-making processes of its citizens when these do not translate into any collective political action against its mode of governance or structure of power. We have argued in this book that the hypostasised 'relatively autonomous' audiences of media theory find in the Internet a venue for collectively voicing their alternative and counter-hegemonic readings, and that such spaces are much less available in the older media, especially that under the operation of state censorship.

While the vast majority of accounts of the Internet in Asia ignore the conventional media (other than the repeated reference to the premise of state control of old media),[59] our analysis of the Internet is embedded in an understanding of the older media context into which the Internet arrived. As Kalathil and Boas have suggested, authoritarian state policy on the Internet is, to a large extent, shaped by its policies about other media, and as such we cannot understand the state's governance of the Internet without reference to national histories and debates about the media. The Internet in Suharto's Indonesia, we argue, was not simply an alternative to the 'old' media but was also articulated into these, pushing print and broadcasting towards certain changes. Finally, and perhaps most importantly, the Internet elided the lines between private opinion and their public expression as the private (individual spectator/listener/reader's) critical readings of propaganda and censored texts found their way into e-mail discussions, available for public consumption. In other words, the Internet provided for public displays of 'misreadings' and demonstrated the media-consumer/citizen's autonomy from the encoding processes, including the process of overt and covert state censorship. In this framework the Internet was not so much an oppositional foil to the old broadcast and print media as a widening of the cracks in the system of state control. This is the second sense in which we see the Internet's role in the dismantling of authoritarian rule in Indonesia.

This is not an unambiguous endorsement of the Internet's ability to foil state censorship and propaganda machines, however. There is a cautionary body of work on computer-mediated communications that sees these as giving ever-greater capacity to the state (and corporations) for surveillance and control of citizens. With sufficient allocation of resources, it is possible for an authoritarian state to track information about citizens necessarily produced in any electronic communication. Based on research on the use of the Internet in nine authoritarian nations that have no or very limited opposition-party presence, Kalathil and Boas document: (a) that, as any casual observer would detect, dissidence online constitutes a very small part of Internet traffic; (b) that most states are willing and able to crack down on political opposition on the net; (c) that some nations such as Singapore are able to provide extensive infrastructure for electronic communication while reproducing within it the same mechanism of content control as operates in the conventional media; and finally (d) that authoritarian states can often use the Internet successfully in their own propaganda.[60] While in theory the Suharto regime had opportunity to use the Internet in the same way, we have documented (in Chapter 3) the inability of its censorship and propaganda practices, honed in broadcasting, to be recast to deal with the new medium. In this contingent and specific failure of the New Order government we see the final articulation of the Internet in the fall of authoritarianism in Indonesia.

The Internet in the production of democracy

The vast majority of the theorising and research on the Internet's democratic potential has taken place not in relation to authoritarianism, but within the context of advanced western democracies. According to Hague and Loader, this line of enquiry emerges from

> first ... a growing perception that current political institutions, actors and practices in advanced liberal democracies are in frail condition and are held in poor public regard .... [and] second ... a belief that the current period of rapid social, economic and political change which may signal an emergent Information Age, provides opportunities hitherto unavailable to rethink, and if necessary, radically overhaul or replace those institutions, actors and practices.[61]

As discussed earlier, a large and powerful body of theory had identified the mass broadcast and print media as major culprits in the erosion of democracy in western capitalist nations. This critique came from three main sources: (i) political economy of media, which pointed to the corporate control of media infrastructure and, through that, the texts and messages it produced; (ii) media imperialism, which demonstrated western economic and therefore cultural control of media messages; and (iii) the Habermasian despondency over the passing of the idealised public sphere as the mass broadcast media took over the function of political and cultural discourse.

To all of these the Internet seemed to provide a perfect answer. The net was spreading so fast that it held the promise of soon embracing everyone in the world. It allowed every user to be producer and consumer of messages at the same time, thus wiping out any sense of state, corporate and even professional control over the words and images that could circulate. The coffee houses of eighteenth-century London had provided Habermas with a prototype of the public space where private citizens would meet and discuss matters of import, free from state and corporate hierarchy. At its most idealised, in the vision provided by Rheingold, Barlow and others, the Internet was an electronic extension of such a forum, comprising a vast network of liberated and equal citizens right across the globe. This electronic global coffee house promised intimacy across thousands of miles and centuries of physical and cultural divide, but laid out no vision of how equality was to be created out of the vast global inequities.

The vision of the global agora has been challenged on several grounds. If print was the foundation of the national 'imagined community'[62] and broadcast media the state's instruments of nation-building, then the Internet, by contrast, is an instrument of both sub-national and supra-national collective identity-making. On the one hand ,the Internet revives the McLuhan promise of the global village like no other medium, but so too 'it makes it feasible to organize smaller or narrower groups. It thus can become a force for polarization, doing more to facilitate organization of neo-Nazi and extreme nationalist groups than broader international constituencies for peace.'[63] A growing body of literature dealing with Asia and

Asian diasporas is documenting the online revival of pre-national, primordial ethno-religious communal identities, often bringing together far-flung diasporas and minorities within particular nation-states.[64]

The euphoria about the fast and uniform global spread of the Internet waned quickly for reasons that are areas of significant concern for anyone working in less developed parts of the world, including Indonesia and most of the rest of Asia. Access to the Internet depended on a much older medium, the telephone, which was unequally distributed not only between nations, but also within them, particularly in the poor nations. Many argued that the networks were simply being 'laid over the same old patterns of inequality'.[65] From this point of view, at best the Information Age would replicate the old lines of inequality, at worst it would intensify these differences by providing the already advantaged with the ever-greater advantages of access to the information superhighway. The differences between the information-rich and information-poor would only grow. Examining Internet usage in Asia in a global comparative framework, Tim Beal suggests that the digital divide both within and between nations is on the whole getting wider.[66] In the same volume (and from our point of view more importantly), D'Costa argues that information technology has developed in Asian nations in such a way that it furthers the interests of the elites, in particular that it links Asian elites to western industries, in effect increasing the gulf between the elites and the rest of the national population.[67]

Non-access is not the only issue at stake in unequal participation on the information superhighway. Literacy and level of education more generally affect the capacity to use the Internet. As Trevor Locke puts it, 'the biggest barrier to mass access to the Internet is the keyboard. The keyboard is an artefact of the literary elite, the technically competent and the highly skilled.'[68] Locke suggests that the prospect for mass participation in interactive communication lies in digital television, with its vastly simpler mode of audio-visual, verbal communication. In the context of Indonesia, Sen has similarly argued that a diversified and dispersed radio might provide a more accessible medium of interactive discourse amongst citizens (some of this is summarised in Chapter 2) than the Internet.[69] As Haywood summarises on the basis of historical experience of the United Kingdom,

> opportunities that easy access to information can bring have never been evenly distributed among the members of any community, rich or poor, large or small. What is probably more important is that despite the convergence of a whole range of new technologies, easy access to the information that can really empower and liberate people still looks likely to be the preserve of an affluent minority.[70]

All of this raises serious questions about the reform and revival of democracy through equal access and equal opportunity within an electronic agora.

The techno-faithful suggest that many previous communication technologies, such as radio and television, which started as elite toys now reach nearly everyone in affluent countries and large and growing numbers in many other parts of the world. There is no reason not to trust that the Internet will follow the same pattern. To this the doubters usually have two responses. The first and somewhat clichéd one is that the majority of the world's population are still waiting to make their first phone call, and as such there can be no inherent logic that guarantees the spread of the net. But secondly and more importantly, even the communication technologies that have spread relatively widely (such as radio and television) have only reinforced the power of the powerful in their wake. The promise that the images and the immediacy of film and television would create a universal language of truth and understanding has been largely displaced as we have learnt that visual languages are almost as divided by culture and politics as language itself. As such, we enter the Indonesian space of the information superhighway with questions about social, political and cultural inequities in Indonesia, across both classes and regions, that will necessarily mark the operations of the new medium.

The chapters

Our first task then is to understand the extent of access that students, NGO and urban middle-class actors had to the Internet and how they used it in building up opposition to the Suharto government. The Internet was introduced into Indonesia at a time of major changes in the Indonesian media as a whole. Chapter 2 places the Internet within this overall context of ferment, globalisation and massive expansion of commercial media in Indonesia. Chapter 3 looks at the growth and spread of critical opinion via the net, which both by-passed the self-censorship of mainstream media and fed back into it in a variety of ways, and the more deliberate semi-underground use of online communication to by-pass government censorship. Chapter 4 describes the spread of Internet and related technologies to identify who had access to these. Together these chapters suggest that the net played a critical role in providing a platform where opposition to the Suharto government was articulated and multiplied. In more general terms these chapters respond with empirical data to theoretical questions about the potency of the Internet in opening up authoritarian regimes.

By all accounts, the transition to a post-authoritarian government in Indonesia has been complex and contradictory. On the one hand democratic institutions of governance are being built; on the other hand exclusivist communal identities are redefining the Indonesian map and threatening the emergence of a pluralist democracy. The later chapters of this book analyse how the Internet is being deployed in this transition. In Chapter 5 we have looked at the implementation of the parliamentary election of 1999 and the beginnings of e-governance in Indonesia. We argue that, while the Internet is clearly not significant either in the development of a mass-based electoral democracy or an instrument for the discursive engagement of citizens into an electronic agora, it nonetheless has played a role in legitimising the election and in the symbolic play of regional autonomy.

Chapter 6 places the Internet in the context of the struggle for Timorese freedom, and Chapter 7 places it in the context of the communal struggle in Maluku. In both cases the presence of the new communication technology was minimal in the actual locations involved. In both cases, though in very different ways, the Internet intensifies global attention to local events. These chapters emphasise the need to move away from any generalised argument about the Internet and the processes of democracy or self-determination, and underline the importance of understanding the specific contexts of its use.

We return in the conclusion to this book to our assessment of the nature and extent of the political transformation in Indonesia across the dividing line of 21 May 1998. We argue that the directions of change can be traced in the discourses of and on the net. We argue that the Internet, and particularly those who had the capacity to wield it against the New Order, might have partially shaped the *reformasi* movement itself and the nature of the democracy that emerged after the fall of Suharto. And as such, neither the fall of Suharto nor its aftermath can be described or fully understood without reference to this new mode of communication.

2 Media in the end of an authoritarian order[1]

Most of the scholarly and journalistic analyses of Suharto's fall see the transformation as abrupt, as if dissidence suddenly broke through dictatorship. But if control of information and communication is both a characteristic of dictatorship and a means to perpetuate a repressive anti-democratic order, then our analysis of the media shows that cracks in the New Order's authority appeared much earlier, as global technological changes on the one hand and the contradictions within the New Order's own principal policies (of political restrictions and economic growth) on the other increasingly put the media beyond the government's control.

This chapter sets out to describe the New Order's system of media control and its slow unravelling from about the late 1980s. The Internet was part of the story of the disintegration of the state's command over the media but the new technology arrived and merged into a mediascape[2] already in ferment. We examine here two main elements in this ferment. Firstly, within the realm of the New Order, the regime's needs for political restrictions were increasingly contested by the demands of the government's own rhetoric of economic liberalisation and growth on the one hand and regime-linked big business's pursuit of media profits on the other. Secondly, changes in media technology and its cultural consequences beyond Indonesia challenged the government's capacity to police national cultural borders. These long and interlaced processes redefined what the media meant in Indonesia and undermined two important instruments of dictatorship: censorship and propaganda.

At the beginning of the New Orders 'Indonesian media' meant newspapers and magazines (few with truly national presence), government-controlled state radio and the beginnings of state television. By the 1990s, the national media included enormous print media conglomerates, over 700 privately owned radio stations and five national private television channels, in addition to the state broadcasters RRI (Radio Republik Indonesia, Radio of the Republic of Indonesia) and TVRI (Televisi Republik Indonesia, Television of the Republic of Indonesia), competing against trans-national television and the newly emerging Internet. In institutional terms, the erosion of the state's control over the mode of media production is most clearly visible in the weakening of the Ministry of Information, the department that had oversight of anything that was defined as 'media'. As Indonesian scholar Daniel Dhakidae pointed out, the Department of Information had been one of the most powerful of the New Order's 'state apparati … because of its double role as an *information apparatus* and an economic apparatus'.[3] But the New Order's own policy initiatives eroded the economic facet of the department to such an extent that, in the final years of the New Order, it could no longer perform its function as an information apparatus either. By the end of the New Order, the ministry, once the guardian of the regime's ideology, was so irrelevant that its elimination from the new administrative structures of the post-Suharto government of President Abdurrahman Wahid produced barely a ripple in the actual operations of the media.

For the rest of this chapter we highlight the main steps in the transition of a relatively small, strictly ordered, national media into a large, chaotic, competing set of technologies, institutions and texts with uncertain limits that did not necessarily map on to the nation's borders.

Ordered press to big business

In Indonesia, as in many other parts of the world, newspapers and news magazines[4] have historically set the political agenda more than any other medium. Despite having a smaller consumer base than the electronic media since at least the 1970s,[5] the print media employed more journalists and concentrated more on news-gathering and dissemination than any other medium, particularly in Indonesia, where radio and TV news-gathering had been, until the end of the New Order, officially the job of the government networks, RRI and TVRI.

We have argued elsewhere that the notion of a non-partisan 'fourth estate' press never held complete sway in Indonesia. Born at the turn of the twentieth century, alongside the emergent nationalism, papers critical of the colonial Dutch quickly became the 'press of political struggle' (*pers perjuangan*), a collective with a partisan commitment to independence. During the early years of independence, the press was dubbed by President Sukarno a 'tool of the Revolution', responsible for energising and mobilising public opinion. The trend for most papers to be linked with political parties was formalised in March 1965 by the Information Minister's instruction that all newspapers affiliate formally with a political party, a 'functional group' or a mass organisation.[6] After the establishment of the New Order, the amalgamation of parties broke the formal party-political connections of the press. Only the government's electoral organisation Golkar retained its *Suara Karya* daily. The government defined the press as its 'partner' in accelerating development, either supporting the government or eschewing political debates, to which most papers complied or were banned.

The New Order extended the system of press permits and controls which it had inherited from Sukarno's Guided Democracy (1957–65) to ensure that the government had the authority to remove publications deemed a threat to security and order but also to control ownership in the industry.[7] Forty-three of the country's 163 newspapers were banned in the wake of Suharto's rise to power in 1965.[8] Again, in 1974 after several days of anti-Japanese and anti-government riots in January, twelve publications were banned, journalists were arrested and dozens were barred from subsequent employment in the media industry. In 1978, after an increasingly truculent press gave sympathetic coverage to student-led protests against the New Order, seven Jakarta dailies and seven student publications were closed as part of a crackdown against students and intellectuals.[9]

The New Order protected particular sectors of the economy, including the media, from foreign ownership or investment.[10] Emasculation of any form of labour organisation, including within the media industry, further aided the development of national corporate structures. A 1969 Department of Information ministerial decree obliged Indonesian journalists 'to become members of an Indonesian Journalists Organisation which is authorised [*disahkan*] by the government'.[11] Until June 1998, the Association of Indonesian Journalists (PWI) was the only such recognised organisation. It was tightly regulated by the government, its leadership often comprising serving or retired military officers or Golkar functionaries, senior members of the profession with cordial working relations with the government, and even owners of publishing houses.[12] The key instruments of the Department of Information's control of the media were clearly developed by the early 1970s. It controlled the quantity of print content by restricting access to newsprint, over which it had a monopoly. It controlled the nature of news content through bans and censorship. It controlled ownership through licensing, and it controlled the industry's labour (journalists and others) through state-sponsored corporate structures.

However, the media industry operated also in an environment of rapid national economic growth and industrialisation through most of the 1970s and 1980s. The de-legitimisation of party-supported media, and the consequent removal of politically partisan readerships, required papers to move away from political journalism aimed at a particular readership to increase their audiences across all political spectrums. More dependent on advertising (once party funding was removed) and therefore chasing mass readerships, the press transformed, as Dhakidae has shown, from a 'message-based' medium into an 'audience-based' one, setting in train the basis for the development of large commercial press holdings.[13] From the mid-1970s, and increasing even more in the mid-1980s, there was a steady rise in reader/consumer numbers, while restrictive licensing kept the number of print media companies limited, in effect helping the concentration of ownership in the hands of fewer companies with growing consumer bases. By the late 1980s, a 'news industry' had developed, consisting of large conglomerate press holdings with cross-media ownership and significant investments in other sectors of the economy.[14]

In the mid-1990s, new digital technologies strengthened the hands of the large cashed-up 'national' papers (overwhelmingly headquartered in Jakarta)[15] in relation to their provincial counterparts. Small provincial papers had survived against competition from big national dailies mainly because they could provide localised stories that did not make national news, and because they could beat the Jakarta papers to the newsstand in their locality. Digital technologies offset the problem of distance in the creation of national markets for the big press holdings. Dubbed the 'long-distance printing system' (*sistem cetak jarak jauh*), a combination of newly available digital and telecommunications technologies allowed a small number of well-resourced national newspapers to be composed in one place and then printed with local inflections in any number of distant provinces.[16] Computerisation and modems also enabled even relatively small papers to improve their coverage of local news and the speed and quality of newspaper production. But the legalisation in 1996 of the long-distance printing system set off a spate of take-overs of provincial papers and local editions of national papers.

By the second half of the 1980s, the press – on the one hand a channel of ideas and information, on the other hand a large national industry – was showing up schisms between the Department of Information's long-established role in regulating the press for ideological reasons, and economic ministries such as the Department of Industry and Trade whose job was to develop domestic industry. As mentioned earlier, all newsprint import and distribution had been regulated and overseen by the Department of Information. In 1985, with the support of the Department of Industry and Trade, a Korean–Indonesian joint-venture company started producing newsprint domestically, ending the Department of Information's monopoly over the most vital raw material for the press. In terms of government policy, the ideological control of Department of Information was being separated from the economics of the industry, which fell under a different ministry.[17]

The policy gap between economic growth of the industry and its ideological control became wider in the early 1990s as the free-market argument was pitched against the foreign investment prohibitions in the Basic Press Law. Entrepreneurs who had invested heavily in the press in the previous decade sought deregulation of the market for capitalisation (by foreign investment where necessary).[18] They also called for a relaxation of the publication permit restrictions to allow the market, not the Department of Information, to determine the viability of their publications. In June 1994, Government Regulation No. 20, initiated by the key economic ministers, opened up various restricted sectors of the economy, including the media, to foreign investment. The Information Minister (Harmoko) had been excluded from the negotiations and refused to allow the application of the new regulation in the media sector on the grounds that it contradicted prior legislation, the 1966 Basic Press Law. Eventually President Suharto threw his support behind the Information Minister, excluding the media from Regulation No. 20 and, for the time being, content control seemed to have priority over open markets in the media sector.

However, in attempting in the 1990s to cordon off the domestic media, the Department of Information faced a more fluid national and international mediascape than in the 1960s and 1970s when its rules and practices had been set. The market was blurring national frontiers as media content moved more freely throughout the world via changes in electronic media technologies. Foreign publications (including the US-based *Cosmopolitan* and, closer to home, women's magazines from Singapore) managed to strike deals with local publishers to bring out Indonesian-language editions and even Indonesian imprints while still apparently adhering to the letter of the law.[19] In the context of the electronic media's breaches of the national cultural frontiers (to which we turn shortly), the foreign investment restrictions on the print media seemed largely useless as a tool for restricting ideas and images from abroad.

By comparison with the two previous decades, there were very few bans or withdrawals of publishing permits (known as 'SIUPP' or *Surat Izin Usaha Penerbitan Pers*) in the 1980s. The relative absence of media bans contributed to a growing assumption by the beginning of the 1990s that the government was fostering a new political 'openness' (*keterbukaan*). The June 1994 banning of three prominent news periodicals – *Tempo*, *Detik* and *Editor* – demonstrated the continuing use arbitrary ministerial authority. But the street demonstrations and the long court-battles that followed demonstrated both that the ideal of a free press was now more anchored in the political discourse of the nation and, more importantly, that the economic viability of the press allowed it a degree of protection against arbitrary government intervention. The Alliance of Independent Journalists (Aliansi Jurnalis Independen, AJI) was formed within days of the banning as the first institutional challenge to the state-sponsored and compulsory PWI.

By 1994, the press had grown into a viable industry, with a workforce that was willing and able to organise itself outside the patronage of the state. Policy differences within the government had severed some of the economic stranglehold of the Ministry of Information over the press. Bans and other government intimidation that had operated for most of the Suharto presidency, together with a myriad of formal regulation and the grid of New Order institutions, to minimise the expression of dissent both in the content and in the organisation of the industry's labour force, were now largely ineffective.

Disorderly radio

When Suharto took power, radio and television broadcasts in Indonesia were under state control. In 1965, RRI had 39 stations around the country, broadcasting to more than a million licensed radio sets.[20] Major towns received both national and regional programming of the RRI. News and other designated special broadcasts were compulsorily relayed to all RRI stations around the country from Jakarta. But beyond this, regional stations were able to accommodate programming both in local languages and of local origin. With no television until 1962 and then only for a few hours in the evening in Jakarta, low literacy levels and a relatively diverse and free press, the incoming government of General Suharto initially saw radio as the state's primary and most centralised medium for mobilising public opinion.

The complete sway of the state over radio waves was, however, already under challenge in 1965. In the early 1960s, political instability and dissatisfaction with RRI entertainment programmes had fostered the growth of a bevy of 'hobby' radio stations, sometimes little more than a handful of individuals operating from a private residence. After the Suharto counter-coup of 1 October 1965, some of these were further politicised and staffed by bands of anti-Sukarno student activists. While technically illegal, such broadcasts were not just condoned, but actively aided by ascendant military factions. Despite low transmission power and very limited audience reach, the existence of 'hundreds of "unofficial" stations … on the air in the vicinity of the capital alone'[21] had effectively broken RRI's monopoly control over broadcasted information and interpretation of the fluid politics of the time.

The New Order government attempted to control this unruly radio by three main means: licensing, restricting political content and strict limits on transmission zones. Three new categories of radio were legalised in 1970 – commercial, community and local government – but the lines between them were never particularly clear. In 1971, all radio stations were required to relay RRI newscasts, and to restrict their permissible transmission area and broadcast content. The 'social function' of radio was described as 'education, information and entertainment' and programs were 'not to be used … for political activities'.[22] As with the press, foreign investment and donation were prohibited. Station-owners had to be Indonesian citizens who had not been involved in the banned Indonesian Communist Party (PKI) and were not office-bearers in any political party or mass organisation. Licences (an allocation of frequency issued by the Department of Tourism, Post and Telecommunications and a separate broadcast permit from the Department of Information) were issued for one year and were renewable for just one year at a time. The New Order government thus sought to depoliticise non-governmental radio, which had emerged out of political opposition and had aided the political rise of the army.

The government also moved to protect the state's monopoly over 'national' broadcast, while legislating to define non-governmental radio as a medium of 'local' 'cultural' communication. A directive of the Minister of Information in 1971 emphasised the local moorings of radio, stating that radio broadcast must be 'local, not national, in character', and that the 'nature, content and purpose of a broadcast reflects the local relationship with the conditions and developments of the area reached by the broadcast'.[23] After 1982, shortwave broadcast by private radio was phased out. Stations opted increasingly for the AM and, from 1987, FM bands, with clearer transmission over shorter distances.[24] Government regulation stipulated maximum transmitter power, which limited the broadcast area to about 100 kilometres for FM and approximately 300–400 kilometres for AM stations.[25] Radio stations were not permitted to create networks.

This policy of 'localisation' had two important but unintended consequences: (i) it kept the commercial potential of radio relatively low, and radio therefore remained in the hands of small business and, in some instances, community groups and non-governmental organisations (NGOs); and (ii) it embedded radio in local communities, tied to the needs and desires of its small, often linguistically and culturally specific, listening publics. In rural areas in particular, the most popular radio shows tended to be traditional forms of oral entertainment, 'tailored to the local cultural tastes of each region'.[26] As Jennifer Lindsay has illustrated, the 'persistent survival of private radio … indicates the vitality of the Indonesian tradition of local community expression through radio broadcasting'.[27] Popular stations, she argues, do not simply broadcast to a given geographical area; they attempt to create and maintain audience loyalty by manufacturing a communal identity and continually refining 'their own interpretations of what is "local"'.[28] In contrast to film and television, where New Order policy virtually banned use of vernaculars, radio broadcasts used local languages extensively in all genres of programming. In the 1990s, two of the Suharto children started to acquire radio stations but, unlike their television oligopoly (discussed on p. 26), their radio operations (about half a dozen stations between them) remained necessarily small in the highly diverse sector.

Given the enormously diverse and dispersed nature of the industry, government censorship and surveillance of broadcast content was always inconsistent and often ineffective. Through most of the New Order period, the Department of Information only intervened forcefully if a station's programming sparked some attention in the print media, which threatened to translate into 'national news' what on radio was by definition merely a 'local' matter. Nor was the licensing system enforceable. Periodic 'sweeps' by authorities were always sure to net dozens of illegal stations, particularly in strife-ridden areas such as Aceh – stations that were able to broadcast without restrictions between such irregular policing. Station-owners and executives were resistant to the requirement to relay RRI news broadcasts, not because of any critical political intent, but due to the widespread belief that audiences tended to turn off the radio when these were relayed. On the other hand, most private stations recognised the audience appeal of alternative news and current affairs programmes and continued to employ staff with responsibility for covering 'current information' (*informasi aktual*) – that is, in any other language, 'news' stories. Under the guise of such 'information programmes', political demonstrations could easily be reported as part of local traffic updates (roads blocked off by demonstrators, for example). The highly sensitive issue of presidential succession was famously discussed by a Yogyakarta radio station in 1995 under the guise of an interview with a clairvoyant!

Pursuing popular ratings and hard-fought advertising money, by the 1990s, many radio stations had started live broadcasts and talkback programmes, although it was illegal to transmit anything from outside of the studio. Even Jakarta's Trijaya FM, owned by Suharto's son Bambang Trihatmodjo, seemed to be constantly pushing the limits of censorship with its weekly 'Jakarta First Channel' programme discussing controversial political issues, while being protected by the assumed immunity of the station-owner. Beginning with the Jakarta riots of July 1996, live reporting from political rallies and riots became the norm for many stations, both in Jakarta and in other cities. The immediacy and transience of radio broadcast made attempts at censorship ineffective. The government was dependent on the industry's self-restraint and the capacity of the PRSSNI (the Indonesian Commercial Radio Broadcasters' Association) to ensure this self-censorship, particularly at moments of political crisis. Attempts by the PRSSNI to enforce the broadcast of particular propaganda or its censorship of broadcast content were never fully heeded. Even senior government bureaucrats recognised that, in radio, 'although normatively there are limits, … in fact they [radio stations] have extraordinary freedom'.[29]

In Bandung, arguably the cradle of the Indonesian brand of cyberdemocracy, Radio Mara Ghita promoted itself as the 'barometer of the dynamics of the population of Bandung'. The comment had initially come to the station's director from a regional military commander as an explanation of why they tolerated, even as early as the 1980s, Mara's hallmark talkback shows, when these were in fact illegal! Mara, the commander had said, was the local military's regular source for understanding depths of local sensitivities over particular issues. Confirmed in the precise role in which the station wished to cast itself, as the voice of the local population, Mara later adopted the army commander's statement as part of its station profile. The station ignored with impunity perhaps the majority of broadcast regulations when it relayed various foreign transmissions for a period of days leading up to the fall of President Marcos in the Philippines. On the eve of Suharto's resignation, Mara announcers and newsreaders called on their listeners to demonstrate peacefully their opposition to Suharto by wearing a white ribbon. From then until Suharto's resignation, the station was inundated with phone calls of support and supplies of white ribbon. A local businessman, reading in this call from the radio station a sign of support for the demonstrating students, contacted the radio station and through it became involved in supplying food and drinks to the protestors.

In the final few weeks of Suharto's reign, many popular stations constantly monitored public opinion by encouraging listeners to ring in and comment on the political mood of their immediate surroundings. As at the beginning of the New Order, so at the end, the lines between political reporting on radio and political action on the streets were largely erased. In 1965, radio as an extension of popular opinion amongst students had aided the legitimation of the New Order; in 1998, it remained a conduit for opinion from the streets, from campuses, from middle-class suburbs, small towns and even slums, against an isolated regime. The simplicity of the technology, the relatively low rate of investment needed, low rates of profit and finally the New Order's policy of keeping radio bound to localised communities (thereby restricting its economic potential) all colluded to allow radio constantly to transgress the New Order's 'order'.

Television: public policy versus private wealth

If radio operated largely outside state control, there were indications by the mid-1990s that the New Order state's project of a televisual cover over the citizenry was also destined to failure. In the last decade of its rule, the government's domination of the audio-visual landscape was seriously challenged, in part due to changing technology, but ironically also due to the business ambitions of Suharto's own family.

In the first decade of the New Order, television grew rapidly with rising national prosperity, and the government invested heavily in the extension of state-owned monopoly television into the far corners of the nation.[30] When the New Order came to power in 1965, TVRI was broadcasting for only about three hours in the evenings, with a single relay station outside Jakarta in Yogyakarta. Real growth started in the 1970s when new regional stations were added rapidly, mainly relaying Jakarta programmes. In 1976, Indonesia launched a domestic broadcast satellite, Palapa, which sped up, expanded and regularised the flow of televisual material throughout Indonesia. In 1983, a more powerful 'Generation B' Palapa satellite was launched, and henceforth all programming was annually predetermined centrally from the Jakarta headquarters of TVRI, effectively relegating regional stations to relay stations.

By the time of the launch of the second satellite, three developments outside of Indonesian borders were beginning to confound Indonesian television policy. Firstly, video recorders were becoming more accessible and more popular amongst the urban middle-class population and it was almost impossible to police copies of foreign uncensored films coming into the country. So for the first time in its history, TVRI had a rival in home audio-visual entertainment. Secondly, residents on the east coast of North Sumatra and West Kalimantan had been able to receive spill-over broadcasts from Singapore and Malaysia since at least the start of the 1980s. But in 1984, Malaysia's first private television station TV3 was launched and became immediately popular in much of North Sumatra, where audiences could tune into its broadcasts with an UHF antenna (which could be rigged up for a few thousand rupiah, the equivalent of a couple of US dollars). Finally, from about 1983, parabolic antennae appeared across the skyline of Jakarta's wealthy suburbs and started spreading to other metropolitan cities.

Everywhere in Asia, satellite-transmitted television was generating new anxieties about cultural border-maintenance. But for Indonesia the technology had conflicting implications. Even with the powerful Palapa B satellite and over a hundred relay stations, TVRI broadcasts covered only about 35 per cent of the nation's land mass and some 65 per cent of the population. Even on the small, densely populated island of Java, there were 'blind-spots' where TVRI signals could not reach. The parabolic antennae created a new problem for the Indonesians' television policy, as they simultaneously threatened to allow vastly more foreign content to permeate national boundaries while also promising to extend Indonesian national television broadcasts to the corners and pockets of the archipelago, beyond TVRI's terrestrial signal range. In 1986, the government legalised private and residential use of parabolic antennae (known as the 'open-sky' policy), with the Department of Information and some regional military commands providing isolated rural communities with parabolas to receive TVRI signals. The decree[31] legalising parabolic antennae restricted their use to receiving broadcasts from the national Palapa satellite but no one seriously expected to be able to police the angle at which the antennae were placed! In any case, foreign broadcasters (such as NBC, STAR and CNN) were also renting transponders on Palapa[32] with financial returns for the Indonesian government and easy access to overseas programmes for the population via the national satellite.

By the mid-1980s also, large business conglomerates, fostered by the New Order, were jockeying for a share of the potentially lucrative Indonesian television market. In particular, the economic interests of members of the First Family demanded privatisation of television. As indicated above, from the point of view of the government, state monopoly over television in Indonesia had been seriously eroded by this time and there seemed no prospect that TVRI would be able to stem the tide of audiences lost to foreign broadcasters. In an era of television privatisation around the world, the introduction and expansion of private networks were promoted by some senior functionaries of the government as the best defence for national culture, which state censorship and ownership could no longer provide in the new circumstances. In that sense, privatisation of television was not a sudden and dramatic move to liberalise the industry; it was, as we have argued elsewhere, a scramble to woo the national audience back to a national media space with a different kind of television from that which TVRI was capable of providing.

Between 1987 and 1995, five private stations appeared, three associated with Suharto family members, the other two with cronies of the President. In 1993, private stations won the right to broadcast nationally via Palapa. Without the financial resources of the private sector and habituated to unimaginative didactic programming, TVRI rapidly lost audiences to private television, its audience share falling to just 6 per cent in some cities by the mid-1990s.

The politically well-connected television entrepreneurs were able to resist attempts by the Department of Information to limit their reach, sometimes with overt presidential intervention in their favour. The tension between the conglomerate's financial interest and the government's ideological concerns was clear during 1996–97 as the Parliament completed Indonesia's first Broadcast Bill. Controversy marked the entire process of the bill's passage through parliament and, for the first time in New Order history, the President refused to sign the bill, returning it to Parliament for reconsideration. The key contention was over the bill's requirement that no station transmit to any more than 50 per cent of the national population, deemed unacceptably restrictive by the industry, which in effect was owned by Suharto's family and friends. Some months later, Harmoko, the longest-serving Minister of Information (1983–97), was replaced by Hartono, a close political associate of the President's eldest daughter, Siti Hardiyanti Rukmana ('Tutut'). After Parliament acquiesced, removing the offending clause, Suharto finally signed the bill in October 1997, his last intervention in the formation of media institutions in Indonesia privileging conglomerate profits over governmental control.

The Department of Information tried to control the content on private television partly through instructions to stations to promote aspects of the New Order's ideology and partly by extending to television the system of film censorship inherited from colonial rule and made more draconian under Suharto. In 1990, a Ministerial Decree required that television programming should support the 1945 Constitution and the state ideology *Pancasila*, and avoid issues that might exacerbate tensions based on ethnicity (*Suku*), religion (*Agama*), race (*Ras*) or between social groups or classes (*Antar golongan*), collectively dubbed 'SARA',[33] in effect extending to television what was already in operation in other mass media. Censorship of television programmes was the responsibility of the Board (later Institute) of Film Censorship (BSF/LSF). From 1995 onwards, the task of actually vetting all pre-recorded programmes going to air would have involved at least 15 hours of material from each of the five stations, seven days a week. The censorship board in fact had two viewing rooms operating for about six hours, five days a week. The government's censorship system, designed for a quite different kind of media, was not equipped to deal with the vast amount of audio-visual broadcast material circulating in the second half of the 1990s.

For a while the government continued its monopoly over television news. As with private radio stations, private television broadcasters were not only barred from producing news, but were obliged to relay TVRI's national news broadcast from Jakarta. Commercial stations quickly started to follow the practice of private radio in casting their own news under the guise of 'information'. All had at least one such evening bulletin, some with high ratings, before the 7 p.m. TVRI news, relayed by all stations. From 1995, private stations were formally permitted to produce their own news. We have argued elsewhere that control of information by the New Order government was implemented not just through the excision of certain kinds of information, ideas and images, but also through a particular form and style of news presentation. Understandably, given the ownership of private television, news content on private television remained supportive of the New Order government's stated policies and politics. However, differences emerged in the style of news presentation that increasingly differentiated TVRI newscasts from those on private channels.[34] These differences, including the private channels' drive for good footage of demonstrations, became politically significant in the final weeks of Suharto's rule. Alarmed by the television coverage of riots and demonstrations, in the week before Suharto's resignation the Armed Forces Commander General Wiranto told the Minister of Information that the army would shut down all private television stations unless they tempered news coverage. The Director-General of Radio, Television and Film instructed private stations to stop filming street political actions, except as part of a team led by a TVRI camera crew. It was a last-ditch – and ineffective – attempt to displace close-up pictures of chaos with the modulated long shots habitually delivered by the national broadcaster. But government control even over TVRI was breaking down: the day after the Trisakti killings, 'even the official TVRI news broadcast incorporated a statement of condolence from station staff', a measure of the extent to which the media were emboldened in their reporting of the crisis.[35]

The New Order government's grip over television and its audiences had been slipping, since the 1980s, through a variety of technological and economic factors. Privatisation – under the control of a few, hand-picked from around the presidential palace – had been expected to deliver to the regime an audience that was tuning out of state television. But this very expansion of the televisual sphere loosened the hold of the state over it. Born in an atmosphere of competition not only against each other, but in part also against international providers such as CNN, BBC and others, private television's programming was honed to a purpose quite different from TVRI's: getting audiences to advertisers. In a time when political dissent against the Suharto leadership was increasingly fashionable amongst the middle classes, including media professionals, economics dictated distance from official voices, notwithstanding the owners' closeness to the regime.

The Internet's promise

Thus, in the second half of the 1990s, the Internet arrived into a mediascape that was already stretching the Indonesian state's capacity to control. The net was also already laden with a discourse of its democratising potential. Even before the establishment of the first Indonesian Internet Service Provider (ISP), works by Rheingold and Rushkoff were widely circulating in photocopied form.[36] (Indeed, we were introduced to Rushkoff by activist students in Gadjah Mada University during a period of fieldwork in 1996.) The parallel and dystopic visions of the Internet, which conceive of computer-mediated communications as tools of state and corporate surveillance, had, by contrast, very little impact in Indonesian discourses on the technology.[37]

By 1994, influential international and domestic print media began to create great expectations regarding the Internet's potential applications and impact. Early articles seemed to create a mystique of development, democracy and prestige around the technology. Features in such regional newsweeklies as *Asiaweek* discussed the effect of Internet uptake around Asia, concluding (in September 1994) that 'there is no doubt: the steamroller is on the way'.[38] In its front page '1994 End-of-year Report on Science and Technology', *Kompas*, then Indonesia's top-selling broadsheet, enthusiastically detailed the wonders the Internet offered to education, business and the general public. The key benefit for all, featured in the article's headline, was that 'The democratisation of information cannot be resisted'. At a time when only one ISP had commenced operations in Indonesia and the number of Indonesians actually connected to the Internet was only a few thousand, the lengthy article opened by noting the importance of adding your personal e-mail address to your name card. 'Apart from the prestige of indicating that you are keeping up with the times and with technological change, you will be able to obtain many benefits, such as access to the most up-to-date information from all around the world; you will also be able to save a considerable amount of money, time and energy, including petrol.'[39] It proceeded to paint a glowing picture of the array of tasks made easier by the Internet, leading the list with the fact that 'you can obtain information which in its country of origin would be tightly censored or "off the record"'. There was a slight note of caution, since 'one could not eliminate the possibility that information coming in might contain elements of terror, subversion or pornographic tendencies'. But such disadvantages were given far less attention in media reports than the benefits the Internet was touted as offering. Earlier, *Kompas* had declared that Indonesia was being 'left behind in the information network', despite the fact that 'everyone, whether they are a student, a researcher or a business person *certainly needs it*' (our emphasis), something 'certainly felt by Indonesians who have studied abroad'.[40] In its front-page feature on 'Internet Mania', *The Jakarta Post* judged breathlessly, 'Getting into the Internet is like entering the magic kingdom' for, although 'there are negative aspects of the Internet which need to be anticipated, … there are great advantages to be gained from the network, if we can make use of it wisely.'[41]

By 1996, the mainstream media, and print media particularly, regularly published stories on both the technical and social aspects of the Internet. They provided a substantial flow of specialised information about Internet technology and its changing specifications, much of it drawn from international technical journals, news agencies or other foreign publications. Specialised magazines, such as *InfoKomputer*, added considerable coverage of Internet technology to their standard fare of computers; some also redesigned their cover and format to broaden their appeal from technicians to the growing general readership keen to learn how to access and utilise the Internet. Detailed accounts were reported of debates and conflicts abroad about the social application of the technology and principles such as freedom of expression on the Internet. For instance, the opposition in the USA to aspects of the 1996 Telecommunication Reform Act – which promoters argued was intended to restrict indecent material on the net, but which opponents branded a breach of freedom of expression – received detailed coverage in national dailies.[42] Newspaper readers were assured that 'the Internet has created a new world for human existence. A virtual world, full of information and connectivity, has emerged with very diverse forms, non-linear and interlinked.'[43] The Internet thus became a site around which to open up questions about freedom of speech and, by implication, its absence in Indonesia.

The Internet did have some critics in Indonesia. Some argued that the uptake of the technology was being driven by foreign economic interests and that such 'high technology' had little practical application in a developing country such as Indonesia, beyond some sectors of business and those fields (education and journalism for example) where rapid access to information had a distinctive value.[44] But, on the whole, enthusiasm about the Internet's potential was overwhelmingly more dominant and, in the increasing political ferment, every aspect of the new technology seemed available for politicisation. Apolitical writings, directed at the business sector, discussing how cryptography enabled the details of financial funds transfers to be kept secure, were read by political activists as pointers to the benefits of encrypting their e-mail messages to maintain secrecy and undetectability.[45] The Internet's arrival and popularisation in Indonesia, largely through the intermediary of Indonesian post-graduate students studying abroad, were seized on as evidence that the new technology was a powerful exploratory tool for educators and researchers, and that by extension it offered the general user access to unofficial information not provided by the mainstream Indonesian media. For some, there was an almost heroic commitment to mobilising the technology. As ITB (Bandung Institute of Technology) spokesperson Onno W. Purbo proclaimed on the Indonesia-L mailing list (known widely as *apakabar*) on 22 August 1996, 'ITB's commitment is to assist and provide Internet access for the world of education and research in Indonesia. It is hoped that ITB can increase its service to community development of the Indonesian nation.' In his frequent newspaper articles popularising the Internet, Gadjah Mada University academic Roy Suryo highlighted the capacity of the net to open uncensored sources of information. He provided lists of such websites, concluding that, 'in the current era of information and globalisation, the existence of homepages containing "alternative" information such as noted above, is regarded as quite important, even if they can't always be believed. […] The old saying "whoever controls information controls the world" seems increasingly more relevant.'[46]

Mainstream print media underscored its own technological weakness *vis-à-vis* the Internet. In December 1995 for example, the newsweekly magazine *Gatra*, ran a feature article on the Internet, emphasising the speed of online news compared to conventional media. It detailed how the Jakarta detention of four political activists, including one with French citizenship, was reported within 12 hours on the then most prominent e-mail list *apakabar* (discussed in Chapter 3), dramatically scooping local Indonesian newspapers, which trailed by a full day.[47] Conventional media organisations recognised that the Internet and Internet-based alternative publications not merely offer faster information, but (as *Kompas* editorialised) also introduce 'an interactive and democratic spirit' into information exchange. This democratic spirit emerged because the relationship 'between the producers and users of information, as well as also within the institution which is developing this system, is not hierarchical or paternalistic in nature. On the contrary, all communication takes place freely and openly.'[48] What the papers did not say, but journalists readily acknowledged in private, was the way in which the Internet both forced the hands of the newspaper editors and provided them with an opportunity to push the limits of state censorship: if an event, however unfavourable to the government, had already become 'news' online, the papers felt obliged to cover it. Moreover, the government needed conventional media coverage to tell its own version once the net had already outed the information. The net not only uncovered stories, but in so doing also enticed and even forced the other news media to cover them.

For individual journalists, the net was an escape from the limits of other news media, whether set by state censorship or editorial policy. News or interpretations that could not get into newspapers increasingly made their way into the Internet and fed back into the conventional media. Staff from two of the newsweeklies banned by the government in 1994, namely *Tempo* and *Detik*, turned to the Internet to launch popular avatars, *Tempo Interaktif* and *detik.com*. Not only did the government not move against these cyberpublications, despite having banned their print predecessors, but state-owned enterprises actively collaborated with *Tempo* publishers to get *Tempo Interaktif* onto the Internet. *Tempo*'s publisher signed a profit-sharing contract with the ISP Idola (PT Linasarta), a partially state-owned company, the major shareholders of which were the Indonesian Central Bank (Bank Indonesia) and the state-owned international telecommunications company Indosat.[49]

Disorder in the House?

Contradictions marked all aspects of the New Order state's response to the Internet, the policy consequences of which are dealt with in the next chapter. At the level of rhetoric, many of the most senior functionaries were endorsing the technology. In December 1995, President Suharto himself launched the Indonesia

Media Network website – a project of the Indonesian Muslim Intellectuals' Association (ICMI),[50] led by B.J. Habibie. On the other hand, an array of government figures and their associates in the media industry questioned the credibility of Internet-based sources of information. The General Chairperson of the government-endorsed Indonesian Journalists' Association's central branch, Sofyan Lubis, dismissed the Internet as 'a garbage bin. In it there may be some good things, just like a garbage heap, but there is also absolute trash, without any redeeming value.'[51] Others projected a moral struggle onto the Internet. After chairing a meeting of the National Broadcasting Council in July 1995, Information Minister Harmoko stressed that the government wanted Indonesian Internet users to look only at 'positive' information on the Internet, adding: 'I am sure that Indonesians have moral, mental and cultural resilience. They are able to discern what is good and what is bad.'[52] Secretary-General of the Department of Tourism, Post and Telecommunications (the department that was substantially responsible for laying and extending the infrastructure of the net in Indonesia), Jonathan L. Parapak, urged Internet users to 'strengthen their own moral resilience' so as to be discriminating in accessing only suitable materials, but added that the government 'would not hesitate to take action against those who spread negative issues' on the Internet.[53] As *The Jakarta Post* reported, Parapak's dilemma was not surprising as 'governments all over Asia are at present watching the rapid growth of this global computer information network with a mixture of hopeful expectation and apprehension'.[54]

The mechanisms of governing the media, inherited by the New Order and developed in the 1970s into a comprehensive policy of restrictive licensing, censorship and propaganda, had, as we have demonstrated, become increasingly ill-defined and ineffective as the technology and economics of the media were transformed. In the last decade of the twentieth century, the content on the vast, commercialised, diversified media was beyond the state's control. These media chased audiences who were by then also disenchanted citizens living under an authoritarian and corrupt government. Deliberately depoliticised in the early years of the New Order, the Indonesian media ironically returned to politics largely for the commercial reason of giving the consumers what they wanted. In the sense that commercialism and technological developments in the end colluded against state censorship, the Indonesian media as a whole contributed to the fall of dictatorship of three decades' standing.

As for the Internet in particular, it was not just that the New Order was unable to contain the Internet within its old structures of censorship and propaganda, but also that there were so many contradictory interests and discourses within the government that it made impossible the development of a coherent position in relation to this new medium. Less than a month before Suharto fell, his last Information Minister, Dr Alwi Dahlan, conceded before the Jakarta Foreign Correspondents' Club the futility of any attempt to regulate the Internet, acknowledging that one of the state's major problems was a 'lack of trust and credibility'.[55]

Suharto's fall appeared to fulfil the techno-triumphalists' predictions about the Internet. Referring to the iconic weapon used by Indonesian independence fighters against Dutch colonial domination in the 1940s, *The Jakarta Post* declared in early June 1998 that the 'Internet replaces bamboo spears in the fight for freedom'.[56] The comparison was apt for, whatever the *technical* efficacy of either bamboo spear or Internet against colonial or authoritarian mechanics of power, they were both widely *perceived* to have been crucial to the respective struggles, and consequently became infused with symbolic power to move the struggle along. Exactly how the 1998 movement grasped its bamboo spear is the concern of the next chapter.

3 Net challenges to the New Order

The most abiding image of the Indonesian struggle for independence from the Dutch is that of the steely-eyed young (usually male) revolutionary (*pemuda*), his long black hair tied back in the red-and-white colours of the Indonesian flag, clutching a sharpened bamboo spear. The image of the *pemuda* still adorns public memorials across the archipelago, representing the romantic revolutionary youth. In May 1998, the *pemuda* were again out in force in the streets of Indonesia, long-haired, and nationalism's familiar red-and-white still around their forehead. But for the students who spear-headed the fall of the former general, Suharto, '[I]nstead of fighting with bamboo spears, swords, guns or tanks, they used banners, placards, the mass media and the Internet.'[1] A 'curious political force, headless and leaderless, without a central organizing force'[2], the movement was, for some, 'the first revolution using the Internet'.[3]

This chapter looks at how the Internet was used to express and spread political dissent against the New Order and opens up questions about the relationship between freedom of speech in cyberspace and citizens' rights in the 'real' political world. As discussed in the previous chapter, the New Order government's capacity to control content of all media had been eroded in the second half of the 1990s through a combination of technological and social transformations. But historically developed political and economic constraints, and the print and broadcast media's habitual self-censorship through much of the New Order, continued to restrict the content of the old mass media. In this chapter we examine the emergence in the mid-1990s of the Internet and associated new technologies – the list-servers, electronic bulletin boards and websites – which were employed by particular sections of the Indonesian community with the specific purpose of disseminating political positions that could not be expressed in the conventional media. Taking into account who used the Internet in Indonesia in 1996–98 in particular, and to what purpose, we try to evaluate the role of this new communication technology in Indonesia's transition from authoritarianism towards a mass-based democracy.

The question we address in this chapter is not whether this new vector of communication, with anarchic freedoms built into the technology, *caused* the erosion of a control that had been maintained for three decades in part by a complex structure of propaganda and censorship. It will always be difficult to pin down such a historic change to one factor or even a small number of factors. We look instead at the Internet as one of the instruments used by groups opposed to Suharto's New Order to communicate publicly, but beyond the state's control. But this deliberate use of the technology needs to be seen within a more complex process of the emergence of an Indonesian 'public sphere' on the Internet.

As discussed in the Introduction to this book, Habermas' theorisation of the public sphere is widely cited in recent critical understanding of the relation between media and politics. The argument, that industrialisation and the attendant commercialisation of the media eroded the 'public sphere' where citizens as collectives could formulate and express their opinion, has been taken up repeatedly in the theorisations of democracy in the west.[4] It is easy to see the Internet as a foil to commercial and state-controlled media – a medium not owned by anyone where therefore everyone can speak, and thus a space where public opinion can be formulated, debated and expressed without being overwhelmed by commercial or state intervention. In Suharto's Indonesia, a public sphere – or in Hewison and Rodan's more limiting (but also more clearly located in the Southeast Asian context) term 'political space'[5] – was highly restricted. As we have discussed in Chapter 2, print and audio-visual media were strictly censored and increasingly in the hands of small coterie of powerful commercial interests. By contrast, the Internet arrived in Indonesia, already valorised as a 'technology of freedom', and became the space where frustrations and aspirations excluded from state and commercialised platforms – not all political, and certainly not all 'democratic' – could be expressed. The chapter is an account of the ways in which the Internet in the 1990s became rapidly anchored in urban Indonesia's political dynamics, and the agents and processes that made it a weapon in the struggle to overthrow Suharto's authoritarian rule.

The arrival of the Internet

Like its Southeast Asian neighbours,[6] the Indonesian government had embraced the 'information superhighway' as part of its developmental dream by the early 1990s. Much of the groundwork for the superhighway in Indonesia was laid by what one industry executive dubbed 'Habibie's kids', a reference to a generation of foreign- and locally trained technologists who benefited from the policies championed, and largesse bestowed, by Baharuddin Jusuf Habibie, Indonesia's influential Minister for Research and Technology for two formative decades (1978–98) and later President. The German-trained doctor of engineering had built a meteoric career with the Messerschmitt Bolkow Blom conglomerate in Hamburg, where he was Vice-President and Director of Technology Application from 1974 until 1978. Returning to Indonesia at Suharto's request, he attempted to build a state research and technology sector through initiatives such as the Bureau for the Assessment and Application of Technology (BPPT) and the Strategic Industries Agency (BPIS). Habibie, who benefited greatly from President Suharto's patronage, was an unapologetic technophile who passionately promoted scientific and high-technology industries (including aeronautics, weapons production and shipbuilding) in the belief that these could rapidly transform Indonesia into a developed post-industrial economy.

As State Minister for Research and Technology, Habibie had in institutions under his authority (or in research institutes of other government departments) an overwhelming majority of all science and engineering researchers in the country. In his push to build a strong research sector, he secured World Bank and Japanese Overseas Economic Cooperation Fund soft loans to provide bright science and engineering students with scholarships to Europe, Japan and the USA.[7] For Habibie, too, the Internet sat easily with his vision of Indonesia's future; he was eventually to become the first Indonesian Minister to have his own homepage.[8] Later, when Habibie was President, a senior aide noted that he would use the Internet 'late at night to read foreign publications and communicate by e-mail', a factor seen by some as contributing to the 'eclectic mix of input into any decision' he made.[9]

Many of the Indonesian students who studied abroad with government-endorsed scholarships were amongst the first of their compatriots to discover the Internet and to appreciate the purposes to which it could be employed. It was from such groups that the first 'Indonesian' mailing list (in the sense of being established by Indonesians and primarily involving Indonesian participants), <Indonesians@janus.berkeley.edu>, emerged in the USA in 1989.[10] Likewise, the first webpage about Indonesia was produced in 1992 as a student project by Budi Rahardjo, an Indonesian post-graduate studying at the University of Manitoba, Canada, on a Department of Education scholarship in the early 1990s.[11] Rahardjo also wrote the first Indonesian-language textbook on Internet use (published in 1994 in the USA).[12]

The development of the Internet in Indonesia from the early 1980s was not a singular or linear process. It was occurring simultaneously in various locations, sometimes coordinated, often independently, experimenting with a variety of emerging communications technologies. From 1983, trials had been under way of 'Uninet', an 'Inter-University Network' linking the University of Indonesia in Jakarta, Bandung Institute of Technology (ITB), Bogor Agricultural Institute (IPB), Gadjah Mada University in Yogyakarta, Hasanuddin University in Ujung Pandang, and the Directorate-General of Higher Education in the Department of Education and Culture, Jakarta (which had funded the venture).[13] In 1986, the National Research Council (Dewan Riset Nasional), chaired by Habibie (and modelled on the US National Academy of Science), recommended the development of science and technology information services. In 1989, this crystallised (under the BPPT) into the design for the information network IPTEKnet.

By the end of the decade, hardware problems and the high cost of the required long-distance telephone connections stalled the Uninet project. But experiments continued at the ITB using amateur radio engineering. In the late 1980s, ITB staff and students developed the computerised transmission of data communication over radio. By 1992, they were using such radio technology to link computers at the Ministry of Research and Technology and the University of Indonesia in Jakarta, with the Indonesian Aerospace Institute in Bogor and Bandung's Institute of Technology, in what was later known as the Paguyuban Network.[14] University of Indonesia staffer R.M.S. Ibrahim developed a protocol that enabled the transfer of data from the 'packet radio' network onto the Internet. Meanwhile, at the Data Centre of the Ministry of Industry (headed by Tungky Aribowo, described as 'the first Indonesian Minister who actively responds to e-mails'[15]), a small bulletin board system (BBS) was developed to provide a free public e-mail service, pioneering electronic public access to an Indonesian government department. In April 1993, the IPTEKnet Planning Committee commenced trials of a Micro-IPTEKnet prototype, involving six government instrumentalities. Several major universities and research institutes around the country joined. During these years, a small Internet community was also growing up in Bandung, which was linked by 1,200 bps packet radio in early 1993.

The costs of such Internet use remained prohibitive. Budi Rahardjo, studying computer engineering in Canada and actively developing Internet networks there, captured the tone of the times when he warned fellow expatriates seeking advice on how to e-mail home to Indonesia: 'Before sending e-mail you have to remember that THEY HAVE TO PAY THE CONNECTION. IT'S VERY EXPENSIVE !!! and they have to pay it from their own pocket. I am not joking. Think TWICE (or 100 times) before sending an e-mail/file(s) !!! [sic]'[16] This cost eased slightly from June 1994 when IPTEKnet began offering member universities global Internet access (and it remained the major non-commercial Internet provider for research and academic work for many years).[17] By 1995, ITB along with some other universities had leased 14.4 Kbps phone links from Telkom for IPTEKnet, and was then integrated easily into the global Internet.

These young computer engineers were the beneficiaries of Habibie's 'grand vision' of a high-tech Indonesia, leapfrogging into the twenty-first century. In the 1980s, they staffed the universities, such as ITB, and the research centres (for example, BPPT, and LAPAN, the Indonesian Aeronautics and Space Institute, both chaired by Habibie) promoting the concept of, and subsequently trialling, the Internet. Path-breaking mailing lists such as <Indonesians@janus.berkeley.edu> abroad demonstrated 'the powerfulness of community building through cyber interaction', and inspired the setting up of additional mailing lists from within Indonesia.[18] By the mid-1990s, such foreign-trained Indonesian computer engineers were establishing the first commercial Internet companies in their homeland.

The three principals of the pioneering Internet Service Provider (ISP) RADNET (PT Rahajasa Media Internet) established their company in July 1994, but immediately encountered government confusion over precisely which department had authority over the Internet and what procedures were required before ISPs could legally commence offering services to the public. Some months earlier, in the absence of any guidelines, PT IndoInternet (known as 'Indo.net') had started negotiations with PT Indosat (the government-owned satellite company) to establish an Internet service.[19] But clarification of procedures only emerged after the issuing of the inaugural ISP licence by the Department of Tourism, Post and Telecommunication (Departemen Pariwisata, Pos dan Telekomunikasi, henceforth Deparpostel) to RADNET in December, enabling its launch of services to the public in May 1995, dubbed the 'Year of the Internet' by *Time* magazine.

By late 1995, demand for the Internet was starting to boom. With IPTEKnet increasingly accessible to academic staff in the major universities, and with the arrival of private commercial ISPs in the metropoles of Java, the Internet was developing a public profile just as the speed and efficiency of the technology were improving exponentially, and the commercial potential of IT investment was being recognised.[20] Businesses that recognised the commercial imperative of acquiring new technologies found highly skilled young technicians staffing the emerging ISP companies who were able to provide the know-how to get medium-sized and large national and multinational companies linked into the net. Concurrently, technological advances were improving the speed and efficiency of Internet communication. In 1994, the connection speed from Indonesia via IPTEKnet, the sole provider, was only 64 Kbps. In 1995, this had increased tenfold to 640 Kbps, and by October 1996, it exceeded 7Mbps.[21]

By the middle of 1996, barely 15 months after RADNET had become the first commercial ISP licensed in Indonesia,[22] the Internet had 'arrived' politically: government, business and radicals were all talking about it. Major daily newspapers such as *Kompas*, *Media Indonesia* and *Republika* devoted regular sections or columns to the Internet and associated computer technologies. Businesses were being assured that '[t]he Internet has changed the parameters of marketing. For half the cost of a full page advertisement in a national newspaper, you can have your own World Wide Web (WWW) server and address and an audience of millions.'[23] The Internet was being touted as offering online employment services, information about the latest medical advances, travel bookings, Indonesian rock music, education and cultural data: a window on the world.[24] Readers could respond immediately and anonymously to opinion polls on various hot political issues, which appeared on websites such as that of the cybermagazine *Tempo Interaktif*.[25] The Internet had been embraced by the technophilic developmentalists in the New Order government, personified by Habibie, and by big business, but in particular by students and the professional middle classes. The Internet thus had a presence in the media and in politics well beyond what the actual numbers of connections (about 0.1 per cent of the total population in mid-1998) might suggest. While much of this attention was being generated in Jakarta, the Internet was quickly branching out – in a very visible manner – changing the streetscapes and the social practices even in some provincial towns.

Indigenisation of the Internet

When the collapse of the Thai financial sector and the floating of the Thai baht in July 1997 sunk the Asian economies in its wake, the ramifications were dramatic for Indonesia. Within twelve months of the commencement of the crisis, the rupiah depreciated by more than 80 per cent, and the inflation rate for 1998 rose to around 13 per cent.[26] But the economic impact was not uniform in all sectors of the economy.[27] For the infant Internet industry it brought challenges and opportunities, which on the whole led to the technology becoming increasingly firmly anchored into Indonesian business and government.

The drastic fall in the value of the Indonesian rupiah drove up the price of all imported computer and Internet hardware. The crisis posed problems for the ISPs who had to pay for their bandwidth (about 40 per cent of their operational cost even before the crisis) in US dollars, while receiving their subscription income in the devalued rupiah.[28] Although the ISPs generally attempted to maintain their subscription fees at the pre-devaluation prices to avoid an exodus of customers, government increases in the cost of timed telephone calls (including connections to the ISP) effectively drove up the costs to the consumer. But the net, then already embedded in the commercial and political life of significant sections of the Indonesian population, did not shrink substantially under the economic strain. The increased cost of new imported materials enhanced the market for the local repair and maintenance of computer hardware. For ISPs, the customer base continued to grow. For instance, IndoInternet (one of the oldest ISPs in operation) lost about 60 subscribers each month in the first half of 1998, about 40 of whom were foreigners presumably leaving Indonesia in the face of the growing political crisis. But at the same time, the company was registering 180–200, mostly Indonesian, new subscribers a month.[29] The industry responded innovatively. The ISP industry organisation, APJII (Association of Indonesian Internet Service Providers), attempted to minimise use of expensive international gateways by maximising mutual exchange of domestic Internet traffic between Indonesian providers, via the 'Indonesia Internet eXchange' (IIX).[30]

Just as importantly, throughout 1997–98 as the economic crisis and political turmoil deepened, the industry managed to present the Internet as both a political and an economic solution to the nation's ills. The print news media generally, and computer-industry-linked publications in particular, repeatedly pointed to the Internet as the single most important medium of unfettered communication, both within the nation and internationally. An article in *Infokomputer*, some weeks after the fall of Suharto, stated: 'Thanks must be given to the ISPs who did not cut or censor the content of Internet traffic. Thus, the idea of people's power from the Philippines could reverberate through some of the chat rooms and mailing lists like *apakabar* and KdP' (both discussed later in the chapter).[31]

Similarly, as businesses faced dire times, they were urged to reconsider their communication practices in order to economise. Industry analysts sought to promote e-mail and the Internet as cheaper alternatives to long-distance telephone and fax contact. Companies were encouraged to do more direct marketing of goods and services on the web, advertising more economically on the Internet rather than in the conventional forms of print, radio and television. The messianic zeal of some of these promotions is evident in the opening lines of one such article: 'In the midst of the economic crisis today, every company and every family is forced to economise in all activities. Nonetheless, the one activity that we cannot do without is communicating. Communicating, whether within the company or within a family, is the life-blood. … A company without communication will fail.'[32] The rest of the article is given over to promoting the Internet as faster and cheaper than all competing modes of communication such as fax and telephone, particularly at a time when prices of international calls were rising rapidly while the ISPs continued to offer Internet services at pre-crisis rates.

By the late 1990s, a variety of pessimistic assessments about electronic communications, including the Internet, had emerged in international academic debates.

In particular, following Foucault's vision of the panopticon, some scholars saw the prospect of new modes of state and corporate surveillance and new limits to the privacy and autonomy of citizens and consumers.[33] But these had no resonance in Indonesia. The period of economic and attendant political crisis in 1997–98 only further embedded the Internet's emancipatory discourse within opposition groups and large sections of the urban Indonesian middle class more generally. The Internet became simultaneously the locus of a critique of dirigism – a proof that the state (*qua* New Order) could not and should not impede the free and international movement of goods and ideas – and a space in which to articulate the anti-statist, free-market and freedom-of-speech arguments.

What follows is a historical account of the ways in which non-governmental organisations (NGOs) and opposition groups, led largely by students and young media professionals, used the Internet – for covert communication, public mobilisation and an alternative source of news and information – in the period leading to the fall of the Suharto regime.

Networks of dissent

We discussed in Chapter 2 the rising tide of opposition to the political and cultural practices of the Suharto regime through the mid-1990s. The networks of dissent, the channels of communication underpinning the 1998 push to topple Suharto, had begun forming well before the opening of commercial ISPs in Indonesia. But it is clear that the informal and covert political opposition in Indonesia recognised the technology's potential soon after its arrival. The main tools were the personal computer (PC) 'clone', produced relatively cheaply in parts of Asia – then imported into Indonesia by the business community and the middle class which embraced it – and associated pirated computer software programs, which were easily duplicated and disseminated in Indonesia's lax copyright environment. From about 1989 onwards, Indonesian students abroad had begun establishing Indonesia-related 'mailing lists', such as IndozNet (Indonesian students in Australia), IsNet (for Muslim students) and ParokiNet (for Catholic students), as they realised 'that cyberspace also afforded them the opportunity to talk about topics considered taboo back home, such as human rights abuses and the repressive policies of the Indonesian government'.[34]

In 1989, the Indonesian Environmental Forum (Wahana Lingkungan Hidup Indonesia, WALHI), an umbrella organisation of environmental groups, became the first NGO to go 'online' internationally, using a Europe-based ISP to communicate with environmental organisations abroad. It was a tentative first step, opening the IT door a crack, but the organisation's expertise was very limited and little use was made of the link. The following year, through its involvement with the Oregon-based Environmental Law Alliance Worldwide (E-LAW), Indonesia's leading human rights advocacy organisation, the Legal Aid Institute (Lembaga Bantuan Hukum, LBH) obtained e-mail facilities using a proprietary American Internet Service Provider, the activist network Institute for Global Communications (IGC) and a San Francisco-based server. The Legal Aid Institute was one of the country's oldest and most respected NGOs, with funding from a wide range of international sources. Its founder, Adnan Buyung Nasution, had been part of the 1966 student movement. By the mid-1990s, LBH had spawned a whole generation of prominent lawyers and, through its long history of providing defence to many critics of the New Order, had justly earned a reputation as one of the longest-standing anti-Suharto NGOs.

As part of their charter, 'E-LAW U.S. Technology Circuit Riders equip environmental defenders around the world with computers, software and modems, and train them to use this equipment [so that] advocates around the world are using cost-effective, fast communications tools.'[35] As <elawjakarta@igc.apc.org>, LBH was able to circulate information on this network, its subscription fees paid by the sponsoring international organisation. The connection was still cumbersome – staff made one weekly direct international phone call to send and receive their batch of e-mails – but LBH became (and, till the close of the New Order, remained) the 'best-connected' NGO in Indonesia, able to relay information rapidly and internationally, acting as a conduit through which a variety of opposition groups communicated news and political developments internationally. Connection became easier once the Indonesian government's satellite management company Indosat established a new firm (with the government's Bank Indonesia), Lintasarta, which provided Internet access for Indonesian customers via the US-based SprintNet, obviating the need for expensive international phone calls. Most users were large or medium-sized companies, but LBH also used this link to send 'urgent action' bulletins on human-rights matters.

Supporters of LBH in the USA smuggled early versions of 'PGP' ('Pretty Good Privacy') encryption software into Indonesia so that LBH could send and receive information securely.[36] As Patrick Ball of the American Association for the Advancement of Science had noted, 'If we are to enable people to monitor violations of internationally recognized human rights, we must be able to communicate anonymously in cyberspace.'[37] Not all of LBH's overseas supporters concurred, with some Americans uncomfortable about the use of encryption because they felt that legal collaborations such as those involving LBH should be open and transparent rather than secretive.[38] The Indonesians involved, however, believed that encryption was needed to secure their freedom of speech and played a vital role in enabling them to distribute sensitive human-rights information under the nose of a repressive government. Thus, on the Indonesian stretch of the information superhighway, the lines between 'underground' political movement and transparent political discourse quickly became blurred.

The earliest attempt by a large national NGO to use new communication technologies domestically was LBH's establishment of LBH-net, a 'Wide Area Network' using 'toolnet' software, 2,400 bps modems, and funds from the Canadian International Development Agency (CIDA). This network enabled LBH to circulate information within its national network of branches, as well as linking to the Internet internationally when necessary. Under the umbrella of INFID (the International NGO Forum for Indonesian Development), this facility was expanded in 1994 into an NGO community e-mail intranet, NusaNet, designed so that select advocacy-oriented NGOs could communicate amongst themselves rapidly and safely, and then post information publicly on the global Internet.[39] Organisations such as INFID began to use this intranet extensively for inter-organisational communication as well as to minimise circulating hard copies of politically sensitive material.[40] The skills base of the NGOs was developed in large measure through trial and error, learning on the job and a small amount of formal training, some of it covert, from international NGOs.

The availability of commercial ISPs from 1995 coincided with one event by which 'cyberspace was finally recognized as a real battleground between the pro-democracy activists and the supporters of the Suharto rule'.[41] The LBH posted a three-sentence 'Urgent Action' calling for protest against the murder of a female labour activist in East Java of which the military were suspected. As one activist involved later wrote, 'In less than six hours after the Urgent Action was posted, the fax machines in the Office of the President, the Department of Foreign Affairs and the Department of Defense and Security were jammed with hundreds of sheets of protest from around the world. This event dramatically changed Marsinah, a young and unknown village girl from East Java, into a workers' heroine known world-wide. It also sparked an NGO-instigated online information war against one of the harshest militaristic regimes in the world.'[42]

Alternative media

About the same time as the Indonesian NGOs were starting to use online communication for their specific advocacy, the first open mailing list exclusively devoted to Indonesian matters emerged, moderated by John A. MacDougall in Maryland, USA. In 1984, MacDougall had established a private research support enterprise, Indonesia Publications, producing and marketing quality research data on various aspects of contemporary Indonesia. During the early 1990s, he contributed to various Internet conferences and newsgroups, which eventually crystallised as a free Internet mailing list on the IGC server. Though more correctly called 'INDONESIA-L', the list became commonly known as *apakabar* after the e-mail address of its founder. As MacDougall noted in his 'Brief History' of the *apakabar* list in those early years, 'Indonesian students studying overseas who subscribed to the then two largest Indonesian-language lists, Isnet and Janus, were sent copies of these postings on a routine basis as a means of keeping them informed on events at home.'[43] In mid-1996, MacDougall added a more comprehensive service, INDONESIA-P, charging an annual fee of $US120.

Apakabar grew into one of the most significant sources of information for contemporary scholarship on Indonesia and, as access to the Internet increased in Indonesia, the majority readership very quickly became Indonesians in Indonesia. The list's content – a mix of 'hard news' on Indonesia from papers and broadcasts from around the world, as well as a variety of commentaries, opinions and snippets of political gossip, mainly in Indonesian languages, not only uncensored but also unedited – established *apakabar* as a valuable means of disseminating information and analyses amongst many NGO activists and the Internet community at large.

MacDougall described the list's editorial policy as 'pluralism, a codeword for the free expression Indonesians did not then enjoy in their own country'.[44]

In the words of one Indonesian academic and newspaper columnist writing in 1996, '*Apakabar* has become a phenomenon. It would not be an overstatement to describe it as a legend on the Internet.'[45] Another writer from a University of Indonesia address stated: 'I am a loyal follower of this fabulous forum and I am pleased that we have such an extraordinary mechanism by which to state our opinions and our thoughts freely and openly.'[46] In late 1995, several prominent articles in the mainstream national print media drew attention to *apakabar*, especially the speed with which politically sensitive news was posted on the list. The weekly *Gatra* wrote, for instance, that news of the arrest and release of some prominent activists was on *apakabar* within hours, but did not make the local papers until the following morning.[47] Press coverage of military statements about the subversive potentials of the Internet inevitably included references to *apakabar*. There were many references to it in the Indonesian print media in the wake of the 27 July attack on the national headquarters of the Indonesian Democratic Party (PDI) in Central Jakarta's Jalan Diponegoro, when the number of people accessing the site rose dramatically.[48] *Republika* daily (associated with the Indonesian Muslim Intellectuals' Association, ICMI, founded by B.J. Habibie in December 1990),[49] obviously following the 'dozens of pieces on the riots … published by John Mac Dougall [sic] on his apakabar@clark.net', quoted from the net the views of radical organisations such as Pijar about the 27 July affair.[50]

It was not possible to confirm the identities of contributors 'posting' on lists such as *apakabar*, as MacDougall went to considerable lengths to ensure the anonymity of all list participants. *Apakabar* mail was circulated by the original and relay mailing lists, local newsgroups and lists, bulletin boards, individual subscribers, groups sharing a single e-mail address, and various other websites in addition to *apakabar*'s archival database, then located at a Stuttgart website. Not only did the system protect the identity of contributors, it was also almost impossible to determine precisely how many people had access. Around the end of 1995, prior to the boom in interest generated by the 27 July 1996 incident and subsequent references to *apakabar* in the Indonesian press, MacDougall attempted to determine the number of identifiable recipients of *apakabar* material and believed it to be about 13,000. He concluded that the majority of users were Indonesians living in Indonesia, followed by Indonesians living or studying abroad.[51] With numbers of subscribers increasing rapidly, in order to service the larger audience the enterprise moved to a commercial host, Ecosoft, with a moderated weblist site at <www.indopubs.com>.

The value to activist groups of *apakabar* was demonstrated in the wake of the 27 July incident. Within hours of the attack, *apakabar* was bristling with urgent postings from a wide range of sources, and including a detailed chronology of the unfolding events.[52] Capturing something of the sense of shared community of the mailing list in his opening salutation 'Dear Apakabarians' (*Apakabarians yth*), 'Pepi Hardiyanto' wrote his initial posting on the basis of 'eye-witness reports from someone at the scene to me by phone about 15 minutes ago'.[53] Hendardi, the

Communications and Special Programmes Director at the Indonesian Legal Aid Foundation (Yayasan Lembaga Bantuan Hukum Indonesia, YLBHI) – the grounds of which had become the makeshift first-aid centre for dozens injured in the attack on the nearby PDI office – quickly posted a detailed press release condemning the attack as a brutal and illegal act which warranted the immediate attention of the United Nations Sub-Committee on Human Rights.[54] The PDI itself posted a poignant appeal on *apakabar* from <pdi.megawati@indonesia.raya>, urging 'brothers and sisters throughout the country' (*Saudara-Saudara Sebangsa dan Setanah Air*) to circulate details of the attack as widely as possible, by e-mailing or printing it out, 'because at the moment all sources of information (newspapers, TV, etc.) have been pressured not to broadcast what really happened'.[55]

The Internet was providing an unparalleled mechanism for the pooling and sharing of information about the event – much of it highly personalised and by apparent non-professionals who witnessed events or their aftermath, but much also from respected NGOs or professional broadcast and print-media reporters. Comparing coverage of the 27 July incident on *apakabar* with two Indonesian and two Australian daily newspapers, Sharon Tickle concluded that *apakabar* 'outperformed the four print publications' with regard to both the 'timeliness' and 'accuracy' of its reports.[56] In this particular case, the speed with which the Internet was able to disseminate information, compared to conventional media, was even more obvious, since the day after the 27 July incident was a national holiday (for the prophet Mohammad's birthday) when no newspapers were printed, no doubt encouraging even greater interest in Internet reports.[57] Given the involvement of the military in either backing or planning the attack on the PDI building, its timing may have been intended to take full advantage of this media holiday.[58]

When the first of the Internet cafés started in Yogyakarta six weeks after the 27 July riots in Jakarta, there were many eager to scan the Internet for information presumed to be unavailable in the national media. In the early weeks of their operation, both privately owned Internet cafés in Yogyakarta, Mega and Pujayo, kept information on hand to assist those customers who wanted help to connect to *apakabar*. The manager of Pujayo estimated that about 40 per cent of Indonesian clients sought out *apakabar* and consulted it regularly.

From the 13,000 users estimated by list moderator John A. MacDougall in late 1995, by mid-March 1998 ten times that number were accessing *apakabar* daily. *Apakabar* became 'by far the largest Indonesian list in the history of the Internet, reaching 250,000 readers in 96 countries' (before it finally closed, for financial reasons, in February 2002).[59] As the *Bangkok Post* observed a month before Suharto's resignation, 'With anti-government street protests rocking Indonesia, opposition parties, students, journalists, and non-governmental groups have been busy posting news and spreading their views on the most important Indonesia-related list, INDONESIA-L [*apakabar*]'.[60]

MacDougall also noted an increased stridency in the postings and 'some of the new themes of the posters, such as very explicit, thorough criticism of Suharto and his family, the rejection of the legitimacy of Suharto's re-election as president and the open mockery of Vice-President Habibie and the new cabinet'. The circle of readers was growing exponentially, with MacDougall claiming that 'postings get printed out, reproduced and distributed in large quantities, bringing the reach of the net far beyond the middle class elite which can afford computers. Postings get read by Indonesian ministers, military officers and diplomats. Some rely on it for "inside" information.'[61]

When, in September 1996, *apakabar* shut down (as it transpired, temporarily) without prior notice, Gadjah Mada academic RM Roy Suryo, in his regular newspaper column about the Internet bemoaned its demise: 'Where can we go now that *apakabar* has closed?' before predicting that 'it is very likely that other "apakabars" will be born based on the same mechanisms'.[62] Indeed, within days the pro-democracy alliance PIJAR expanded the mailing list for its news bulletin *Kabar dari PIJAR* <KdP@usa.net>, filling something of the void left (for the few weeks) during *apakabar*'s absence. Playing a similarly complementary role was the Joyo News Service, a limited mailing list in English and Indonesian, begun in the northern summer of 1996 by an anonymous Indonesianist with thirty years' association with the country, who produced the list from a New York apartment. This list grew from initially only six friends of the founder in 1996 to 4,000 recipients in 1998.[63]

It has often been suggested that the Internet was difficult to censor in part because of its capacity to 'repair' itself: the technology is such that if one connecting node was severed, information would automatically be re-routed along other nodes. The efficiency and speed with which KdPnet replicated some of the functions of *apakabar*, albeit with a much smaller subscription list (517, about half using Indonesian e-mail addresses, the rest with either non-Indonesian or untraceable addresses).[64] was the result of political action rather than the technology's inherent capacity, of course. But Internet technology and the politics of freedom of speech and information had become so enmeshed in the last days of the New Order that such events confirmed the net as a self-repairing form of connectivity. We return again and again through this book to this 'techno-social' nature of the Internet, which makes it impossible to separate the impact of the technology on Indonesian politics from the way the technology was socially conceived and constructed at each stage.

Politics underground

From the point of view of the New Order government, by far the most problematic aspect of the growing Internet usage within Indonesia was the need to identify the sources of uncensored political information that appeared online and, indeed, to halt its distribution. If the government closed down a domestic site or news-posting group, another would spring up at some other location. From the point of view of political analysis, as our earlier discussion of LBH suggests, online activism in the late 1990s obfuscated the lines between open and underground politics in Indonesia. In this section we look at the way underground groups were making their political presence immanent by going online.

The Democratic People's Party (Partai Rakyat Demokratik, PRD), a small pro-labour, largely student-based and unregistered political party was accused by the authorities of planning the 27 July riots. It was demonised as an attempted revival of the Indonesian Communist Party, PKI, banned since 1965. The New Order government made concerted efforts to crack down on the PRD (together with its various affiliated mass organisations) after 27 July, arresting the party leadership and harassing and intimidating the rank-and-file.[65] The party and individual members continued posting on the web and on *apakabar* from an ISP outside Indonesia, maintaining its political presence nationally and internationally and thumbing its nose at the government. Representatives of the PRD abroad, with the support of local sympathisers in both Australia and the Netherlands, maintained a party website with regularly updated bulletins and information, and mirrored on a server in each of these countries.[66] The military's spokesman on social and political affairs, Lieutenant-General Syarwan Hamid, reportedly acknowledged this presence in a meeting with the major Jakarta NGOs and professional and religious organisations some weeks after the 27 July affair. He commented that the PRD's considerable power is 'evident in its activity on the Internet. Their writings are published at least twice a week. If they are prepared to show themselves on the Internet, it means they are strong. If they were not strong they would not be visible.'[67] Virtual political presence was thus being equated with real politics by both sides: the Internet's invincibility protecting the underground political activists, and simultaneously allowing them a public presence while marking the limits of the New Order's power against a banned political party.

Activists from the PRD initially learnt how to use e-mail from colleagues in some of the large, well-funded NGOs, such as the LBH. Even before the government crack-down on the PRD after 27 July, cadres were already using the net, but it was difficult, expensive and rare, since very few members had access to computers or only to those with slow, cumbersome modems. Support from some sympathetic academics meant that it was possible to use university facilities to send and download e-mails, a technique increasingly used when communicating with supporters abroad. Some secreted laptop computers with PCMCIA modems[68] into the *wartel* (phone kiosks or privately owned public phone facilities, discussed in Chapter 4) dotted around Indonesian cities since the 1980s. Typically the work was done in groups of three, with one member keeping look-out and two shielding the computer from sight inside the *wartel* phone booth. They would connect the laptop to the phone cable, sing or laugh to drown out the distinctive modem connection tones, and then rapidly upload and download their e-mails before a hasty exit.

The Internet, at this stage, was gaining in importance for the PRD's international linkages, but access remained occasional and it was of no use in any internal party communication within Indonesia. However, those members who could gain access to the Internet would download and copy material, then circulate this in 'hard copy' to others, eluding the government's attempts to restrict the movement of certain types of critical information in and out of the country. With the establishment of local ISPs, access became cheaper and Internet use increased. By 1996, when the 27 July incident sent many party cadres, mostly university students, into hiding, they were able to use the local ISP Idola to distribute material, canvass ideas and coordinate cadre activities via the Internet. While constantly on the move to avoid capture and detention, they developed a variety of strategies to access the net daily, while avoiding both detection and subscription fees. Some cadre members would subscribe to an ISP using a fake ID card (KTP) and mailing address, so that they could avoid paying the monthly bill. The next month they would move to a different ISP or sign up under a different 'identity' with the same provider. By this stage, they also had the capacity to encrypt their communications for secrecy, using software such as 'PGP'.

In the crack-down after 27 July, for the PRD activists (at least those in regional towns such as Yogyakarta) the net became 'the most effective communication medium – because it was very fast accessing information, cheap, and immediately deliverable to all'. During their years underground, it was to remain 'the most appropriate medium' for their anti-Suharto struggle. Chronologies of events, photos (which they would 'zip' for ease of transmission), political protest actions and anti-Suharto campaigns were written up, edited into a journal or bulletin to be then posted on *apakabar* and e-mailed to sympathetic mailing lists to foster the broader protest movement. This use by activists of the net developed in tandem with the spread of Internet cafés (*warnet*), providing increasing numbers of public-access points and bringing down the cost of access. In the words of one PRD cadre member, then based in Yogyakarta, '[w]e launched a guerrilla struggle via the Internet'; these public venues provided anonymity, ease of access and rapid transmission of writings locally and internationally for those 'on the outside' (that is, not underground).[69] The experience of those party members arrested also reinforced their collective confidence that the Internet was one arena in which the PRD had the upper hand in its struggle against the New Order: they gained the distinct impression that their interrogators, and even the prosecutors and judges, lacked any appreciation or even knowledge of Internet and e-mail technologies. It was clear to them that the activist community was much more astutely aware of the mobilising possibilities of the net than were New Order government security agencies.

For secret internal party purposes, the PRD continued to rely substantially on trusted couriers who moved around the country from cell to cell, circulating strategic information. While e-mail was useful for certain kinds of communication, it did not totally replace such personal human contact, needed for building solidarity and resilience in the struggle. Nonetheless, as a communication tool, the Internet was seen as more secure than the telephone (which users always suspected of being tapped) or 'pagers'. Even PRD groups outside of Java, as far afield as north Sumatra, north Sulawesi and West Papua, were comfortable using the Internet and e-mail for most political communication.[70] Within the party, which had a strong base on campuses including amongst communication and technology students, the skill required to use IT spread almost by osmosis amongst cadre members, without any formal party training programme or structured learning, though foreign sympathisers provided sporadic training in higher-order skills such as PGP encryption and webpage development. Members of the party generally encouraged each other to develop increasingly higher-level skills to maximise their use of improving technologies and software. Some members who had managed to flee overseas, usually on forged documents, tried to develop their computer skills before returning home.

The experience of the PRD in moving onto the Internet demonstrates a more common phenomenon amongst broader non-parliamentary opposition groups in Indonesia at this time. While the PRD was more radical, more covert and probably more efficiently organised than many, the pressures and opportunities that made the Internet so attractive to the PRD were also operating on many other groups of activists pursuing political reform.

From early 1996, a variety of political organisations within Indonesia started their own mailing lists, most of them cross-posting with each other and with *apakabar*. The Centre for Information and Reform Action Network (PIJAR), an organisation established by student activists as a 'mechanism for democratic struggle' in September 1989, was the first explicitly reformist political group to establish its own mailing list and website. The group pursued its aim of social and political justice through a programme of publications, education and training, and public advocacy. Its print periodical, *Kabar dari PIJAR* [News from PIJAR] (*KdP*), was one of a number of unauthorised publications that circulated amongst students, mainly in Jakarta. After the banning of three prominent newsweeklies – *Tempo*, *DeTik* and *Editor* – in June 1994 for their critical stance on various government policies,[71] there was a heightened public interest in political publications such as *Kabar dari PIJAR*. For two months immediately following the press bans, *KdP* appeared daily and illegally, without the then obligatory publishing permit, and maintained its strident critical stance at a time when the government was cracking down further on any public criticism.

In July 1995, *KdP* editor Tri Agus S. Siswowihardjo (known as 'TASS') was charged with insulting the President in an article in the magazine, and spent two years in jail. Office-bearers of another underground publication, *Independen*, the organ of the Alliance of Independent Journalists (AJI), were also jailed around the same time for spreading 'hostility, hatred and contempt' towards the government in their unlicensed publication.[72] *Independen* had been established by a group of journalists and students to counter 'the atmosphere in the Indonesian press of repressive control by the government and the dictates of a small group of owners of capital'.[73]

Unable to distribute on the streets after the mid-1995 crack-down, *Kabar dari PIJAR* went online in early 1996 as a mailing list called KdPnet, which also made it possible for PIJAR to distribute its messages much more easily to NGO groups outside Jakarta, to expatriate Indonesians and to international human-rights groups. Like many of the fully legal publications going online in this period, PIJAR used a server outside Indonesia, in this case provided by the Association for Progressive Communications (APC) in the United States.[74] The online version of AJI's *Suara Independen* (formerly *Independen*) also appeared on the same server at the same time. Part of *KdP*'s success was due to its strong links with former student press activists, whose careers had taken them into the mainstream media. As *KdP* editor TASS explained, '[I]f there was information from our journalist mates in the mainstream press which they could not write up because of the restrictions on their medium, they would pass the information on to us. We would write it up, and we'd publish it. So we could get complete information.'[75]

Several cyberpublications were produced by a core half-dozen activists associated with the Institute for the Free Flow of Information (Institut Studi Arus Informasi, ISAI), established by former *Tempo* journalists under the leadership of editor Goenawan Mohamad. Mostly young journalists with some older NGO activists, those producing such Internet material went to great lengths to keep their activities, identities and funding sources secret. Collectively, they produced a range of bulletins with differing emphases. The most enduring of these was *SiaR-list*, which started with the aim of becoming an 'alternative news agency' trying to reproduce what its founders saw as standard journalistic practices which were being corrupted by censorship and propaganda of the New Order government. SiaR News Service fostered other sub-lists including *Bergerak* (meaning 'move' or 'take action', in solidarity with the jailed PRD activists), *MateBEAN* (supporting independence for East Timor), *MeunaSAH* (on Aceh) and *MamberaMO* (on West Papua).[76]

By mid-1997, more than 20 other pro-democracy organisations in Indonesia had their own websites, most linked electronically to each other and to major international human rights networks abroad, such as the Global Democracy Network <www.gdn.org>.[77] The importance of these groups is not in how, or whether, individually they constituted a challenge to the Suharto regime or to the mainstream news media (which were also going online at the same time), but rather in the ways they functioned together as a forum in which to discuss, question and supplement what was formally defined as news. News stories that journalists wrote but could not get printed in newspapers regularly got posted on one or more mailing lists. Letters to editors that could not be printed, either for editorial policy or through lack of space, could easily be accommodated on a bulletin board. The online newsgroups were a constant reminder that censorship could be got around and much that could not be said in the formal media – whether for state-imposed restriction, or commercially or politically driven editorial policy, or simply lack of page space – could be circulated on the Internet. On the net, also, one did not have to be limited to a particular source of news (a particular paper): one webpage was necessarily an entry point to another.

The Internet also provided a highly targeted mode of communication for student activists. Though concentrated largely in Jakarta, organisers of the two major activist groups – the Jakarta Student Senate Communication Forum (FKSMI) and the City Forum (Forum Komunitas Mahasiswa se-Jabotabek, known commonly as Forkot) – began to mobilise nationally, contacting sympathetic students on campuses around the country. Several foreign observers in Indonesia at that time noted the centrality of the Internet in this organisational process. One noted that '[e]-mail and mobile phones gave the students and their supporters an additional opportunity to coordinate with each other and to make their viewpoints widely known. It [the net] also provided them with information about real or alleged examples of abuse of power by the Armed Forces, the authorities, and Soeharto and his family and friends.'[78] Another pointed out that '[d]uring the weeklong occupation of Parliament which led to Suharto's resignation, representatives of more than 40 universities met separately – a feat which would have been virtually impossible without online communications. And Internet postings ... reached thousands of other Indonesians as well.'[79] And yet another wrote: 'Bypassing the government-controlled television and radio stations, dissidents shared information about protests by e-mail, inundated newsgroups with stories of President Suharto's corruption, and used chat groups to exchange tips about resisting troops. In a country made up of thousands of islands, where phone calls are expensive, the electronic messages reached key organisers.'[80] Abigail Abrash of the Robert F. Kennedy Memorial Centre for Human Rights in Washington writes that, in the final days of Suharto's reign, while thousands of students had occupied the parliament building, her organisation was receiving reports that appeared to come from 'someone [who had] brought a laptop inside Indonesia's parliament building, and went on-line while [the Parliament was] surrounded by armed troops'.[81] The momentum was maintained in the weeks after Suharto's resignation with one observer noting that students 'downloaded overseas commentary on the movement, printed the most compelling posts, and plastered them on bus stops all over Jakarta'.[82]

Government failure

The flip-side of the story of enormous success of NGOs, student opposition and underground political groups was the failure of the New Order government's machinery of censorship and propaganda honed in the 1970s to control broadcast and print media pre-dating digital and satellite communication. In Chapter 2, we have described the ways in which the media as a whole were becoming increasingly difficult for the New Order state to control. The New Order mode of state censorship and later the control of content through concentration of ownership could not work in relation to the new technology.

The Internet posed a definitional problem in the context of the Indonesian government's departmental divisions: was it a broadcast medium which would be primarily under the Department of Information (Deppen), or was it an extension of the postal service to be placed under the Department of Tourism, Post and Telecommunications (Deparpostel)? Like radio and television, the new medium became the joint responsibility of the two departments. While 'content', and therefore in large measure all organisational matters relating to the two older electronic media, was in the hands of the Department of Information, in the case of the Internet the departmental arrangements remained unclear.

Policy differences between these departments reflected the tensions within the Indonesian bureaucracy from the mid-1980s onwards about how to respond to ideas and technologies of globalisation. In the last decade of Suharto's rule, the army and other security departments sought barricades against global influences; on the other hand, some of the economic ministries saw many aspects of globalisation as new openings for growth and development. The Department of Information, one of the old powerful ministries of the New Order, responsible for censorship and propaganda, fell into the former category. Deparpostel, a new portfolio created in 1983 with its primary function in international services (tourism, post, telecommunications) and infrastructural development, was in the latter category. Caught between two discursive positions, the Indonesian government, like many others in the region, was simultaneously enabling an expansion of computer networking capacity, while at the same time trying to control the informational content on the Internet. In the early 1990s, Deparpostel embraced the information technologies and their economic potentials with evident enthusiasm. The Departments of Information and of Defence and Security remained primarily concerned with regulation, monitoring and control of the information flows made possible by new technologies.

The Department of Information had formal responsibility for the content on the net but had great difficulty coming to grips with a medium whose broadcast capacity exceeded all other media (since any message can be sent instantly throughout the world), but which could simultaneously 'narrow-cast' down to a single individual. In September 1996, department officials participated in regional discussions in Singapore regarding Internet control but, while expressing support for the principle of strict control agreed upon in such forums, the Indonesian Department of Information never had the legal or technological means to enforce direct monitoring of Internet usage, or official restricting of particular sites, such as had been undertaken by the Singapore government.[83]

Reports circulated that ISPs were visited frequently 'by military officers, searching for the names of certain users', but prominent ISPs such as RADNET denied that they had been asked to restrict anything other than pornographic materials.[84] Journalists writing anonymously for the various cyberpublications believed strongly that the military were actively trying to identify them and track them down, with one journalist–activist writing that military spokesperson Brigadier-General Amir Syarifudin was 'busy trying to locate journalists who continue to write uncensored news reports', and that intelligence officers had been assigned 'to search office by office, editor by editor, to find Internet-based journalists who reported to the outside world'.[85] As with many newspapers and television stations, there were also rumours that intelligence staff were employed within the ISPs to monitor information on behalf of the Department of Information. Chapter X of the Broadcast Act, approved by the President in October 1997, appeared to be an attempt to legalise such modes of surveillance. Titled 'Investigation', the section stated: 'Apart from the police ... particular civilian employees of departments whose work and responsibility involves broadcast, are given special authority as investigators under Act No.8, 1981 of the Criminal Code [Hukum Acara Pidana]'.[86] The civilian investigator's duties start with 'receiving reports or complaints from individuals regarding criminal acts in the area of broadcasting' and include questioning and fingerprinting the suspect. Much of the bill was never put into operation.

Censorship in the Indonesian media, particularly from the early 1980s, had been effective in large measure because of self-censorship within media industries, rather than through consistent government action. But this self-censorship depended on the threat of punishment. In the case of the Internet the target, for such punishment was hard to define: who was to blame for a critical, anti-government message? The author? The ISP through which the message was transported? The reader who downloaded the message from a website? Moreover, webpages of entirely legal media outlets and even in one instance of a government department could provide links to many 'underground' ones, confusing even further the issue of responsibility. In a new industry, whose global *raison d'être* was unhampered flow of information, ISPs located in Indonesia needed to be internationally competitive in ensuring client confidentiality and access to information. Otherwise, for the price of a brief international phone call, Indonesian consumers might prefer to use ISPs located outside the Indonesian territory. Many Internet users, including some of the largest semi-underground mailing lists as well as legal newspapers and magazine websites, did use ISPs located abroad. In May 1996, Human Rights Watch/Asia regarded the Internet as freer than any other mass medium in Indonesia, 'thanks to an absence of laws, regulations, or ministerial decrees concerning its use'.[87] Suharto's last Information Minister, Alwi Dahlan, was only stating the obvious when he told the foreign press, just weeks before the president's fall, that 'I do not see how you could regulate the Internet'.[88]

Online propaganda was also a complete failure. In October 1995 the Indonesian Armed Forces, ABRI, established a special Internet unit, to go online as 'HANKAM/ABRInet'.[89] Its stated aim was to 'correct inaccuracies' in international information about Indonesia. ABRInet's real target was not so much the ill-informed foreigners, but locally gathered information that was quite correct but which contravened government interpretations and circulated on mailing lists such as *apakabar* and, later, KdPnet, SiaR and other virtual news-pools after 27 July 1996. The ABRInet site never achieved credibility or popularity. But political activists widely assumed that much of the pro-government material placed on popular bulletin boards or mailing lists came from staff in ABRI's Internet unit, as part of what one columnist described as 'ABRI's "Information War" in Cyberspace'.[90]

In an April 1997 speech, Suharto, in a veiled reference to the Internet and related technologies, warned that, though 'the free flow of global information' was bringing countries closer, 'this enables people to receive foreign values that can erode their sense of nationalism. So extreme is the impact of foreign influences, some people no longer care about maintaining their nation's unity.' According to at least one account, presidential advisers believed that such 'global information' was partly to blame for riots that had just broken out in central Java.[91]

Net effect on activism

While the Internet was, as we have described, particularly amenable to being used for concerted and covert activism, it was only one of the arenas where the activist groups discussed in the previous section transmitted their critique of the government. The same groups also arranged for the material to be printed out, photocopied and distributed in a variety of creative ways. Publications were tossed into crowds or demonstrations from passing motorbikes, left under seats on city buses, even sold by children hawking mainstream newspapers on street corners.

There were a variety of unconfirmed reports of people, including children, being detained by police for distributing material downloaded from the Internet. In August 1996, Human Rights Watch protested to the Indonesian government at the arrest of Prihadi Beny Waluyo, a lecturer at Duta Wacana Christian University in Yogyakarta, by soldiers of the district military command. He was

> accused of distributing e-mail messages and also of sending messages relating to the July 27 riots to a destination in Holland. His arrest came after an unidentified person gave an officer, photocopies of e-mail messages that were traced to Drs. Waluyo. The person claimed the printouts came from a store in Kebumen [a small town in Central Java].[92]

The Waluyo case – the only incident of which we are aware where someone was detained specifically and solely because of their Internet use – points to some useful ways of understanding the place of the Internet in the movement that brought down Suharto: firstly, that the impact of the Internet may not be fully understood simply by looking at the population with access to the net. Once downloaded, material was readily circulated in the form of photocopies, even through shops in small provincial towns such as Kebumen, with no public-access Internet facilities of its own at that time. Merlyna Lim has provided further evidence of linkages between cyberactivists and the wider community by systematically tracking the dissemination process of George Aditjondro's detailed listing of Suharto's wealth from Internet into the non-networked public.[93] Aditjondro's article appeared first as a series of four postings on *apakabar* on 31 January 1998, and continued its cyberspread through KdPnet, SiaR, and subsequently linked to many other websites. Then there followed a suggestion on one homepage that the document be printed out and faxed or passed on to non-Internet users. By April, it was appearing as faxes 'into private and public offices in major cities in Indonesia'. It was posted on *warnet* noticeboards and circulated beyond Internet users through a myriad of social and political networks. Lim argues that 'layers of mediators' connected elite informants such as Aditjondro (who had privileged access to information) with 'ordinary people' and concludes that 'the interconnectedness of all actors from all of these layers created the necessary multiplier effects for information dissemination to result in mass mobilization and political reform'.[94]

Secondly, the Waluyo case draws attention to the ready access of staff and students to the Internet, which made universities a major source of contraband information and in effect underwrote the leadership role of students and intellectuals in the political movement. Indonesian students have always been credited with initiating major political transformation in Indonesian history, from national independence,[95] to the fall of Sukarno, to the many uprisings in the three decades of New Order rule. To this historic role students and their teachers and mentors had now added a new claim to leadership, turning a specifically educational tool into a protest mechanism. In 1974 and 1978 when the students had marched on the streets against Suharto, the government had responded by legislating to restrict student participation in politics outside of the university. This time the weapons of resistance were inside the campuses and so legitimised in the technophilic discourse of the developmentalist New Order that, even if the military did come to fear the Internet, the provision of these through the education system kept expanding throughout the period of anti-Suharto activism.

Lim may be quite correct in thinking that the Internet was part of the process of integration of the different layers of informational conduits into a 'mass mobilization' for political reform. But equally, the technology was best understood and best utilised by students and middle-class urban professionals, and secured their leadership of the anti-authoritarian movement in 1997–98. The students did march on the streets against Suharto and get shot by the army in 1998, as they had marched against him in 1974 and 1978 and as they had marched against Sukarno in 1966, and as indeed they had taken up arms against the colonial Dutch in 1945. But beyond being student-*qua*-guerrilla fighter or student-*qua*-demonstrator, in the late 1990s the Internet made the student-*qua*-student, with their knowledge-technology, a key in the informational chain and therefore leader in a struggle that was centrally around control of information.

When one looks at the use of the Internet from the point of view of anti-Suharto activists who used it (as we have done in this chapter), the technology seems to have had a central role in the demise of the New Order. Some observers have taken a more cautious line to suggest that the Internet was 'an escalating factor' which 'fast-forwarded things' but did not change the outcome.[96] The political activists who used the net and the members of the regime who tried to block and blunt its efficacy both seem to insist on the centrality of the Internet in the fall of the Suharto dictatorship. This can seem surprising given the tiny reach of the technology. But the very acknowledgement of the role of the Internet necessarily identifies the leadership of the revolt against Suharto: a rebellion of university students and urban professionals who had the privilege of access to their colleagues around the world, through a new and (for the majority of Indonesians) exclusive communication technology. The role of the Internet in this context is therefore probably best understood by acknowledging the limits of the anti-Suharto movement, which did not involve the mass mobilisation across classes (or, with few notable exceptions, across regions). In the collapse of the New Order, the efficacy and reach of the net and the web within the urban middle class were more pivotal factors than their relative *in*accessibility beyond such groups.[97]

The Internet technology could have been used for purposes entirely different from regime change, as indeed it has been by the commercial sector both before and after Suharto's fall. But in the crisis-ridden Indonesian polity prior to May 1998, Gold and Platinum 'Corporate Net' lines advertised by the ISPs[98] seemed far less important than the wired *warnet* and their motorbike-riding student clients, who turned the state-supported educational and business tool into a weapon against the Suharto regime. In that sense, the political function of the Internet was defined by the growing middle classes and their discontents, both spawned by the New Order. In other words, the definition of the Internet as a 'political medium' was determined not by the technology per se, but by political agency of a section of the society whose leadership of the anti-Suharto movement may indeed have been boosted by their technology of choice.

It is easy to argue that a Habermasian public sphere was born in the discursive freedoms of the Internet in Indonesia. It was untarnished by both commercial interests and government interventions. But, like the public sphere idealised by Habermas, it was an exclusive space – only a small minority with the privileged technical access and knowledge could become full members of the new Indonesian public sphere. In the experiment with a mass-based democracy that followed the fall of Suharto, the role of the Internet and the public sphere it underpinned (and contained) in the last days of the New Order need to be judged again in relation to who was in and who was out of the net, and we turn to this in the next chapter.

4 Mapping the Internet in Indonesia

The global spread of the Internet has been uneven – flooding America and parts of Europe while barely even trickling into Africa and the Middle East.[1] Even within developed nations many authors argue that the technology will never become entirely universal.[2] It is therefore unsurprising that, within a developing economy such as Indonesia, access to the Internet has been highly unequal. In the context of an increasing expectation within both governments and the private sector that 'new technologies' such as the Internet will bring broad social and economic benefits to countries adopting them, the consequences of such inequitable access in Indonesia are significant. In particular, any assumptions by technophiles and bureaucrats in Jakarta that the Internet offers Indonesia unparalleled economic, political and social gains need to be tempered by a realistic assessment of the costs of the technology and other limits to access.

Like the Internet itself, research *about* the Internet in Indonesia is in its infancy.[3] Many elementary questions have yet to be answered and the pace of change overtakes easy answers. Much of the writing about the Internet in Indonesia concerns either highly technical aspects of digital communications hardware and engineering infrastructure, or thinly veiled marketing, promotional or business management material touting vast profits to be made from investment in dot.com businesses of various kinds.

Focussing on public-access rather than business or commercial applications, this chapter seeks to provide the empirical basis for dealing with the more analytical questions later in this book. How many people use the net? Where, and how, can the Indonesian public gain access? To what use do they put the Internet? We assert that Internet use in Indonesia may differ from that in the western developed nations that have been the focus of most research to date. In Indonesia, statistics on connectivity do not give an accurate picture of *who* uses the Internet, or even *how many* users there are, much less *how* they use the Internet. In a community where it is estimated that one copy of a newspaper is read by at least six people, there is extensive communal use of this much more expensive medium of information.[4] This chapter suggests that where and how one accesses the technology may substantially determine the use to which the technology is put. Thus the communal locations from which most Indonesians access the Internet might, to some extent, shape the social and cultural consequences of the technology here.

The chapter is divided into three sections. It begins by attempting to measure the growth of Internet use in Indonesia. The second section focusses on public-access Internet facilities, which emerge as the major locus of Internet use in Indonesia. It discusses their uneven diffusion throughout the archipelago, their ownership and potential for increasing user numbers. Thirdly, having established the geographical territory encompassed by the Internet and the dominant mode of connection to it, we tease apart possible profiles of Internet users and their patterns of usage.

Net growth

Global use of the Internet has increased a hundredfold since 1991. In 2002, the International Telecommunication Union estimated that there were around 590 million Internet users globally, with more than one-third in Asia, including about four million in Indonesia.[5] As with the rest of Asia, the Internet started growing substantially in Indonesia in the mid-1990s.[6] Like other governments in Southeast Asia, the 'developmentalist authoritarian'[7] government of Indonesia under then President Suharto (1966–98), and particularly B.J. Habibie, as Minister of Technology, later Vice-President and finally President (May 1998–October 1999), embraced the Internet as a conduit of national development. According to the Department of Tourism, Post and Telegraph (Deparpostel) estimates, in 1995–96 the Information Technology market in Indonesia was worth more than 100 billion rupiah (approximately US$43.5 million) with about 40 per cent of this being in the banking and finance industries.[8] In 1997, Indonesia was included by the magazine *Inter@ctive Week* as one of the 'Emerging 20' nations offering 'a plethora of untouched opportunities for expanding the Internet'. The Latin-American, Asian and Eastern European countries listed were noted for having 'two qualities that make them extremely attractive to U.S. equipment providers: All are in their technological beginnings and all are headed by governments that realize the vital need for advanced communications to sustain an economy in the new Internet frontier'.[9] While projections of growth were consistently optimistic in these early years, the expansion of the Internet in Indonesia remained relatively slow compared to its near Southeast Asian neighbours Malaysia and Singapore. Through its last decade, the Suharto government seemed committed to extending the Internet both horizontally across the regions and vertically across the socio-economic classes.

Lack of basic communication infrastructure constrained uptake. For Indonesia, where even in mid-2000 the population of 210 million shared only 7.5 million telephone connections, 3 million of which were in Jakarta, national teledensity (that is, the number of phone connections for the total population) of 3.6 per cent was also well below that of Thailand (7–8 per cent) and neighbouring Malaysia (20 per cent).[10] Indonesian rural areas typically have very degraded infrastructure and scarce phone lines. Of about 72,000 villages in Indonesia in 2003, 42,000 were not reached by landline connections. While in Jakarta, the ratio of public telephones to population is around 61 phones per 10,000, in some outer regions this plummets to only one–six phones per 10,000.[11] Constrained by such infrastructural limits, connecting to an Internet Service Provider (ISP), particularly from rural areas, remains extremely difficult. It involves at least a long-distance call to a nearby town, with connections subject to frequent breaks and very slow transmission speeds, often less than 10 Kbps.[12]

The exact number of Internet users at any given time in Indonesia is notoriously difficult to establish, with an International Telecommunication Union study noting that 'there is a serious shortage of ICT [information and communication technology] market information for Indonesia'.[13] Nonetheless, the trajectory of Internet growth is clear and dramatic. Prior to 1995, Internet use in Indonesia had been restricted to a handful of science students in the major universities; by the end of 1995, there were an estimated 15,000 Internet users, serviced by five commercial ISPs and the initial university-based network, IPTEKnet. By the middle of the following year, there were 15 ISPs in operation and 40,000 subscribers. By May 1997, the government had issued permits to 41 ISPs, of which 32 appeared to be operational.

Over the following year, as the Asian financial crisis hit, the growth in subscription numbers slowed and remained at about 85,000 through 1997–98.[14] Indonesia experienced economic problems that were 'exceptionally serious by any historical or contemporary standard' and 'certainly much deeper than any other Southeast Asian nation'.[15] Nonetheless, figures in September 1999 from the Association of Indonesian Internet Service Providers (APJII) indicated that growth had resumed, with 250,000 paid-up subscribers, a sixfold increase in the two and a half years since the end of 1996.[16] Indonesian Internet traffic also grew disproportionately, with APJII figures indicating a ninefold increase in traffic between January and October 2000.[17] In 2001, APJII listed 55 active ISPs (out of 147 with licences).[18] Growth in user numbers exceeded predictions, reaching more than 4 million in 2001–02, to over 8 million (again exceeding predictions) by the end of 2003 (Table 4.1).[19]

Other measures generally confirm similar growth.[20]

Table 4.1 Indonesian Internet growth: subscribers and users (cumulative)

Year	*Subscribers*	*Users*
1996	31,000	110,000
1997	75,000	384,000
1998	134,000	512,000
1999	256,000	1,000,000
2000	400,000	1,900,000
2001	581,000	4,200,000
2002	667,002	4,500,000
2003	865,706	8,080,534
2004*	1,300,000	12,000,000

Source: These figures are drawn from APJII's website, <www.apjii.or.id/dokumentasi/statistik.php?lang=ind> (accessed 4 June 2004) and earlier versions.

*estimate for 2004

The Internet boom has encouraged a raft of ISPs. While 150 ISP licences had been issued by June 2001, only 60 were actually operating.[21] By March 2003, the number of ISP licences had risen to 186, but only 121 of these had registered as members of APJII, indicating a likelihood that their business was active.[22] Despite this multiplication of ISPs, ten major providers dominate with nearly 80 per cent of market share. Some of these large ISPs enhance their positioning through their own chains of Internet cafés; others offer fierce competition to conventional telephone companies by offering cheaper VoIP (voice-over Internet protocol) phone services.[23]

Another common measure of national Internet growth is the increase in 'Indonesian' domain names: that is, Internet addresses ending with the Indonesia-specific '.id'.[24] During the early years of the Internet in Indonesia, these doubled annually. To some extent, the increase in the number of Indonesian domains was enhanced by a June 1997 APJII-sponsored agreement to establish the Indonesia Internet eXchange (IIX). Prior to this agreement, virtually all Indonesian Internet traffic, even between servers physically in Indonesia, used international connections. By re-routing communications directly between Indonesian ISPs, the IIX minimised the use of more expensive international connections, and consequently reduced ISP operational costs and increased transmission speed.[25] Nonetheless, in 2001, the number of new '.id' domains began to decline, in what APJII regarded as part of a global slowing in dot.com enterprises (Table 4.2).

Table 4.2 Indonesian domain names (new and cumulative)

	Rahardjo		*APJII*	
Year	*New domains*	*Total domains*	*New domains*	*Total domains*
1995	87	87		
1996	240	327		
1997	722	1,049		
1998	1,484	2,533	1,479	1,479
1999	2,163	4,696	2,148	3,627
2000	4,266	8,962	4,219	7,846
2001			3,478	11,324
2002			3,183	14,507
2003			3,764	19,167
2004 (March)			994	20,161

Source: This table is compiled from two primary sources. Figures up to 1998 are from Budi Rahardjo, 'Indonesian Internet Statistics', unpublished report, PT INDOCISC & PT Insan Infonesia, version 1.7, dated 2001, downloaded from <www.insan.co.id/indonesia-internet-statistics.pdf>, 3 September 2002. Figures from 1998–2004 are from <www.apjii.or.id/dokumentasi/statistik.php?lang=ind> (accessed 4 June 2004).There are minor discrepancies between these two sources, but they are not significant.

Table 4.3 Indonesian domain distribution

Sub-domain	*Total*	*percentage*
ac.id (academic)	291	2.97%
co.id (company)	6,115	62.50%
mil.id (military)	6	0.06%
net.id (provider)	130	1.32%
or.id (others)	1,571	16.05%
sch.id (school)	578	5.91%
web.id (web)	1,059	10.82%
war.net.id (*warnet*)	34	0.34%
Total	9,784	99.97%

After excluding the small number of Indonesian government sub-domains ('go.id'), in March 2001, the break-down of the distribution of '.id' domain names showed commercial enterprises dominated the sector (as 'co.id', 'net.id', 'web.id' and 'war.net' sub-domains) with 75 per cent of the Internet presence (Table 4.3).

These statistics do not capture any domains which may be registered without the Indonesian '.id', such as companies using the 'generic' or 'universal' domain pattern without an identifier linking them to any country (for example, '.com', or '.net' only). The drift of Indonesian businesses to '.com' rather than 'co.id' domain names caused APJII and the Indonesian Country Code Top Level Domain (ccTLD) administration to investigate public perceptions of the reliability and security of 'co.id'. Their report noted that 'there is a perception in the community generally which infers that the use of the .COM domain as the representation of, or identity for, an e-Business on the Internet holds a more prestigious value compared with the use of a co.id domain'.[26] It seems that, while Indonesian businesses were developing a presence on the net, they were not always keen to be identified as 'Indonesian' when they did so, preferring the more prestigious 'universal' address.

Perhaps the most dramatic measure of the expansion in the Indonesian segment of the Internet is the volume of 'traffic' it carries (in Megabytes per second). Between February 1999 and March 2003, the peak traffic carried by the Indonesia Internet eXchange increased a massive 300-fold, from 2.05 Mbps to 620.595 Mbps in four years, doubling again by December 2003 (Table 4.4).

However, even with this burgeoning user-base, with parallel growth in Indonesian domain registrations and total Internet traffic volume, 'dial-up' subscribers still amounted to only about 0.4 per cent of the country's 210 million inhabitants at the end of 2003.

Subscription numbers, however, provide only a very incomplete picture of the extent of Indonesia's Internet usage. Corporate connections are invariably used by more than one staff member, and within a home several members may use the same subscription, raising the number of people with access to the net substantially

Table 4.4 Indonesia Internet eXchange (IIX) peak traffic

Date	*Peak traffic*
February 1999	2.05 Mbps
January 2000	3.07 Mbps
May 2001	40.96 Mbps
March 2002	245.76 Mbps
March 2003	620.595 Mbps
December 2003	1.2 Gbps

Source: <www.apjii.or.id/dokumentasi/statistik.php?lang=ind> (accessed 4 June 2004).

above the total of financial subscribers. In Indonesia the practice of sharing passwords and accounts is common. What seems apparent, from APJII estimates at any rate, is that *total user numbers* are growing at a much faster rate than subscribers, from a factor of 3.5 in 1996, to 6.75 in 2002 to 9.4 in 2003, suggesting a much greater uptake of non-subscriber access modes over subscriptions. As a percentage of total population, too, Internet users have increased substantially in recent years, comprising about 4 per cent of the population in 2003, up from 2 per cent in 2001.

Indonesia's low teledensity and poor Internet connection speeds have been referred to above. Income levels make personal computer ownership levels low, even by Southeast Asia's standards.[27] Wage figures from the Indonesian Central Bureau of Statistics (Badan Pusat Statistik, BPS) suggest that the price of the cheapest personal computer is well over the median monthly earnings of the overwhelming majority of working Indonesians.[28] Our observations and anecdotal evidence suggest that the price of a personal computer was well over the monthly income of all but senior executives and successful professionals. All of this accounts for a relatively slow rise in subscriptions.

Public-access Internet facilities

While Indonesian personal computer ownership figures might be low, a burgeoning expansion of public-access points has put the technology within reach of some people who could not afford their own computer (or even a telephone connection), which explains in part the consistent estimate of industry insiders that the number of Internet users greatly outstrips the number of personal computers in the country.[29]

The popularity of public-access Internet emulated an earlier boom in public telephone and facsimile services, through government-owned and private telecommunication kiosks. In the early 1980s, it was not uncommon to have to queue even in lower-middle-class areas of Jakarta to make a call from the sparse scattering of public telephone booths. While public phone booths (common on street corners and shopping malls in western cities) remained sparse in Indonesia, mass public access to telephony began in the mid-1980s when the '*warung telekomunikasi*', commonly called *wartel* and best translated as 'telecommunication kiosk', began to dot the Indonesian urban landscape, providing local, national and international phone and fax links. The *wartel* are more or less elaborate versions of the corner shop, mostly privately owned, often with several phones arranged in booths to allow for a relatively private conversation. By the early 1990s, there were 25,000 public phones and 800 *wartel* around the country.[30] This expansion of the *wartel* continued, with the number of *wartel* phones soaring 23 per cent nationally in the period 2000–2001 alone.[31] *Wartel* provide a greater access to telephony than do non-*wartel* public phones. In Jakarta, for example, the ratio of *wartel* phones and public phones was 115 compared to 61 per 10,000 population. In the least-serviced outlying regions, *wartel* still provide between five to 25 phones per 10,000 population, compared to only one to six public phones per 10,000.[32] For the vast majority of Indonesians without personal phone access, the *wartel* is their local provider of phone services. The relative privacy of the *wartel* made possible a degree of clandestine use of phones and, by extension, the use of the Internet for underground political work (described in the previous chapter).

In more recent years, personal telephone access has been expanded through a proliferation of mobile carriers. In 2001 alone, cellular phone subscriptions rose nationally more than 41 per cent to an estimated 7.4 million mobile subscribers by mid-2002[33] (higher by some estimates) and to 18.2 million by the end of 2003.[34] But, while mobile-based net connections and the myriad of other wireless services are widely promoted in advertising targeting the Jakarta elite, there appears to be only modest uptake of such services and, for the present, these constitute only a tiny fraction of national Internet connections. The vast majority of Indonesian netters use landlines, either from home or office, or from a public Internet access point.

With the arrival of commercial Internet Service Providers in Indonesia in 1995, many *wartel* added Internet to their existing telecommunications facilities and adopted the name *wartelnet* (Internet telecommunication kiosks) or, increasingly, *warnet* (Internet kiosks). More commonly in the early years of Internet growth, cafés or *warung* (roadside stalls selling food, the word from which the *warnet* takes its name) set up a couple of tables with computers for customers who might pay 1,000 rupiah for a cup of coffee and 5,000 rupiah for an hour of web access. In her study of *warnet*, Merlyna Lim has argued that 'the *warnet* has emerged as a reincarnation or contemporary form of the *warung*' which had long been 'simultaneously a point of commerce, a meeting place, and an information network for the households in the neighbourhood. Not just a place to eat, the *warung* is where people meet to chat and to gain and spread information.'[35] The accelerating popularity of these *warnet* provided one of the major drivers of the growth of access to the Internet, despite the post-1997 economic malaise in Indonesia.[36]

By the end of 1998, the Internet was accessible to subscribers in more than a hundred cities and towns with public-access points in most provincial capitals.[37] One industry study estimated that, by the end of 2000, there were 1,500 *warnet* operating in cities and town across Indonesia.[38] Even more optimistic was AWARI (the Indonesian Internet Kiosk Association), which estimated that, by the end of 2000, there may have been as many as 2,500 *warnet*, increasing at a rate of 30 per cent per annum.[39] As this sector of the industry expanded, there emerged a variety

Table 4.5 Internet users – Indonesia 1999

Place of access	*ACNielsen*	Tempo Magazine
Office	52%	30%
'Warnet'/public rental	26%	62%
School/campus	19%	18%
Relative's home	13%	2%
Own home	11%	23%
Friend's home	n/a	7%
Totals	121%	142%

Source: *Media Scene 1999/2000*, PPPI, Jakarta, p.32. Origin of data not provided. The totals exceed 100 per cent since some users may use different access points at different times.

of organisational support structures for the Internet kiosk-owners, such as AWARI and other local associations of operators. Books and webpages appeared, detailing how to start up and manage such operations. Public-access venues were heavily promoted by 'techno-activists' such as US-trained engineer-turned-Internet-guru Onno W. Purbo, who campaigns to 'socialise' the Internet by providing detailed guidelines and free personal advice on how to set up and run cheap, community-based *warnet*. Despite their relative ubiquity in metropolitan cities such as Jakarta or Surabaya and university towns such as Bandung and Yogyakarta, there is very little statistical data on who used the *warnet* in the late 1990s. However, there is little doubt that, by 1999 (as figures from two separate sources show), a significant proportion of Indonesians using the Internet – somewhere between one-quarter and two-thirds – used *warnet* (compared with a quarter or less dialling up from home) (Table 4.5).

Geographical concentration

If there is an economic divide in Indonesia between wealthy subscribers dialling from home and others using the public *warnet*, unequal access also has a geographical dimension. About 75 per cent of Internet subscribers and users are believed to be located in Jakarta, 15 per cent in Indonesia's second city, Surabaya, with another 5 per cent elsewhere in Java, leaving only the remaining 5 per cent scattered across the rest of the archipelago.[40] The concentration of financial resources and infrastructure, primarily in Jakarta and on the island of Java, through the New Order years is well documented. Address lists in the Indonesian Yellow Pages indicate that the overwhelming majority of the Indonesian ICT companies are located in Jakarta (1,414 in 2003), followed by Surabaya and Bandung, Java's other major industrial centres. Very few ICT companies appear to be located outside of Java: 42 in Medan, the largest city in Sumatra; 32 in Bali; just six in Makassar; and four in Palembang. *Warnet* also have not escaped the Jakartacentric economics of the New Order, despite the regional autonomy legislation of the post-Suharto period designed to move away from the concentration of economic and political power in Jakarta.

The locations of the identifiable *warnet* thus provide an index of exclusion of some sections of the population. In August 2000, AWARI listed 364 *warnet.* It had a comprehensive list of these in Jakarta and the surrounding area – 265 in all – but only a handful in other cities in Java and Bali. The Idaman.com website (owned by another association of *warnet*) provided a more representative list of 340 public-access points across the archipelago. Given that membership of these groups and the provision of information to such websites are voluntary, no such list was exhaustive. But 314 *warnet* on the Idaman list provide sufficient information for verification of their existence. Of these, 264 or nearly 85 per cent were located on the island of Java, where a little over half the Indonesian population live. On this list, the capital Jakarta accounted for 80 (or just under a quarter) of all public-access points, though only about 5.5 per cent of the nation's population live there. Another 105 were in three provincial capitals (Surabaya, Bandung and Semarang) and 42 in Yogyakarta and Solo, the old university towns and the cultural heartland of Java. The remaining 37 were spread across several district capitals. Outside of Java, we found no listed public-access Internet outside of large provincial capitals and the Bali tourist areas.

In mid-2001, an industry study, using data from the Warnet Directory (at natnit.net), claimed that1,151 *warnet* had registered on the online directory, but declared that the actual number across Indonesia may be more than 2,000, since many 'do not yet have a license to operate'.[41] An Indonesian Cyber Industry study noted that more than 50 per cent of the *warnet* they identified were in Jakarta, where the ratio was more than one *warnet* per 20,000 people.[42] Although it found that 'the number of *warnets* available throughout Indonesia is quite a considerable amount', the ratio fell to around one *warnet* per million inhabitants in places such as West Nusa Tenggara, Sumatra, Sulawesi and Maluku.[43]

Data from 2002 reinforce this general mapping of *warnet* predominantly on Java. The government's Centre for the Study and Application of Information Technology and Electronics (P3TIE) provides a breakdown of 1,480 *warnet* (based on natnit.net data), which indicates that 35 per cent are in Jakarta, 25 per cent in West Java, 15 per cent in Central Java and Yogyakarta, 11 per cent in East Java, 6 per cent in Sumatra, 3 per cent in Bali and the West Nusa Tenggara, with 2 per cent each in Kalimantan and Sulawesi and the remaining 1 per cent spread across Maluku and Irian Jaya.[44] *Warnet* are clearly spreading through Java and Bali, but not yet to the corners of the archipelago, drawing all citizens equally into a cyber-community.

Nonetheless, all evidence confirms that the growth of *warnet* has been much faster than the rise in subscriptions. The increase – like the geographic concentration – is most evident on Java. In Yogyakarta, for example, a Central Java town renowned as a centre of tertiary education and one of the fastest provincial capitals of Internet up-ake, the first three *warnet* opened in September 1996, growing to at least 31 by mid-2000. Similar growth was evident in Malang in East Java, also with a high proportion of students among its population of about 700,000. Like Yogyakarta, Malang's first *warnet* opened in September 1996; within four years the number had grown to 52, of which 38 were near one of the town's several universities. In a micro-study of the *warnet* industry in Malang and Blitar undertaken in September–October 2000, Paul Harvey calculated that there was one *warnet* computer for every 2,360 inhabitants of Malang and every 5,833 in Blitar.[45]

To believers in the transformative capacity of the Internet, the growth of *warnet* had seemed to be the answer to the problem of the enormously unequal distribution of technology (generally, and IT in particular) both across regions and across social classes in Indonesia. A deputy minister in the Megawati government, J.B. Kristiadi, claimed that farmers in several locations throughout Indonesia were using the Internet to monitor price fluctuations for their agricultural commodities, thereby maximising their market price.[46] The data above on regional distribution of *warnet* and other modes of connectivity cast grave doubts, however, on the prospects of an ordinary farmer in the regions accessing the Internet currently or in the near future. There is little to suggest that Indonesia is any exception to Harold Thimbleby's quip that 'serfs don't surf'.[47]

Local *warung* or multinational centres

As indicated in the last chapter, the Internet developed in Indonesia as the preserve of the young, technophilic, new entrepreneur – and the New Order government seemed committed to keeping it that way. In the mid-1990s, the Department of Tourism, Post and Telecommunications (Deparpostel) appeared to be issuing only a limited number of ISP licences and these only to companies run by technically competent young IT entrepreneurs, who were explicitly outside the politically well-connected conglomerates that dominated the domestic economy and, as discussed in Chapter 2, the media in particular.

In February 1996, the Deparpostel Minister, Joop Ave, stated explicitly that 'the government remains consistent, in that ISP [licences] will not be given to conglomerates'. Department Director-General, Djakaria Purawidjaja, denied that the policy was hostile to big business and suggested that it was designed to maximise the entrepreneurial potential of IT graduates returning from training abroad. He emphasised that there was no prohibition against conglomerates 'supporting' these entrepreneurs, 'provided such help did not influence the decisions of those who held the [ISP] licences'.[48] But very quickly, some novice companies were drawn into various financial arrangements with the major conglomerates or state concerns. RADNET, for example, with a leadership that was very young (the oldest of the founders was 33) and highly qualified (all three principals had postgraduate degrees), developed political connections rumoured to include Bustanil Arifin, a former minister in the Suharto government (1988–93) and head of the national Logistics Board, and to a lesser extent Admiral Sudomo, the former Commander of the all-powerful Kopkamtib (Command for the Restoration of Security and Order), and President Suharto's son-in-law Prabowo Subianto. The company quickly established itself as a market leader in Jakarta and Surabaya.

This trend of large business empires acquiring ISPs continued. By1997, Suharto crony Liem Sioe Liong's BCA Group appears to have had an interest in CBN, and other large conglomerates like the Centrin, Napan and Lippo business groups were involved in the ISPs Centrin, Central On-Line and LinkNet respectively.[49] But many ISPs remained in the hands of small businesses until the end of the decade.

When *warnet* started appearing from around 1996, these were also overwhelmingly established and run by small local operators, not owned by the ISPs or other big business. The only large commercial entity involved was the government postal company, PT Pos Indonesia, in partnership with its own ISP, Wasantara.net.[50] In 1996, PT Pos Indonesia had joined with Telkom (formerly a state monopoly and the largest telecommunications company in Indonesia) and the Telecommunications Technology College (STT Telkom) to establish the ISP Wasantara.net (privatised in June 1995), to offer Internet services through local nodes in every provincial capital and other major cities. Pos Indonesia had been using the Internet internally from about 1988 but, around 1993, it began exploring the possibility of offering public Internet services, developing plans for *Warpostron* (electronic mail kiosks) at post offices, extending the existing arrangements for long-distance fax and telephone facilities. It established small Internet stalls – sometimes with only three or four terminals – in public post offices around the country, quickly spreading into the widest network of *warnet* in the country. The *warnet* was a logical extension of Wasantara's ISP service and part of an ambitious national strategy to supply Internet access via local nodes in all Indonesian provinces, paralleling conventional postal services. In 2000–01, Wasantara.net linked about half of the major post offices (154 out of 314)[51] to the Internet, but it did not reach its expansive plans for 288 outlets nationally.[52] By mid-2002, financial difficulties forced it to close many of its *warnet* and local dial-up ISP in many areas, leaving only about 75 cities in the network.[53] However, Wasantara retains the largest geographic spread of any Indonesian ISP and remains the most extensive provider of *warnet* facilities. If a town has only one Internet kiosk, it is most likely to be in the central post office and owned by Wasantara. When other ISPs and large operators did enter the *warnet* market, these were almost exclusively in the large capital cities as points of presence familiarising the would-be subscriber with the ISP brand name.

Most commonly, in the mid to late 1990s, *warnet* developed as a high-tech 'cottage industry', with individual small business operators opening usually just one Internet café but sometimes a small chain of half a dozen around a town. Until at least 2000, the industry was the province of what are referred to in Indonesia as 'UKM' (*usaha kecil dan menengah*, small and medium enterprises).[54] Yogyakarta and Malang provide good instances of patterns of *warnet* growth.[55] In Yogyakarta, the first three *warnet* were opened within days of each other. Wasantara's *warung pos Internet* (Internet post kiosk) opened on 12 September 1996, with three computers tucked away in a ground-floor corner of the city's Central Post Office. Wasantara had only begun offering dial-in services for business and individual clients in Yogyakarta in February that year and by September had a clientele of about 700.[56] The other two *warnet*, owned by local business people, were established on the borders of the largest university in the town, Gadjah Mada (UGM). On Jalan Colombo, the main road connecting UGM to some of the biggest private universities in the city, the Maga *warnet* opened on 17 September, offering free access for the inaugural week. And in that week, its seven booths were constantly in use throughout the opening hours: 9 a.m. to 10 p.m. Less than a kilometre away, on Jalan Simandjuntak on the western edge of the UGM campus, about 300 metres from the university's own Internet computer centre GAMA-net, another Internet café, Pujayo.C@fe.Net, had opened on 9 September. Its eight computer terminals were dramatically visible through the four glass walls, which carved out a third of the downstairs floor space of Pujayo's popular eatery and karaoke lounge. Both of the private kiosks were stylish, appealed to students and drew a constant high volume of patronage.

In Malang, the first *warnet* was established by Wasantara.net, but quickly others appeared both in the town centre and around the various universities. While the majority (70 per cent) were not actually managed by the owners, particularly in the university environs it was common to find *warnet* being established by recent graduates who would pool their funds to buy the computers and other equipment necessary to start up. Like those who established the first ISPs, those who established and ran the first *warnet* were also young, male and relatively highly educated. The *warnet* generally had about six or seven computers, each at a cost of about 4.5 million rupiah if new (or 3.1 million rupiah if second-hand), representing a modest 'start-up' cost of less than $US2,000.[57] The likelihood of forging a profitable small enterprise with steady cash-flow was good, as the market and demand expanded steadily in those early years. Harvey estimated that more than 4 per cent of Malang's population used the *warnet* and, more remarkably, about 25 per cent of the city's university students did.[58]

From about 2000 onwards, international IT companies began to move into both the Indonesian ISP and the *warnet* market. In mid-2000, the multinational MIH (Myriad International Holding) moved into the Indonesian market as 'M-Web Indonesia'. Its homepage claimed that it was a substantial enterprise:

> Established in South Africa in 1986, MIH (www.mih.com) has grown into a multinational company with operations in more than 50 countries. For the Internet market, the spearhead of MIH is M-Web Holding Limited, a portal and Internet Service Provider company, which leads the online market in South Africa with more than 250,000 customers. The M-Web Group was established in October 1997, and grew to lead the Internet marketing South Africa within two years. […] After its success in South Africa, the M-Web Group (www.mweb.com) broadened its portal and ISP business globally starting in Thailand (www.mweb.co.th), China (www.mweb.co.cn), Namibia (www.mweb.co.na), Zimbabwe (www.mweb.co.zw) and Indonesia (www.mweb.co.id).[59]

In May 2000, M-Web acquired a small ISP named Cabinet and then, just two months later, Satunet, one of the biggest portals in Indonesia. In August, it launched <www.mweb.co.id>, adding enhanced search engines, finance, and travel operations by the end of the year. In January 2001, it acquired PT Warnet Gemilang, the biggest network of privately owned Internet centres in Indonesia, and <www.astaga.com>, one of the country's most popular portals. In March, it signed agreements with the Surabaya Institute of Technology (ITS) and Gadjah Mada University (UGM) Yogyakarta, initially for the development of campus-based 'student Internet centres', with Malang's Brawijaya University and others following.[60] By June 2001, the company had invested $US10 million in Indonesia (in the hope of generating half that figure in revenue within a year). It owned more than 600 Internet-linked computers in the key cities of Jakarta, Yogyakarta and Surabaya. Its strategy was to establish student Internet centres on major campuses. The University of Indonesia Psychology Faculty M-Web centre, for example, had 120 screens and charged students 5,500 rupiah per hour.[61] News of these large, fast and well-equipped Internet centres filtered out of the campuses and attracted other users.[62] After a hectic two years of expansion, M-Web declared itself 'the largest Internet center operator in Indonesia' and the 'largest online service provider, providing total Internet solutions for corporate, SME [small and medium enterprises], as well as individual users'. It had expanded its operation to nearly 1,400 screens in 20 centres across Java.[63]

In July 2002, it began shedding staff and selling off ISPs in restructuring operations that failed to achieve profitability.[64] Closing the door on Indonesia in March 2003, MIH sold off M-Web Indonesia's assets (including Astaga.com, Kafegaul.com and satunet.com) to PT Indonesia Media Technologies (IMT).[65] While MIH's flamboyant foray into Indonesia had lasted less than three years and was not in itself a business success story, investors such as M-Web signalled the possibility that public-access Internet could be undergoing a transition from local *warung* to branded multinational centres.

The Internet centres, often using satellite links to facilitate reliable high-speed connections, threatened the smaller operators, around 75 per cent of which used slower, more erratic dial-up ISP links.[66] When M-Web initially opened on UGM campus, the local branch of AWARI, the Yogyakarta Internet Kiosk Association (AWAYO), launched a public protest campaign, including a spirited debate on the AWARI mailing list. In May 2001, 100 AWAYO members passed a motion condemning M-Web's arrival in Yogyakarta. With a high density of small *warnet* in the university precinct, AWAYO Chairperson Stephanus Edi Pambudi declared, 'We are worried that if M-Web enters the UGM campus it will set a tariff which will kill off the competition from *warnet* in the campus surrounds.'[67]

Other big (and often well-connected) investors had entered the *warnet* scene about the same time as M-Web. These included Indonesia's national Telkom, Myohdotcom, the powerful Indonesian Lippo Group (through the holding company Across Asia Multimedia Ltd, chaired by Jonathan L. Parapak, former Secretary-General of the Tourism, Post and Telecommunications Ministry during the last years of the New Order period), and PT Semesta Citra Intan (owned by Rini M.S. Soewandi, the Minister for Trade and Industry in the Megawati Sukarnoputri Cabinet). Most large companies primarily targeted eager university students, who had a high demand for, and familiarity with, Internet use. Telkom started its own campus Internet centres early in 2001, signing collaborations initially with the University of Indonesia Economics Faculty and the Bogor

Agricultural Institute, under the brand name 'Cyber Campus'. Under these agreements, the facility remained the property of the university but Telkom provided the network access. PT Semesta Citra Intan, with its public-access Internet branded 'Planet Digital', also eyed the potentially rich campus market, initially through Muhammadiyah University in Malang, but increasingly concentrated in middle- and upper-class shopping malls, such as Jakarta's Blok M Plaza.[68]

Strategically located public-access Internet provided such companies with a ready cash-flow. For example, David Burke, Director of Marketing and Sales of M-Web Indonesia (which, as noted above, had wide interests in portals, mobile phones, business solutions, website hosting and ISPs), noted that its Internet centres generated a very substantial 20 per cent of the company's total revenue, and had the distinct advantage of providing a strong, immediate, regular cash-flow.[69] For such integrated IT companies, the push into the *warnet* market had considerable promotional benefits. As Rudi Rusdiah, Chairperson of AWARI, observed, '*Warnet* are important for Internet companies because 50 per cent of portals or sites are accessed from *warnet*.' Furthermore, the company share price is leveraged by its 'point of presence', enhanced by recognition through *warnet*.[70]

The only national commercial operator to attempt expansion beyond capital cities was the local ,publicly listed company Myohdotcom Indonesia. It collaborated with a multinational company, Hewlett-Packard (providing the hardware), and the Office of the Minister of State for Research and Technology (KMNRT) in an attempt to spawn a national network of small franchises operating 9,000 'technology and information stalls' (*Warung Informasi dan Teknologi, warintek*). These would be akin to *warnet* but also provide IT education and training and marketing opportunities for local products. In the project, called 'Warintek 9000', launched in February 2001, the ambitious aim was to have the *warintek* operating across all of Indonesia's 8,000 sub-districts (*kecamatan*), with an additional thousand in regions of high population density, by 2004.[71] According to Myohdotcom Indonesia's Corporate and Marketing Director Rendra Hertiadhi, the aim was 'to make technology down to earth'.[72] Six months after the concept launch, Myohdotcom claimed to have opened about 90 *warintek*, mostly in Java and Sumatra, with more than 1,000 terminals, and to have received more than 2,000 applications from potential franchisees to join the project. Universities such as the Medan State University (*Universitas Negeri Medan*) were among the early participants. The UNESCO office in Bangkok also backed the concept, joining with the local government in South Sumatra to

> establish WARINTEK in South Sumatra Province as an access community center ... to provide rural and remote communities with public access to information technology, especially the Internet, and with the training to utilize it effectively. The ultimate goal of this project is the empowerment of community members and the use of such technologies for a variety of applications benefiting sustainable human development.[73]

Under their business model, Myohdotcom (which charged a franchise membership fee) projected that a franchise holder would break even within about 1.7 years, assuming that the *warintek* operated eight hours a day, charged an hourly tariff of only 3,000 rupiah and maintained an occupancy rate of 50 per cent.

With the support of the Research and Technology Ministry, the *warintek* project targeted non-urban areas, attracting interest from the private sector as well as schools and government agencies. In a further attempt to draw people outside of the major cities under the IT mantle, in August 2001 the Research and Technology Ministry launched its first 'mobile *warintek*'. From Surabaya, the small minibus toured rural areas of East Java and Bali, demonstrating multimedia and information search applications using onboard computer facilities and satellite Internet link.[74]

The Warintek 9000's ambitious targets had to be pruned back when, at the end of 2002, Myohdotcom complained that the banks were loath to provide sufficient finance for the *warintek* as 'small and medium enterprises'. Only 4,000 of the target 9,000 *warintek* had been established.[75] Though still mainly on Java, some were dotted across 30 provinces. Local governments, empowered under the post-Suharto regional autonomy provisions, were taking some initiative, with the East Nusa Tenggara government, for example, reportedly urging district heads (*bupati*) in 14 regions to allocate funds (of about 20 million rupiah each) for the establishment of a district *warintek*.[76] Utari Budiharjo, the Assistant Deputy for Information Network Development (*Pengembangan Jaringan Informasi*) in the Ministry for Research and Technology, reported requests from Papua for the development of 500 *warintek* spread around its *kabupaten* (districts), though few appear actually to have been completed.[77]

The entry of big business notwithstanding, the overwhelming majority of *warnet* around Indonesia and even in Jakarta have remained in the hands of small businesses. A major study by ICT Watch in five cities around the country demonstrates that many *warnet* indeed remain *warung*. ICT's survey was carried out in August 2003 in Makassar (Sulawesi), Medan (Sumatra), Bandung (West Java), Yogyakarta (Central Java) and in suburban Jakarta. Detailed interviews with ten *warnet* proprietors in each city revealed that a large majority (including in Jakarta) were operating without any formal business documents (many did not know that any legal documents were required), with between one and five employees (the largest in Bandung had 16) and, except in Jakarta, remained open 24 hours a day or for irregular hours. The largest of the *warnet* included in the study had 65 work-stations (Yogyakarta), but the majority had fewer than 20, many under a dozen. Most of the software used appeared to be either shareware (that is, where no licence fees are payable) or pirated – as licences were regarded by most as too expensive.[78]

Our own earlier observations and more recent work by Merlyna Lim have drawn on the analogy of the simple, small-scale *warnet* as an organic extension of the traditional food-stall *warung* located socially within 'the historic cultural context of Indonesian life'.[79] That little corner food stall, it seems, had not been swamped by the 'business centre'.

However, by the end of 2002, the growth in *warnet* in general (including the big chains) had come to a halt. The discrepancy between numbers of subscribers and numbers accessing the Internet remained. By APJII estimates, quoted on p.

57, there were over 8 million users in 2003 and just 865,706 subscribers. But the proportion of users connection to the cyberworld via Internet kiosks had declined markedly. An ACNielsen survey in August 2000 had found that 52 per cent of Indonesia's Internet users gained access through a *warnet*, 42 per cent through their workplace, 13 per cent from home and 12 per cent from schools, universities or colleges. Another survey in the same year put access via *warnet* at 60–70 per cent of total access. But in 2001, Internet kiosks accounted for 42 per cent of access, down to 26.8 per cent in 2002, and to just 3.2 per cent in 2003.[80] Discussions in the media suggest that part of this decline may have been due to a large increase in the provision of Internet in schools and universities, with APJII estimating that in 2003, about 32 per cent of the users were students logging in via schools and universities.[81]

That the local *warnet* appears, to a degree, to be being superseded by networked schools and colleges rather than by big commercial interests alone may be a good thing – and is widely supported by the Internet activists who have promoted egalitarian distribution of the technology through educational institutions amongst other forms of public access for nearly a decade now. This apparent expansion of the net through the educational infrastructure, however, needs to be understood in the context of the inadequacies of that system. Figures from UNESCO released in Jakarta in April 2004 claim that some 44 million, that is, almost 47 per cent, of school-age children (between 7 and 15 years) are not receiving primary education. The National Bureau of Statistics estimates that 5.9 million Indonesians between the ages of 10 and 44 years are illiterate.[82]

If the educational system does not provide the prospect of universal access to this new communication technology, nor does it allow the kind of communicative freedoms that the widely distributed, easily accessible, cheap and autonomous *warnet*, promised, and to some extent delivered, in the last years of the Suharto regime (which we have described in Chapter 3). Such user-autonomy cannot be fully replicated in the more institutionally restricted context of schools and universities. The spread of the net through universities, and even more through technical colleges and schools, returns the Internet in Indonesia securely to the role that the New Order technocrats had planned: a tool of technical education to promote economic development. *Warnet*, the institution that held the greatest promise of the Internet becoming the technology of a relatively inclusive discursive space, is itself in decline.

User profiles: who and why

Theorists who analyse the way the Internet is changing us and our world are on the whole highly selective about whose and which use of the Internet they take into consideration. Not only is much of this work done in the context of western societies but, even within that, the focus has been on the formation of sub-cultural groups coming together in some form of interactive reciprocal relationship that the Internet makes possible, indeed perhaps even encourages.[83] Ideologically, much of this work is committed to finding in the net the possibilities of new kinds of community which are reciprocal and non-hierarchical and bound by a common commitment to a cause. Chapter 3 of this book, describing the pro-democracy discourses on the Internet in Indonesia, and most of the chapters that follow similarly focus on the use of the net by relatively small and select groups. In this present chapter we summarise some existing research on who uses the net in Indonesia and why, to place in a wider context our own more focussed observations of specific kinds of usage.

Most of the available research indicates that the majority of Internet users in Indonesia, possibly up to 75 per cent, are males and relatively well educated.[84] This gender distribution appears to be in line with the Asia–Pacific region as a whole, but very different from developed western nations such as the USA where there seems to be little gender difference in terms of user numbers.

As discussed earlier, the Internet initially entered Indonesia (as with many other countries) through the universities and research institutes. And by 2003, educational institutions were once again central in providing net access to Indonesians. Figures from 2000 indicate that virtually all Internet users had at least an upper-secondary school education (Table 4.6).

The most ambitious Indonesian Internet industry study to date of why and how people use the net was carried out by PT Pacific Rekanprima in 2001. It interviewed 1,500 individual Internet users across ten Indonesian cities (with follow-up focus-group discussions, including some with industry insiders). The sample comprised 65 per cent men and 35 per cent women, across three age bands: 32 per cent 14–25 year-olds, 38 per cent 26–35 years and the remaining 30 per cent in the 36–55-year bracket.[85] The object of the research was to determine usage levels and reasons so as to provide the analytical basis for expansion of the 'cyber industry and market' in Indonesia. Like hundreds of similar market research all over the world, Pacific Rekanprima's research team sought to identify the 'demographics, lifestyle and habits' of Indonesia's Internet users through surveys. It identified six broad user types by disaggregating the sample according to 'technographic'

Table 4.6 Educational level of Indonesian Internet users

	percentage of total users
Bachelors degree (*Sarjana*)	43%
Upper secondary college (*SLTA*)	41%
Masters degree (*Sarjana muda*)	9%
Higher degree (*Pasca Sarjana*)	5%
Primary or lower secondary college (*SD/SLTP*)	2%

Source: Mars-e, *Potensi Bisnis & Perilaku Penggunaan Internet di Indonesia*, June 2000, cited in P3TIE (2002), Indikator Teknologi Informasi dan Komunikasi Tahun 2002, Badan Pengkajian dan Penerapan Teknologi, Pusat Pengkajian dan Penerapan Teknologi Informasi dan Elektronika (P3TIE), Jakarta, (downloaded from <www.apjii.or.id/dokumentasi/arsip/indikator/siti2002.pdf>, accessed 28 July 2003), p.17.

segmentation: that is, 'categorization on the basis of motivation, desire and capability to invest in technology'.[86]

Categorised as 'light users' with 'entertainment orientation' were the teenagers, who comprised 10 per cent of the sample. They regard the Internet not as signifying personal status, but rather as a communal good, perhaps reflected in their tendency to frequent Internet kiosks, which provide net access without interference from figures of authority such as parents. Also relatively light users were the 'young socialites', 24.7 per cent of the sample, aged in their twenties, who use the Internet (and mobile phones) to enhance their communication with peers for social and entertainment purposes, but for whom the Internet has not become fundamental to their social life. 'Medium users' included 9.3 per cent of 'traditionalists', aged between 26 and 35, who use the Internet at their office but do not prioritise personal computer purchase or use. A substantial 36 per cent of the sample were characterised as the 'digital hopeful technofamily', again 26–35 years old, but with an enhanced interest in the benefits of new technologies and higher priority for technological goods in their purchases, particularly where they can be enjoyed by the whole family. The two 'heavy user' groups were both relatively small. 5.7 per cent of the sample were described as 'Bossy' or 'Hand-shakers': that is, they tended to be 36–55 years old, in established career positions which make them relatively independent and strong forward-planners (including in the purchase of other high-tech products). Finally, 13.7 per cent were regarded as 'techno-strivers' or 'young executives' who had 'a positive attitude towards modern technology' and a strong motivation to mobilise such tools to boost their personal success.[87] They used Internet for both work and social purposes.

Despite the quirky labels, the Pacific Rekanprima analysis does sketch some of the age/sex segmentation in the otherwise undifferentiated population of Internet users in Indonesia. It needs, however, to be read within the limits of its objectives and methods. The research was undertaken to assist the IT industry to develop more effectively by identifying areas of market potential and impedance 'for those who plan to exploit the challenges and opportunities of this dynamic industry'.[88] Socio-economically, the Pacific Rekanprima sample was also restricted to users with a minimum total monthly expenditure of one million rupiah, 63.5 per cent of whom had a PC at home (compared to about five PCs per hundred households nationally) and 48.9 per cent a mobile phone – not a normal cross-section of the Indonesian population.[89] Like most research dependent entirely on surveys, this research was marked by how the subjects wanted to be seen, rather than what they did and why.

Harvey's micro-study of *warnet* in Malang and Blitar provides a different way of looking at which Indonesians are actually doing what online. Harvey's categories of who accesses the Internet are given in Table 4.7.

Based on a limited selection of *warnet* computers' 'history' files, he found that the overwhelming majority of the sites accessed could be categorised as 'entertainment'. In the university town of Malang, 45 per cent of the usage was for entertainment and in the smaller town of Blitar, where many of the *warnet* were located near high schools, up to 75 per cent of the usage appears to have been for entertainment.

Table 4.7 Internet users in Malang and Blitar

Customer category	*City centre (percentage)*	*University environs (percentage)*
University student	35%	83%
Teenager	22%	9%
Business person/office worker	18%	6%
Other employment	9%	2%
Tourist	15%	—

Source: Table drawn from P. W. Harvey, 'Bisnis Warung Internet di Malang dan Blitar', unpublished Field-study Report, Australian Consortium for 'In-Country' Indonesian Studies, Perth [2000], p. 36, which provides estimates given by the *warnet* managers rather than precise statistical analysis. Harvey excludes from his survey Internet facilities actually on the university campuses.

This included access to pornographic sites: about 30 per cent (less in the university surrounds) of websites accessed through *warnet* in Malang, rising to 55 per cent in Blitar.[90] By contrast, in Blitar only 1 per cent of web access was for education and just 2 per cent for news; in Malang this was 3 per cent (city centre) to 5 per cent (university area) for education and 3 per cent (university area) to 6 per cent (city centre) for news.[91]

Interviews with *warnet* owners and users rarely reveal this degree of pornographic usage. In interviews with Harvey (as with us in Yogyakarta in 1996), the *warnet* managers played down the use of the net for pornography, yet 10 per cent of the *warnet* in Malang used pornographic screen savers, and none had a policy of prohibiting or limiting access to online pornography.[92] Nonetheless, when asked to volunteer Internet usage patterns, no *warnet* manager in Harvey's study admitted that their customers primarily used the Internet to view pornography.[93] Similarly, when ICT Watch interviewed 100 *warnet* owners in 2003, every one of them denied that their clients accessed pornography, while also saying that they did not and would not consider putting any restrictions in place. Architecturally, the *warnet* designs tended to give absolute primacy to client privacy and only about one in ten maintained records of log activities of clients – all of which make both research, and perhaps more importantly surveillance, of Internet use extremely difficult.

Harvey's findings for Malang and Blitar are on the whole supported by Adi Nugroho's study of Internet cafés in Makassar, Sulawesi, over the last week of January 2001, though its methods are very different, making direct comparison of data impossible.[94] The most accessed site, according to this study, was the search engine Yahoo.com (which does not give clear indication of reasons for use). However, a close second was 'yimg.com', a hardcore 'pornoheaven' photo download site (6.77 per cent accessed this site). Another popular porn-site was '17tahun.com', containing stories or text materials in the Indonesian language rather than visual pornography, accessed vastly more often than major Indonesian-language news media sites such as *Kompas* or *Detik.com*.

Onno Purbo has undertaken a detailed analysis of the most popular e-group site <http://groups.yahoo.com>, to compile a more comprehensive picture of what he calls 'the Indonesian community in cyberspace'.[95] In 2001, he estimated, that there were about 49,000 e-groups, making this form of net communication one of the largest and most concentrated. He undertook an initial evaluation of more than 25,000 of these, eventually restricting his sample to the 1,170 (4.5 per cent) with memberships greater than 100 (several of which have more than 8,000 subscribers). The sample incorporated a substantial total of 425,478 subscribers (including an unspecified number of multiple users). His statistics demonstrate that, contrary to widespread belief, neither pornography nor politics completely dominates net groups, although pornographic groups attracted a significantly disproportionate number of subscribers (14.1 per cent of subscribers to 6.2 per cent of groups), suggesting a greater interest by e-group members in pornography compared to religion, hobbies or politics. Purbo demonstrates that such pornographic sites tend to be relatively passive, generating only 2.6 per cent of total *messages* while consuming a massive 40.7 per cent of total e-group *bandwidth* due to the downloading of images.[96] In other words, a very large amount of Indonesian cyberspace is taken up with non-interactive usage, which reproduces the hierarchy of conventional broadcast media with large numbers of consumers, and a very small number are message or image producers (Table 4.8).

Purbo argues that the majority of Indonesian subscribers are using the e-groups for social, general educational or business purposes. He identifies the five mailing lists that carried the highest number of messages during 2001, namely, the hobby site 'ahli' (57,540 messages, despite having only a modest 204 members), the political list 'proletar' (with 44,871 messages), the computer technology list 'mailplus' (37,517), the literary list 'penyair' (23,001) and the business list

Table 4.8 Subject of (Indonesian) e-groups (with over 100 subscribers)

	percentage of groups (total: 1,170)	*percentage of subscribers (total: 425,478)*
Social functions (alumni, community, family, friends)	27.7	19.4
General knowledge (incl. IT)	20.9	19.1
Business (incl. import/export, employment)	14.9	15.5
Religion	12.6	12.7
Hobbies	9	11.1
Politics	7.4	7.1
Pornography	6.2	14.1
Economics	1.2	0.9
Total	99.9	99.9

Source: Statistics from Purbo, 'Kekuatan Komunitas Indonesia di Dunia Maya' [file 08c.html].

'export-product-indonesia' (21,723). After three decades of suppression since 1966, Marxists and socialists have a strong presence on the Indonesian net, with nine mailing lists. The largest, 'indo-marxist', has 618 members but low traffic of only between one and five messages per month. The party most actively using e-groups.com was the Justice Party (*Partai Keadilan*), which had strong support from Muslim intellectuals, including former activists of the HMI (Islamic Students' Association, *Himpunan Mahasiswa Islam*). The party generally identifies itself by using a 'pk' prefix in list names. Associated lists include: 'partai-keadilan' (534 members), 'pk_linkbisnis' (528 members), 'pk-bandung' (167), 'pkjaksel' (114), 'pk-pesanggrahan' (107) and 'pk-info', the largest with 1,064 members.[97]

In all of these usages, the interactivity of the net is of critical significance, the process throwing up a new kind of leadership whose authority, Purbo suggests, depends not on their position in government or bureaucracy, but on 'their skills, their expertise, their wisdom in the fields in which they occupy themselves. They are different from "leaders" in the real world, in government, the majority of whom are career bureaucrats who have their own [ready-made] mass following.'[98] We will return to this broad question of changing social relations and practices in the age of the Internet in Indonesia later in the book. Overall, what is clear from the foregoing is that only a relatively small portion of the Indonesian population is putting the Internet to use in a very wide range of political, social and cultural activity, to receive and provide information in ways that are not available in older traditional modes of communication or in the older media.

Conclusion

Though our mapping of the Indonesian cyberspace both geographically and socially is tentative and incomplete, some of the trends are nonetheless clear. The number of Internet users is growing but, on current trends, universal access will not be achieved in the foreseeable future with Indonesia's current technology and political economy. By the most optimistic accounts, no more than 4 per cent of the population, in only parts of the nation, is currently reached by the new technology, and this access can be easily disrupted by small changes in the provision of public access. At best then, the Internet has been unable to escape the social and regional inequities that marked the last 30 years of Indonesian development; at worst, it is adding a new dimension to inequality in Indonesia.

If Rheingold's new electronic 'social commons' are open only to a tiny section of the Indonesian society, how will the members of these commons relate to the majority of the population that lives outside it? Even the language used in Indonesian online communication in e-groups – more English than either the regional or national languages of Indonesia[99] – puts fences up around these commons that the average Indonesian living in Indonesia cannot breach, while at the same time laying them open to Indonesians and others living in western nations with access to the technology.

Manuel Castells has argued not only that '[t]echnology is a fundamental dimension of social change', but also that the 'kind of technology that develops and diffuses in a given society decisively shapes its material structure'.[100] Much of the growing body of literature on the Internet celebrates the capacity of cyberspace to provide alternative identities and communities outside, and alternative to, the lived context of individuals. If that is so, then will the Indonesian members of the cyber commons identify with different collectives from the one that the nation forges? And on a more empirical level, what, if any, are the uses of this unequally distributed technology in the hands of the political and economic elite, in the process of institutionalisation of mass democracy in Indonesia since 1998? This is the question to which we turn in the next chapter.

5 Communication technology for a new democracy

Under the constraints on communication imposed by the New Order, the Internet in the hands of a small group of dedicated activists had presented the possibility of relatively secure communication between and within opposition groups, both within the nation and beyond national borders. Whatever the failures of the post-Suharto governments to live up to the aspirations of the 1998 'Reform' movement, there is no doubt that much of the explicit and covert government control over the operations of the mass media has been removed, and open political discussion is now the norm. The post-*reformasi* explosion in publications and radio and television stations allows a vastly greater variety of political and cultural positions to emerge in the national and regional media, which have the potential to reach far larger audiences than the Internet in its current state of distribution in Indonesia. In the new politics, where state censorship is non-existent or ineffectual and the Internet's limited reach does not make it an appropriate vehicle of mass mobilisation, does this new medium, valorised as the technology of democracy, contribute to the development of democratic governance in Indonesia?

This chapter attempts to answer this question by surveying (a) the ways in which the Internet was used in the 1999 general elections, especially for public scrutiny of Indonesia's first democratic elections since 1955, and (b) efforts after the 1999 elections to implement e-governance in Indonesia.

Elections

The 7 June 1999 general elections in Indonesia were not *conducted* online, in that voters did not register their ballot directly onto the Internet. It was, however, the first occasion when Indonesian voters were able to confirm, through a search of an independent publicly accessible Internet site, the calculation of the poll statistics, from tens of thousands of individual polling stations, through all levels of government from district (*kabupaten*) to the final centralised national tally. Some scholars have argued that the Indonesia's first democratic elections in 40 years represented a new mode of legitimising the position of the same power elites that had been produced by the New Order.[1] Others heralded it as 'a benchmark for the transition towards democracy'.[2] Starting from the assumption that electoral transparency, while not sufficient to ensure a thriving democracy, is a prerequisite for any democracy, we document the use of the Internet in underpinning some of the critical markers of a democratic election.

The abiding features of all New Order elections were the high degree of predictability and lack of public accountability and credibility of the processes of results. Much has already been written on this.[3] Pre-poll speculation in the New Order focussed not on which party would win – a victory for the regime's electoral machine, Golkar (*Golongan Karya*, Functional Groups), was never in doubt – but on what *percentage* victory the government would choose to orchestrate. The New Order permitted only two opposition parties in addition to the ruling Golkar, namely the PPP (Development Unity Party) and the PDI (Indonesian Democratic Party), and the final results of elections always appeared with great speed. By contrast, the 1999 elections were contested by 48 parties, they got a clean bill of health from international and domestic monitors, they were arguably 'a model of decorum and transparency',[4] and it took nearly two months to get the final results.

Critical to the New Order's management of election results was its control over the transmission of ballot results from the voting booths to the national tally centre without any external scrutiny. State-controlled television tended to play out images of efficiency where a 'sophisticated network of radios, satellites and computers, all hooked into a command centre at the military's Cilangkap headquarters in south Jakarta, … had election results pouring in from all over the country from the moment the polls closed'.[5] Not surprisingly, during the New Order, there was a widespread public perception that 'votes went into a "black hole" somewhere between the ballot box and the national result announcements'.[6]

When B.J. Habibie inherited the presidency on 21 May 1998, he faced strident calls for an immediate, fair and open election. Although constitutionally he could have claimed to have inherited a presidential term valid till the next scheduled five-yearly elections in 2003, Habibie bowed to the unrelenting pressure for widespread reform and expedited elections. Some have even argued that 'Habibie took a personal interest in the reforms, apparently wanting to be remembered as a president who brought Indonesia out of an authoritarian system and into a democratic era'.[7] Ushering in a period of liberal government, three pivotal political laws were passed by Parliament on 28 January 1999 to permit the free establishment of political parties, reform the election process and reform the two national representative bodies, the DPR and MPR.[8] Within months, more than 180 fledgling political parties had collected the required 50 signatures, registered with the court and the Department of Justice, and, having thus had their existence formalised, were then recorded in the Government Gazette (*Lembaran Negara*). Of these, 48 proceeded to meet the preconditions for participation in the forthcoming general elections, namely an active organisation in one-third of Indonesia's 27 provinces and half of the districts within these provinces.[9]

The 1999 General Election law came into effect on 1 February for elections slated for 7 June. Since elections were held simultaneously for the People's Representative Council (DPR) and the provincial and district parliaments, 413 million ballot papers had to be produced and distributed to 300,129 polling stations across the archipelago for Indonesia's 121 million eligible voters.[10]

The implementation of general elections under the New Order had been entirely under the control of government-appointed committees at all levels down to the villages, and headed ex officio by particular bureaucratic positions. The General Election Board (Lembaga Pemilihan Umum, LPU) had always been appointed by the President and had scripted the succession of highly dubious Golkar 'victories' in the six general elections under the New Order. The 1999 Election Law replaced the LPU with a semi-independent General Election Commission (Komisi Pemilihan Umum, KPU). The KPU, charged with administering the election, consisted of one representative (usually chairpersons or secretaries-general) from each of the 48 contesting political parties, with five additional government-appointed members (who each held nine votes to ensure parity between party and non-party members). Though established under the January law, the KPU did not actually become operational until early March, leaving only three months for the challenging task of implementing a massive and complex election.

Campaigning online?

In the 1997 elections, the three political parties contesting had all developed Internet sites. The move was led by the Muslim PPP party, which launched its site, <www.ppp.or.id> on 25 April 1997, declaring in its 'editorial' that it aimed to provide a means of rapid, economical party communication to disseminate information about activities and party views, in a manner not possible via its monthly print publication which circulated mainly to party functionaries. The following month both Golkar (<www.golkar.co.id> and <www.indocon.com/golkar>) and the PDI (<www.banteng.org>) had followed suit.

The 1997 campaign had been even more restrictive than previous New Order elections with severe limitations on public rallies, and radio, television and print media circumscribed by campaign protocol dictated by the Minister of Information. The nation was divided into six campaign regions, with two of the three political parties scheduled to campaign in any one of these at any one time. In effect, a political party could thus campaign for only nine of the 27-day campaign period in any particular area. The massive street rallies which had characterised previous elections were outlawed. Each party also had nine broadcast slots on state radio (RRI) and television (TVRI), to be simultaneously relayed on all private stations. The material for broadcast had to have prior approval of the newly established Committee for Election Campaign Material (*Panitia Naskah Kampanye Pemilu*) and be submitted to the Minister of Information (Harmoko, then also the General Secretary of the ruling party, Golkar) prior to broadcast. No additional campaign advertising was permitted in the broadcast media.[11] Much of the broadcast had to be in the form of debates between parties under the new concept of 'dialogic' campaigning, with pre-recorded debates on a restricted range of topics, moderated by government appointees.

However, none of the new campaign regulations mentioned the Internet. In this context, given the surrounding discourse about the democratic potential of this technology, the Internet could have offered the PPP and especially the PDI, which did not even have a regular print periodical, new opportunities.[12] Unlike the small but increasingly vocal students and non-governmental organisations (NGOs) whose online activism against the New Order during this same period is described in Chapter 3, the formal political opposition seems to have made very little impact via this new medium. The outcome of the 1997 election was that PDI's votes were substantially reduced and, as in the previous years, Golkar's majority increased even further (from 68.1 per cent in 1992 to 74.51 per cent). In the context of New Order elections, with their foregone conclusion of a steady increase in Golkar votes, it was very difficult to judge the campaign value of the new technology. But more generally, the party leaderships understood, as the PPP campaign coordinator, Yusuf Sjakir, pointed out in an interview, that 'those who got PPP campaign information through the Internet are not the masses who are sought via conventional campaigns such as rallies and meetings'.[13]

In 1999, only a small minority – according to Ahyani, only nine – of the 48 parties contesting the elections had their own websites.[14] The API Foundation directory of 141 registered political parties (not all of which qualified to participate in the elections), listed nine parties with e-mail addresses but no webpage listed; one with a webpage but no e-mail; and only six with web and e-mail.[15] None of the three New Order parties – Golkar, PPP or PDI(-P) – listed either e-mail or website in this listing, though they did have sites operating.

Of the new political parties, the National Mandate Party (PAN, Partai Amanat Nasional), with its strongest appeal to urban, middle-class, university-educated voters, was the first to launch its website (<www.amanat.org>) in August 1998, the day after its formal establishment, featuring a photograph of founder Amien Rais, and bilingual (English and Indonesian) sub-pages. By March 1999, as the campaign hotted up, the party claimed around 3,000 visitors per day. However, most regional branches of the party, even in Java, had no access to the Internet and made no use of the technology in any way at all in their local campaigning, despite the importance of the urban, educated middle class in their support base throughout the country.[16] Media reports about the sites of most of the major political parties, including PAN, Abdurrahman Wahid's National Awakening Party (PKB, *Partai Kebangkitan Bangsa*) (<www.pkb.org>) and Megawati's PDI-P (<www.megawati.forpresident.com>), suggested that they were all plagued with slow, frequently broken transmission, sometimes days of stalling, and programming glitches which proved a turn-off for netters.[17]

Golkar – arguably the party with the strongest organisational structure and finances of any party going into the 1999 elections because of its position of privilege for the previous three decades – employed a public relations firm (ISA-PR) to develop a new Internet website (<www.golkar.net>) and to help design its overall media campaign, under the control of the party's central committee. According to the PR company, Golkar campaign managers regarded the Internet as the least important of the media, and much less important than face-to-face contact with supporters in mass rallies. Released from New Order restrictions, radio became the most important electronic medium for reaching the largest sections of the Indonesian population. On private radio stations, dispersed throughout the nation and with localised content and concerns, campaign pitch could be locally targeted, often using local spoken dialects and languages.[18]

The new Golkar site was launched at the end of April and, in July, ISA-PR provided a report regarding its use during the campaign. Even through the most frenetic period of the election campaign and the peak of polling, the site attracted an average of only 209 visitors per day, many from overseas.[19] Most of the report consists of a sample of 60 e-mails from the Golkar site 'guest book' expressing opinions about the party. About a third were clearly pro-Golkar, and about half highly critical. Some of the messages were thick with abuse for the party that had dominated Indonesian politics for so long. 'Gunawan' recommended: 'It would be best if Golkar was disbanded because it has deceived the people for at least as long as I have been alive.'[20] Some comments left on the site were exceptionally abusive to Golkar, individual members of Golkar and the Suharto family. Two aspects emerge clearly from these electronic messages. Firstly, the site was not being used for any serious feedback to the party in a way that even remotely opened up the prospect of an emerging discursive space where serious political issues could be aired and ideas exchanged. Secondly, in Suharto's Indonesia, the Internet had been the space for expressing opinions and views without the constraints applied to other public discourse, whether imposed by state or space or socially accepted standards. After the opening up of the media to diverse political and cultural views, the Internet remained a medium where extreme personal positions and emotions could be given public airing in ways that could not happen in any other media. (We will return to this highly emotive use of the Internet in Chapter 7.)

The tiny Democratic People's Party (Partai Rakyat Demokratik, PRD) used the Internet more actively than any of the other political parties during the 1999 elections. It had a sophisticated appreciation of the technology's potential, partly because the party's base was in the radical student movement of the early 1990s, and because it used the Internet extensively during its period underground in the closing years of the New Order (see Chapter 3). Once formally registered for the election in 1999, the party invested much of the KPU election funding support of 150 million rupiah into buying computers for their regional offices (to facilitate rapid e-mail communication) and funding their Internet communication. But the PRD did not even come close to winning a seat, running 40th out of 48 parties with a national DPR vote of only 78,730 (or 0.07 per cent of valid votes) compared to the PDI-P's leading tally of over 35.6 million.[21]

On the whole, there was minimal use of Internet in campaigning strategies. Given the low penetration rate of the Internet, campaigns mostly directed at winning over a 'mass' base concentrated on the older media and other conventional campaign methods. The Internet was so insignificant as a campaign tool that a major post-election survey by the International Foundation for Election Systems (IFES) did not even refer to it when questioning respondents about their sources of election information.[22] Even parties such as Golkar, which did have extensive Internet connections throughout its regional offices, did not employ e-mailing lists to generate two-way communication with sympathisers or to attract potential voters,[23] nor, as we have noted above in relation to the Golkar site, did the websites generate any serious political discourse. As a campaign tool, the Internet was of no particular consequence.

Communications technologies and the electoral process

New communication technologies were, however, at the heart of the newly established electoral process. From the start, the KPU was faced with two interrelated challenges: firstly, to administer an election which a highly sceptical public would regard as free and fair; and secondly, to this end, to devise and implement an effective, transparent and credible method of vote-counting and reporting. The New Order election results had always been published by the LPU a few weeks after the voting and these results were the 'final and legally valid outcome of each election, not the vote counts reported directly from the polling stations'.[24] In 1997, the old election board, LPU, set up a database for tabulating election results to which only five senior government officials, including President Suharto and the Golkar chairman Harmoko, then Minister of Information, had access. Heads of the two opposition parties were denied access to this database, ostensibly because of concern about costs.[25]

The post-Suharto KPU thus had to devise a viable, highly secure and publicly verifiable mode of tabulation of results. There was no question that a sophisticated computerised system would have to be at the heart of this process. Computer systems consultant Dhana Dharsono, Chairperson of the KPU's Computerisation Working Group (Ketua Pokja Komputerisasi KPU), was given only two months to develop a functioning network, based on pre-existing technologies readily available in Indonesia, that could be operational within that very limited time span.[26] There were three contenders. One was the Garuda Indonesia airlines reservations network, but it was deemed inadequately broad, with penetration only down to provincial capitals. The second was the public Internet system (via Telkom), capable of both voice and data transmission and with very good coverage to more than 90 per cent (or nearly 300 out of 316) of the nation's district-level (*kabupaten*) administrative units, plus about 400 out of its 4,029 sub-districts (*kecamatan*). However, with its limited bandwidth and speed, and its 'open' system, it was regarded as inadequate for the huge volume of traffic that was anticipated on election day – a reservation which proved well-founded since demand for the public election site alone virtually gridlocked the nation's Internet traffic capacity.[27] There was also serious concern that an open Internet system would not be secure enough for such data, with a high exposure to interference and 'hacking'.

The final option was the national banking computer system. It was based on secure satellite (rather than landline) links, and was a private closed system, specifically devised for massive data collecton and exchange. In addition, for the previous three to four years the banking network had been adapted to register applicants for the annual Muslim pilgrimage, the Haj. Known as Siskohat (Sistem Komputerisasi Haji Terpadu, Integrated Pilgrimage Computerisation System), it was regarded as safe from interference and able to channel statistical information rapidly from nearly 300 districts around the country in which it was operational. In Dharsono's view, the Siskohat was eminently capable of being adapted for use by the KPU and offered several added benefits. It did not require procurement of substantial additional equipment and could, instead, be leased by the KPU at a cost of about $US2.6 million for the several months required for data collection. Since the bank staff who input the data for the Siskohat were specifically trained for such tasks, they were capable of election data input with only minimal additional instruction, obviating the need for special recruitment and extensive training. Such training as was required was given via their branch offices and consisted of little more than a single sheet of instructions on how to key in poll results. The Japanese government provided funds and two consultants to review the KPU's needs and then design, translate and monitor a trilingual (Indonesian, English and Japanese) website, which contained full transcripts of all electoral legislation, regulation and forms (<www.kpu.go.id>) and later the polling data. The KPU's electronic system was the backbone of the electoral tabulation and monitoring process.

On election day, reflecting 'their faith in the new electoral mechanisms', 93.5 per cent of eligible voters turned out to vote. There were 104 million votes cast in 300,129 polling stations around the archipelago.[28] Reports of violence or major breaches of the election regulations were minimal. The *Economist* observed:

> The next day, the stockmarket joined in the celebration. With their hopes for a clean election apparently realized, investors poured money into local shares, driving up prices by 12 per cent, to their highest level since mid-1997, when the region's financial collapse began. The IMF [International Monetary Fund] too was pleased, and approved the release of another $450m [US] in loans. … After the violence and turmoil of the past year, it seemed enough that the elections had got off to a free, fair and friendly start.[29]

After the close of polling, ballots were counted before authorised witnesses and election monitors at the individual polling stations, before being transferred to the next (village) level for consolidation. From there, they were passed manually to the next sub-district (*kecamatan*) level for further aggregation, until the ballots and the results sheets from these lower levels reached the district (*kabupaten*) level where all the figures (down to the individual polling stations) were entered into the KPU database. Staff from the government-owned Indonesian State Bank (BNI, Bank Negara Indonesia) and Indonesian People's Bank (BRI, Bank Rakyat Indonesia), from district level, input data continuously in three shifts over the 24-hour cycle. (The hard-copy aggregations then followed, being tabulated right up to national level.) These statistics were then available virtually immediately at the central KPU server at their Jakarta headquarters in Jalan Diponegoro. Apart from the server at the KPU, there was a second host mirroring server for back-up at the Department of Religion. A complex back-up network enabled the system to re-route in the event of a crisis.[30]

Once data had reached the central KPU host server from the district data-entry sites, it took about one hour for them to pass through a series of security features to become accessible to the public via a high-capacity server located at the Indonesia Internet eXchange (IIX) at the Gatot Subroto Automatic Telephone Central Exchange. According to Budi Rahardjo, the Internet specialist in charge of this public-access site, it was subject to several hacking attempts, all unsuccessful. As a further safeguard, the same data were also copied to the Asiatel Network at the Cempaka Putih telephone exchange, providing the public with another access point to the results. Via the KPU site, the public could trace results right back down to individual polling stations, thereby verifying the accuracy of the data transmission and allaying concerns about vote-rigging or statistical tampering. Dharsono, head of KPU computerisation, summed up the key principle:

> If the community can see the official vote data right to the polling station level, they can reconcile their notes of the vote counting at the polling station where they cast their ballot with the data being broadcast by the KPU. If there is a discrepancy, they can lodge a protest by facsimile or phone or Internet.[31]

The KPU site was in extraordinarily high demand. For the fortnight following the poll, there was a daily hit rate of around 860,000, with up to 30,548 Mbyte of data being accessed each day.[32]

Television, radio and print media carried regular updated statistics. Freed from the shackles of decades of government constraint as part of the Habibie reform process, the media took an intense interest in the elections, giving them broad, generally balanced and in-depth coverage. In the lead up to, and wash-up after, the elections, many of the country's news media included election sites, usually hyperlinked to a KPU site, on their webpages, containing far greater detail than was being published or broadcast by conventional media. A week before the poll, Reuters published a list of 17 election sites (in addition to the KPU) set up by 'non-government organisations, academics and other groups'.[33]

In a world-first, members of the public wanting more immediate figures could also dial in to a telephone data distribution system, called SPRED (SMS Programme for Retrieving Election Data) to retrieve the latest results across the country. The SPRED system was sponsored by the Government of Finland and the multinational telecommunications giant Nokia, whose mobile phones feature prominently in the Indonesian market. Despite advertisements run in the newspapers prior to the election explaining how it worked, this telephone information system was considerably less popular than the website, as it required a complicated sequence of keystrokes and voice prompts to identify specific local poll results, and phone calls were charged at the premium rate, with up to two hours required to get comprehensive figures, all of which made it much less attractive than the Internet connection. Though it was in no way comparable to the web-based KPU system in its efficiency or depth of coverage, 32,000 people, nonetheless, reportedly received via mobile phone data equivalent to a total of 178,000 pages in the fortnight after the election.[34]

External checks were in place to enhance the credibility of the KPU results. The United Nations Development Programme (UNDP) had commissioned an independent audit of the KPU computer coding programs and networks, with multinational Andersen Consulting subsequently undertaking this, just prior to election day, to ensure transparency, accuracy and fairness.[35] In addition, recognising the crucial importance of informed, accurate media coverage of the elections, the KPU established a Joint Operations and Media Centre (JOMC) at the central Jakarta Aryaduta

Hotel. The JOMC provided statistical information directly to the public and the media. Two separate but official routes for the transmission of results were thus established. As indicated above, the KPU's tally (dubbed 'formal and official') was aggregated manually from each polling station, through administrative levels up to the district, where it was entered into the banking computer system to become accessible via the KPU national database. Parallel but separate to this, results from the sub-district (*kecamatan*) level were also transmitted (usually by fax or telephone, protected by a PIN code) directly to the JOMC in Jakarta, which was serviced by 220 special phone lines, 600 data-entry computers and 50 fax machines capable of simultaneous receipt of data.[36] This enabled the JOMC to provide regular updates (termed 'informal and official') directly onto the Internet and to the national and international media. This rapid release of reliable, if informal, data to the media and the public, separate from the KPU's official statistics, enhanced public confidence and demonstrated a high degree of accuracy. The UNDP reported that 'provisional results produced by the JOMC one week after polling day were within 4 per cent of the final results in accuracy',[37] while a KPU verification team compared KPU results with those of the JOMC and other election monitors to conclude that the discrepancy between the JOMC and the KPU tallies was statistically insignificant.[38]

Public scrutiny

The astounding degree of public scrutiny that gave these elections their democratic legitimacy was not, of course, entirely premised on the electronic gaze via the Internet and the World Wide Web. As indicated above, there were three stages of vote, counting and tabulation prior to the beginning of data digitisation. The new election laws provided for the presence of one party monitor from each of the 48 political parties to attend at every polling station. There were 119 national and 20 international organisations accredited as election monitors.[39] The presence of numerous civil society organisations made this, in the words of the UNDP report, the 'biggest election-monitoring effort the world has ever seen'.[40] More than half a million election monitors were mobilised on election day.

Based largely on the model of NAMFREL,[41] the citizens' election monitoring organisation which emerged in the Philippines during the Marcos dictatorship, in Indonesia too a handful of civil society organisations had attempted to monitor elections prior to 1999. With varying degrees of success, they had publicised breaches of election legislation and attempted to document serious hindrances to free and fair polling, usually at considerable risk. The Independent Election Monitoring Committee (KIPP, Komite Independen Pemantau Pemilu), established in March 1996, won international acclaim for its professionalism and courage in the face of intimidation and harassment during the 1997 election when it had about 40 monitoring offices around the country with about 9,000 volunteers.

In 1999, KIPP was joined by several other kindred organisations, two of the largest of which had national reach and had emerged from the campuses that had been at the forefront of the anti-authoritarian reform movement.[42] The Rectors'

Forum (*Forum Rektor*) was regarded as having 'the advantages of being part of "the establishment" [with] access to university resources and contacts and legitimacy in the eyes of the electoral authorities and other parts of the government'.[43] On election day it was able to get nearly 220,000 monitors at polling stations around the country – the largest contingent of any organisation.[44] Not surprisingly, given that the universities were the initial entry site for the Internet in Indonesia in the early 1990s, the Forum had an impressive website to document and promote its activities.

Under the slogan 'Pemilu Jujur di Tangan Kita' ('An honest election is in our hands'), UNFREL (University Network for a Free and Fair Election) was able to mobilise more than 96,000 volunteers, mainly students, through some 22 branches across Indonesia. About half of these branches were connected to the Internet, the remainder communicating by phone or fax to their Jakarta headquarters. Able to draw upon volunteers from the university sector with high levels of expertise in Internet technologies, UNFREL maintained a website complete with newsgroup, details of its monitoring activities, click-on e-mail facility to send criticisms and suggestions, and an online form on which the public could submit complaints of breaches of electoral regulations and procedures.[45]

Foreign governments and a string of international NGOs provided funding, advice and technical support to these and other Indonensian NGOs undertaking election monitoring. Prominent amongst them were the US-based National Democratic Institute for International Affairs (NDI), IFES, the UNDP and sympathetic foreign governments such as the USA, the UK, Japan, Canada, Germany and Australia. For organisations such as the NDI, IFES and the UNDP, having a website was an important communications tool. In its report on the elections, the UNDP noted that, together with its periodic printed newsletters, its website 'added to the credibility of the Programme in the eyes of the media and the broader NGO community'.[46]

While the Internet proved a valuable tool in providing public information and soliciting responses from those with Internet access, communications with outlying areas remained a major hurdle for most organisations. Most poll-observers in the more than 300,000 polling stations across the archipelago relied on older, more established means of transport and communication. The UNDP had provided funding so that most UNFREL branches at the district level could get access to a phone line, fax machine and, if available, an Internet connection, for the six months around the election. Election monitors were also assisted by the multinational phone company Ericsson, which donated 76 mobile phones through the UNDP.[47] However, the mobile phones reportedly did not work in some isolated locations such as Aceh, where coverage was poor. On occasions, when trying to get materials to and from those branches, election monitors resorted to asking passengers at airports to courier packages for them. In at least one instance, on the island of Sumbawa, an UNFREL observer found that, in one village polling station not even a motorbike was available, so that he had to go by horseback to a fax machine in a district centre to transmit the information to the central office in Jakarta![48]

Legitimacy of the digital process

The final results were not officially announced until 4 August, after two months of agonising waiting and complaints. There was criticism of the process of data collection and transmission of official results from various sources. The physical examination and counting of votes and their manual collation through to the point of computer entry was slow. The pace with which the computer links could register the data was out of kilter with the laboriousness of the ballot count itself.

The KPU's central committee itself (known as the Indonesian Election Committee, or PPI) expressed considerable dissatisfaction with the computerised system of data transmission. The committee, which had invested an enormous amount of faith in the computerisation being able to deliver fully authenticated results, refused in the end to accept the results on a variety of grounds, including the failings of the electronic process. Post-election commentary from some of the members of this body suggested that they were not convinced about the accuracy of the computerised tabulation of as much as 30 per cent of the total votes, and were concerned about the cost-benefit effectiveness of computerisation from the point of view of overall public good.[49]

Under Article 65 of the 1999 Election Law, the official declaration of the poll results required signing off by a two-thirds majority of the members of the KPU, 48 of the 53 members of which were effectively party representatives. Over subsequent weeks, as the figures became firm, parties attempted to trade their endorsement of the final results for greater political advantage in the future government. After weeks of negotiations, only 22 party representatives on the KPU, together with the five government appointees (but excluding the Chair), were prepared to confirm the results.[50] Eventually, with the KPU unable to muster the required two-thirds majority, President Habibie stepped in to sign off the results (with Presidential Degree No. 92, 4 August 1999). Of the 48 parties that contested the poll, only six obtained more than 2 per cent of the tally. Of these, three were the residual political organisations from the New Order period: Golkar, PDI-P and PPP. Joining them were three 'reform era' newcomers, namely the PKB, PAN and the Islamic Moon and Star Party (PBB, Partai Bulan Bintang). While the parties may have disputed the division of spoils and the electronic tabulation that underlay the results, the President was able to intervene to resolve the crisis,[51] in part because of community acceptance of the fairness of the polling, and the transparency and credibility of the tabulation of results, despite some serious complaints of corruption and malpractice, particularly from distant provinces.

A post-election study of a cross-section of the population in Jakarta by IFES suggested that, in general terms, 86 per cent of the public regarded the count of votes to be honest and fair: this, despite 17 per cent believing that the KPU itself was politically biased. Significantly too, trust in KPU had increased during the conduct of the election from 38 per cent of respondents prior to the election to 59 per cent after the poll. Similarly, trust in the democratic system as a whole had risen through the election. While prior to the election only 33 per cent of respondents believed that Indonesia was 'primarily a democracy today', by August the response had more than doubled to 74 per cent and the proportion of those who 'don't know what democracy means' declined from 15 per cent to 8 per cent.[52]

How much of this sentiment was an endorsement of the electronic tabulation whose processes were on constant public display is difficult to gauge precisely. Clearly, the continuous webcast of the unfolding election count assisted individuals and civil society groups, driven by urban middle-class, computer-literate activists, in their monitoring of the electoral process. It is not surprising that several of the most extensive domestic election monitoring organisations (such as UNFREL and the Rectors' Forum) were based on the campuses, precisely the initial entry sites of the Internet into the community and the best placed to mobilise the new technologies in the service of political reform. Both within the Election Commission itself and amongst the civil society organisations that had been mobilised to monitor the election, there appeared to be a strong view that the community had accepted that computer networked technologies assisted in the transmission of results and enhanced the transparency of calculations.

Much of the public criticism of the slow and, at times, corrupted results' transmission and tabulation procedures was directed at the delaying role of party monitors and the poor preparation and determination of official supervisory teams (*Panwas Pemilu*).[53] Of the thousands of complaints received by the KPU, few could be classified as primarily against the electronic tabulation or web delivery of the results per se. Complaints were all about human error, corruption, money-politics and procedural issues. Nor were there any serious suggestions about reducing the role of computer-mediated communication in the tabulation and monitoring of elections in future. On the contrary, two widely circulating suggestions for improving the tabulation system both required extension of computerisation. The first suggestion came from academic and columnist Roy Suryo, who recommended a decentralisation of the system so that each province would have its own tabulated results on a provincial database and website, which would simply be connected to the national election database and website for a final collation. The second suggestion related to an extension of the computerised counting right down to the polling stations to help speed up transmission and to avoid hand-transcription errors, which had generated a substantial number of the complaints. The KPU's own computer verification team recommended:

> in order that the next election be conducted in an honest, secret, and fair manner, the calculation of votes would be better undertaken using a computer system located directly at each polling station, and with the voters able to enter the political party of their choice directly into such a computer system on providing their fingerprint identity details.[54]

An independent study of the elections undertaken across eight provinces similarly included the recommendation:

> To improve the transparency and speed in the process of vote counting, the results at the KPPS [polling station] level should be directly sent to Jakarta through on-line computer technology. By cutting the steps of compiling

ballots and counting them at the subdistrict, regency and provincial levels, the system would be less prone to illegal manipulation or careless mistakes. A central information center would be necessary to increase transparency of such a vote counting system.[55]

The foregoing suggest that the legitimacy of the election depended in some measure at least on the visible role of these technologies, which were not marred by their association with the New Order like many of the personnel of the Election Commission, or the politically self-interested party representatives.

Democratic governance and communication technologies

Parliament online

In October 2000, a cable television station, Swara (*Suara Wakil Rakyat*, Voice of the People's Representatives) was established by PT Jaring Data Interaktif, with the support of IFES and the Secretariats of the MPR and DPR, to broadcast exclusively from Parliament and its various commissions and forums. Swara transmitted 24 hours daily, without any censorship, free to air, but requiring a digital decoder and mini-parabola, throughout the country. These proceedings were initially accessible via the website <www.swara.net>, hyperlinked from Parliament's own homepage.[56] Problems of restricted bandwidth led to the broadcast being discontinued by mid-2002.[57]

A modest stream of visitors persevered on swara.net and the MPR site, which provided a comprehensive list of e-mail addresses for party leaders, parliamentary commissions, Secretariat and research staff.[58] The MPR site had a Discussion Forum facility at <www.mpr.go.id/diskusi>,[59] inviting public comments. A number of the commentators, while supporting the principle of the discussion list, expressed grave doubts about its effectiveness on the grounds that the MPR members had neither the requisite computer skills nor any real intention of reading the inputs.

On the whole, these assessments that the electronic mechanism for public access to parliamentarians was more window-dressing than a real part of parliamentary business were borne out by our own interviews with decision-makers from the major parties. Only a minority of the elected politicians appeared to have the requisite skills to access the Internet themselves; most either did not have an e-mail address or had an address that was accessed by a secretary only. Some members – such as PAN's Deputy Secretary, General Alvin Lie, one of a small number of parliamentarians under the age of 40 (and with a Masters degree in International Marketing from Glasgow's Strathclyde University) – had an e-mail address, but admitted to downloading only about once a month, 'because I find it very time consuming. You can imagine we have to sort out junk mail and every time I open the Internet to check my e-mails … I cannot afford to lose time for nothing like that.'[60] One parliamentarian estimated the number of MPs 'comfortable' with e-mail at only about 20 per cent of the House. A similar pattern appears common in the regions. While the 358 branch offices of the PDI-P, for example, are generally equipped with computers, one estimate indicates that less than 20 per cent of its office-bearers have the requisite skills to use Internet communication technologies optimally, though the party leadership is attempting to rectify this by incorporating Internet communications skills in cadre training programmes.[61]

This very limited use of the Internet and electronic mail by politicians contrasted starkly with the widespread adoption of such technologies by civil society groups and activists, particularly NGOs, which, as indicated in Chapter 3, had used cyberspace to publicise their critique against the New Order internationally. For large national NGOs in particular, which depend on funding and other forms of support from international organisations, Internet use now seems both habitual and essential.[62] By contrast, parliamentarians are dealing with their largely non-connected constituencies. Even within those parties that had access to Internet technologies for intra-party communication, this technology was seen as less flexible and less suited to the demands of rapid communication than the mobile phone. Voice calls on mobile phones are vastly more expensive than using the Internet, but the capacity to send cheap, short text messages (SMS) to either individuals or specified groups meant that Internet and e-mail had a serious rival technology in the mobile phone. During an interview, Alvin Lie showed us that SMS could extend to the distribution of rather lengthy texts requiring ten or twenty 'screens' of a mobile phone, such as an urgent report to senior party officials from someone inside a sitting parliamentary commission. Leaders of parliamentary factions use SMS in the DPR sessions to coordinate effective voting alliances on key issues.[63] The mobile phone numbers of MPs are easily available to the public and they receive a cascade of text messages most days, from both party insiders and constituents. Pramono Anung, Deputy Secretary-General of PDI-P, the largest parliamentary faction to emerge from the 1999 election, estimated that he receives about 150 text messages daily, compared to only about five–seven e-mails.[64] While the e-mail may be the perfect vehicle for a clandestine report on state corruption or a long research document on an impending environmental disaster, in its current state of technical development it seems less efficient than mobile telephony in the cut-and-thrust of Indonesian parliamentary politics.

Moreover, more than 90 per cent of political party representatives elected to the parliament in 1999 were over the age of 40. Some of the smaller parties had no representatives under the age of 40. By its very nature, democratic representation in Indonesia means that the majority of parliamentarians hailed from the regions rather than the large cities. As indicated in Chapter 4, Internet and related technologies in Indonesia (as indeed in many other parts of the world) are the domain of the young and well educated, living in the metropolitan centres. By their age, location and inclination, the party politicians were not part of the net scene.

Government online

The limits of the electronic communication in the business of the new democratically elected legislature notwithstanding, a Presidential decree (Inpres No. 6, 2001) on 'the development and utilisation of telecommunications in Indonesia', signed by Abdurrahman Wahid, laid out the principles of 'government online' in Indonesia. In

2003, a further Presidential decree, signed by his successor Megawati, committed 'ministers, heads of statutory authorities, head of the secretariat of the Highest State Institution (MPR) and [other] High State Institutions,[65] Commander in Chief of the Indonesian Armed Forces, Chief of the Indonesian Police, Attorney General, Governors, [and] district regents/city mayors' to 'take all necessary steps as appropriate in their respective role, function and responsibility to implement the development of e-government nationally, based on the Strategic National E-Government Development Plan appended to this Presidential Instruction'.[66]

The Strategic E-Government Plan, appended to the Presidential Instruction, starts with a series of reasons why the 'government *must immediately* implement the process of transformation towards e-government' (our emphasis).[67] The four main 'objectives' of e-government as stated in this document can be summarised as: improve public information and public service by government departments, improve government links with the business community to enhance the latter's international competitive position, create mechanisms 'to facilitate public dialogue so that the community can participate' in policy decision-making processes, and create a transparent and efficient system of governance at all levels. Like many such planning documents, this strategic plan mentioned nothing of the real limits of access to electronic communication amongst the population.

The newly created State Minister for Communication and Information (a position established in the August 2001 'Gotong Royong' Cabinet) was responsible for the overall implementation of the plans. The decision by President Megawati Sukarnoputri to create this ministry was unpopular, as it was seen as the revival of the much-hated Information Ministry of the New Order which President Wahid had abolished. For the moment, however, the new Ministry, charged under this Presidential Instruction with 'assisting the President in formulating policy and coordination in the field of Communication and Information nationally', appeared to be defining its role as supporting the dissemination of information rather than censoring it.[68] The Ministry's website bears the English motto 'increasing the quality of public services trough [*sic*] the use and development of information and communication technology', while the Indonesian banner declares the goal of 'increasing the quality and flow of communication and information transparently, ethically and responsibly to enlighten the nation'.[69]

In 2002, the Ministry formulated a conceptual framework for a 'National Information System' (SISFONAS) to be developed by 2010, integrating information exchange vertically and horizontally across the nation, and began actively to promote the role of 'e-government'. It established a national task force for e-government development and held a National Coordination Meeting (drawing in 500 participants from all levels of government and academe, along with technical experts and commentators). It encouraged provincial and local authorities to set up websites, standardised the URL pattern (as <www.*placename*.go.id>) and produced a detailed *Guide for the Management of Local Government Websites*. Introducing the Guide in August 2003, the Minister expressed his pleasure at the way district and provincial governments had taken the initiative to launch websites, totalling more than 350 by June that year (Tables 5.1 and 5.2).[70]

Table 5.1 Official province websites

Number of provinces	30
Number with websites	19 (63%)
Accessible	12 (40%)
Unable to be opened	7 (23%)
Number without websites	11 (37%)

Table 5.2 Official websites of town and district (*kabupaten*) regional governments

Number of town/district regional governments	414
Number with websites	166 (40%)
Accessible	139 (34%)
Unable to be opened	24 (6%)
Number without websites	248 (60%)

Source: *Panduan Penyelenggaraan Situs Web Pemerintah Daerah*, Kementerian Komunikasi dan Informasi RI [Jakarta], 2003, <www.kominfo.go.id/kebijakan.asp?cid=90> (accessed 7 August 2003), Appendix, pp.34–5. Figures adjusted for mathematical error.

The minister Syamsul Mu'arif himself, despite having only very limited personal experience of electronic communication (and being a rare user of e-mails or the Internet),[71] became the first Indonesian minister to participate in an Internet chat session (on 6 August 2003). According to reports, the minister was questioned about information policy and e-government for over two hours, in a session moderated by the Secretary-General of the Association of Indonesian Internet Service Providers (APJII) and involving contributors from distant islands and overseas (namely Singapore and Germany).[72]

E-government objectives, as stated in the national strategic plan, are fairly standard claims for e-governance plans anywhere in the world. In the case of Indonesia, however, there was a special urgency around the issue of transparency. Middle- to low-level bureaucratic corruption in New Order Indonesia was related to the lack of clearly visible rules and regulations. Adequate provision of information to the public was itself a way in which the post-Suharto governments could measure their progress towards openness and transparency. By the end of 2003, a massive amount of regulation relating to all aspects of political and business life was online on relevant departmental and local government websites, which were linked together for easy navigation. Every departmental site has lists of bureaucrats and their job descriptions and all relevant legal documents, on the surface at least providing an insight into rules and personnel that was never publicly available in the New Order. Some of the sites list the e-mail contact addresses of all senior administrators, including ministers. All sites have at least one e-mail address through which the public can contact the department.

Who precisely is being served by this massive amount of online information and how are difficult to establish. Those national government departmental sites that keep a record of hits suggest that some of these sites get large numbers of visitors, the largest being recorded by the Department of Industry (Perindustrian) – over 1.4 million between the creation of the site in September 2000 and May 2004. Several other departments recorded about half a million (though the period covered is not clear, and some of these are more recent). It is impossible to know precisely where the hits are coming from and whether those accessing these websites are Indonesian or foreign residents. About half of the sites have 'discussion forums' (of one kind or another) and, while only a very small minority of visitors participate in these, the discussions are exclusively in Indonesian and names (where available) are Indonesian. Similarly, most of the polling on these sites is conducted in Indonesian. This might suggest that the users of the government sites are, in the main, Indonesians – that small minority of Indonesians with access to the Internet identified in Chapter 4 (the implications of which we return to in the concluding chapter of this book). But does this imply a discursive participation by citizens (even a small number of them) in the governmental decision-making processes, as was the stated aim in Megawati's Presidential Instruction regarding e-governance?

Regional e-government

By the time the Indonesian Government's strategic plan was devised, many central government departments and regional governments had already begun to install their webpages with different degrees of interactivity. At the provincial and district level, the greatest encouragement to stake a spot on the information superhighway came from both local commercial interests, seeking to market their products more widely, and specialist IT companies, including multinational firms marketing web-based templates designed for local-level government entities. Foreign governments, and international institutions such as the World Bank, UNESCO and even the computer giant Microsoft, appear to be funding and supporting Internet training and connectivity at various local government levels.[73] There are clear discrepancies in local government's capacity for connection to the world via the web. An ICT-Watch report in early 2004 indicates that, while in most provinces of Java and Bali 80 to 100 per cent of the district governments have websites, this falls to below 20 per cent in most of Sulawesi, Papua and Central Kalimantan, and down to 0 in the strife-torn province of Maluku.

Decentralisation was seen as a crucial part of the post-Suharto process of political and economic reforms. Decentralisation (specifically Laws Nos. 22 and 25, 1999, introduced in 2001) devolved authority to *kabupaten* (district-level) regional administrations.[74] Under this regional autonomy, the rewards of local economic development, particularly through locally imposed taxes, theoretically accrued to the districts. Many district-level governments saw the World Wide Web as a way to connect local enterprises to prospective partners and consumers across the nation and, indeed, around the world, by-passing Jakarta and the national commercial structures that had been so centralised under Suharto.

Through April 2004, we looked randomly at 20 provincial, district and district-capital official websites, including six that had been nominated for the E-Government Awards for 2003 by Indonesia's most prestigious financial journal, *Warta Ekonomi*. Every one of these sites prominently displays local resources and industries on its welcome page, most linking to pages with detailed information on those industries. The characteristic welcome message on the Kota Bontang webpage (only launched in early 2004) starts: 'Kota Bontang is a strategic area. As an autonomous region, Bontang holds great promise for investors in business opportunities, with abundant natural resources.'[75]

The emphasis on 'the local' is such that, in some instances, the homepage of the district government makes scant reference to the province in which it is located. Takalar district (in South Sulawesi), remarkable for its provision of e-government services, probably best encapsulates this spirit of regional autonomy and global connection in its webpage welcome:

> Welcome to the new site of the regional government of Takalar. Takalar has adopted an initiative in the new mode of governance, based in a global technology. This has been implemented to provide maximum service and the easiest possible access to these services for the community. … The information provided on this site demonstrates the commitment of this regional government to its responsibility of accountability to the society, both in Takalar and outside Takalar. For this reason, you are most welcome to inspect this site as part of your participation in caring for Takalar.[76]

Those addressed in this welcome are from Takalar or beyond. The rest of South Sulawesi and the Indonesian nation are addressed only as 'outsiders'. There is no mention of the district's provincial or national location anywhere on the homepage, where the cybervisitor first steps into Takalar.

It is clear that the levels of service and efficiency of the various regional e-government processes are very uneven. In Takalar, the first regional government to trial a system of digitised issuing of permits (Takalar calls it the SIMTAP system), there are reports of astounding gains in efficiency and local government revenue generated in that process. Using a similar system of electronic processing, Kutai Timur, the winner of the E-Government Award in the 'city government' category, is said to have cut down the time for issuing some permits from days to 36 minutes.[77]

The majority of local governments do not as yet have this level of implementation of e-government. It is most common for sites running in mid-2003 to early 2004 simply to reproduce government documents, lists of government branch offices and staff contact details, without enabling visitors to undertake any particular business (such as extending or issuing licences or permits) or monitor government performance in any respect via the site.[78] When we followed up some specific cases of queries and complaints in 'guest books' or 'discussion forums' of local government sites, none of the individual complainants had received any response from the relevant authorities. At any one time, there are dozens of polls running on local government sites, some addressing national issues, many with local questions and even particular policy decisions of governments. Our observation suggests that, compared to the total population, only a tiny minority (usually only a few hundred people, self-selected and limited by access to technology) respond to these polls. It is impossible to judge how much such polls determine policy, but they do clearly provide the government with sources of popular opinion and popular discontent, to which it would not otherwise have such direct access. For instance, the Blitar town government site conducted an opinion poll on the quality of the services of the town administration, which was rated 'poor' by 62 per cent of the 1,062 respondents![79] Likewise, responses were overwhelmingly negative to the Bantul government's weekly poll on whether their district's telecommunications infrastructure was adequate, with only 8 per cent of the 95 respondents being positive.[80]

The Internet in general and e-governance in particular have been seen everywhere to hold the promise of participatory democracy, allowing citizens a method of discursive engagement with political processes. Even in the heartlands of democratic government, analysts have concluded that local government use of 'telecommunications technologies concentrates primarily on *information provision*, not the communication linkages that might improve the quality of democratic discourse'.[81] Suharto's New Order, seen by many scholars as an 'autonomous state' with a 'self-preserving and self-aggrandising impulse', was indeed dependent on the suppression of popular will.[82] A critical test for the new democratic process and regional autonomy was therefore the rebuilding of channels of communication from citizens to the bureaucracies and elected representatives. We look briefly here at the extent of inclusion of platforms for discussion on local government sites and the kind of the use that the citizens were making of such platforms.

A cursory move across the local government sites we had been visiting through April 2004 suggested that about half of them provided some kind of open-access platform where visitors could leave messages. The number of messages on these pages, mostly called *buku tamu* (guest book) or *pesan dan saran* (messages and suggestions) varied greatly: some had just one or two over the entire period of the site's existence, while others had up to 20 a week. Local users everywhere clearly felt able to vent their grievances. The <www.bantul.go.id> 'guest book' included several messages to the local authorities, urging action on such matters as air pollution from a local sugar factory, repair of a village road, and corrupt payments to local officials.[83] Most such forums also contained cmplaints (and sometimes compliments) about private companies, various indirect promotions of small local businesses selling goods and services, and announcements of local events and meetings. One or two of the 'guest-book' pages had also been reduced to meeting-places for young people, with brief SMS-style messages, organising dates and entertainment. On most of the sites, there appeared to be neither any attempt by the local government to direct the conversations, nor indeed any indication that anyone in any government department was even looking at the comments.

East Kalimantan, one of the three provincial governments nominated for the E-Government Awards in 2003, appears to be at the forefront of the development of e-government. Its districts won two out of three district-level nominations. Nine of East Kalimantan's 13 districts have local government websites, five of which have archived and active online discussion forums. The number of postings ranges from just one on one district site to a dozen or more a week on another. Many of the messages (up to half on two of the sites) originate from universities in other parts of Indonesia, mostly Java. The capital city of East Kalimantan, Samarinda, has one of the best set-up and most informative e-discussion forums of all the local government sites we visited. The Samarinda 'city forum' site carries long and thoughtful contributions on various issues to do with government policy, popular participation and e-government, along with a range of other subject matter, such as health and the environment. There are, however, very few responses to any of the postings. Even on topics that clearly generate an interest, such as e-government, there were only three postings in the archives, while there have been 358 viewers of the messages. Another much-read string of messages was 'participatory government', which had seven messages and over 400 viewers.

As Kalathil and Boas have observed elsewhere, e-government measures might 'improve citizen services while simultaneously strengthening bureaucratic cohesion and efficiency', yet may 'not necessarily provide societal oversight of government affairs'.[84] Our observation in Indonesia suggests that e-government does provide a better source of information for the small minority with access to the Internet. It also has a degree of symbolic value in the assertion of local autonomy, connecting provincial towns directly to the world, by-passing Jakarta. But discursive participation of citizens cannot be presumed simply on the basis of a technological provision. Even within the small minority of the Internet-connected population, far too few (counted in dozens in a population of millions) are participating in electronic mechanisms of democratic discourse, even where such a platform is available.

Conclusion

As King has noted, 'In so far as the 1999 Election experience can serve as a microcosm of the larger political system, it suggests that regime change is indeed under way.'[85] The 1999 election may also be a microcosm of the political roles of Internet technologies in Indonesia (and potentially at least in other post-authoritarian states with similar Internet penetration rates). The Internet had no direct impact on party results in the 1999 ballot. It was not central to the game plan of any of the political parties, and there appears to be no correlation between the volume of visitors to party websites and the final percentage of votes won.[86] But, through the mediation of the Internet, this historical event in the life of the Indonesian nation was more fully displayed for the world to watch than had been any previous Indonesian election. The display, largely funded by overseas governments, was not just to legitimise the election before a world community, though this was undoubtedly part of the equation. The numerically small but politically influential young urban students and professionals, having set up the networks of dissent mobilised so effectively against Suharto, retained a strong conviction about the Internet as a democratic technology. They had seen their victory in the information war against a dictator. Now, the election on the Internet, to some extent, authenticated the newly emerging democracy in their eyes. On the eve of the election, Onno Purbo, making an explicit link between politics on the streets and on the net, called on the 'community' to use the Internet to express their opinion rather than go out on the streets and face the military. The Internet in Indonesia had become a space from which educated middle-class liberal democrats could mobilise armies of volunteers to monitor the ballot across the archipelago, but, more importantly, it was an avenue through which they could then scrutinise the progress of their new democracy and determine whether it warranted their support. For them, at least, the Internet provided a platform for a shared experience of this most important of democratic symbols.

In the assertion of regional autonomy, the Internet again plays an important symbolic role. We have argued here that local government websites allow at the very least an illusion of autonomy from Jakarta – in cyberspace, the foreigners (particularly the foreign investors!) can come straight to Bantul or to Takalar or any of the other 400 or so districts, without having to stop in Jakarta or even at any other physical port of entry. The economic impact of these shifting lanes and byways between the distant regions of the far-flung archipelago and the world outside cannot be part of this research. But one thing is clear: cyberspace is providing a context for the reworking of citizens' identities around the 'region', while also embedding that identity in a sense of global connectivity.

On the other hand, introduced into Indonesia at a moment of sharpened political conflict, the Internet seems to remain a space for the expression of opposition, critique and even anger and frustration to a degree not possible in any other public media. It seems much less amenable to developing into an electronic village square, where citizens come together to reach consensus after sustained discussions of serious issues. The Internet, particularly in the web-discussion format we observed on local government sites, allows individuals to make extreme positions public, without acknowledging their identity or taking any responsibility. This may in some ways seem convenient in a nation where for over 30 years the culture of political debate had been suspended, and where many have argued the practice of open debate had never developed. Both the culture of the net and its technology mean that the chances of identification and reprisal for political views expressed online are relatively low. In this context, the Internet may function better as a tool of opposition (for getting around restrictions of all sorts undetected) than as a vehicle for building consensus out of diverse opinions and identities openly expressed.

6 East Timor

Communication technology for a new nation[1]

This chapter starts in Indonesia and ends in the new nation of the Democratic Republic of Timor-Leste.[2] Timor-Leste, or East Timor, provides a striking example of how a protracted independence struggle adjusted to the new strategic possibilities of the Internet, how these new technological possibilities could exert international political leverage and how they can be applied by a nation on the path to independence. In many ways, this chapter needs to be read in tandem with Chapter 3, not only because it covers some of the same period, but also because both chapters are histories of small determined struggles to break the cordon on national media set by the New Order.

Much has been written about the movement for an independent East Timor.[3] Less has focussed on the strategies, and particularly the technologies, employed in the international diplomatic lobbying that accompanied the local guerrilla resistance.[4] This chapter is not a detailed history of the local struggle in East Timor but will attempt to plot the incorporation of Internet (and related) technologies into that struggle. It discusses how the Internet provided a unique opportunity for East Timor to claim 'independence in cyberspace' as part of a spectrum of Internet-related activist strategies, sometimes dubbed 'hacktivism'. In the final section, the chapter traces the role of the Internet and other new technologies in the months before and after the referendum of 30 August 1999, sponsored by the United Nations.

The study is thus an attempt at a (partial) technological history of East Timor's resistance movement, examining how political strategies and the new telecommunication technologies converge in the service of the struggle. We argue that, in East Timor where the control of communications with the outside world was central to the New Order government's hold over the territory, the new digital and satellite communication technologies (we focus on e-mails and the web, but mobile and satellite phones played a role too), in breaching that control, were a significant new weapon in Timor's struggle for independence from Indonesia. As Huntley and Hayes have argued, '[t]he political clarity of contemporary humanitarian imperatives, in the face of traditional appeals to national interest, highlights an important emerging new feature of international relations: the pivotal role that can be played by civil society armed with new technologies of communication.'[5]

The battle for information

East Timor's independence struggle can be plotted alongside the history of the new computer-mediated technologies themselves. On 6 October in the year Bill Gates and Paul Allen licensed their BASIC computer language and founded Micro-Soft (before they dropped the hyphen), Indonesian 'volunteers' attacked the East Timor border region village of Batugade. This year, 1975, was thus both the birth of the personal-computer revolution that formed the basis of the Internet's open future[6] and, for East Timor, the beginning of one of the most brutal covert international invasions of the second half of the twentieth century. It was not until two months later, on 7 December 1975, that Indonesian forces officially entered East Timor, barely a week after the primary pro-independence party, Fretilin, declared the territory's independence on 28 November. But, within ten days of the initial 6 October attack by Indonesian irregulars on Batugade, five Australian-based journalists had been targeted and killed in the aftermath of an assault on Balibo by a 'mixed force of 3,600 *Kopassanda* (Indonesian commandos) and Timorese supporters'.[7]

Australian Labour Prime Minister Gough Whitlam heard of the murders within about ten hours from Australian intelligence agencies monitoring Indonesian military radio signals. But Whitlam and his senior ministers accepted intelligence advice not to reveal publicly any knowledge of the deaths. If the Indonesian military had an acute interest in controlling the flow of information out of East Timor, neighbouring governments, most notably Australia, colluded in this, routinely withholding intelligence in their possession unless such information had become public through other means. For much of the next 24 years, in their public postures, successive Australian governments appeared not to know anything unless the Indonesian government made it public first. The eventual media revelation of the journalists' fate focussed international attention on this largely unreported half-island and ensured a periodic return to the subject in the media – at least the Australian media – for the next quarter of a century.[8] These deaths were but one of several reasons why Australia was to play a leading role in international public and media coverage of East Timor. Simple proximity together with a historical memory of the sacrifice paid by East Timorese protecting Australian soldiers against Japanese attacks in the Second World War played their role, as did the presence in Australia of a growing East Timorese refugee community.

The logistics faced by the five ill-fated journalists illustrated how difficult communications were in 1975. 'The only way of getting a message out of Balibo was for someone to carry it by road,' wrote Ball and McDonald, as the

> Fretilin troops in Balibo had no radio. There was no telephone line. From Maliana [20 kilometres east and 45 minutes by road] a single phone line ran to another town further into East Timor, from where telephone calls were relayed by radio link to Dili. Maliana also had Fretilin's nearest radio post. A telephone service also linked Atabae, on the north coast, with Dili, but this town was several hours drive from Balibo.[9]

In the months preceding the Indonesian invasion, Fretilin's military wing, Falintil, maintained its own radio communications network but made extensive use of the civilian telephone network (which used some wire connections, but mainly radio relay), both of which were subject to interception by Indonesian military signals intelligence.[10]

During the next 24 years of struggle against Indonesian occupation, the primary strategic concern of the East Timorese pro-independence guerrillas was survival against a far stronger and better-equipped occupation force. The guerrillas were supported by their designated representatives abroad, notably José Ramos-Horta who, beginning with his arrival at the United Nations Organization in New York on 11 December 1975, travelled the world to maximise international protest against the Indonesian invasion. The movement was supported abroad by a committed, if sometimes chaotic, array of sympathetic groups, non-governmental organisations (NGOs) and individuals, who agitated for East Timor's self-determination. During at least the first 15 years of their campaign, a crucial challenge for such activists was securing access to information about what was happening in East Timor itself.[11]

It was an often insurmountable challenge, for '[f]ew countries in the contemporary era have been so hermetically sealed as East Timor was in the years following the invasion'.[12] Pro-independence forces experienced considerable difficulty in communicating with the outside world – or even broadcasting information within East Timor. Dili's civilian telecommunications hub, the Marconi Centre, was one of the first targets for destruction by the invading forces. The local Dili radio station, which had been broadcasting as Radio Fretilin or Radio Maubere, was quickly captured by Indonesian forces, whose broadcast announced: 'Fretilin is no more. Radio Maubere is dead ... Long live the people of East Timor with the Republic of Indonesia!'[13] Several American-made Second-World-War portable radio transceivers, left by the Portuguese Army, together with some later-model pack radios, and transceivers supplied several weeks earlier from Darwin by Australian sympathisers,[14] were carried off by the guerrilla forces. Despite constant difficulties maintaining these mobile radio units, they were capable of transmitting to northern Australia from the resistance's mountain retreats and were used regularly for messages over three years. The messages to Australia, when necessary using a primitive (and ultimately ineffective) code in an attempt to maintain secrecy, were then taped, transcribed and either phoned (or, from March 1976, telexed) to key Fretilin contacts in Mozambique, Portugal and elsewhere. The efficacy of the radio link depended on the existence of mobile radio reception and transmission equipment being used by the Campaign for an Independent East Timor (CIET) in Australia's Northern Territory. While it was permissible to receive, it was illegal to transmit from Australia without a licence, which the Australian government steadfastly refused to issue. Instead, after a long-running cat-and-mouse chase, the government eventually succeeded in confiscating the CIET equipment. Within East Timor, the surrender in December 1978 of the Fretilin Minister for Information and Internal Security led to the seizure of Fretilin's transmission equipment and the severing of its vital radio link to the world outside.[15]

Pro-independence forces had other ways of circumventing the Indonesian government's blanket of silence over East Timor, including through family or church contacts. Throughout the 1980s, following the cessation of radio contact, letters and messages giving details of human rights abuses and military clashes, sometimes scrawled on the torn-out pages of school exercise books, were smuggled out of the territory. Once information had been secreted out of East Timor, international support groups actively disseminated it through any means available, to the media, to sympathisers and to like-minded political organisations around the world. Such material occasionally made it into the mass media, but its veracity was questioned by the Indonesian government,[16] and third-party verification was virtually impossible. As new technologies became available they were readily used. A small number of satellite phones were smuggled into the territory, for example. One, reportedly brought into the territory by a Japanese activist, was used by Falintil Commander Konis Santana[17] (until it broke in 1995; maintenance of equipment was a constant problem).

However, the 'opening up' of East Timor by the Suharto regime in January 1989 did facilitate a greater flow of information and intrepid investigators across the borders.[18] The first demonstration to capture international media attention was when banners were unfurled at an open-air mass being celebrated by Pope John Paul II during his visit to Dili in October 1989. Another striking success was Robert Domm's September 1990 interview with the leader of the National Council of the Maubere Resistance (CNRM) in the mountains of Ainaro, which introduced Xanana Gusmão to the outside world and demonstrated that the resistance movement had a powerful intelligence apparatus capable of outwitting its Indonesian counterpart.[19]

During the years of East Timor's forced silence, computer-mediated communication technology was advancing steadily. In 1979, the first two American campuses were linked via phone line by Usenet (short for User's Network), a 'collection of networks and computer systems that exchange messages, organized by subject into newsgroups'.[20] Within a few years, Usenet connections extended to Europe and Australia, and the subject-based 'newsgroups' organised on the Usenet grew to cover an ever-wider range of topics, although most of the 60,000 Usenet users were still in military installations, universities or technology corporations. By the time Indonesia 'opened up' East Timor in 1989, civilian networks for a general consumer were emerging, using a common networking protocol (known as TCP/IP[21]) to create what was collectively known as the 'Internet'.[22] In 1990, the newsgroup 'reg.easttimor' was started by several activists and human rights groups, using the Association for Progressive Communications (APC) system as a medium. The APC (which included member networks such as PeaceNet and GreenNet) 'provided the wires but the initiative, content, and promotion was all done by NGOs and individuals', including TAPOL in the UK and groups in the USA that later coalesced in the East Timor Action Network (ETAN/US).[23] This facility enabled e-mailed information about the East Timor situation to be disseminated around the world to like-minded organisations. In Australia and elsewhere, key activists were beginning to recognise the potential of this technology. By 1991, Usenet was hosting more then 35,000 nodes, producing nearly ten million words of discussion daily.[24]

In another path-breaking innovation, researchers in the European Laboratory for Particle Physics (CERN) revolutionised the linkage, storage and retrieval of information (using HTTP, HTML and URL as building blocks[25]). From its introduction in 1991, this system, called the World Wide Web (WWW), together with the 'browsers' and 'search engines' that soon followed, enabled users to get rapid access to vast, virtually unlimited amounts of data. Once information was entered on the Internet, the WWW would enable rapid retrieval from any linked computer.[26] The Internet had become, in the term popularised by future US Vice-President Al Gore in 1990, an 'Information Superhighway'. Its application grew exponentially with use of the original WWW server at CERN, increasing tenfold per annum between 1991 and 1994.[27] By 1994, the underground resistance was beginning to use e-mail from inside East Timor – clandestinely to avoid Indonesian military attention. For the most part, however, the fledgling technology remained rare within East Timor, with more conventional methods used to pass on information (and material) between the guerrillas and underground supporters in Indonesia (for example the National Resistance of East Timorese Students, RENETIL, founded in 1986) and abroad (such as the various human rights and East Timor lobby groups).[28] Even internationally, for the vast majority of independence supporters, 'snail mail', fax and phone remained the most common means of communication.

The Indonesian government's gradual enhancement of the telecommunications infrastructure in the territory provided some benefits for those wishing to breach the information cordon. Corroborating details of the 12 November 1991 Santa Cruz massacre were got out of East Timor by telephone calls to supporters and international aid organisations such as the Red Cross in Jakarta and elsewhere, reinforcing reports from foreign journalists who had fled East Timor after witnessing the massacre.[29] Accounts were subsequently disseminated around the world via newsgroups such as 'reg.easttimor' and mailing lists such as John MacDougall's *apakabar* (discussed in Chapter 3). But it was the potent images of the massacre filmed in the cemetery on a micro-camera by Max Stahl, the striking photographs by Steve Cox and the vivid descriptions by journalist Allan Nairn that distilled the brutality of East Timor into a single graphic event for the international mass media. Cut into sound-bites, screened repeatedly around the world, Stahl's footage of the Santa Cruz massacre reinvigorated the pro-independence movement abroad and brought the campaign back into the mainstream mass media.

The profiling of Xanana, his capture by Indonesian forces in November 1992 and his subsequent trial generated international protests, now including e-mailed bulletins, and attracted further media attention.[30] Xanana provided a sharp focus for both television and press coverage. From his Jakarta prison he was able to maintain his contacts with the independence struggle outside (aided by a mobile phone smuggled into the jail). Select key supporters were given intensive training in the use of computer-mediated communications technologies overseas from a computer expert who had been involved in setting up the 'minihub.org' network for the use of civil society organisations. With such skills, Xanana's supporters in Jakarta could then send e-mail messages using 'PGP' ('Pretty Good Privacy') encryption (which, as mentioned in Chapter 3, was also used in semi-clandestine communication by critics of the New Order within Indonesia) to East Timorese contacts abroad, such as Ramos-Horta. Until local Internet Service Providers (ISPs) were established in Indonesia, these activists logged on to the Internet by dialling internationally, usually to Pactok, a low-cost electronic mail network for NGO movements in the Asia–Pacific region set up in 1991. The ease of encryption offered users greater peace of mind than telephone conversations that could easily be tapped. The ability to transmit large amounts of information instantaneously had the added advantage of cost efficiency.[31]

Internationally, Internet usage was increasing amongst the broader public as the technology became more 'user-friendly'. The public release in August 1993 of a point-and-click graphics browser (that is, one that required a single 'click' of the mouse rather than a string of arcane computer text instruction) dramatically simplified Internet entry and use, and consumer interest grew accordingly.[32] For example, by 1994, a single online service provider, America Online, had four million members, mainly inexperienced, mainstream members of the public. While the vast majority of activists using sources such as 'reg.easttimor' were users of APC or academic networks, simplified software and expanding network access enabled even computer novices from around the world readily to access a vast array of materials on the net, including information about East Timor.

TimorNet at the University of Coimbra, Portugal, for example, provided links to information on the history, geography and culture of the territory, key UN documents, details of human rights violations, online articles and publications, ideas and mobilisation advice for activists, news archives and online discussion groups.[33] One of the most enduring mailing lists to emerge was produced by ETAN/US,[34] which had been catalysed by the Santa Cruz massacre and had mobilised existing networks and the Internet to achieve a nationwide presence in the USA, with 'a dozen local chapters and several thousand members' by 1996.[35] The group provided e-mailed action alerts on issues such as 'the need to lobby congress, severe human rights violations and the like', with postings averaging about two or three a month. In addition, 'reg.easttimor' routinely contained postings from the CNRM, ETAN/US and support groups in Australia, Portugal, Canada, Ireland and elsewhere.[36] 'Reports and translations from various wire services, the Indonesian, Portuguese, Australian, British, US and Irish press also regularly appear[ed] there, along with UN and other official documents' totalling about six to ten postings daily. There were Internet 'conference' and 'newsreader' facilities and weekly news summaries. Interested parties could be automatically e-mailed daily updates or select to receive a newsletter, *Network News*, of six to ten pages five times per year, delivered either electronically or on paper. From 1991 to 1995, ETAN/US published a 'roughly semi-monthly paper publication', *Documents on East Timor*, of selected articles from 'reg.easttimor', that was mailed to people who did not have e-mail access. 'By 1995 email access was ubiquitous enough that the paper publication ceased.'[37]

Internet was enabling pro-independence East Timor activists from around the world to work collectively, 'coordinating closely with East Timorese leaders both inside the occupied territory and in exile',[38] in a honed way unimaginable in the early years of Indonesian occupation. For some supporters at least, the very newness and capacity of the medium itself, with the startling advances in communication it offered, engendered a new confidence in their own capacity to organise and mobilise support. The speed, currency and volume of communication that the Internet offered gave activists their own 'mass medium', which in turn encouraged greater activist response.[39] Once information – even a snippet secreted individually from East Timor – was fed into this electronic network, it became further ammunition in the global battle for public opinion. In the commercial media, 'accounts of the suffering of the Timorese were sporadic, and rarely came into sharp and sustained focus'. By contrast, electronic networking, made possible by Internet technology, assisted in maintaining nodes of informed activists and beyond them a broader 'group of sympathisers ready to respond if and when some development re-ignited the issue'.[40]

By 1994, just as 'point-and-click' browsers were stimulating a proliferation of organisational and personal homepages on the web, Indonesia itself was being wired to the Internet. As mentioned earlier in this book, from 1995, commercial ISPs, including the popular wasantara.net established by the national postal system, fanned out across the archipelago. Anti-New Order activists in Indonesia began using the Internet as a virtual 'news-pool', through which they could distribute their materials globally. Among such civil society organisations were a growing number who had taken up the cause of a free East Timor since the early 1990s. These included Infight (Indonesian Front for the Defence of Human Rights), Lembaga Penegakan Hak-hak Asasi Manusia (LPHAM, Institute to Uphold Human Rights) and Hidup Baru (the Christian 'New Life' organisation). By the mid-1990s, they were joined by PIJAR (Center of Information and Action Network for Reform), Yapipham (an inter-religious organisation), the Jakarta Social Institute, the Joint Committee for the Defence of the East Timorese (JCDET) and others.[41]

East Timorese students studying outside the territory had long provided a vital conduit for information, together with Catholic Church channels and sympathetic 'tourists' visiting Timor.[42] Some of the new communication infrastructure of the NGO movement and universities in Indonesia was available to the members of the Timorese underground, who were studying in Java and Bali. An East Timor Internet news network was established. Working with Indonesian supporters, learning together to use laptops as mobile Internet servers and how to use virtually unbreakable encryption software to maintain secrecy, members of the student underground were in daily contact with colleagues within East Timor who were sending out stories of human rights abuses, intimidation and resistance, which could immediately begin to circulate in the international public domain.[43] Using the Internet, mobile phones and existing older forms of underground communication, there emerged a 'complex two-way flow of information and decision-making structures reaching from Cipinang Prison in Jakarta where Gusmão was confined, to East Timor and beyond to CNRT [National Council of Timorese Resistance] external leadership and the ever-increasing numbers of impressive activists and intellectuals emerging from East Timorese diaspora communities around the world'.[44]

Within East Timor, too, the speed and anonymity of e-mail communication contrasted with the lack of confidentiality and ease of surveillance of public fax access, particularly for getting information out of the territory. Such public-access communication was risky, and many young East Timorese activists had been arrested and jailed when caught faxing or phoning out information.[45] Even in 1997, the quasi-government Telkom office, frequented by intimidatory Indonesian military and paramilitary, remained the only public place in Dili from which to send an international fax.[46] By November 1998, activist organisations such as the Student Solidarity Council, located in a little house near the Santa Cruz cemetery, had computers and an Internet connection through which they could send regular e-mails, despite the fact that the 'local server was so slow that it took an hour just to download ... hotmail'.[47] Unlike paper press releases, e-mails could be tailored to various readerships and adjusted rapidly as circumstances changed. For example, on 6 April 1999, a statement from Xanana Gusmão, then under house arrest in Jakarta, was circulated to the foreign media in response to escalating militia and Indonesian army violence against civilians in East Timor; the initial heading, 'Brink of war in East Timor', was quickly altered to 'FALINTIL resumes their mission in defence of the people' to avoid falling into the trap of reinforcing the Indonesian government position that civil war was breaking out in the territory.[48]

During these final years of the struggle, according to Ramos-Horta, information on the internal situation in East Timor sometimes came directly from guerrillas, 'written on laptops in the mountains'.[49] In July 1999, for example, the military cantonment of Falintil commander Taur Matan Ruak (now commander of the East Timor armed forces) was equipped with satellite phones and at least two laptop computers.[50] He and his staff were able to follow international reports about East Timor on the Internet (and on satellite television).[51] But in the campaign for East Timor's independence, the Internet was not simply a mechanism for distributing information and exchanging military intelligence. It was a virtual 'territory' and battlespace in its own right. It is to this strategic use of the Internet as a site for a new form of conflict, or 'cyberwar', that we now turn our attention.

Independence in cyberspace

Twelve months after the Nobel Prize for Peace was awarded to José Ramos-Horta and Bishop Carlos Felipe Ximenes Belo, on the opposite side of the globe to East Timor, *The Irish Times* reported on 17 November 1997 that

> East Timor might not exist as [a] country due to the Indonesian invasion, but next month it will achieve independence in cyberspace, thanks to an Irish Internet Service Provider. East Timor's own top-level domain ('.tp') has been taken up and registered, and Connect Ireland will administer it in conjunction with East Timorese people currently living here. They intend to hand over the domain to East Timor on independence.
>
> We are reserving all appropriate names for the future [East Timor] government such as government, subdomain government and all related activities

> such as education, health etc' a spokesman [sic] for the East Timor Ireland Solidarity Campaign says. The domain's official launch date has been set for December 7th, the invasion's anniversary.[52]

In a linked document defining 'the social and political aspiration for the East Timor domain', Connect Ireland Project Director Martin Maguire noted that the domain rules '*acknowledge our obligations to the people of East Timor, the Diaspora from this country and their continued call for freedom*' (italics in the original). Furthermore, '[t]he domain registry and applicants for services under this domain (.tp) hereby affirm East Timor's inalienable, indefeasible, and sovereign right to choose its own form of Government, to determine its relations with other nations, and to develop its life, political, economic and cultural, in accordance with its own genius and traditions.' The domain-name hostmaster team at Connect Ireland were responsible for the domain, which they established 'following well established and developed policies and procedures based on Internet standards, on discussions with service providers and network experts both within and outside East Timor, and on experience'.[53] What the document did not mention at the time was that the application for the registration of the domain, smuggled into Cipinang prison for approval, designated Xanana Gusmão as the official contact for the domain.[54] The rules of the Internet Assigned Number Authority (IANA) require, as the technical administrator, someone with an address and telephone line in East Timor, so the application listed the phone number of the barracks of the Indonesian Military Commander in Dili where Gusmão spent his last night in East Timor![55]

By 1997, the Internet had become such a common venue for the communication of ideas and information between East Timor activists that the claim for an East Timor domain name was a logical assertion of the nation's 'virtual' rights, rights vehemently contested by the Indonesian authorities. The Indonesian embassy in London responded that, while Indonesia fully respected the freedom of cyberspace, it was 'concerned that this freedom has been misused by Connect Ireland to spread a campaign against Indonesia .... The handover of the domain to the government of East Timor is beyond imagination since the government of East Timor will not exist.'[56]

Adverse Internet publicity was alarming the Indonesian military. Indonesia's commander in East Timor, Colonel Slamet Sidabutar, used the occasion of a visit by the US military attaché on 13 August 1997 to stress to the press that East Timor's security was not as negative as depicted in Internet news.[57] Internet coverage of East Timor was also worrying members of Indonesia's Parliament (Dewan Perwakilan Rakyat, DPR), some of whom urged the government to open up the territory to European mass media 'so they do not need to take information about East Timor from the Non-Governmental Organisations which often have a negative perception of Indonesia'. A member of the DPR and of the National Commission on Human Rights (*Komnas HAM*), B.N. Marbun, advocated opening the territory because '[w]e have to counter the negative influence of East Timor news in Internet'.[58] The Indonesian government was recognising the adverse potential of the Internet as a source of information and was casting around for strategies to counter it. In the hands of civil society activists, the Internet offered more than just a rapid method of distributing information. Maximising the net's political impact was becoming an activist art in itself, with considerable potential for escalation. The Indonesian government's expressed anxiety over the domain registry and its suspected attempts at hacking (the latter described in the next section) suggest that the occupying forces saw East Timor's independence in cyberspace as very much a part of the reality of the struggle on the ground.

Hacktivism as political strategy

Dorothy Denning, in a paper examining the Internet as a tool for influencing American foreign policy, identified three broad classes of Internet-related activism:

> The first category, activism, refers to normal, non-disruptive use of the Internet in support of an agenda or cause. [This] includes browsing the Web for information, constructing Web sites and posting materials on them, transmitting electronic publications and letters through e-mail, and using the Net to discuss issues, form coalitions, and plan and coordinate activities. The second category, hacktivism, refers to the marriage of hacking and activism. It covers operations that use hacking techniques against a target's Internet site with the intent of disrupting normal operations but not causing serious damage. Examples are Web sit-ins and virtual blockades, automated e-mail bombs, Web hacks, computer break-ins, and computer viruses and worms.[59] The final category, cyberterrorism, refers to the convergence of cyberspace and terrorism. It covers politically motivated hacking operations intended to cause grave harm such as loss of life or severe economic damage. An example would be penetrating an air traffic control system and causing two planes to collide.[60]

After 1997, East Timor activism on the net included actions which fit into Denning's second category, with cyberattacks becoming increasingly common. Information (including disinformation) placed on a website by either party in an international conflict was open to hacking and manipulation. In 1997, hackers[61] breached several official Indonesian government websites, posting pro-independence messages and linking them to pro-independence websites. As reported by the *South China Morning Post*, the Indonesian government was now 'waging war against a new breed of freedom fighter for East Timor – the computer hacker'.[62] With the net-name 'Toxyn', a hacker from the group 'Portuguese Hackers Against Indonesia' breached the military's website and scrawled 'propaganda' across it. According to computer guru Onno W. Purbo, breaches had occurred earlier to various government sites including those of the Department of Foreign Affairs, the Indonesian government's Research and Technology (IPTEK) computer system and the Surabaya Institute of Technology. The penetration of the military site was quickly rectified, but hacktivism had become a proven strategy in the East Timor struggle. So substantial and so frequent were the anti-Indonesian government hacks of 1997 that (along with breaches of the websites of NASA, the British Conservative Party and the Spice Girls) the campaign was declared one of the 'Hacks of the Year' in an international survey of the past quarter-century's computer milestones.[63]

On 11 July 1998, Portuguese hackers known as 'kaotik' penetrated the Indonesian Department of Security site, replacing it with the slogan 'Free Xanana Gusmão'. They declared:

> This attack is not against indonesian [sic] people but against its government and their opression [sic] towards the republic of Timor. These actions were made to honour and remember all the 250 people killed in Dili on the12November [sic] 1991. WE DONT [sic] FORGET WHAT THEY HAVE DONE !!!!![64]

Over the first two days of August 'kaotik' hacked 45 Indonesian domains, in what appears to be one of the largest single co-ordinated hack-attacks ever.[65] In a media interview, one of the group in his early twenties, known only by the hacker name 'Secretos', outlined the political agenda of the group: 'We have hundreds of servers we could hack, and we don't. ... The main objective of our hacking pages is to transmit the message [of East Timor independence]. It is not, "We are groovy, we have power".'[66] For 'kaotik', cyberattack was part of a broader political strategy.

The Toxyn attack triggered a revenge strike by a group dubbed the 'Indonesian Street Fighters' who claimed to have crashed Toxyn's server (although Toxyn denied this, countering that they were simply 'down' while upgrading). What appears to be another group, 'IndoHack', reportedly attempted to attack Portuguese sites, but was unsuccessful. In another counter-attack, Indonesian 'ByteSkrew' succeeded in penetrating the server of Portugal's University of Coimbra, which hosted the TimorNet Information Service.[67] The attacks were part of a growing hacking culture developing in Indonesia, in which the practitioners dubbed themselves 'electronic cockroaches' (*kecoak elektronik*). But some of the young Indonesian hacktivists who were initially hostile, above all towards Portugal, gradually changed this position. According to one report on the *kecoak elektronik* homepage, exchanges of abuse between Toxyn and ByteSkrew softened into an 'alliance' between them as the Portuguese hacktivists explained their political point. The article, by a self-confessed hacker, concluded that the majority of Indonesian young-generation hackers 'are anti-establishment and anti-oppression. And a tyrannical government like Indonesia is justifiably seen as the enemy by them.'[68] Portuguese hackers' criticism of Suharto's folly in East Timor seemed to find sympathy amongst Indonesian hackers caught up in the growing mood of domestic opposition to the President in late 1997 and 1998.

However, even after Suharto's resignation on 21 May 1998, Internet attacks against sites supporting East Timor continued, some of which were highly coordinated and, in the opinion of Timor activists, officially sanctioned. When 'cyberspace saboteurs' forced the ISP Connect Ireland offline in January 1999' the company, which had been acting as a server for sites using the East Timor domain name, protested to the Indonesian Embassy in London. Connect Ireland Project Director, Martin Maguire, stated that their servers had come under systematic attack from at least ten different sources in a strategy he believed was organised by the Indonesian government. The attacks, over more than nine months, were not directed at a single website but at the top-level domain for East Timor, '.tp'. In what was described by one Irish newspaper as 'the most sophisticated [cyber-attack] ever recorded in this country', 18 separate hackers apparently operated in unison throughout the night of 19 January to break into Connect Ireland's security system. Maguire believed that 'the attack was so well organised, so deliberate and so skilful that whoever was doing it must be getting paid. The value to them is not one of kudos.'[69] Indonesian authorities denied any involvement in the incident, but Maguire persisted in his suspicions, claiming: 'It's a regime that has shown little regard for human life. Attacking an Internet service would not be outside their moral boundaries.' After the attack, Maguire declared that 'we received support from many Indonesians – who translated our statement(s) [sic] into the many languages that are used within that territory and circulated these widely'.[70] The incident attracted extensive international attention in the mainstream print and electronic media and Maguire was inundated with 'some 14,000+ email offering support'.[71] If the attack on Connect Ireland had been officially sanctioned, it was probably not known by the President, for Habibie had already informed his ministers on New Year's Day that he would accept independence for East Timor if that was the outcome of a 'popular consultation'. This dramatic shift was announced publicly by Foreign Minister Ali Alatas and Information Minister Yunus Yosfiah on 27 January, eight days after Connect Ireland temporarily shut down.[72]

On 21–23 April, the Indonesian proposal was formally presented at talks with Portugal and the UN Secretary-General, to be formally signed off on 5 May with a 'popular consultation' agreed for August.[73] An Australian parliamentary inquiry noted that in East Timor 'human rights abuses decreased [after Suharto's resignation] and security forces did not interfere with public rallies and demonstrations in major towns'. The end of Suharto's reign had inspired a greater boldness amongst the pro-independence students and the underground resistance but, as the inquiry added, 'this more tolerant approach did not last long and serious abuses became more frequent from late 1998'.[74] The prospect of a referendum injected a new uncertainty. While, for its part, Falintil observed a unilateral ceasefire, militias – transparently created, funded, armed and directed by the Indonesian military – attempted to terrorise the UN into abandoning East Timor and to intimidate the population against a free vote in the referendum.[75]

Amidst this heightening terror, even as the United Nations Mission in East Timor (UNAMET) prepared for the ballot, the Internet battle for East Timor took a new turn. On 17 August, Ramos-Horta – himself the target of an earlier e-mail death threat, regarded by the CNRM as being 'from an Indonesian with likely links to the military intelligence'[76] – reportedly threatened to unleash a 'desperate and ferocious' Internet campaign if Indonesia refused to honour the results of the 30 August referendum. He claimed that more than one hundred computer hacktivists had prepared a dozen special computer viruses capable of bringing Indonesia to a standstill for weeks by infecting electronic communications systems, including aviation. Reportedly, Ramos-Horta had claimed that hackers, mostly teenagers in Europe and the USA, stood ready to attack Indonesia's banks, stock exchange and government computer systems.[77] Such assertions were doubted by many, including some close to Ramos-Horta. Indonesian officials declared that they would take 'preventative action' against Ramos-Horta's threats, which they viewed as 'extremely serious' and which were referred to the Ministry for Political and Security Affairs. Dino Patti Djalal, a senior official in the Indonesian Foreign Ministry, was quoted as retorting, 'This is terrorism against democracy.'[78]

Martin Maguire, victim of the Connect Ireland hack, quickly disassociated his organisation from Ramos-Horta's tactic, declaring that 'we do not condone attacks of any kind on the Internet or other similar technologies. We believe in the freedom of speech and in everyone's ability to conduct their communication for their own legitimate purposes. We ... believe there is more to be gained by maintaining the opportunities that can be developed through free speech than in conducting cyberwarfare.'[79] But the sense that Indonesia could be on the brink of a cyberwar was growing within some sections of the country's political elite as the leading English-language *Jakarta Post* editorialised that 'the employment of the Internet for political expression and conflict is an inevitable consequence of the information revolution. ... It is indicative of cyberspace that a territory the size of East Timor is at the center of what has become a global issue, and has attracted participants worldwide.'[80]

There is nothing to indicate that Ramos-Horta ever acted on his threat, even during what he dubbed 'the darkest days of my life' during the post-referendum violence.[81] Irrespective of whether he was able technologically to unleash the attack, to do so may well have been judged diplomatically counterproductive. Of her three categories of Internet activism, Denning had noted: 'There is a general progression toward greater damage and disruption from the first to the third category, although that does not imply an increase of political effectiveness.'[82] It may be that, just as Gusmão stayed Falintil's hand, containing it to agreed cantonments rather than risking civil war and withdrawal of international support for the referendum in the face of murderous militia provocation, so too, in the final instance, Ramos-Horta judged that a cyberattack on Indonesia would only weaken his nation's moral claim to vital international military intervention. What is important here in our quest to understand the relationship between cyberspace and real politics is that hacktivism and the discourse around it in the context of East Timor were not just a game in cyberspace, not an escape from real identities as it is often theorised, but part of a life-and-death war of independence, where the Internet was a weapon alongside machetes and machine-guns.

As the diplomatic temperature increased in the weeks prior to the referendum, cyberterrorism – at least at the level of threat – had become another strategy in the East Timor conflict. That referendum and its traumatic aftermath highlighted the pivotal role that new communication technologies were playing in media reporting and international responses to the crisis.

Referendum and new technologies

With large numbers of observers and journalists arriving in the weeks before the referendum, getting information out of East Timor by the Internet, or by any other means, took patience and determination. The single ISP in East Timor was the national postal service's 'wasantara.net', operating only in Dili.[83] Despite the general reliance on an over-stretched wasantara.net, the Internet had become an integral part of a converging, if still rudimentary, local media. When the world's largest organisation of journalists, the Brussels-based International Federation of Journalists, and two of its key Asian affiliates, the Alliance of Independent Journalists in Indonesia and the Media, Entertainment and Arts Alliance in Australia, opened a Safety Office for Media in East Timor (SOMET), its email address was <somet@dili.wasantara.net.id>.[84] Also, prior to the referendum and until it was forced to close and its operators flee to the bush, Fretilin's own radio station Radio Vos de Esperance took much of its news from Internet sources, which it then translated into the local Tetun language for broadcast.[85]

We have indicated earlier in Chapter 4 that Indonesia's telecommunications infrastructure was both underdeveloped in comparison to many of its Southeast Asian neighbours and inequitably distributed across provinces. In East Timor, one of the least developed regions, teledensity (that is, the number of phones per head of population) was one of the lowest amongst Indonesia's provinces. Most ordinary citizens had to rely on rare and poorly equipped public-access telephone kiosks (*wartel*) of which districts such as Baucau only had three – one run by the quasi-government Telkom and two private kiosks. Mobile cell phones had become increasingly popular in the preceding years. From key student activists to militia leaders, the 'handphone' had become a reasonably common accessory, at least in Dili and the one or two other urban centres in which they functioned. Even Xanana, still detained in a prison house in Jakarta, was only a phone call away.[86] However, the two Indonesian mobile-phone companies, Telkomsel and Satelindo, were unable to cope with the booming demand from consumers, leading to a complete log-jam at times of high demand. Key players, such as Falintil, continued to rely on satellite phones, for example to report atrocities to the International Committee of the Red Cross.[87]

Many of the outsiders who flooded the territory to facilitate and observe the referendum brought their own mobile communication equipment. The international media, and even individual election monitors or observers, were able to be in voice or Internet contact, via satellite or mobile phones, albeit with somewhat frustrating coverage. After a visit to Gleno, about 30 kilometres southwest from Dili, the head of the Australian Observer Delegation, Tim Fischer, commented that '[l]ocal communications were next to zero even though telephone or mobilenet links existed, although mainly for the area around Dili'.[88] International monitoring teams in the field, IFET (International Federation for East Timor) for example, depended on satellite phones (though landlines were available in Dili where the IFET office had six). It was through such links that organisations such as IFET accessed the Internet (via Indonesian servers) and communicated with the outside world. Nonetheless, news of militia atrocities was rapidly transmitted around the globe via satellite video link, often from the roof of Dili's Mahkota Hotel, which functioned as a virtual studio for the international media who 'had brought in container loads of equipment for their satellite links back to their home newsrooms'.[89]

Attacks on the general population continued to escalate, with a significant pause on the referendum day itself. By 1 September, some Dili residents were seeking the relative security of the UNAMET compound. On 4 September, the retaliatory offensive against the independence movement went into high gear, with buildings burned in large numbers throughout the territory. By mid-September, 300,000 refugees were in hiding within East Timor and another 150,000 – eventually swelling to 250,000 – were herded across the border into West Timor.[90] The world watched the security of East Timor unravel before their eyes. In the days after the referendum, international radio and television stations were conducting 'live to air' phone and video-link interviews with personnel, even those held virtual hostage in the surrounded UNAMET compound. Journalist John Martinkus wrote of the UNAMET compound at the close of the first week of September:

> the regular phone lines were cut off, and mobile phones started working only occasionally and only on a certain network. Satellite phones had become the only real means of communication with the outside world … [We] found out later that the whole UN contingent had been relying on three satellite phones for communication with the outside world.[91]

For the independent Indonesian media covering the referendum and its aftermath, the challenges were equally overpowering.[92] When the Indonesian government declared a state of martial law in East Timor on 7 September 1999, as the military-backed militia razed the territory and virtually depopulated Dili, Indonesia's largest daily newspaper, *Kompas*, took the unusual step of informing readers that, under the relevant 1959 legislation *(UU Nomor 23/Prp/1959 tentang Keadaan Bahaya*), the

> military emergency authorities, among other things, have the right to control all postal infrastructure and telecommunications equipment, such as telephones, telegraph, radio transmitters, and other equipment which is related to radio broadcasting and which can be used to reach the general population.[93]

As *Kompas* warned its readers, 'the military emergency authorities have the right to "censor" the news which will be filed by journalists who are currently still in East Timor', for all printed material was similarly subject to military control. But despite such regulation, and intimidation of journalists, some Indonesian media organisations continued to receive information out of East Timor by Internet or mobile phone and to disseminate non-official versions of stories about East Timor within Indonesia. After the militias drove most journalists from the territory and after the arrival of the International Force for East Timor (InterFET) on 20

September, Jakarta-based independent Radio 68H continued to receive reports from freelancers in East Timor. These reports were distributed by Radio 68H to 150 stations in its network across Indonesia, using both Internet and radio transmission.[94] Suspicions that anti-independence hackers were active resurfaced in Jakarta on the day the UN evacuated all but 84 of its staff from its compound, leaving Dili (in the words of a departing Portuguese journalist) 'a ghost city'.[95] On the afternoon of Friday 10 September, *The Jakarta Post* website's opinion poll mysteriously crashed. The poll, on the heated question of whether Indonesia should invite an international force into East Timor, had registered 3,720 votes before crashing, with a staggering 94 per cent in favour of an international deployment. Faced with the apparently inexplicable site crash, the editor could only announce: 'our IT people are still trying to find out the cause. … We regret the inconvenience'.[96]

While all forms of media coverage of the referendum and pillage of East Timor contributed to the considerable weight of international public opinion, the well-established activist Internet networks provided a powerful infrastructure for the dissemination of up-to-the-minute information on unfolding events. As one observer noted: 'East Timor was the first country born of the Internet Age, thanks to the sophisticated information bombardment of its committed supporters. … Part of the reason for the turn of events in September 1999 when President Clinton and Prime Minister Howard relented to armed peacekeepers going to East Timor was the level of Internet outrage on embassy systems at the White House, in Portugal and the Australian Parliament.'[97] It was a view endorsed by Ramos-Horta, who declared that the ultimate acceptance by President Habibie of an international force 'illustrates the power of the media, the power of images, the power of the Internet'.[98] He believed that 'it was the weight of world public opinion – and shame – that finally liberated East Timor'.[99] In turning this shame into a political victory, and in mobilising international political and military support, the Internet has proved a sophisticated tool, and one of great assistance in the period of reconstruction.

Indonesia's 'scorched earth' policy left the territory without most basic infrastructure. In post-referendum East Timor, one of the early logistical requirements of both the military peacekeepers and the international NGOs was the establishment of secure, reliable Internet and e-mail communication. The US InterFET contingent ensured secure Internet access to their Defense Department's classified network for military information.[100] Following the experience of the US military, which in 1995 began linking its overseas service personnel with their home bases and families via Internet in what was dubbed 'Operation Home Front', InterFET quickly set up an Internet café for its staff in Dili.[101] Oxfam International / Community Aid Abroad linked their Dili field office by e-mail to the rest of their international organisation abroad.[102] Local community and religious organisations (such as the Carmelites) established their own Internet connections, initially using superseded computers from aid dispatches (described by one journalist as 'old stuff that might ordinarily be destined for the scrap yard').[103] The technological and Internet 'savvy' of international supporters continued to have a role. The East Timor

Institute for Reconstruction Monitoring and Analysis, La'o Hamutuk (meaning 'Walking Together'), for example, was set up to 'monitor, to analyze, and to report on the activities of the principal international institutions present in Timor Loro Sa'e ... [and] to facilitate greater levels of East Timorese participation in the reconstruction and development of the country'.[104] In producing its regular bulletins and e-mail updates, this local initiative was assisted by ETAN through its homepage at <www.etan.org/lh>.

The rewards of Internet connectivity for the new state have been much-promoted, with Ramos-Horta declaring in February 2000 that his country would turn to the Internet to generate trade and investment as it integrated with the world:[105]

> In this global economy, you don't have to have really an enormous space and population of your own. ... You sit at the computer and you trade anywhere around the world. You can buy, you can sell, just at the touch of a keyboard. We are part of the global economy. ... [and] as a small nation we have to look at the world through the Internet, meaning surf the rest of the world for business opportunities to sell, to buy, to invest.[106]

Establishing that connection to the global economy is proving challenging, however. In the transition to independence, the East Timor Transitional Administration (ETTA) sought potential Internet Service Providers for East Timor. Its policy was that 'there should be regulation with a light touch aimed at ensuring the protection of the customer (quality of service; privacy), adherence to the principles of fair competition and network integrity',[107] and it called for tenders for a 'Build Operate and Transfer project for the construction and operation of a complete Telecommunications system for East Timor', with the successful tenderer promised an exclusive licence for ten years. Significantly, the provision of Internet services was explicitly excluded from this exclusive licence and, after a maximum transitional period of three years, there was to be 'full liberalisation of the ISP market'. Prospective ISPs were warned that 'only a small number of the population has, at present, access to computers. Moreover their computer skills are very low. Although this is likely to change quite rapidly in the future it is not expected that the development will be immediate.' With an illiteracy rate of at least 15 per cent (according to some figures as high as 50 per cent) and an economy and infrastructure in tatters, it is likely to be some time before the Internet in peace time plays as important a role for the people of East Timor as it has during the struggle for independence.

'In March 2003, telecommunications in East Timor (fixed lines, mobile and Internet) were turned over to a partly Portuguese-owned monopoly called Timor Telecom (TT).'[108] It now registers the '.tp' domain names that had played such a symbolic role in the independence struggle, though many of Timor's governmental websites continue to be hosted outside of East Timor. Timor Telecom used its monopoly to shut down all other ISPs, including the subsidised Internet access that the United Nations Development Programme (UNDP) had been providing to NGOs. As a result, many NGOs can no longer afford dial-up access.

Commercial or individual use of the Internet by the Timorese remains very limited. There is for all practical purposes no service outside of Dili. Even in the capital city, at a rate of about US$3 an hour ('half a day's wage for casual work') in Internet cafés, cyberspace is beyond the reach of the overwhelming majority of the Timorese. Nor does Timor have the necessary infrastructure to support a fast spread of new communication technologies: 'Electric power is intermittent or non-existent, and computers are in very short supply – no surprise in the poorest country in Southeast Asia.'[109]

Conclusion

Australian journalists Don Greenlees and Robert Garran observed that the Internet

> played a significant role as an alternative communications network for East Timorese activists, keeping the issue alive when the attention of the mainstream media was elsewhere. Developments in East Timor quickly generated a flood of e-mails to journalists, politicians and others, replacing the cumbersome medium of newsletters. These changes in communications compounded other pressures on Indonesia to open up East Timor.[110]

As MSNBC Washington correspondent Brock Meeks reflected more colourfully in early 1998:

> The slaughter of innocents in East Timor might get 45 seconds on the network news and two minutes more on MSNBC or CNN. And then, as a news story, it dies. However, take that same story to the Internet and it not only lives, it proliferates, millions of times a day. It refuses to die. It refuses to go unnoticed. And when enough people generate enough talk, generate enough letters to enough of the right people, things start to happen. This is the power of the Internet.[111]

It was a power mobilised to unanticipated effect by supporters of an independent East Timor. But it was not the technology of the Internet that sustained an international campaign for East Timor. The technology was simply employed by activists who would (and did), in its absence, maintain a concerted strategy of diplomatic and political leverage with whatever technologies were at their disposal. In this articulation with a range of other technologies – 'new' and 'old' – the Internet is seen as a powerful tool in the service of civil society.

We can only speculate on the effect such a tool may have had in triggering Indonesia's policy shifts. In the complex interplay between military strategies and political leverage, many factors contributed to the ultimate success of the movement for self-determination in East Timor. Fukuda has noted, among other elements, the importance of the guerrilla forces in symbolically maintaining the Timorese fighting spirit and identity, the contribution of Indonesia in creating an educated (but ultimately under-utilised and frustrated) youth who consequently 'gravitated to the forefront of the resistance movement', and the decisive leadership of Gusmão in initiating strategic shifts from armed guerrilla conflict to underground resistance and non-violent civil protests.[112] Ultimately, however, Fukuda argues that a 'commitment to nonviolence came first and foremost in building the self-reliance of the resistance movement',[113] and that this was crucial in enabling leverage to be exerted over Indonesia, both internationally and within Indonesia, through sympathetic human rights and pro-democracy organisations.

For the first 15 years, before the Internet, such civil society organisations used 'snail mail', telephone and fax to sustain their campaign for East Timor's self-determination. Internet and e-mail were articulated almost unconsciously into the activists' armoury, so surreptitiously that some of the most active in the campaign have difficulty recalling precisely when they adopted one information technology or another. But, equally, the technology itself was not merely incidental. As one long-time Australian activist mused,

> the new media were TOOLS (which enhanced the effectiveness of activism/resistance) rather than stimulating/causing political work. But was there something in the one-off 1990s novelty/new-ness/wonder of the medium itself which offered/stimulated, outside immediate resistance and activist circles, a broader direct engagement with the Timor story (and which ultimately had a political impact)? And even among activists, did not the medium engender a confidence-building increased sense of power? I suspect it did.[114]

In the final years at least, '[a]ccess by independent eye-witnesses to instantaneous communication media – cell phones, satellite transmissions, Internet-based networking – made it possible to generate widespread public awareness and conviction in "realtime": that is, while such awareness could still make a difference.'[115] If we recall here the description earlier in this chapter of the painstaking, expensive and above all slow process of getting information out of East Timor in the early years of Indonesian occupation, then we might argue that the global communication revolution was one of the markers of the difference between the world in which Timor was occupied and the one in which it gained independence.

Warf and Grimes have argued: 'The Internet obviously does not guarantee the emergence of counterhegemonic discourses, but it does facilitate the opening of discursive spaces within which they may be formulated and conveyed.'[116] In the battle over East Timor, the Internet enabled individuals and local groups to draw effectively upon skills and resources from far-off supporters. It focussed international attention on events that the occupying army was attempting to keep secret. Though only a microscopic minority within East Timor had access to the technology, the Internet was an instrument in the translation of their long marginalised struggle into a mainstream global political issue.

7 Communal conflict

Maluku online

The fall of Suharto was marked on the one hand by euphoria about democratic decentralisation of government and society and on the other by separatist and inter-communal violence that tested the parameters of the national boundary. In earlier chapters we have examined the new communication technology's articulations into the new democratic processes and institutions in Indonesia, and its part in the birth of the new nation of East Timor. In this chapter we examine the Internet in the context of the longest continuing communal conflict after the fall of Suharto, in an effort to identify further the links between politics in cyberspace and the politics of the street.

The Maluku archipelago in eastern Indonesia has experienced a continuous cycle of communal violence since January 1999. In her study, Birgit Bräuchler describes how organisations such as the (Christian) Crisis Centre of the Diocese of Ambon (CCDA) and the (Muslim) Laskar Jihad deployed the Internet for their respective causes after the outbreak of hostilities. She demonstrates how structured associations with an organisational existence and operations 'on the ground' extend their activities into cyberspace.[1] In Chapters 3 and 6 we have looked at such deliberate online activism in the movement of opposition to Suharto and the independence of East Timor.

Here we turn that question on its head and ask how the discourses and relationships in cyberspace are transformed by events on the ground. The main empirical content we use to answer the question is our (ethnographic) observation[2] of the Yahoo! e-group, ambon.net, the oldest (and longest-surviving) of the more than 70 e-groups explicitly related to Ambon or Maluku. Over five years, from its establishment in late 1998 and through the period of the communal wars, we observed the emergence of a sense of online identity amongst unorganised, randomly coalescing, individual participants in an open, publicly accessible forum. The 'ambon' e-group was not established explicitly to support the work of a designated membership, association or religious constituency; it evolved out of a social mailing list of a handful of friends originally from, or with family links to, Maluku. By tracking the e-group's postings over more than five and a half years, we endeavoured to trace how it was transformed, in tone and content, as well as in the number and type of participants involved, by the unfolding conflict in Maluku. In broad terms, this chapter is concerned with the degree of autonomy of cyberpolitics in the context of violent conflict.[3]

Maluku in communal conflict

In providing the background to the specific 'cyberethnography' later in the chapter, we have drawn on several academic studies that examine the sequence of events in the Maluku wars.[4] Maluku (also known in English as the Moluccas) is a group of 1,208 islands, which colonial trade since the beginning of the sixteenth century made famous as the 'Spice Islands' for their rich supply of nutmeg and cloves.[5] They cover about 850,000 square kilometres (90 per cent of which is sea) to the east of Borneo and to the west of Papua, running north of Timor-Leste through to the border with the southern Philippines.[6] Until the Moluccan archipelago was divided into two provinces – Maluku and North Maluku – in September 1999 under President Habibie, it had been Indonesia's most extensive single province. Ambon city (on the island of the same name), the capital of the old undivided province of Maluku, remained the capital in the new Maluku province, with Ternate as the capital of the poorer, more remote North Maluku.[7] At the time of the division into two provinces, the archipelago's population of just over two million, about 830,000 of whom were in North Maluku, amounted to less than 1 per cent of the Indonesia's total population.[8]

As in several of the outlying areas of Indonesia, so in Maluku separatism has long simmered and on occasion burst into flame, to be quickly suppressed by Jakarta. In 1950, an armed movement proclaimed the independence of the Republic of South Moluccas (Republik Maluku Selatan, RMS) in Ambon. Several months of military operations followed, resulting in Indonesian troops effectively crushing the RMS movement, which was mainly, but not exclusively, supported by pro-Dutch, Christian Ambonese. About 12,000 Ambonese eventually repatriated to Holland, where they maintained an on-going claim for an independent Moluccan state. Some remnants of the RMS held out in an inaccessible part of the archipelago until 1962. On the whole, the RMS failed to attract the attention of the international community, despite four violent hijacks and hostage-taking incidents in Holland between 1970 and 1978.[9]

Notwithstanding the Moluccas' history of separatist resistance to Jakarta, the archipelago had a reputation during the New Order for enjoying relatively harmonious relations between its very large Christian minority (41 per cent) and the Muslim majority (59 per cent). While Christians had been in the majority until the 1980s, since then the Muslim numbers have been increasing in part through migration from other parts of Indonesia.[10] Individual incidents of violence – occasional gang-fights, incidental skirmishes on the boundaries of contested territory – did form part of the background of inter-religious relations in Maluku, but these were generally sporadic and readily reconciled within overall harmonious relations between the two communities. Most experts were baffled when (by most interpretations) a relatively minor traffic incident in January 1999 triggered a string of violent conflicts between Muslims and Christians, spilling over from Ambon city to the corners of the Moluccan archipelago.[11]

With the dismantling of the New Order's iron-fisted controls, communal and religious tensions between the nation's 87 per cent Muslim population and the

Christian and other minority faiths began to surface and to be expounded more vocally by the media, freed from the censorship that had constrained all discussion of ethnic, religious, racial or class divisions. In contrast to the other political hotspots in Indonesia, the conflict in Maluku is not fundamentally a centre-versus-region battle. It is, on the surface at least, distinctly religious, which on this scale has never happened in post-colonial Indonesia. Estimates of casualties in an on-going civil war are necessarily difficult. On best available figures, somewhere between 4,000 and 10,000 people died in the two years after January 1999, with up to 860,000 displaced.[12] Van Klinken estimates that the mortality figures (to 2001) meant that the Maluku conflict was the worst case of 'collective violence since Indonesia's 1965–1966 bloodbath', with the sole exception of the Indonesian invasion of East Timor.[13] The Indonesian government has sponsored various peace strategies, but observers, such as the International Crisis Group, note that in Maluku province 'there is no expectation that natural reconciliation will be achieved quickly'.[14] Fresh outbreaks of violence in April 2004 muted optimism further.

The roots of the violence and the details of the ensuing wars are both complex and contested.[15] Bubandt cautions against simplifying the crisis into 'one homogenous event, explainable by one motive or one social history', arguing instead that it was more akin to 'an erratic wildfire ... emerging suddenly and ferociously in one place, only to jump to another and yet another'.[16] Below we summarise some of the well-documented events from the end of 1998 to 2003 (on the basis of secondary academic sources) to enable us to map online actions of the 'ambon' e-group onto acts of violence on the streets.

One of a number of incidents of civil unrest in the aftermath of the New Order occurred in Ketapang, central Jakarta, on 22 November 1998, when rivalry over a gambling house between two (largely Ambonese) gangs – one Muslim, the other Christian – erupted with fatal consequences, killing 14 and destroying a mosque and 27 churches.[17] After many gang members involved subsequently returned by boat to Ambon, there was reportedly an increase in tensions within that region. There, on Idul Fitri (19 January 1999), the celebration following the Muslim fasting month of Ramadan, an altercation between a Christian busdriver and a Muslim youth quickly escalated into a cascade of major clashes around Ambon city, involving many hundreds of people.[18] As van Klinken has noted, 'At first it tended to be defined (especially by Protestant Ambonese) as an attack by "indigenous" Ambonese against non-Ambonese "newcomers" who happened to be Muslim. But it quickly acquired a purely religious, rather than ethnic or geographic, character.'[19] Homes, markets, shops, and places of worship were torched by mobs adopting the colour signifiers of their faith: white for Muslims, red for Christians.

In the wake of the initial incident in Ambon city, violent clashes, often between neighbouring villages, cut a swathe through the south of the archipelago, even on outlying islands. The previously inter-mingled population of Muslims and Christians was polarising, with those under threat either fleeing or attempting to establish secure, defendable communal strongholds. After largely peaceful general elections were concluded in June, a second riot broke out in Ambon city on 24 July

1999. Considerable fighting centred on a 300-metre stretch of territory within half a kilometre of the harbour in the heart of Ambon, as the opposing militias battled between the Al Fatah mosque on the one side and the Maranatha Protestant church on the other.

Five months later, the day after Christmas 1999, a third riot occurred with the Protestant Silo church in central Ambon being burnt down (a graphic photo of which illustrates one of the more militant Christian websites),[20] followed the next day by the burning of An-Nur mosque. While the previous January rioters had few firearms (and those largely home-made), by this third riot semi-automatic weapons had become available, in addition to various locally manufactured or home-made, but nonetheless lethal, weapons. At the same time (27 December) in Tobelo, North Maluku, fighting triggered 'the worst single massacre in the Maluku wars', when Christians slaughtered between 4,000 and 5,000 mainly women and children in two mosques in neighbouring transmigration villages.[21] Communal segregation had become so pervasive that, after various killings on inter-island ships, Christians and Muslims travelling to Ambon took different routes (via Makassar for Muslims and Kupang for Christians) and disembarked in separate harbours in Ambon Bay.

Such incidents dramatically fuelled the calls for a militant Muslim response, with thousands of Laskar Jihad (Holy War Brigade) militia beginning to arrive in the islands from their training base in Java from May 2000.[22] On 27 June 2000, following further riots in Ambon and in the Galela district of north Halmahera, the Abdurrahman Wahid government declared a 'civil emergency', giving the police and military extraordinary powers while still under the civil authority of the provincial governor. This remained in force until rescinded by the Megawati Sukarnoputri government on 15 September 2003.[23] By the time the 'civil emergency' was imposed, nearly a third of the archipelago's population had become refugees, most in refugee camps that had become 'concentrated pools of resentment and bitterness'.[24]

After initially failing to intervene in the clashes, as the community polarised so too did the military, units of which began to support rival religious militia. There were even accounts of fighting between police and military units.[25] Civilian partisans obtained military weapons, either supplied covertly by sympathisers or through the raiding of arms depots.[26] In June 2000, a Balinese Hindu was appointed regional military commander in the hope that he would be regarded as neutral in the conflict and therefore more capable of diffusing inter-communal tensions.

Throughout 2001, some progress was made towards the cessation of hostilities, though major clashes occurred in Ambon after the 19 January second anniversary of the initial riot, and again in June. On both occasions, military attempts to intervene were accompanied by fire-fights in which both civilians and soldiers died.[27] Sporadic shootings, bombings, and attacks on places of worship continued, with an occasional major incident. But, overall, by the beginning of 2002, violent mass conflicts of previous years had started to abate.[28] In October 2002, Laskar Jihad and its sponsoring organisation, the Communication Forum of the Followers of the *Sunnah* and the Community of the Prophet (FKAWJ, Forum Komunikasi Ahlus Sunnah wal Jama'ah), were disbanded.[29]

In February 2002, with encouragement and facilitation by the Indonesian government, Muslim and Christian leaders meeting in the south Sulawesi town of Malino signed a peace accord that provided an agreed framework for moving forward. The agreement was not without its sceptics. But in stark contrast to 1999, in 2003, Idul Fitri passed without incident with thousands of Muslims praying on 25 November at Ambon's largest mosque, Al Fatah, to celebrate the end of the Ramadan fasting month. The press reported that '[p]olice and Indonesian Military (TNI) security personnel could still be seen safeguarding the event, but most were unarmed, a notable difference from previous years'.[30]

In 2002, a broad movement (known as BakuBae) had emerged, encouraging 'bottom-up' reconciliation with some positive results,[31] notably the establishment of (initially two) 'neutral zones' for 'economic activities, education and health services' located at the intersections of Christian and Muslim districts, where members of both could safely inter-mingle and benefit from common facilities. The establishment of a non-partisan 'Maluku Media Centre' (MMC), sponsored by the national Alliance of Independent Journalists (AJI) as a safe space in the neutral Mardika district of Ambon, was another tangible outcome of the reconciliation movement.

Some analysts have argued persuasively that the military – either centrally in Jakarta, or more locally in Maluku – orchestrated the wars, or at least, maintained skirmishes for their own political and economic interests.[32] In his detailed study, van Klinken discounts several such interpretations that the violence was somehow initiated, or at the very least exploited, by Jakarta forces behind the scenes: either the Armed Forces aspiring to regain the political influence they enjoyed during the Suharto period, or politically based thugs (*preman*) operating to destabilise the emergent democracy, thus providing an opportunity for pro-Suharto interests to re-emerge. He dismisses similarly interpretations that stressed external provocation of the crisis through the despatch to Maluku of militant Islamic organisations, such as Laskar Jihad, or Netherlands-based supporters of the 1950s' separatist movement, the RMS.[33] He argues persuasively for the 'fundamentally local character' of the Maluku wars. External forces may have interests that intersect and support local ones, but the triggers that ignite, and the fuel that feeds, this conflict are logically local, if complex and entangled, ones.

Communal conflict in the Maluku media

A study of the local Maluku media undertaken by the Internet-based 68H Radio News Service indicates the way in which the media was transformed in the process of the communal conflict.[34] Prior to the outbreak of violence in January 1999, Maluku had only one local newspaper in Ambon, *Suara Maluku* (*The Voice of Maluku*) owned by the Surabaya-based Jawa Pos media conglomerate,[35] and three commercial (and, by definition, local) radio stations, in addition to the national television network TVRI and the national radio network RRI. The national networks and the newspaper employed staff of both religions, but had offices located in Christian sectors of the Ambon city that eventually became unsafe areas for Muslim staff. Initially, as had been the practice of the media in general when reporting on sensitive religious, racial or class conflict during the New Order period, the newspaper's reports were cautious and non-inflammatory, naming villages involved, but refraining from any religious identification of the parties in dispute or interviewing those involved.

Between the second and third Ambon riots of July and December 1999, the religious schism deepened, and the city of Ambon split into distinct Muslim and Christian neighbourhoods, making it very difficult for journalists to traverse, and therefore to report across, the religious divide. This was exacerbated after Muslim journalists left *Suara Maluku* in July to open the new *Ambon Ekspres* newspaper (also owned by Jawa Pos). The 68H study noted that 'the publishing of two newspapers for the two separate communities marked the total segregation of the Ambon community – previously there had been segregated transport and segregated markets, eventually there were segregated media'.[36]

From December 1999 to the declaration of the 'civil emergency' in June 2000, the conflict escalated from village-level violence to well-armed attacks by opposing communities designed to take absolute control over Ambon.[37] The two newspapers became explicit mouthpieces for their particular religious communities, and circulations increased. This period also saw a further expansion of the media in Maluku, with eight new papers and four new radio stations commencing between October 1999 and November 2001, all aligned with one or other religious community.[38] From late 1999 also, other media were increasingly employed by both religious communities, with amateur video compact discs (VCDs) being mass-produced for distribution and sale, containing inflammatory 'close-ups of oozing wounds, bullets protruding from body parts, maimed and charred corpses, and the bodily contortions, moans, and screams of people's suffering too painful to watch', yet produced, multiplied and distributed to be 'watched, over and over again'.[39]

The period from June 2000 until the Malino Accord of February 2002 was 'marked by the intervention in the conflict of outside forces as fighters arrived in Ambon and further fanned the flames'.[40] The new publications and radio stations that had opened were firmly aligned to particular religious communities and more vociferous and provocative than their more established competitors. The International Crisis Group noted in July 2000 that a 'propaganda war of sorts is being fought on the Internet and in the newspapers' (and, clearly, also the radio), adding that such sources 'should be treated with greater than usual care' because of the difficulty in confirming their veracity.[41] Radio SPMM (*Suara Perjuangan Muslim Maluku*, Voice of the Maluku Muslims' Struggle), for example, was established in mid-2000 by the Public Relations division of the militant Islamic group Laskar Jihad, which had recently arrived in Ambon.[42] On 14 June 2001, the station was destroyed in a raid by the military's crack *Yon Gab* (Joint Batallion), but was re-established within days, quickly broadcasting a 'fatwa' by Laskar Jihad leader Ja'far Umar Thalib, declaring a Muslim's obligation to kill the Balinese military commander I Made Yasa.[43]

The 68H study is optimistic about what it described as the 'fifth phase' in the development of media (in tandem with communal conflict) in Maluku, which started with the inter-religious Malino Accord in which leaders of the two communities committed to halt the conflict and seek a peaceful resolution to their differences. Common workshops for the training of journalists from all religious camps in 'peace journalism', the establishment of new publications without clear religious affiliations and the establishment in 2002 of a new daily, *Koran Info* (*Info Paper*), employing both Christian and Muslim staff, were interpreted as encouraging signs of more fair and balanced reporting.[44] Contributing significantly to the breaking down of sectarian barriers to non-partisan reporting, through its provision of a neutral meeting place (and, if they chose, a work space) for all journalists, was the Maluku Media Centre, established in October 2001. Re-emerging too after the Malino Accord was a sense of professional solidarity between journalists, to some extent over-riding religious differences. Whereas previously individual papers had sometimes led the call on the authorities to crack down on rival publications, as journalists began to inter-mingle and appreciate their common interests in assisting in a resolution of the crisis, they tended to resist attacks on the media and speak out against harassment and intimidation of journalists (as professionals, rather than as Christians or Muslims).[45]

In the context of such a communalised media, the Internet could have been regarded as another kind of 'neutral zone', akin to those promoted by the BakuBae movement, much like the markets or health centres on the borders between Christian and Muslim neighbourhoods. The cyberspace resided in no particular group's physical domain, being equally accessible (or, one might suggest, *inaccessible*) from both Christian and Muslim enclaves. Potentially at least, all sites (that is all neighbourhoods in cyberspace), could be open to both communities. Equally, as Birgit Bräuchler observed in her study of the Internet's role in Maluku, the online environments offered 'ideal playgrounds for the construction process of individual as well as group identities, the latter providing means for the imagination of communities, which constitute part of the Moluccan conflict'.[46] These emerging 'virtual communities' – shared-interest groups that evolve through the exchanging of information, perspectives and debates online – 'provide powerful identities, which influence the national and international audience and thus the ongoing conflict'.[47]

Maluku online

As one might anticipate from our earlier account about the unequal spread of the Internet in Indonesia, the Internet is not widely available in the provinces of Maluku and North Maluku generally or even in the capital cities. There were just two public-access Internet points in the whole of Maluku in its two port cities (also the provincial capitals), Ambon and Ternate. In mid-2004, North Maluku appears to be one of only three provinces with no provincial government website. We were not able to establish the precise number of subscribers in Ambon. But in 2000, the local manager for Wasantara.net, the main provider in the region, indicated that the level of connectivity was very low compared to Java and had dropped by about 50 per cent since the start of the religious wars in January 1999. It appears that, for a period early in the communal war, the Internet service had broken down completely in Maluku as the Wasantara staff were unable to travel from their homes in one religion's stronghold to the Wasantara office in another. Gradually, some parts of the service resumed and the Ambon *warnet* was operating again by September 2000. On the other hand, since the beginning of the religious strife, the presence of Ambon and Maluku on the information superhighway has risen sharply.

Generally, the range of sites with substantial reference to Maluku fall readily into two categories: the distinctly partisan sites siding with one or other religious community, and those belonging to national or international, secular non-governmental organisations (NGOs) that are committed to neutrality. Many international aid organisations and peace and reconciliation bodies – such as the International Crisis Group, Human Rights Watch, the Harvard Program on Humanitarian Policy and Conflict Resolution, or the United Nations[48] – have Maluku-related information and links on their sites. Other neutral sites may display the efforts of well-intentioned individuals, without institutional support. For instance, the 'Ambon Information Website', hosted in Canada, was set up in 2000 by W. Richard Rowat, former Ambon coordinator for the international emergency organisation Médecins Sans Frontières (MSF) from May 1999 until February 2000.[49] The site avoids explicit religious allegiance, providing population statistics, maps, and links to sites it considers unbiased and reliable: the Indonesian Alliance of Independent Journalists' Maluku Media Centre, Human Rights Watch, the US State Department's Country Reports on Human Rights Practices (in Indonesia), the International Crisis Group's reports on Maluku, the Liberal Islamic Network (Jaringan Islam Liberal) in Indonesia, and the Crisis Centre Diocese of Amboina. It provides an English translation of both the text of the 'Declaration of War' by Laskar Jihad Commander Ja'far Umar Thalib (broadcast originally in Indonesian on Ambon's Radio SPMM in May 2002), and the text of the 'Mailino [*sic*] II' Agreement signed by 35 Muslim and 35 Christian delegates in February 2002 as part of a strategy of peace-building and reconciliation.[50]

However, a large amount of the online traffic relating to Maluku is of an overtly partisan nature. March 1999 was dubbed by one Indonesian commentator as the month the 'war via the Internet' commenced in Maluku.[51] Hundreds of sites centrally concerned with Islam or Christianity began to include information – online media articles, individuals' postings – referring to the religious conflict in Maluku and taking up the cudgels for their fellow believers in Maluku. The 'Project Open Book' site, for example, dedicated to 'Documenting the Persecution of Christians in the Islamic World', included information on places as diverse as Maluku and the Maldives, Sudan and Palestine.[52] The 'Christian Portal News' covered the massacres in Ambon, alongside papal news, and reports about the Christian Coalition in the USA backing the then presidential aspirant George W. Bush.[53] Within the national frontiers, Surabaya's Petra Christian University hosted a 'discussion forum' that often posted Maluku-related information for the two years of the conflict.[54]

Internet reports were seen, by some, as playing a role in the conflict, feeding back information – correct or otherwise – into a highly volatile atmosphere. In its report on the disturbances in Tobelo and Galela, in Halmahera in December 1999, for example, the SAGU Foundation claimed that 'the background to the mass conflict at Tobelo began with the circulating of rumours of a bloody Christmas and news from the Internet about the [Laskar] Jihad program'.[55] Bubandt argues that, in general, the 'infectious nature of the violence ... was to a large degree created by these rumours [of extreme violence by one side or the other], which were as often as not disseminated by partisan media reports or by rumours on the Internet'.[56]

Dozens of Maluku-specific Internet sites began emerging after 1999. 'Djangan lupa Maluku' ('Don't Forget Maluku')[57] provides one window into the range of these. It listed not only 16 specifically named 'Maluku Sites', with another 12 Moluccan sites listed under other sub-headings, but also a further nine sites named after specific islands or villages in Maluku! Of the sites listed on Djangan Lupa Maluku, 'Ambon Berdarah On-Line' ('Bloody Ambon Online') is the most popular Christian site expressly dedicated to 'News and Pictures about Ambon/Maluku Tragedy'.[58] A deft example of committed, partisan use of an Internet website, it operates in English and Indonesian from various mirror-sites and continues to be regularly updated, even several years after the initial surge of international interest in the events in Maluku.[59] It has a search facility, extensive archives, maps, references, and links to other like-minded sites. The site's religious affiliation is flagged with a cross on the opening page and it regularly runs appeals for donations to various Christian organisations in Maluku, Jakarta and internationally. A 'moving window' appears periodically with a photo of Laskar Jihad leader Ja'far Umar Thalib above the words 'Wanted for Terrorism and Crimes in the Moluccas'.

Ambon Berdarah On-Line's site counter indicated nearly 50,000 'visitors' in the 12 months from August 1999. A statistical breakdown of the 'top domains' (that is, usually, the countries) of the 17,027 visits in the five months till April 2000 – an average of 109 visits a day – revealed that the origins of 24 per cent were 'unknown', 25 per cent were from the Netherlands (home to a Moluccan diaspora that has grown to more than 40,000) and 17 per cent were from Indonesia, with the remainder being statistically insignificant.[60] Bräuchler has noted the importance of the Internet as the main source of information on the conflict for the international community, particularly for expatriate Moluccans in Holland, whose perception of the conflict, she claims, is directly shaped by the Internet.[61] That a diaspora such as the Moluccans in Holland may be relying increasingly on the Internet would fit with Tekwani's observations (of the Tamil diaspora) that such sites are commonly 'hosted and maintained by members of ethnic diasporas who have settled in the West and use the Internet to maintain links with the homeland and other members of the diaspora, while simultaneously drawing the world's attention to the plight of their ethnic or religious group in their homes countries'.[62]

Islamic organisations were also establishing webpages. By mid-2000, the Laskar Jihad of Ahlus Sunnah wal Jama'ah were using a 'www3.cybercities.com' host address to solicit donations and members, who could register online. Visitors to the site could download Laskar Jihad 'wallpaper' for their computer screens, subscribe to the linked e-group mailing list or read Laskar Jihad news in Arabic as well as Indonesian about the 'more than 3,500' Laskar Jihad militants then in

Maluku.[63] The 'Jihad Homepage' was linked also to sites such as 'Suara Ambon Online' ('The Voice of Ambon Online'), with its photo gallery of ruined mosques, Muslim refugees and slain Muslims swathed in white bandanas.[64]

Bräuchler has focussed her study on three major organisations both directly involved in the Moluccan conflict and maintaining a continuous presence on the Internet: the (Catholic) CCDA (Crisis Centre Keuskupan Amboina, which sends out newsletters and reports to recipients who register with it); the (Protestant) Masariku Network which maintains an e-mail list that can be viewed by anyone; and the (Muslim) FKAWJ from which the Laskar Jihad emerged, and which has also managed a publicly accessible e-mail list.[65] Such groups frequently employed common strategies in their varying uses of the Internet, but Bräuchler found that 'while the Muslims direct their appeals mainly to the national Muslim community and the world *ummat* [religious community], the Christians plead mostly with international Christian associations, the international community, and the United Nations'.[66] Both parties appeared to regard 'Internet homepages documenting the felt atrocities perpetrated by the opposing group' as pivotal in an international climate 'where media documentation is an important aspect of gaining world sympathy and hence international aid and support'.[67] Bubandt suggests that, for some Moluccans, it was as if 'the conflict in their province was a global event', part of the same apocalyptic battle that was being fought out simultaneously in conflicts such as the 1999 Gulf War.[68] And to join the global battle they needed to employ a global medium of communication.

The same web infrastructure enables both Masariku's and Laskar Jihad's stations on the information superhighway; both use the 'Yahoo! Groups' facility, at <groups.yahoo.com>. Both the CCDA and Masariku apply mechanisms to limit access to their information; one needs to contact the organisation to request to be supplied with their newsletter or to gain admission to the mailing list. While admission may be virtually assured, there is theoretically the possibility of having one's request refused. In the case of the Masariku list, membership is 'restricted', and while it is unmoderated and all members may post, the group's archives are not open to the public and one must 'join' the list to gain access.[69] As a non-member, one has no access to the exchanges taking place between the list members. It is, in that sense, a relatively 'private' portion of cyberspace. By contrast, membership of the Laskar Jihad mailing list was open, but content on the list was controlled by the moderator who vetted all messages and was the only one permitted to post. Yet the archives were public and open to all to read. This combination of settings make the Laskar Jihad list a passive 'public', but highly controlled, Internet space.

In May 2004, the 'Yahoo! Groups' facility was host to at least 76 e-groups relating primarily to Maluku or Ambon.[70] However, 27 had only ten members or fewer, and only nine had 'public' archives, including the only three with memberships of more than 200, namely 'laskarjihad' (1,209), 'islamkristen' (406) and 'ambon' (250).[71] For the rest of this chapter, we focus the 'ambon' e-group, which we have observed, visiting periodically, from its inception in 1998 well before the first January 1999 incident in Ambon, to see how its content and its social role were transformed by the intervention of the communal war. This e-group has been selected for several significant reasons. It is the oldest of the 'big three' publicly archived e-groups (mentioned above), and the only one established specifically as an Ambon/Maluku group, with the other two – 'islamkristen' and 'laskarjihad' – being formed around a religious rather than a Maluku-specific orientation. Apart from having the longest history, its archives hold a very substantial volume of traffic, with 32,777 postings during its first five years and eight months (though somewhat less than the 38,317 postings on 'islamkristen' in its first five years and one month).[72] It was significantly also not a pre-existing organisation that sought to promote its view in cyberspace, but merely a coalescence of 'random' individuals with no previous institutional or organisational form who simply gravitated around a common interest in the topic of 'Ambon'.

The 'ambon' e-group

An 'e-mail group of the Global Moluccan Community and its Sympathisers' (*Masyarakat Maluku Sedunia dan Para Simpatisan*), initially known as AMBONnet and from its second anniversary as 'ambon.COM', was established on 31 August 1998, on the first anniversary of the related website <www.ambon.com>, and, at the time of writing in 2004, remains an open list.[73] It was one of the first two Maluku-related (Yahoo!) e-groups to appear, beginning a fortnight after 'eage-watch', which really focussed much more broadly on the Brunei–Indonesia–Malaysia–Philippines–East ASEAN growth area, and was maintained institutionally by an apparently well-endowed Philippines-based non-governmental organisation, Initiatives for International Dialogue (IID).[74] By contrast, the 'ambon' e-group was a much more modest affair, emerging barely two years after the Internet had begun to be publicly accessible in Indonesia through the growth of Internet kiosks (discussed in Chapter 4). It was more like a circle of friends, and certainly bore none of the hallmarks of institutional support or intent that were so evident on 'eage-watch'. Like thousands of small casual groups congregating on the Yahoo! e-groups platform, it initially linked just a handful of individuals in America, the Netherlands, Germany, Ambon and Jakarta. By mid-August 1999, it had a membership of 192, which had grown to 334 by early August 2000.[75] Although this membership had declined to 250 by May 2004, it remains the third largest Maluku-related Yahoo! e-group. It is unmoderated, it primarily uses Indonesian (sometimes with Moluccan inflections, not understood by standard Indonesian speakers) with a high volume also of English postings, and its archives are public. The archive and statistics provide a valuable insight into the changing traffic and focus of the group, thereby enabling us to undertake a reasonable longitudinal study of this particular e-group's activities.[76]

In the opening posting on 31 August 1998, P.C. ('Noce') Wattimena, who established the list, addressed the three other initial members, informing them that 29 others had been contacted to encourage them to join and asking his friends if they were aware of any other Ambonese mailing lists. Though it is not evident to outsiders reading the postings, Philip Christian Wattimena was born in Ambon in October 1950 and trained as a master of ocean-going vessels. He was employed in

Jakarta as Operations Manager of a marine company, PT Sakareksa Pacific Lines.[77] He was not a professional church-worker, though he has served as lay chair and secretary of his local Jakarta congregation. His interest in Christian teachings and his international orientation are evident from his follow-up posting to the list on 2 September, when he exhorts 'Elya' (E.G. Muskitta) to post meditational 'Daily Reflections' (*Renungan Harian*), 'Linda' to 'occasionally include humorous stories from wherever', and 'to Clint, how about economic perspectives on Indonesia, specifically Maluku'.

There were no symbols of Christian militancy (for example, unlike Ambon Berdarah On-Line,[78] there was no crucifix, other Christian symbol or biblical quotation), although clearly it was a space for Christians to commune on spiritual issues. Of the 84 postings in August and September, the first two months of operation, 54 (64 per cent) were 'Daily Reflections' from E.G. ('Elya') Muskitta on Bible passages. Muskitta, a US-based 'consultant' active in his local Los Angeles church, had been born in Jakarta of Ambonese parents and was living in California with his wife and children.[79] Intensely personal postings (such as the three on 'My joys and sorrows today' [*Sukaduka saya hari ini*]) were only occasionally interrupted by restrained, and studiedly non-sectarian, political statements. For instance, Wattimena re-posted an open letter (originally on the Christian Paroki-net) from the Indonesian Christian Communication Forum (Forum Komunikasi Kristiani Indonesia, FKKI) to President B.J. Habibie urging him to investigate and prosecute those responsible for damaging churches during his presidency. The letter detailed the attacks on 15 churches in Java, far from Maluku (the ostensible geographical focus of the 'ambon' e-group) – but did not blame any community for these attacks.

The non-personal postings were not only non-sectarian but, at least on the surface, also non-religious. These included two reports of a student demonstration (one from the print media, the other based on a radio broadcast), two exchanges about the value of the rupiah against the US dollar and five exchanges about the concept of a federal (as opposed to a unitary) state.[80] All but four of the first two months' 84 postings were by either Muskitta or Wattimena, with only two others participating. Neither Muskitta nor Wattimena was living in Maluku. They were writing as and addressing Malukan expatriates, either in Jakarta or abroad. A close reading of the correspondence shows that this was a dialogue within a group of Christians, known to each other, and linked by their faith and their ethnicity but not by their actual residence. The group showed only a peripheral interest in the politics of religion in taking up the cudgels for other Christians under threat. And, while from the beginning the group seems aware of an identity that is both global and unique, there is nothing in the early postings to indicate animosity for other religions or a sense of embattlement or marginalisation.

Although there were only 26 messages in December 1998, after the November incidents in Jakarta, the number of active contributors, together with the breadth, variety and political tenor of the postings, had increased noticeably. There were postings (some forwarded from other lists, like Paroki-net, mentioned earlier) not just about violence against Christians in Ketapang (Jakarta), but also about national politics unfolding in Jakarta more generally, and open letters of protest to Parliament from the Jakarta-based Maluku People's Voice Forum (Forum Suara Rakyat Maluku).[81] The original non-sectarian voice in the group continued to emerge in such postings as one from Wattimena announcing that the Jakarta alumni of an Ambon government high school were to celebrate both Christmas and the closing of the Muslim fasting month, both events organised by the same committee.[82]

On New Year's Day 1999, Mickey Soukotta sent his greetings from 'NYC-USA' (New York City – USA).[83] With the salutation 'Hello to my nation' (*Hello Bangsa*),[84] he wrote of his hope that 'in the coming year life in Indonesia, especially in Maluku, will become better', but ended (in English) with 'Only God knows!!!!'[85] His concluding flourish was an ominous opening to the year, for the increase in the pace and volume of traffic on the 'ambon' e-group list from only 26 in December 1998 to 192 in January 1999 ran parallel to the escalating conflict in Maluku, which came more and more to determine the volume and tenor of traffic on the list. Rioting broke out in Ambon in mid-January. Eight were killed in Dobo, southeast Maluku, on 14 January, beginning a string of battles and conflagrations that, by the end of March, had already resulted in hundreds of deaths, with tens of thousands rendered homeless.

By January 1999, the majority of the month's 192 postings were materials drawn from other mailing lists (such as the Federation of Indonesian Christians in America's FICA-net), news organisations (for example, the *Far Eastern Economic Review*, Associated Press, Antara news agency), or political and activist groups, both international and national, self-consciously mobilising on the Internet.[86] Many postings were foreign-sourced. There were now 17 active participants ranging from frequent posters such as 'tali_hulaleng' (with 60 postings), 'Noes Souisa' (from Holland, 59)[87] and 'Samuel' (30), to eight individuals who posted only one message each for the month. Only six of the 192 postings were from Noce Wattimena, and none were by Elya Muskitta, whose 'Daily Reflections' had provided 64 per cent of the 'ambon' e-group's first two months' traffic.

Included in the postings were several 'eye-witness' accounts of the violence in Ambon, which appear not to have been published in the commercial (print) media, but which originated from Ambon itself. 'Petrov', using the e-mail address of Ambon's Pattimurra University computer technology unit (UPT-Komputer), posted a second-hand account (passed on by telephone) of the murder of four members of a Christian church by 'hundreds of people armed with long swords [*golok panjang*]'. There is no mention of the religion of the assailants, though the account makes clear that victims were killed because they were Christians. The posting refers to the 'atmosphere of racial hatred [*suasana permusuhan rasial*]', but does not attribute blame to any particular religious community.[88]

Over the following months, there were other postings too from people (evidently) in Ambon, expressing hope and optimism for the future.[89] In his May 1999 posting from a wasantara.net address in Ambon, for example, 'Alto' sent an English-language poem, urging readers to:

> Be understanding to your enemies,
> Be loyal to your friends.
> Be strong enough to face the world each day.

Be weak enough to know you cannot do everything alone.
Be generous to those who need your help.
Be frugal with what you need yourself.
Be wise enough to know that you do not know everything.
Be foolish enough to believe in miracles.
Be willing to share your joys.
Be willing to share the sorrows of others.
Be a leader when you see a path others have missed.
Be a follower when you are shrouded by the mists of uncertainty.
Be the first to congratulate an opponent who succeeds.
Be the last to criticize a colleague who fails.
Be sure where your next step will fall, so that you will not tumble.
Be sure of your final destination, in case you are going the wrong way.
Be loving to those who love you.
Be loving to those who do not love you, and they may change.
Above all, be yourself.

Most postings, however, still appeared to be sent from outside of Ambon. The links with a broader Christian congregation were evident, for example, with Elya Muskitta's re-appearance in early March, informing the readership of a Memorial Service for Ambon, being held in Los Angeles by the American–Moluccan Friendship Association (Himpunan Persaudaraan Maluku-Amerika; HPMA).[90]

Rivalries and factions within the expatriate Moluccan community bubbled over into the mailing list. In May 1999, for example, 'Pattimura Muda'/ 'Andarinyo' (who gave an Ambon suburban postal address but, according to the founder of the list, sent his e-mails via a series of American proxy-servers, which suggested he lived in the USA) fired off some cutting criticisms of the behaviour of pro-RMS activists abroad, specifically at a recent University of California Riverside seminar. The ensuing debate led to two active members of the US-based community, Elya Muskitta and (his distant uncle) Helmi Wattimena, coming out publicly at loggerheads over such parochial issues as schisms within the HPMA and rivalry over membership of the local Indonesian Consulate's Overseas Election Committee for the June 1999 general elections.[91] Some angry exchanges ensued, primarily between Helmi Wattimena and 'Andarinyo' (whom some on the list believed to be a pseudonym for Elya Muskitta), paraded before the small (largely expatriate) readership. Some members of the group were neither familiar nor concerned with conflicts of expatriate Moluccans in the US. 'Miranda manusama' bemoaned, 'I have only just joined this mailing list because I was interested and wanted to feel "part of the Ambon family" [in English in original]. But I was very startled to receive the following email. What is going on? Why does there have to be swearing, anger and hostility? Aren't we all relations (one family)? Please explain.'[92] She received several responses, with a number echoing her concerns. List-founder Noce Wattimena stepped in, urging an end to the bickering in the name of the 'common cause' of Maluku.[93] He also appealed for a shift away from the diaspora, appealing to members to approach relatives *who were actually living in Ambon* and surrounds to encourage them to join and contribute their suggestions and ideas to the discussions, indicating clearly that he regarded the current membership of the group to be non-Ambon residents.[94]

In the wake of the 7 June general elections in Indonesia, postings on the list were frequently articles from the Indonesian and English-language international press about the poll. While some posters such as 'Noes Souisa' and 'Lita Nanulaitta' continued to contribute biblical readings or prayers, the list preoccupation had largely gravitated away from spiritual matters, swamped by expatriate rivalries, and now drawn to national political events, such as the elections. It was the media, not the Bible, that was providing most traffic. That June, the number of postings rocketed to 878, more than five times the previous month's 151. Postings subsequently dropped back to between 300 and 400, until January 2000 when they increased to 736, nearly doubling to the list's heaviest monthly volume of 1,431 in July 2000, immediately after the declaration of the civil emergency by the Jakarta government (Table 7.1).[95]

As violence escalated in Maluku, the 'ambon' e-group, which started as essentially a chat group for a handful of friends, was being transformed into a relatively high-volume communal forum, containing a great deal of criticism about the Indonesian press coverage of events from what members of this group saw as the 'Muslim angle'.[96] When the second Ambon riot broke out in late July 1999, forwarded Indonesian and international press reports were supplemented by individual messages about the violence, some ostensibly from Ambon, but only a few clearly identifiable by their ambon.wasantara.net.id e-mail address.[97] Most of the personal accounts were anonymous, forwarded by second parties.

Most frequently, however, requests by group members for updates on the latest situation in Ambon elicited only published media reports rather than 'first-hand' accounts. Over time, first-hand accounts from Maluku or even personalised 'second-hand' reports seemed to decrease. On 25 August, for example, 'papilaja' appealed, 'Who can send news about the situation in Maluku today?', a call echoed by 'WATTIMENA_BETAUBUN' the following day. Despite these and Noce Wattimena's earlier call for more input from contributors in Ambon itself, of the 74 postings listed in the last week of August, almost all of the information about events in Ambon was sourced to other publicly available media. Of the 74 messages, 50 per cent (37) were published media reports (23 per cent English; 27 per cent Indonesian) and 23 per cent were individuals posting opinions or comments unrelated to Moluccan issues (on such topics as Papua, East Timor, the Taliban, largely very personal views of individual participants, and so on). Only 11 might be categorised as personal contributions concerning the situation in Maluku. Most of these were expressions of sympathy at the death of a particular individual killed in the conflict. Only two of the 74 (or less than 3 per cent) really provided additional information regarding internal events in Ambon that was not available elsewhere in the mainstream media: one was a press release from the Crisis Management Centre of the Federation of Indonesian Churches (Pusat

Table 7.1 Traffic on the 'ambon' e-group

Year	*Jan*	*Feb*	*Mar*	*Apr*	*May*	*Jun*	*Jul*	*Aug*	*Sep*	*Oct*	*Nov*	*Dec*	*TOTAL*
1998									51	33	19[a]	26	129
1999	194[b]	120	86	74	151	878[c]	480[d]	358	373	399	326	330[e]	3769
2000	736	851	572	626	748[f]	970[g]	1431	1017	901	1223	752	424	10251
2001	267[h]	274	548	325	420	315[i]	554	601	590	662	459	288[j]	5303
2002	230	439[k]	454	623	645	351	411	517	854	494	452	470	5940
2003	544	389	405	431	358	152	64	231	285[l]	317	392	415	3983
2004	526	485	883	1086	445								

Source: <http://groups.yahoo.com/group/ambon> (accessed 24 May 2004).

Notes:

a Katapang Incident
b 1st Ambon riot
c general elections
d 2nd Ambon riot
e 3rd Ambon riot at Christmas
f Laskar Jihad begin to arrive
g 'civil emergency' declared
h 2nd anniversary clashes
i major clashes in Ambon
j burning of Ambon parliament
k Malino Accord
l 'civil emergency rescinded'

Penanggulangan Krisis, PGI), and the other a report from the Sala Waku Foundation (Yayasan Sala Waku) on 'The Situation in Ambon, Wednesday/Thursday 25–26 August 1999'.[98] There was not one piece of information that was local or experientially specific to the posters.

By January 2000, postings were becoming more anti-Islamic and strident in their tone. But at the same time, people identifying themselves as Muslims began to post on the group. For example, 'zUlFaN K' from the 'Moslem Netter Association' provided a radical counter-point to the dominant perspective within the group.[99] On 6 January 2000, he described the previous month's conflict:

> … approximately 3,000 Muslim victims who died were slaughtered sadistically by the barbaric Christian dogs. Many who died were burnt alive. One holy fighter from the Justice Party was murdered cruelly and his genitals were severed and put in his mouth, and he was then barbarically crucified in the church where the Christians worship Christ Jesus who they say teaches love.
>
> A large number of the female victims were raped first in the streets and then murdered like dogs. The refugees were burnt alive in the trucks transporting them. …
>
> One group of men, women and children, numbering in their dozens, was locked in the Jami mosque and burnt alive. All the Islamic buildings were doused in petrol and burnt to the ground. All of this took place intentionally only one day after Christmas, which the Christians claim is a day of love, and at the time of the Holy Month of Ramadan leading to the Lebaran festival. …
>
> Then the leaders of the heathen Christians in Jakarta twisted the facts through the mass media and TV networks which they own and which they have built up since the New Order, including [the newspapers] *Kompas*, *Media Indonesia*, *Jawa Pos*, [and the television stations] SCTV, Indo Siar, RCTI assisted by the non-governmental National Commission for Human Rights.[100]

As indicated in Table 7.1, the escalation in Maluku, with the arrival of the Laskar Jihad in May 2000 and the declaration of 'civil emergency' in June, increased traffic on the 'ambon' list to 1,431 messages in July, the largest of any month since its establishment. There had been conscious attempts by members of the group to stop the escalation of communal sentiments on the 'ambon' e-group. As early as 23 January 1999, one of the regular posters, Noes Souisa, had cautioned members (initially of the Christian FICA-net, but then cross-posted to the 'ambon' e-group) against being provoked by one 'Devin', who had appeared on other online Christian forums. Souisa wrote, 'He [Devin] is not Ambonese. He is a follower of the devil … . What he writes is false propaganda, he wants to enrage the peoples of Indonesia, especially the Moluccans and the Papuans.'[101]

Devin appeared as the first unashamedly violent sectarian in the group. Writing from an e-mail account named 'devil', he introduced himself on the 'ambon' e-group on 30 March 1999 with a detailed and passionate account of his life and work as 57 years old and 'totally blind for the last 27 years'. He recounted his life, 'born a free American to free American parents', but staked his claim to a role in the communal conflict on the grounds of his family's long history in Maluku:[102]

> My father died of malaria and heart attack on Ambon Island while in missionary service to the people of Maluku.
>
> I grew up in Maluku, and saw these proud and noble people bent and broken by their unprincipled oppressors (who have been consistently backed by the Pentagon) all my life. Instead of teaching Indonesia the principles of democrasy [sic] and freedom, the United States has been arming and training the Jjavanese [sic] military elite to torture, kill and deceive under such programs as 'counterinsurgency training', 'psychological warfare', etc. ... I was also a missionary in Maluku, where I paddled hundreds of miles in outrigger canoes, and crossed islands on foot (sometimes on bare feet because I was not able to obtain footware capable of standing up under that kind of treatment for more than one or two days). Death threats are not new to me, because people also threatened my life for preaching the Gospel in the Moluccan wilderness.
>
> So, as I have told my friends, the decision to stand up to Indonesia and its CIA and Pentagon backers is my own free choice, taken as a free American. I perceive them only as criminals who lack the honor I might ascribe to a dog. I was born a free American, I have lived a free American, and I will die a free American. And thanks to the Internet, there is no way anyone can touch me outside due process of law without the entire world knowing what they have done. Small comfort perhaps, but pretty good when you compare this with the fate of Christian friends in Ambon.

In the high volume of exchanges in July 2000, Devin was the dominant voice on the 'ambon' e-group. In the first week of July, he posted 14 per cent of the 400 postings with identifiable authors (e-mail addresses). There were 51 identifiable participants (plus four with 'no author'), of whom 14 posted ten or more messages. While the majority of posters whose religious affiliation is able to be determined (with at least some degree of certainty) appear to be Christian, 38 per cent (ten out of 26) are Muslim.[103] In stark contrast to the total absence of Muslim participation in the early years of the e-group's existence, by July 2000 two of the four most active posters were Muslim. Christian Devin led with 57 messages, followed by Muslim 'Oemar-Moyo' (36), Christian 'anandadesa' ('village kid', which appears to be Helmi Wattimena's address) (32), and Muslim 'zUlFaN Z' (28). 'Oemar-Moyo', who appears to have only joined the e-group (with a test message) on 2 July, had contributed 36 messages by 7 July. His frequent anti-Ambonese racist slurs included derogatory descriptions of Ambonese as resembling chimpanzees, and veiled threats of rape (in locally inflected language).

On 1 July 2000, 'Chaumont (Joe) Devin' (whose other screen names include 'devil' and 'Tete') posted a message in English addressed to 'Dear Moluccan Friends Worldwide'.[104] He quoted a conversation he had had with 'a Moluccan "Christian"' in California whom he had approached 'to ask for money to buy guns'.[105] The person declined, and Devin was scathing in his condemnation of his co-believers who, 'having gained the safety of the US, … turn their backs upon their fellow Moluccans in Ambon and say, "We are very sorry, but it is clear that Jesus wants you all to die, there is nothing we can do, and to help you by sending you guns with which to defend yourselves would be a sin."'[106]

On 3 July, a heated exchange triggered by a posting from Devin (using his other *nom de guerre*, 'Tete') led to threats of warfare and sabotage strategies on the net. When Septiaji Eko Nugroho ('adjie') forwarded from a Muslim list a piece entitled 'Does Pope Condemn the Christians [*sic*] Barbarity in Maluku?', Devin responded aggressively, addressing his readers as 'Moluccan comrades', inviting them to 'silence the lying dog [adjie]'. He also called on 'Moluccans, all around the world, at this moment [to] send empty (e-)mails in their thousands to [the Muslim list] istiqlal-subscribe@egroups.com? Wouldn't this crash their server? What do you say we try it? Come on, not just one individual by themselves, but let's wait until we have a general agreement, and then we can all hit them at once and not give them any rest for dozens of days. What do you reckon?'[107]

Adjie responded by highlighting the futility of the gesture: 'Oh, gee! Don't do that. If the istiqlal server crashes, this mailing list ['ambon'] will also crash. (We're both on eGroups). And then where would our discussion go? Wouldn't it be better to just hack it (or even hot it up a bit [*lho kok malah manasin*])'.[108] For some reason, the mutuality of the infrastructure was readily visible in cyberspace even after the common infrastructure of Ambon city had been all but destroyed by the preceding months of animosity, though the recognition of this 'common interest' did not in any way change the tenor of the exchanges.

The tone set by these most active posters was one of vitriol and verbal violence directed at the 'other', most commonly defined according to religion, but often too with ethnic connotations. The dark complexion and crinkly hair of the ethnic Ambonese was mocked by (ethnic Javanese Muslim) 'ali-susanto74' (five postings) who, harking back to the Lebaran (December) 1999 event that triggered the violence, asserted passionately that 'it's fair enough if we massacre [you] because you attacked us first during Lebaran two years ago. Do you still remember?????? So don't whine if you're now the ones being slaughtered like rats.'[109] Devin, the Honolulu-based 'free American', remained one of the most belligerent on the list and before too long, on behalf of what he called his 'Eastern Alliance for Freedom', was soliciting for 'people willing to undertake the dangerous task of infiltrating the Moluccas in special boats in order to set up chains of command, weapons transport systems, and military attack squads'.[110] In a characteristic racial attack, his posting of 13 July states:

> Say, you Javanese have real guts when it comes to torturing unarmed and innocent victims, or dismembering women and children. I just can't wait to see what the Moluccans do to you when we get them some real guns. That should be VERY INTERESTING INDEED, and amighty [*sic*] good show! I've always been kind of interested in such things. I can still remember watching my mother butcher chickens when I was a boy. Really interesting

> stuff, and all kinds of pretty colors inside! Sometimes I kinda wonder if you Javanese are like that. But I don't suppose you have gizzards. No, I don't think you would have gizzards at all.[111]

But after playing a dominant role in the e-group, posting some of the most inflammatory messages, Chaumont Devin seems to have disappeared from the list, with a final note on 15 August 2000 giving no hint.

Arguments on the list were often couched within a polarised nationalist debate. Muslim posters often regarded Christians as inevitably supporters of the (separatist and largely Netherlands-based) RMS.[112] Meanwhile, Ambonese (Christian) ethnic nationalists, such as Helmi Wattimena (from the e-mail address 'anandadesa'), regarded their opponents as imposing a process of 'Javanisation' and 'Islamisation', and called for support for a Moluccan (or Alifuru) nation ('Viva Alifuru Nation').[113]

Not all messages spoke with communal and violent language. Some, such as the posting signed 'Willy' and addressed to 'Dear friends in Sydney [Australia]' (re-posted from the 'anandadesa' e-mail address), provided a description in relatively non-emotional language of a series of running skirmishes in the area around Ambon. Entitled 'A Letter from the Ambon battlefield', it was clearly a Christian perspective but was measured and controlled, for example describing those conducting the aggression neutrally as *perusuh* (rioters, terrorists) and not identifying the rioters in any explicit religious category.[114] Similarly, a posting by the 'Masariku Network' (from 'peter') described an attack on a Christian area of Ambon by 'rioters' whose religious or ethnic identity was not specified. This kind of linguistic neutrality – that is, ways of stating problems without overt ethno-religious identification – had been honed in the media under the New Order, when such neutrality was often the only way of writing about a social conflict. But on the 'ambon' e-group it had become impossible to speak from a neutral position. Peter's vague reference to terrorists necessarily invited demands for clear positioning. An immediate response from a Surabaya Muslim 'elha' asked: 'Just who are these "rioters"? And who is being terrorised?'[115]

The postings on the 'ambon' list had clearly become open for challenge and debate, to be picked apart and trawled over for signifiers of religious allegiance and complicity. Patricia Spyer, in her exploration of the emotional climate 'of fear, insecurity, and mental and physical exhaustion which Ambonese inhabit everyday' as a consequence of the conflict, coined the term 'hyper-hermeneutics' to describe this 'compulsive need to interpret and mine just about everything for hidden meaning, to see any trivial occurrence as a sign or omen of what might come'.[116] The 'ambon' e-group participants were applying to cybercommunication the same forensic linguistic discrimination that had come to characterise face-to-face communication in Ambon itself, where 'strongly segregated youth socialization leaves its adherents with a sufficiently distinctive vocabulary, so that locals claim they can instantly identify someone's religion if they hear that person speak'.[117] Postings similarly betray the writer's linguistic milieu, dotted with either recognisably Muslim or Christian names, greetings, terms or associated images.

As the broader political context within which the e-group operated became ever more antagonist, so too did the list polarise, leaving little space for non-partisan exchange. The barest hint of an affiliation lay a participant open to strident criticism from posters with opposing loyalties. Expressions of disaffection and disappointment continued, with the list's preoccupations and personal vituperation leading one wag to comment: 'This mailing list is gradually getting less and less worthwhile. There's no point in you trying to manage Ambon; at least it might be a start if you could get yourselves in order!'[118]

There had been a dramatic transformation in the 'ambon' e-group during the two years since its establishment in August 1998. From a spiritual forum for a few friends scattered around the world, it had developed into a vitriolic sectarian battlefield in which loyalties to religion, state, nation and ethnic group were all open to vilification and attack. Some early participants were still active. For example, 'tali_hulaleng', who had been the most prolific poster in January 1999 with 60 of the month's 192 messages, still had nine postings between 1 and 7 July 2000. But there was little trace that July week of founders P.C. ('Noce') Wattimena and Elya Muskitta, though both were still members of the list. In his role as list administrator, P.C. Wattimena appeared very rarely, taking no apparent part in discussions.[119] Elya Muskitta returned only occasionally for bitter exchanges with his old foe Helmi Wattimena and others.[120] Those participants active in 2000 were mobilising to raise money for their compatriots' military operations. They were seeking to crash or hack opponents' Internet access. They were striving to use this new technology to mobilise an international community in support of their faction in a local civil war, tranforming the 'e-group' into another of what Tekwani has dubbed the 'autonomous nodes in a militant network'.[121]

Some of the initiators of the 'ambon' e-group moved on to other patches in cyberspace. Wattimena, who had established the 'ambon' list in 1998, became a contributing member of the Christian KADnet ('Kawanua Advent se-Dunia') website, established by the Indonesian Adventist Community, which included team members in Indonesia (Jakarta, Ternate, Surabaya Manado, Balikpapan, Papua and elsewhere), Canada, Australia (Sydney), the Philippines (Manila), Germany, the Netherlands, the USA (California and Seattle) and elsewhere.[122] Helmi Wattimena ('anandadesa') had also set up another Yahoo! group on 7 March 2000, called 'Maluku', 'For Communication between Moluccan [sic] around the World'.[123] According to this e-group's homepage ,it also had open membership, public archives, and was unmoderated. But by contrast to the 'ambon' e-group, its membership remained tiny (only nine in November 2003), with virtually all postings by Helmi Wattimena himself. In October 2000, there was a hiatus, with the flow ceasing until revived in April 2001 with sporadic messages from Dutch-based Papuan activist Ottis Simopiaref. Wattimena re-engaged in September 2001, when postings included a press release from the USA's Moluccan Sovereignty Front (FKM-USA), of which he was the chairman. The document called, among other points, for the release in Indonesia of detained FKM Executive Chairman Dr Alex Manuputty, a campaign also taken up on the 'ambon' e-group.[124] The press release appeared also on the FKM-USA's own site, established in 2001 which, unlike

Wattimena's 'Maluku' e-group, had dozens of new postings through 2003.[125] Traffic on the 'Maluku' list remained sporadic and unfocussed and, by October 2003, though the list continued to be available, the latest postings were from all-too-familiar multi-million-dollar Nigerian financial scams, or material unrelated to Maluku, such as postings about Papua by Simopiaref.[126]

In contrast to the fitful history of Helmi Wattimena's 'Maluku.com' list, the original 'ambon' list continued to attract new participants to its changing clientele. By February 2002, the month leading up to the Malino Accord, the e-group was settling back to a slow but steady, and somewhat predictable, flow of press reports and criticisms of Islam. There were only 230 messages that month, the lowest since May 1999. Most active was 'Marinyo Maluku' (with 13 postings, most of which were English-language press reports, with a couple of reports from the Diocese of Amboina Crisis Centre) and 'Bengs' (most of whose six postings were religious homilies). In addition, there were two contributions each by 'flip noija' (a Christmas greeting and cross-posting from the Christian FICA-net) and 'Achirrani' (quotations from Patrick Henry's 'Give me Liberty or Give me Death', in English with Indonesian translation). The three remaining postings by individuals included an advertisement from a Makassar computer store, and two Christian criticisms of 'the anti-Christ' and 'Jihad'.[127] There were no apparent postings by Muslim members, and the general tone was restrained and confident, in the manner of correspondents sharing Christian-oriented information with those of like mind. It was an illusory peace, however, for as soon as a Muslim participant posted a seemingly innocuous message analysing the possibility of a multi-level marketing business strategy conforming to the *Syari'ah* (Islamic law), the response from 'Moluccan Whip' was immediate and antagonistic.

> Don't you bring that *syariah* bullshit to this Ambon group. The Ambonese are sick of hearing that crap. You should sell that shit idea to your other mates in Indonesia. Moluccans are not Indonesians. That nation is a nation of colonialists, the TNI is an army of occupation that must be fought until the Banda Sea turns dry. *Comprehende*? The Islamic Scholars' Council, the Association of Indonesian Muslim Intellectuals, the Indonesian Committee for Islamic World Solidarity, the Islamic Defenders' Front, and the Laskar Jihad are all involved in the slaughter of 8,000 of the Maluku nation. So we don't need that *syariah* bullshit![128]

While the list gave extensive attention to the Malino Accord of February 2002, with dozens of postings of press reports on the negotiations and agreements, the overall thrust of opinion was defensive, pessimistic, anti-Muslim and suspicious, with participants such as 'Marinyo Maluku' regarding the accord as a victory for:

- The creator of Maluku conflicts itself such as Green Army/TNI based in Java
- The Laskar Jihad, Laskar Mujahiddin and MUI [Indonesian Muslim Scholars' Council]
- And of course the 'Colonial Indonesian Government'.[129]

Helmi Wattimena ('anandadesa') was posting critical material, such as that by Dr Alex Manuputty, Executive Chair of the FKM in Ambon, condemning the Accord as a 'Javanese satanic conspiracy'.[130] Others (such as the poster 'Ambon'), though highly critical of militant Muslims, nonetheless posted, without particular derogatory comment, numerous statements and documents from the Laskar Jihad Online site authorised by its parent body the Central Leadership Council of the FKAWJ, no doubt confident that in the particular context of this e-group any document associated with Laskar Jihad would be read only to be criticised and rejected.[131]

By July 2003, incidence of violence in Maluku was declining as the Malino Accord and other peace and reconciliation efforts, such as the BakuBae movement, took effect. List traffic that July slowed considerably, with only 64 messages – the lowest monthly tally since 1998. Three of the eight posters in July contributed ten messages or more. Most prolific was 'AreopagusVII',[132] whose 25 postings (40 per cent of the month's traffic) were mainly items from the print media (including *Kompas*, *Tempo*, *Sinar Harapan*, *The Jakarta Post*) but included six news bulletins from the FKM.[133] Almost as prolific was 'Ambon RMS' (whose postings were sometimes signed 'HARLEY CYBER WAR') with 19 messages (30 per cent), many of which were American-sourced news items, and included a dozen photographs of demonstrations outside the Indonesian Ebassy, pressuring the USA to continue to withhold military aid from Indonesia.[134] An elderly left-wing Indonesian émigré living in exile since 1965, A. Umar Said, contributed ten postings (15 per cent) from his home in Paris. Most of these could be described as historical 'thought pieces', including commentaries on the Indonesian legal and justice system and memoirs of a former political prisoner held after Suharto's military coup of October 1965.[135] Lesser contributions were made by 'Moluccan Whip' (whose three postings were of media reports, but included abusive 'subject' taggings berating the Indonesian unitary state and Muslim 'cockroaches'![136]), 'Nitram Rehtul' (or 'Martin Luther' written backwards) who posted two outbursts against Indonesian Army violence,[137] and 'madju95' who circulated two statements presented to the United National Working Group on Indigenous Populations from the 'Maluku Alifuru nation'.[138]

Five years after its establishment, with only a handful of the postings it generated in its heyday during 2000, the tenor of the list was unflinchingly firm and once again relatively homogeneous politically. There were no religious homilies, no poems about peace, no Bible readings, no individualised 'personal reports' of, or pleas for help from, the trauma of the Maluku wars. Those few accounts (ostensibly from Ambon) that do appear are institutionalised: press releases from the FKM. There was no obvious dissent from the list's dominant voice, which was anti-Muslim and supported independence for Maluku. As was the case during its early months of existence, the e-group's active posting circle was again under a dozen, all – with the possible exception of AreopagusVII (posting on behalf of the FKM) – emanating from outside of Maluku. The vitriol that had emerged in the group's exchanges between Muslims and Christian posters during the height of the war in Maluku had evaporated and the Muslim participants had withdrawn, leaving the field to the pro-independence FKM and other Moluccan nationalist spokespeople whose very e-names – such as 'Moluccan Whip' and 'Ambon RMS' – flagged something of their political stance. There was no space for political equivocation. Anyone interested in ideas, debates and discussions had left the field to those with little interest in any exchange, but with sharp axes to grind and political points to score.

Conclusion

Cyberoptimists have put great store on the socially transcending characteristics of Internet technologies. They suggest that

> the changing politics of identity characterised by the breakdown of social class, patriarchal and racial modes of political organisation and their replacement by a diverse range of movements championing social difference may also be finding expression in cyberspace. In this context cyberspace is regarded as the medium through which to explore concepts of emancipation, empowerment and the transcendence of physical subjugation.[139]

We found no such clear autonomy in areas of the cyberspace that had identified itself with Ambon or Maluku. Nor indeed was the 'subjugation' of the 'ambon' e-group to Ambon city and Maluku province entirely straightforward. The 'ambon' e-group transmitted information about events in Maluku to Moluccans outside of their archipelagic homeland – either elsewhere in Indonesia, or in Europe, the USA or Australia. The volume, pace and tone of its traffic could be mapped into the battles within the physical border of Maluku itself. On the other hand, the 'ambon' list was not a forum for current residents of Ambon to talk either amongst themselves or directly to compatriots outside. It was a place for people outside of Maluku speaking about them, on behalf of them, trying to take up in cyberspace – from scattered keyboards around the world – the physical battles being fought on the soil of the province.

The Internet did not provide a neutral zone where Muslims and Christians could meet, not even in the midst of the BakuBae efforts to create neutral areas on the ground. Indeed, the cyber 'ambon' was peculiarly divorced from the specific events of life in Ambon itself – no first-hand accounts, no breaking story, no urgent churning of the rumour mill fomenting (as Patricia Spyer elegantly demonstrates) immediate actions on the ground. There was little information on the 'ambon' e-group that was not re-cycled from the mainstream mass media, or history books, other than the occasional very personal vitriolic excesses of foreigners and expatriates. It was certainly not a vector to amplify, for global attention, local voices excluded from the mainstream.

As we watched the few hundred people on the 'ambon' e-group, a very global technology was harnessed to foster the formation of primordial identity, at once intensely parochial and also trans-national. The net helped (sadly) the constant interlacing of Maluku's local woes to the Huntingtonian 'clash of civilisations', without bringing to the global sphere anything uniquely local to Maluku.

8 Conclusions and more questions

It is more than a decade since the first Indonesian language newsgroups were starting up to celebrate the arrival of a new medium/weapon in the struggle to rid the country of an old authoritarian ruler, and almost a decade since the first Internet Service Providers (ISPs) were being established in Indonesia and the earliest *warnet* began promising equal access to the new technology. In the heady days of the anti-Suharto demonstrations, the Internet established its reputation as the fastest and most accurate of the 'news media' amongst the young, the urban and particularly amongst the anti-New Order activists. When large street protests and civil unrest occurred, it was to the Internet that these people turned in the hope of information and critical analysis.

From the websites to the *warnet*, citizens' demands took precedence over fear of government crack-down, in part perhaps because there was no clear policy or practice laid down by the old, tired, contradiction-ridden New Order government, but partly too because a certain conviction about the anarchic character of the Internet seemed to permeate the discourse about the technology. At the level of the local Internet *warung*, the hand of government regulation rested lightly. Permits to open Internet cafés were no more difficult to obtain than those required to open the computer rental businesses that dotted the surrounds of the campuses, providing hourly rental rates. Public Internet access points appeared not to restrict clients' access to their desired websites. Even Wasantara, which because of its association with the government's postal service might have been security-conscious, required no independently verifiable details of users, no identity card (KTP) or address, and did not block or monitor access to any sites, either for political or 'moral' reasons. In Yogyakarta on a fieldwork trip in 1996, we ourselves had no difficulty accessing every radical political website and newsgroup (in any language) we knew.

In those early days of the Internet's spread into Indonesia (which coincided with the final years of Suharto's rule), it was not so much the content of the political discourse on the net that seemed important, but the sense that absolutely anything *could* be said and *was* being said online with impunity. The very freedoms of the Internet became a constant reminder of the constraints on the other media. Universities' Internet facilities, intended for academic purposes, were equally suited to coordinating student political action around the country. The same infrastructures that the New Order government promoted to serve big business and technological education could be utilised with equal ease by small, disparate groups to disseminate their views and information. The human skills-base produced by the Habibie-driven technology training policies of the New Order produced the technicians who staffed both the hi-tech offices in the skyscrapers of Jakarta and the stuffy backrooms of the community action groups around the country. Smart university graduates set up ISPs such as RADNET, but also the 'alternative' cyber-publications such as *Tempo Interaktif.* The speed of expansion of the Indonesian stretch of the information superhighway, and the amount and disorder of its traffic, seemed to make policing it almost impossible. Seen thus, the Internet successfully breached the censorship and restrictions on freedom of expression imposed by the New Order government.

Such an upbeat conclusion, in tune with much of the popular writing in and on the net in Indonesia and Asia more generally, would be a correct but incomplete reading of the place of the Internet in democratising Indonesia. The points of translation between the freedoms of the cyberspace and politics of streets, parliaments and ballot boxes within a particular nation are neither direct nor essential. And though a decade is not nearly long enough fully to take stock of how Internet and politics have shaped each other in Indonesia, the lines of their connections are clear enough to raise further questions.

This book

Our interest in the Internet was first generated in 1996 by the dissident and optimistic students in Yogyakarta engaging the new technology in pursuit of democracy in Indonesia. We followed the activities of the networks of dissent as they were growing online and watched political activists utilise those capacities of the technology that disabled state censorship and enabled freedom of speech. We have described some of these networks in Chapter 3. There is little doubt that there was some overlap between the students who used the *warnet* in Yogyakarta and Bandung or at their universities in Jakarta, and those who stormed the parliament on the eve of Suharto's resignation. But we claim no singular causal connection between these networks and the demise of the New Order.

Indeed, we suggest that the social and political consequences of the Internet cannot be understood by treating it in isolation from other media. Here our work stands out from the majority of published accounts of the Internet and the World Wide Web in Asia, which characteristically cast these 'new' modes of communication as the polar opposite of print and broadcast media, operating with no reference to existing media forms and institutions. Our introduction to the Internet in Indonesia was, however, in the midst of a previous research project to identify dissident, anti-establishment practices within the conventional media, against the command model and mechanisms developed by the New Order government since 1966. That research (as summarised in *Media, Culture and Politics in Indonesia*[1]) indicated clearly that, by the 1990s, there were many lines of fracture in the New Order's control of the media. We have re-visited some of these issues in Chapter 2 of this book to argue that the Internet's early history in Indonesia is best understood in relation to the growing breaches and rips in the New Order's theory and practice of ordering the media, rather than as a sudden, entirely new oppositional force. The Internet, we maintain, amplified and extended the elements of dissent against the New Order government that were already present in the texts and institutions of the older media. Indeed, the political significance of the new medium was precisely in the many points of its articulation into the older media, so that, despite its own very limited reach, the Internet's role in the transition from authoritarianism was palpable, even if it is not quantifiable.

There is a more general point to be made here. It has been the common practice of media studies to attempt to measure impact by isolating a particular medium from other social and cultural practices. In the early 1970s, in his classic work *Television: Technology and Cultural Form*, Raymond Williams critiqued the then dominant mode of television studies: 'The most significant feature of this discussion has been the isolation of the medium.'[2] Williams went on to argue against the 'simple cause-and-effect identification' of television's agency in social and cultural change:

> What is significant is not the reliability of any … particular identifications …. What is really significant is the direction of attention to certain selected issues – on the one hand 'sex' and 'violence', on the other hand 'political manipulation and cultural degradation' – which are of so general a kind that it ought to be obvious that they cannot be specialised to an isolated medium but, in so far as television bears on them, have to be seen in a whole social and cultural process.[3]

While Williams is talking about analysis of television in the western 'advanced industrial societies' in the mid-twentieth century, an echo of this analysis, changing only 'political manipulation' to 'political activism', rings entirely true in relation to a good deal of writing about the Internet in Asia in the early twenty-first century.

Following the assumption that no medium can be understood in isolation from the wider social, cultural processes (what elsewhere in his book Williams refers to as 'all that men [sic] ordinarily see as history' (Williams p. 127)) we have tried, as indicated above, to place the politics of and on the Internet into the framework of the media in Indonesia. We have tried also to understand the role of the Internet in relation to political movements and conflicts in the context of Indonesia's transition from an authoritarian rule to democracy. Such an analysis of the Internet, embedded within particular political struggles, means that our specific arguments about the use of the technology in the *reformasi* movement's bid for democracy in Indonesia (Chapters 3 and 5) or in East Timor's struggle for independence (Chapter 6), cannot necessarily be generalised across the Indonesian archipelago. If Chapters 3 and 5 show that the Internet provided a space for like-minded citizens to come together in defiance of a powerful government and begin to set up the institutions of democratic governance, and Chapter 6 suggests that it echoed East Timor's calls for freedom around the world, then Chapter 7, placing the Internet in the context of the bloody communal conflict in Maluku, suggests that the net's benefits are available as much to liberal democrats struggling against dictators and moderate nationalists seeking self-determination as to right-wing religious extremists of every variety. The internet's predominant feature is its capacity to transport information, in the form of digital material, and it does so even-handedly – it does not choose between democratic principles, economic innovations or communal histories. As Denise Murray has observed, while in its infancy the internet may have been the preserve of a tight core of academics and scientists with a 'shared social consensus', the net's embrace by now of many tens of millions of netizens means that 'the same destructive and deviant behaviour found in the real world is found in the virtual one'.[4]

Methodologically, global, macro approaches to the Internet have tended to obfuscate the content and the actors and have focussed on the uniqueness of the technology. The mainstream of 'Internet theory' (as it has emerged since the mid-1990s) has been more driven by imagining what the technology can do and will do, rather than looking at the 'observable record' (to borrow a phrase from McChesney's classic work on *Rich Media, Poor Democracy*) of its social and political use. Our own study here fits into a small minority of Internet research where the actions of the netizens, rather than their tools, are the primary concern. If the Internet does leave a political mark on a society into which it is introduced, then it does so in ways that are not technologically predetermined. The issue of agency is thus central to this book. Rather than thinking about the 'impact' of the Internet, we have sought to understand it in terms of the opportunities afforded by the new technology, and of who took up which ones of these. And if agency is important, then so is the issue of access. Chapter 4 charts the growth and spread of access to the Internet in Indonesia from 1996 to early 2004. Unsurprisingly, we found inequities both regionally across the nation and hierarchically across social differences in income and education. That the lines of inequities should fall along the lines of other social inequities produced by the New Order is also not surprising. What is notable is that there are now clear signs of decline in the sector that provides Indonesians with cheap public access to the net. In Chapter 4 we have described the emergence of a very indigenous version of the global Internet café, the *warnet*, which replicated the traditional Indonesian suburban and rural corner shop and held the best promise of increasing access beyond the urban rich. Not only has the growth in this sector halted, but the sector is also being transformed. The public-access sector's transition from small 'downmarket' *warung* to upmarket, corporate-owned 'computer centres' in city malls is now eroding any hope of wide-spread access across the archipelago.

Access to the Internet is not, of course, determined only by financial or communication infrastructure capacities. The net is the domain of the literate: the better one can write or type, the better one's access to the Internet both as consumer and, even more, as producer of ideas and information. We have argued in Chapter 5 that its limited distribution and its typographic mode make the Internet insignificant in the mass politics of elections and parliaments since the New Order. Our analysis of local government websites suggests that they are used primarily by these governments in the symbolic display of regional autonomy and to a lesser degree for the distribution of information. Their role in the process of engaging citizens in any meaningful dialogue, let alone any real engagement in decision-making (which in policy rhetoric has been the *raison d'être* for e-government), is negligible. Far fewer residents in Indonesia receive information via the Internet than via the conventional media. More importantly, most of those who enter the net do so as observers and consumers – replicating online the readers and spectators of conventional media – rather than as the idealised, active discursive citizen of net theory.

Closing questions

Increasingly, activists in Asia themselves have become aware of the contradictory political possibilities of the Internet. Their attention is shifting from a valorisation of the technology of freedom to a focus on protecting the freedoms of the net users against state and corporate interventions, which are increasingly evident.[5] Too little is said, however, beyond the obligatory mention of inequity, about the political consequences of this unequal access to the Internet. Where the net's discursive space leaves out many nationals, how will the discursively active relate to those who are not 'in'? In the last days of Suharto's Indonesia and in the final years of Timor's independence struggle, we have seen local political networks on the ground elaborated, echoed and transported into global networks online. But beyond those events, and in relation to democratic politics in Indonesia after the end of authoritarian rule, many questions remain about the nature of the relationships that might develop between those who are globally connected (to their social or professional peers across the world) and their fellow citizens (living in neighbouring suburbs) who are not. If the electronic agora does not, and in the foreseeable future cannot, include most citizens, then it is arguable that the very existence of such a privileged and exclusive space is in fact a hindrance rather than a help to the formation of a democracy that is inclusive of all citizens. Analysis across Asian economies is showing clearly the increasing gap in growth and productivity between sectors, which are and are not integrated into new information technologies.[6] Are there parallels to be drawn about the increasing political clout of netters *vis-à-vis* the others? And if cyberspace operates in defiance of state boundaries (as it clearly does) and yet conditions of entry into it are set (as we have seen) by state-determined infrastructure, then who will address the issue of entry into this space?

Specifically in the context of the Indonesian *reformasi*, these normative questions need to be addressed. There is little doubt that the Internet is capable of delivering social, economic, political and cultural advantages to its users – whether these users are individuals setting up cottage industries in defiance of the multinationals, or communities practising alternative medicine, or fundamentalist religious groups running roughshod over the individual human rights of those who live around them. The users of the Internet played a role in bringing down the repressive Suharto regime – *and* they privileged themselves in the eyes of the world by being *seen* (by their 'virtual' presence) to be at the forefront of the democratic movement. But if we think of democracy as inclusive of all citizens, then in Indonesia today the Internet may be at best yet another index of inequality, at worst yet another impediment to equal participation in an emerging democracy.

We return finally to something that has been implicit through much of this book, as indeed it is in many other discussions of the media and democracy: Habermas' conceptualisation of a public sphere, which underpins his notion of 'discursive democracy'. As we mentioned in the Introduction, these concepts are a frequent point of reference in many discussions of democratisation in the west and in Asia; Indonesian intellectuals have also evoked the German philosopher. Critiquing the nature of the emerging democracy in his own nation, Ignas Kleden has written:

> The basic assumption of "deliberative democracy" is that citizens' participation in the democratic process [has] a rational character; that voting, for example, should not simply aggregate preferences but rather follow on a process in which citizens become informed of the better arguments and the more general interest.[7]

It is easy to understand the affinity that intellectuals such as Kleden and other leaders of the *reformasi* movement might feel for a deliberative and necessarily intellectual form of democracy where political decisions emerge exclusively from reasoned arguments competing on the basis of their truth value. As Sidel writes of the Muslim intellectual leadership in particular (but which applies equally to the rest of the *reformasi* leadership), 'they had spent long years of the Suharto dictatorship engaged in Habermasian discussions and debates on the seminar circuits and newspaper editorial pages of Jakarta'.[8] It is easy to see why such a leadership would embrace the keyboard and the screen as its preferred weapons in a battle again Suharto's military rule, and for the primacy of the deliberative or discursive modes over other ways of acquiring and exercising power. It isn't entirely flippant to suggest that the cybercafés and their Indonesianised counterpart, *warnet* – as well as the online chat rooms, websites and mailing lists – are not unlike the eighteenth-century English coffee shop, which was Habermas' archetype for the public sphere: that is, they are spaces for information-sharing, opinion and gossip, but also where skills of reading and writing, the elegance of arguments and intellectual sophistry matter more than mass appeal.

In practice, however, the Internet in Indonesia seems to have failed the test of both mass-based and discursive democracy. On the one hand the typographic access to the net keeps out many, making the net necessarily privileged and therefore undemocratic. On the other hand it, is not restricted to the civic-minded leadership of the Indonesian reform movement of the 1990s, but available to many forces that are extremist, illiberal, anti-democratic, and not necessarily 'civil', society. In the end, the Internet might be understood as Castells has suggested, 'in the realm of symbolic politics, and in the development of issue-oriented mobilizations by groups and individuals outside the mainstream political system',[9] while it is the mainstream that must be engaged in securing democratic institutions in a large and complex nation such as Indonesia.

On the other hand, the Internet has put the ideas of 'interactivity' and 'networks' at the centre of media theory, policy and technology. The key words in national media policy (in Indonesia and elsewhere) have shifted from 'broadcast' and 'impact' to 'network' and 'feedback'. The digital industry is creating new hardware and software for 'network platforms'. In media theory too, the early 1990s' buzz-word 'media convergence', which drew research to the interaction and interlacing of technologies, is beginning to be replaced by 'network media', where the social practice (interaction and interlacing of people) has conceptual precedence over the technological form. In Indonesia as well, perhaps the Internet's best contribution is that it has been one of the vehicles for the imagination of a less pedagogic and more discursive and decentralised mode of communication. How networks of and in the media are materialised in Indonesia will depend not so much on the spread of the Internet (which we have argued is unlikely to extend very far, very fast), but on how radio and television, by far the most accessed media, are transformed in the context of Indonesia's new democratic politics on the one hand and changing global media technology on the other. These mediatised networks do not, of course, promise to be havens of liberal democratic discourse. But at least they might be places, literally, to air local issues and, in the cacophony, drown out any possibility of the centralised voice from Jakarta with which the New Order government ruled Indonesia.

Notes

1 The global information highway in a national context

1 Many would argue, of course, that the notion of any medium being 'national' is fraught in a globalised media system, with a constant flow of media content across national borders.
2 See B.N. Hague and B.D. Loader (eds), *Digital Democracy: Discourse and Decision Making in the Information Age*, Routledge, London and New York, 1999.
3 P. Ferdinand (ed.), *The Internet, Democracy and Democratization*, Frank Cass, London, 2000, and S. Kalathil and T.C. Boas, *Open Networks Closed Regimes: The Impact of the Internet on Authoritarian Rule*, Carnegie Endowment for International Peace, Washington, 2003.
4 See Reporters without Borders, 'The Internet Under Surveillance', 2004 Report, available online at <www.rsf.org> (accessed 24 June 2004).
5 In the early hours of 1 October 1965, an abortive coup by a group of middle-ranking military officers, which resulted in the killing of six senior officers, was quickly overthrown by Major-General Suharto's forces, who then conducted a massive pogrom against leftist and nationalist groups, with up to one million killed. For details, see R. Cribb, 'Problems in the Historiography of the Killings in Indonesia', in R. Cribb (ed.), *The Indonesian Killings, 1965–1966: Studies from Java and Bali*, Centre of Southeast Asian Studies, Monash University, Melbourne, 1990.
6 For dates of accession to these posts, see R. Cribb, *Historical Dictionary of Indonesia*, The Scarecrow Press, Metuchen and London, 1992, pp. 530–1. For a description of this transition, see R.E. Elson, *Suharto: A Political Biography*, Cambridge University Press, Cambridge, 2001, pp. 121–2.
7 Suharto's resignation speech is translated in G. Forrester and R.J. May (eds), *The Fall of Soeharto*, Crawford House Publishing, Bathurst, 1998, pp. 246–7.
8 On the attack on the PDI headquarters, see K. O'Rourke, *Reformasi: The Struggle for Power in Post-Soeharto Indonesia*, Allen & Unwin, Sydney, 2002, pp. 9–15.
9 See H. Hill, 'The Indonesian Economy: The Strange and Sudden Death of a Tiger', in Forrester and May (eds), *The Fall of Soeharto*, pp. 93–103.
10 M.C. Ricklefs, *A History of Modern Indonesia since c. 1200* (3rd edition), Palgrave, Houndmills, 2001, p. 404.
11 The circumstances surrounding the fall of Suharto are graphically depicted in O'Rourke, *Reformasi: The Struggle for Power in Post-Soeharto Indonesia*. On Suharto's response to the Asian financial crisis, see particularly pp. 22–51.
12 On the General Session of the MPR, see K. van Dijk, *A Country in Despair: Indonesia between 1997 and 2000*, KITLV Press, Jakarta, 2001, pp. 137–60.
13 Ibid., p. 164.
14 See I.N. Bhakti, 'Chronology of Events Leading to the Fall of President Soeharto', in Forrester and May (eds), *The Fall of Soeharto*, pp. 239–45.
15 Robison and Hadiz suggest that the powerful oligarchy of business interests that largely controlled the New Order had come to regard Suharto as an impediment to their continuing power, and had determined to jettison him in order to preserve their teetering financial empires.

See R. Robison and V.R. Hadiz, *Reorganising Power in Indonesia: The Politics of Oligarchy in an Age of Markets*, RoutledgeCurzon, London, 2004.

16 E. Aspinall, 'Opposition and Elite Conflict in the Fall of Soeharto', in Forrester and May (eds), *The Fall of Soeharto*, pp.130–53.

17 Ibid., p. 136.

18 In the decade between 1982–83 and 1992–93, for example, enrolments in state universities nearly doubled from 275,000 to 427,000, while in private universities they increased more than fivefold from 170,000 to 1,000,000! See Thee Kian Wie, 'Determinants of Indonesia's Industrial Technology Development', in H. Hill and Thee Kian Wie (eds), *Indonesia's Technological Challenge*, ISEAS, Singapore, pp. 117–35: data from Table 6.2, pp. 122–3, 1998.

19 D. Bourchier and V. Hadiz (eds), *Indonesian Politics And Society A Reader*, Routledge, London, 2003, p. 254, fn. 2, provide a list of some key LSMs, in a coalition called IN-DEMO (Indonesian NGOs for Democracy).

20 P.J. Eldridge, *The Politics of Human Rights in Southeast Asia*, Routledge, London, 2002, p. 121.

21 Eklöf, S., *Indonesian Politics in Crisis: The Long Fall of Suharto 1996–98*, NIAS, Copenhagen, 1999, p. 166.

22 Ibid., p. 170. See also O'Rourke, *Reformasi: The Struggle for Power in Post-Soeharto Indonesia*, pp. 69–70.

23 O'Rourke, *Reformasi: The Struggle for Power in Post-Soeharto Indonesia*, p. 44.

24 Eklöf, *Indonesian Politics in Crisis: The Long Fall of Suharto 1996–98*, p.108.

25 'Broker BEJ pun berdemo', *Jawa Pos Online*, 20 May 1998 <http://202.149.241/jplalu/mei98/20 mei/de20mi4.htm> (accessed 30 January 1999).

26 O'Rourke, *Reformasi: The Struggle for Power in Post-Soeharto Indonesia*, p. 38.

27 K. Evans, 'Economic Update', in G. Forrester (ed.), *Post-Soeharto Indonesia: Renewal or Chaos?*, Crawford House Publishing, Bathurst, 1999, pp. 105–27: quotation from p. 116.

28 Ricklefs, *A History of Modern Indonesia*, pp. 408–21 provides a useful overview of these issues.

29 For details of decentralisation legislation, see M. Turner and O. Podger (with M. Sumardjono and W.K. Tirthayasa), *Decentralisation in Indonesia: Redesigning the State*, Asia Pacific Press at the Australian National University, Canberra, 2003.

30 D. McCargo, *Media and Politics in Pacific Asia*, RoutledgeCurzon, London, 2003, p. 41.

31 For details of some of these confrontations, see O'Rourke, *Reformasi: The Struggle for Power in Post-Soeharto Indonesia*, pp. 181–4.

32 Till 2004, Indonesian presidents were indirectly elected by the MPR: that is, the joint sitting of the DPR (Dewan Perwakilan Rakyat, People's Legislative Council) and regional and functional group delegates. As part of the reform process, the Indonesian Parliament in 2003 passed new electoral laws for direct presidential elections, which took place for the first time in 2004.

33 For a detailed discussion of the political manoeuvrings from May 1998 to July 2001, see D. Kingsbury, *The Politics of Indonesia*, 2nd Edition, Oxford University Press, Melbourne, 2002, Chapters 12 and 13.

34 For details, see A. Ellis and E. Yudhini, *Law on the General Election of the President and Vice-President passed by the DPR on 8 July 2003: A Short Guide*, National Democratic Institute for International Affairs (NDI) Jakarta, 2003, located at <www.accessdemocracy.org/library/1622_id_presidentialelectionPDF.pdf> (accessed 27 November 2003).

35 A. Ellis and E. Yudhini, *Law on the Structure and Composition of the MPR, DPR, DPD, and DPRDs (Susduk Law): A Short Guide*, National Democratic Institute for International Affairs (NDI), [Jakarta?], 2003 located at <www.accessdemocracy.org/library/1621_id_lawstructurePDF.pdf> (accessed 27 November 2003): quotation from p. 4.

36 A.Budiman, B. Hatley and D. Kingsbury, 'Introduction' (pp. i–viii), in A. Budiman, B. Hatley and D. Kingsbury (eds), *Reformasi: Crisis and Change in Indonesia*, Monash Asia Institute, Clayton, 1999: quotation from p. iv.

37 H. Crouch, 'Political Update 2002: Megawati's Holding Operation', in E. Aspinall and G. Fealy (eds), *Local Power and Politics in Indonesia: Decentralisation & Democratisation*, ISEAS, Singapore, 2003, pp. 15–34: p. 33.

38 V.R. Hadiz, 'Reorganizing Political Power in Indonesia: A Reconsideration of So-called "Democratic Transitions"', *The Pacific Review* , 16:4, 2003, pp. 591–611, particularly p. 121. See also Robison and Hadiz, *Reorganising Power in Indonesia: The Politics of Oligarchy in an Age of Markets*.

39 In the 5 April 2004 Parliamentary Elections, Golkar got the largest percentage of any party (21.6 per cent) in the national vote (followed by the PDI-P with 18.5 per cent). Two out of the five presidential candidates in the July first round of the presidential elections were former generals (Wiranto and Susilo Bambang Yudhoyono) associated with the New Order regime, with Yudhoyono winning the run-off against Megawati in September.

40 J. Sidel, 'It takes a Madrasah: Habermas meets Bourdieu in Indonesia', *South East Asia Research*, 9:1, 2001, pp. 109–22, quotation from p. 114.

41 H. Antlöv, 'Not Enough Politics! Power, Participation and the New Democratic Polity in Indonesia', in E. Aspinall and G. Fealy (eds), *Local Power and Politics in Indonesia: Decentralisation & Democratisation*, ISEAS, Singapore, 2003, pp. 72–86: p. 75.

42 M. Poster, *The Second Media Age*, Polity Press, Cambridge, 1995, p. 3.

43 H.I. Schiller, *Information Inequality*, Routledge, New York, 1996, p. 43.

44 H.I. Schiller, *Culture Inc.: The Corporate Takeover of Public Expression*, Oxford University Press, New York, 1989, and Schiller, *Information Inequality*; R.W. McChesney, *Rich Media, Poor Democracy: Communication Policy in Dubious Times*, University of Illinois Press, Urbana IL, 1999.

45 McChesney, *Rich Media, Poor Democracy*, p. 3.

46 J. Habermas, *The Structural Transformation of the Public Sphere*, Polity, Cambridge MA, 1989, p. 27.

47 Ibid., pp. 33–5.

48 Ibid., p. 186.

49 Ibid., p. 187; p. 188, our emphasis.

50 Ibid., p. 194.

51 See, for instance, I.M. Young, *Inclusion and Democracy*, Oxford University Press, Oxford, 2000, Chapter 5.

52 For one of the most recent and sophisticated versions of this kind of analysis, see G. Rodan, *Transparency and Authoritarian Rule in Southeast Asia: Singapore and Malaysia*, RoutledgeCurzon, London, 2004.

53 A. Sreberny-Mohammadi with K. Nordenstreng, R. Stevenson and F. Uboajha (eds), *Foreign News in the Media: International Reporting in 29 Countries*, UNESCO, Paris, 1985.

54 M. Castells, *The Rise of the Network Society*, Blackwell, Oxford, 1997, p. 374.

55 Kalathil and Boas, *Open Networks Closed Regimes: The Impact of the Internet on Authoritarian Rule*, p. 11.

56 On audiences, see, for example, I. Ang, *Watching Dallas: Soap Opera and the Melodramatic Imagination*, Methuen, London and New York, 1985; and T. Leibes and E. Katz, *The Export of Meaning: Cross-cultural Readings of Dallas*, Oxford University Press, New York, 1990. Through the late 1970s and early 1980s, one of the dominant critical positions in film studies (as articulated, for example, in issues of the most important film studies journal, *Screen*) was the notion that spectators did and could read 'against the grain' of surface meaning of films. See also S. Hall, 'Coding and Decoding in the Television Discourse', in S. Hall *et al.* (eds), *Culture, Media, Language*, Hutchinson, London, 1980.

57 K.B. Jensen, 'Conclusion', in K.B. Jensen (ed.), *News of the World: World Cultures Look at Television News*, Routledge, London, 1998, p. 188.

58 K. Sen and D.T. Hill, *Media, Culture and Politics in Indonesia*, Oxford University Press, Melbourne, 2000.

59 See, for instance, the country profiles in M. Rao (ed.), *News Media and New Media: The Asia-Pacific Internet Handbook*, Eastern Universities Press, London and Singapore, 2003, Chapters 13–25.

60 A similar set of observations emerges also in various chapters in K.C. Ho, R. Kluver and K.C.C. Yang (eds), *Asia.com: Asia Encounters the Internet*, RoutledgeCurzon, London, 2003.

61 Hague and Loader, *Digital Democracy: Discourse and Decision Making in the Information Age*, p. 4.

62 B.R. Anderson, *Imagined Communities: Reflections on the Origin and Spread of Nationalism*, rev. edn, Verso, London and New York, 1991.

63 H.H. Perritt, 'Cyberspace and State Sovereignty', in *Journal of International Legal Studies*, Summer 1997 <www.kentlaw.edu/perritt/publications/3_J._INT%27L_L._STUD._155.htm> (accessed 21 November 2003).

64 A.S. Rai, 'India On-line: Electronic Bulletin Boards and the Construction of a Diasporic Hindu Identity', *Diaspora*, 4:1, 1995, pp. 31–57; S. Tekwani, 'The Tamil Diaspora, Tamil Militancy, and the Internet', in Ho, Kluver and Yang (eds), *Asia.com: Asia Encounters the Internet*, pp. 175–92.

65 T. Haywood, 'Global Networks and the Myth of Equality: Trickle Down or Trickle Away', in B. Loader (ed.), *Cyberspace Divide: Equality, Agency and Policy in the Information Society*, Routledge, London and New York, 1998, pp. 19–34, particularly p. 22.

66 T. Beal, 'The State of Internet use in Asia', in Ho, Kluver and Yang (eds), *Asia.com: Asia Encounters the Internet*, pp. 23–43.

67 A.P. D'Costa, 'Catching Up and Falling Behind: Inequality, IT, and the Asian Diaspora', in Ho, Kluver and Yang (eds), *Asia.com: Asia Encounters the Internet*, pp. 44–66.

68 T. Locke, 'Participation, Inclusion, Exclusion and Netactivism', in Hague and Loader (eds), *Digital Democracy: Discourse and Decision Making in the Information Age*, pp. 211–21, particularly p. 220.

69 K. Sen, 'Radio Days: Media-politics in Indonesia', *The Pacific Review*, 16:4, 2003, pp. 573–89.

70 Haywood, 'Global Networks and the Myth of Equality: Trickle Down or Trickle Away', p. 26.

2 Media in the end of an authoritarian order

1 This chapter draws heavily on K. Sen, 'Indonesia: Media and the End of Authoritarian Rule', in M.E. Price, B. Rozumilowicz and S.G. Verhulst (eds), *Media Reform: Democratizing the Media, Democratizing the State*, Routledge, London and New York, 2002; and K. Sen and D.T. Hill, *Media, Culture and Politics in Indonesia*, Oxford University Press, Melbourne, 2000.

2 This term was introduced by A. Appadurai, 'Disjuncture and Difference in the Global Cultural Economy', *Public Culture*, 2, 1990, pp. 1–24, to encompass the global cultural economy – the 'mechanical global infrastucture' as well as the globally circulating repertoires of images and narratives – within which national media (or any particular media industry or text) must necessarily be understood.

3 D. Dhakidae, 'The State, the Rise of Capital and the Fall of Political Journalism: Political Economy of Indonesian News Industry', unpublished doctoral dissertation, Cornell University, 1991, p. 432. Italics in original. Dhakidae provides an incisive study of the political economy and ideological functions of the Department of Information in Chapters 11 and 12 .

4 For histories of the Indonesian press, see A.B. Adam, *The Vernacular Press and the Emergence of Modern Indonesian Consciousness (1855–1913)*, Southeast Asia Program, Cornell University, 1995; E.C. Smith, 'A History of Newspaper Suppression in Indonesia 1949–1965', doctoral dissertation, University of Iowa, 1969; Oey Hong Lee, *Indonesian Government and Press During Guided Democracy*, Centre for Southeast Asian Studies, University of Hull/Inter Documentation Co, Zug, 1971; D.T. Hill, *The Press in New Order Indonesia*, University of Western Australia Press/ARCOSPEC, Perth, 1994; and Y. Hanazaki, *Pers Terjebak*, Institut Studi Arus Informasi, Jakarta, 1998 (Indonesian translation by Danang Kukuh Wardoyo and Tim Cipinang of 'The Indonesian Press in the Era of Keterbukaan: A Force for Democratization', doctoral dissertation, Monash University, 1996).

5 In 1996, there were 283 newspapers and magazines of all kinds in Indonesia, with a total circulation per edition of about 13.5 million copies, of which the 165 daily and weekly newspapers amounted to about 8.5 million copies. This compared poorly with an estimated 40 million radio sets, and 20 million televisions, the latter reaching an estimated audience of 100 million: B. Subakti and E. Katoppo (eds), *Media Scene 1995–1996 Indonesia: The Official Guide to Advertising Media in Indonesia*, PPPI, Jakarta, 1996, pp. 27–9. In early 1997, one Minister of Information appeared to believe the discrepancy was even greater, with radio reaching 95 per cent of the population and 'electronic media' (in this context, presumably meaning 'television') reaching 75–80 per cent: 'Deppen Kembangkan "Community Newspaper"', *Kompas Online*, 28 January 1997, posted on KdPnet <kdpnet@usa.net>.

6 The Ministerial Decision No. 29/SK/M/65 determined '[t]he Basic Norms for Press Enterprises within the Context of the Promotion of the Indonesian Press'.

7 Under its powers after the martial law declaration of 14 March 1957, the Supreme War Command (Peperti) issued Regulation No. 10 (Peraturan Peperti No. 10/1960) in 1960 specifying the obligations of press publications. These were reinforced in a 1963 Presidential Directive (Penpres No. 6/1963), which required papers and magazines to hold a publication permit. This directive was only withdrawn with the passing of the 1966 Basic Press Law (UU No. 11) which stated (in Article 20) that 'for a transitional period' publishers required a publication permit (*Surat Izin Terbit*, SIT), obtainable from the Department of Information. In 1982, legislation was passed to replace the SIT with a press publication enterprise permit (*Surat Izin Usaha Penerbitan Pers*, SIUPP); this change was implemented two years later. From 1965 until 1977, an additional printing permit (*Surat Izin Cetak*, SIC) had to obtained from the military security authority, Kopkamtib.

8 Atmakusumah, *Kebebasan Pers dan Arus Informasi di Indonesia*, Lembaga Studi Pembangunan, Jakarta, 1981, p. 169, fn. 3.

9 For further details, see Hill, *The Press in New Order Indonesia*, pp. 37–9.

10 The classic study of the political economy of the New Order is R. Robison, *Indonesia: The Rise of Capital*, Allen & Unwin, Sydney, 1986. The 1966 Basic Press Law (No. 11, Article 13) stated: 'The capital of press companies has to be entirely national capital, and all founders and managers have to be Indonesian citizens' and 'Press companies are prohibited from giving or receiving services, help or contributions to or from foreign interests, except with the agreement of the Government after hearing the opinion of the Press Council.'

11 No.02/PER/MENPEN/1969, chapter 1, article 3.

12 For further details see Hill, *The Press in New Order Indonesia*, pp. 67–73.

13 Dhakidae, *The State, the Rise of Capital*, p. 74.

14 See Dhakidae, *The State, the Rise of Capital*, and Hill, *The Press in New Order Indonesia.*

15 However, Jawa Pos, one of the biggest newspaper empires, is centred in Surabaya.

16 See Sen and Hill, *Media, Culture and Politics in Indonesia*, pp. 65–7.

17 The newsprint conflict is discussed in more detail in Sen and Hill, *Media, Culture and Politics in Indonesia*, p. 62. See also Dhakidae, *The State, the Rise of Capital.*

18 S. Bachir, 'Bisnis Pers di Tengah Arus Globalisasi', *Kompas*, 10 February 1992. On Soetrisno Bachir's media interests, see Hill, *The Press in New Order Indonesia*, pp. 97–8.

19 *Kosmopolitan* (modelled on Hearst's *Cosmopolitan*) was brought out by the publishing company PT Higina Alhadin, which paid Hearst an (undisclosed) 'copyright' fee. See 'Advertising: Cosmopolitan Girl Dresses up for Summer Debut in Indonesia', *The Wall Street Interactive Edition*, 9 April 1997, posted on 'soc.culture.indonesia' and 'alt.culture.indonesia' newsgroups on 9 April 1997; 'Cosmopolitan: Gaya Helen Brown di Higina', *Gatra*, 41:3, 30 August 1997, on <www.gatra.com/III/41/med–41.html>, posted on Indonesia-p, 31 August 1997; and 'Ada Kemungkinan Artikel Indonesia Terbit Di Luar Negeri', *Antara*, 6 August 1997, posted on Indonesia-p on 6 August 1997.

20 D.O. McDaniel, *Broadcasting in the Malay World: Radio, Television, and Video in Brunei, Indonesia, Malaysia, and Singapore*, Ablex, Norwood, 1994, p. 218. McDaniel makes the point that statistics on *licensed* radios considerably underestimate actual usage, since many owners may seek to avoid paying the licence fee.

21 McDaniel, *Broadcasting in the Malay World*, p. 223.

22 Government Regulation (Peraturan Pemerintah) no. 55, 1970, cited in K. Sen and D.T. Hill, *Media, Culture and Politics in Indonesia*, Oxford University Press, Melbourne, 2000, p. 84.

23 *Surat Keputusan Menteri Penerangan Republik Indonesia Nomor 39/KEP/MENPEN/1971 tentang Petunjuk-Petunjuk Umum tentang kebijaksanaan penyelenggaraan acara serta isi siaran bagi radio siaran non-pemerintah*, Bab II Ketentuan-Ketentuan Khusus, Pasal 4, Sifat Siaran, paragraphs (1) and (2).

24 Laws and regulations concerning radio broadcasting appear in PRSSNI, *Petunjuk Radio Siaran Swasta Nasional '95*, Pengurus Pusat PRSSNI, Jakarta, 1995 and other PRSSNI publications such as PRSSNI, *Kumpulan Peraturan tentang Radio Siaran Swasta di Indonesia: Tahun 1970 s/d 1992*, Sekretariat Pengurus Pusat PRSSNI, [Jakarta], 1992.

25 J. Lindsay, 'Making Waves: Private Radio and Local Identities in Indonesia', *Indonesia*, 64, October 1997, pp. 105–23, specifically p. 114, fn. 40. These stipulations are widely disregarded, with Lindsay noting that, while FM transmitters should be no more than 100 watts, 'most FM stations broadcast with at least 5 kilowatt transmitters, and some as much as 20 kilowatt'.

26 A. Susanto, 'The Mass Communications System in Indonesia', in K.D. Jackson and L.W. Pye (eds), *Political Power and Communications in Indonesia*, University of California Press, Berkeley, 1978, pp. 229–58, specifically p. 237.

27 Lindsay, 'Making Waves', pp. 115–22, provides an excellent analysis of the local role of private radio, with several valuable case studies: quotation from p. 115.

28 Ibid., p. 116.

29 The former head of TVRI, Ishadi, is quoted in 'Perlu Regulasi di Bidang Penyiaran Media Radio', *Kompas*, 4 July 1996, p. 10.

30 On Indonesian television, see P. Kitley, *Television, Nation and Culture in Indonesia*, Ohio University Southeast Asia Series, Athens, 2000.

31 Decree of the Minister for Tourism, Post and Telecommunications, Republic of Indonesia, No. KM 49 Year 1986, on Parabola Antenna Reception of Television Broadcast. Like radio and the Internet, responsibility for the television broadcast system lay with the Department of Tourism, Post and Telecommunications (Deparpostel).

32 W. Atkins, *Satellite Television and State Power in Southeast Asia: New Issues in Discourse and Control*, Centre for Asian Communication, Media and Cultural Studies, Edith Cowan University, Perth, 1995, p. 25.

33 Minister of Information, Decree No. 111, 1990.

34 For detailed analysis, see Sen and Hill, *Media, Culture and Politics in Indonesia*, pp. 125–31. See also Kitley, *Television, Nation and Culture in Indonesia*.

35 E. Aspinall, 'Opposition and Elite Conflict in the Fall of Soeharto', in G. Forrester and R.J. May (eds), *The Fall of Soeharto*, Crawford House Publishing, Bathurst, 1998, pp. 130–53: quotation from p. 144.

36 H. Rheingold, *The Virtual Community: Homesteading on the Electronic Frontier*, William Patrick, Reading MA, 1993; and D. Rushkoff, *Media Virus!: Hidden Agendas in Popular Culture*, Random House Australia, Sydney, 1994.

37 Drawing on Foucault's concept of the panopticon, some of the more scholarly work (see, for instance O. Gandy, *The Panoptic Society*, Westview Press, Boulder, 1994, and L.A. Friedland, 'Electronic Democracy and the New Citizenship', *Media, Culture & Society*, 18:2, April 1996, pp. 185–212) pointed out the dangers in the electronic footprints left by all users and therefore capable of being used in surveillance of citizens and consumers with great potential for 'loss of autonomy in the realms of political, cultural and social life' (Friedland, 'Electronic Democracy and the New Citizenship', p. 186).

38 Anon., 'Paving the Highway: The Information Revolution is Coming and Part of It Is Here', *Asiaweek*, 14 September 1994, pp. 35–8: quotation from p. 38.

39 Anon., 'Demokratisasi informasi tak dapat di bendung: Catatan akhir tahun 1994 bidang Iptek', *Kompas*, 26 December 1994, p. 1.

40 Anon., 'Indonesia di tengah jaringan Internet', *Kompas*, 23 October 1994, p. 9.

41 T.S. Gunawan, 'Internet Mania Hits Indonesia', *The Jakarta Post*, 12 July 1995, p. 1.

42 For example, R.L. Pattiradjawane, 'Demonstrasi di Jaringan Internet', *Kompas*, 7 February 1996, p. 16. On the Telecommunications Reform Act and opposition to it, see C.J.P. Moschovitis, H. Poole, T. Schuyler and T.M. Senft, *History of the Internet: A Chronology, 1843 to the Present*, ABC-CLIO, Santa Barbara, 1999, pp. 206–7.

43 L.E. Nugroho, 'Internet dan peranan komputer masa depan', *Kompas*, 3 April 1996, p. 17.

44 An example of such criticism is J. Kuncoro, 'Internet: Demi Teknologi Atau Informasi?' *Media Indonesia*, 25 July 1996, p. 14.

45 For example, A. Andoko, 'Tempat bertemunya pedagang dan pembeli', *Kompas*, 17 August 1996, p. 21.

46 R.M.R. Suryo, 'Ke mana setelah' 'apakabar' 'ditutup', *Media Indonesia*, 5 September 1996, p. 10.

47 A.N. Basral, 'Ini Milik MacDougall', *Gatra*, 2 December 1995 (circulated on <apakabar@ clark.net> on 28 November 1995).

48 'Tajuk Rencana: Agenda Pers Indonesia di Tengah Tumbuhnya Paradigma Baru Media Massa', *Kompas*,11 November 1995 (circulated on <apakabar@clark.net> on 12 November 1995).

49 See S.B. Ridwan, 'From TEMPO to TEMPO *Interaktif*: An Indonesian Media Scene Case Study', paper presented at Third Australian World Wide Web Conference, 5–9 July 1997, Southern Cross University, Lismore, Australia, available online at <http://ausweb.scu.edu.au/aw97/papers/ridwan/paper.htm>, sighted 26 March 2004.

50 Anon, 'Bisnis Dunia Maya: Target pasar perlengkapan Internet di Indonesia US$ 2 juta', *Gatra*, 16 December 1995 (posted on <apakabar@access.digex.net> on 28 December 1996).

51 'Ketua Umum PWI Pusat Sofyan Lubis: Masyarakat dan Pejabat Belum Sepenuhnya Memahami Pers', *Suara Pembaruan Online*, 13 February 1997 (circulated on <Indonesia-p@igc.apc.org> on 13 February 1997).

52 'Internet users warned over immorality', *The Jakarta Post*, 12 July 1995, p. 2.

53 Gunawan, 'Internet Mania Hits Indonesia'.

54 'The Specter of Internet', *The Jakarta Post*, 16 June 1995, p. 4.

55 'Information "Key to Restoring Indonesia's Credibility"', *Straits Times*, 1 May 1998, available online at <www.asia1.com.sg/straitstimes/pages/stsea4.html> (accessed 1 May 1998).

56 H. Agustine, 'Internet Replaces Bamboo Spears in Fight for Freedom', *The Jakarta Post*, 8 June 1998, p. 7.

3 Net challenges to the new order

1 H. Agustine, 'Internet Replaces Bamboo Spears in Fight for Freedom', *The Jakarta Post*, 8 June 1998, p. 7.

2 S. Mydans of *The New York Times* quoted in A. Craddock and B. Lintner, 'Indonesia's Net War', *Wired News*, dated 29 May 1998, available online at <www.wired.com/news/politics/0,1283,12609,00.html> (accessed 17 September 2003).

3 W.S. Thompson quoted in D.L. Marcus, 'Indonesia Revolt was Net Driven', *Boston Globe*, 23 May 1998, reproduced in E. Aspinall, G. van Klinken and H. Feith (eds), *The Last Days of President Suharto*, Monash Asia Institute, Clayton, 1999, pp. 73–5. On the fall of Suharto, see also K. van Dijk, *A Country in Despair: Indonesia between 1997 and 2000*, KITLV Press, Jakarta, 2001, pp. 161–216.

4 J. Habermas, *The Structural Transformation of the Public Sphere*, Polity, Cambridge MA, 1989.

5 K. Hewison and G. Rodan, 'The Decline of the Left in Southeast Asia', in R. Miliband and L. Panitch (eds), *Socialist Register*, Merlin Press, London,1994, pp. 235–40.

6 See G. Rodan, *Information Technology and Political Control in Singapore*, Working Paper No. 26, Japan Policy Research Institute, Cardiff USA, November 1996, for Singapore, and K. Sen, 'Australia, Asia and the Media', in G. Jones (ed.), *Australia in its Asian Context*, Academy of the Social Sciences in Australia Canberra, Occasional Paper No. 1, 1996, pp. 44–9.

7 T. Shiraishi, 'Rewiring the Indonesian State', in D.S. Lev and R. McVey (eds), *Making Indonesia: Essays on Modern Indonesia in Honor of George McT. Kahin*, Studies on Southeast Asia, Ithaca, 1996, pp. 164–179: p. 170.

8 On 3 January 1997, Habibie launched his homepage <http://habibie.ristek.go.id> and, within three weeks, about 1,200 logons had been recorded (according to INDONESIA-L, 21 January 1997, sourced to *Tempo Interaktif*, 'Ketika Habibie Mejeng di Internet', <http://www.library.ohiou.edu/indopubs/1997/01/20/0045.html, sighted 31 march 2005.

9 D. Greenlees and R. Garran, *Deliverance: The Inside Story of East Timor's Fight for Freedom*, Allen & Unwin, Sydney, 2002, p. 91.

10 O.W. Purbo, *Digital Review of Indonesia*, electronic document (indonesia-digital-review–11–2002.zip) dated November 2002, available online at <www.bogor.net/idkf>, p. 3, sighted 30 August 2003.

11 Budi Rahardjo initially established 'The Indonesian Homepage' at <www.umanitoba.ca/indonesian>, later shifting it to <http://indonesia.elga.net.id> (accessed 20 August 1999). He first set up the page around 1992, recalling that it was 'before there was Netscape, before there was Apache, when there was only Mosaic'. Rahardjo had a scholarship to study for a Master's degree, but

supplemented this by working for the University of Manitoba as a computer services systems administrator, thereby getting access to the server on which the homepage was located (personal e-mail communication, dated 20 September 2003).

12 Budi Rahardjo, *Buku Pegangan Sistem Unix dan Internet*, Open Pathways, Bellingham WA, was published in May 1994 (see advertisement posted 11 May 1995, archived on <www.library.ohiou.edu/indopubs/1995/05/11/0014.html>, accessed 30 September 2003).

13 Y. Ikawati, 'Dr Joseph FP Luhukay: Perintis Internet di Indonesia', *Kompas*, 30 December 1995, p. 20.

14 Purbo, *Digital Review of Indonesia*, pp. 1–2, discusses the early history of the Internet, with particular reference to Bandung.

15 Quotation from Purbo, *Digital Review of Indonesia*, p. 2. Tungky Aribowo was Minister of Industry from 1993 and became Minister of Industry and Trade when the two ministries were combined in December 1995, a post he held till March 1998 (see van Dijk, *A Country in Despair*, p. 540).

16 Rahardjo's advice is found in <www.library.ohiou.edu/indopubs/1993/07/29/0005.html>, posted on 29 July 1993 (accessed 30 September 2003). He also provides a detailed list of the various net connection modes available in Indonesia, and notes that some private companies, such as IBM, have their own Internet access, though these were not publicly available.

17 Information on IPTEKnet is taken from <www.iptek.net.id/background.html> (accessed 31 January 1997), with a comprehensive list of member organisations given on <www.iptek.net.id/member.html>. We are indebted to Mr Tri Kuntoro Priyambodo, Network Manager of GAMA-net, the Gadjah Mada University Internet facility, for information of the university sector's early development of Internet technologies. Interview, Yogyakarta, 18 July 1996.

18 Purbo, *Digital Review of Indonesia*, p. 3.

19 IndoInternet applied to Deparpostel in February 1995 and received the third ISP licence that August. Information on IndoInternet from company spokesperson, Sanjaya. Personal e-mail, 28 February 1997.

20 See O.W. Purbo, 'Ceramah Ilmiah: Komunikasi Internet dan Dunia Pendidikan', in *Duta Wacana menyongsong Budaya Teknologi*, Dies Natalis ke34, Duta Wacana Christian University, Yogyakarta, 31 October 1996, pp. 43–7.

21 Ibid. A kilobyte is a thousand 'bytes'; a megabyte is a million 'bytes'.

22 Information on RADNET taken from 'RADNET (PT Rahajasa Media Internet) Company Profile' (9 pp, undated typescript), provided by Feraldi W. Loeis, of RADNET, Jakarta, 18 November 1996.

23 Advertisement for Fujitsu Internet Web Servers, *Kompas*, 10 July 1996, p. 17.

24 See, for example, 'Sartono Tawarkan Cari Pekerjaan Lewat Internet', *Kompas*, 26 September 1996, p. 3; 'Memanfaatkan Jaringan Internet', *Media Indonesia*, 3 September 1996, p. 14; 'Kanker di Internet', *Media Indonesia*, 1 September 1996, p. 18; 'Indonesian artists leap onto Internet', *The Jakarta Post*, 28 June 1996, p. 2; 'Data Pendidikan Indonesia Dapat Diakses di Internet', *Kompas*, 11 November 1996, p. 20.

25 *Tempo Interaktif* was an incarnation of the country's most prestigious newsweekly print magazine, *Tempo*, banned by the Suharto government in June 1994 in a highly controversial and contested crack-down banning three outspoken news publications.

26 J.S. Djiwandono, 'The Rupiah – One Year After Its Float', in G. Forrester (ed.), *Post-Soeharto Indonesia: Renewal or Chaos?*, Crawford House Publishing, Bathurst, 1999, pp. 144–52, particularly p. 150.

27 See Embassy of the United States of America, 'Indonesia Economic Trends 1999 – Signs of Life', on <www.usembassyjakarta.org/econ/trends99–2.html> (accessed 2 September 1999).

28 'Para ISP Makin Terengah-Engah', *Info Komputer Online*, June 1998, at <http://www.infokomputer.com/0698/bisnis/bisnis.shtml> (accessed 27 January 1999).

29 Ibid.

30 Ibid.

31 S.E. Baskoro, 'Peranan Internet dalam Reformasi Indonesia', in *Info Komputer Online*, June 1998, at <www.infokomputer.com/100798-l.shtml> (accessed 19 December 1998).

32 P.M. Winarno, 'Peran Internet di tengah krisis', *Info Komputer Online*, 13 April 1998, available online at <www.infokomputer.com/analisa/130498-1.shtml> (accessed on 19 December 1998).

33 See, for instance, L.A. Friedland, 'Electronic Democracy and the New Citizenship' (pp. 185–212) and several other articles in special issue of *Media, Culture and Society*, 18:2, April 1996.

34 Tedjabayu, 'Indonesia: The Net as a Weapon', *Cybersociology*, Issue 5, 1999, available online at <www.socio.demon.co.uk/magazine/5/5indonesia.html> (accessed 23 September 2003). Unless otherwise noted, information on the early use of the Internet by NGOs and activist groups is drawn from this source, or from a confidential interview (Jakarta, 3 December 2001) with an NGO activist closely involved in these developments.

35 Quotation and details of E-LAW from their website, 'About us', at <www.elaw.org/custom/customPages/viewPage.asp?WebPage_ID=24> (accessed 14 October 2003).

36 Phil Zimmermann, the inventor of PGP, was under investigation in America from 1991 to 1996 for posting PGP on Usenet in June 1991, thereby breeching the International Traffic in Arms Regulations (ITAR). The case was finally dropped in January 1996 after the US Attorney's Office found there was no evidence that he personally 'exported' PGP. See C.J.P. Moschovitis, H. Poole, T. Schuyler and T.M. Senft, *History of the Internet: A Chronology, 1843 to the Present*, ABC-CLIO, Santa Barbara, 1999, pp. 158–9.

37 Ibid.: quotation cited on p. 159.

38 Confidential interview with Indonesian activist then working at LBH, Jakarta, 3 December 2001.

39 Tedjabayu, 'Indonesia: The Net as a Weapon'. Despite the array of services provided by commercial ISPs since 1995, NusaNet survived until 2001, when it was finally disbanded.

40 S. Tickle, 'Assessing the "Real Story" Behind Political Events in Indonesia: E-mail Discussion List Indonesia-L's News Coverage of the 27 July 1996 Jakarta Riots', unpublished Master of Arts thesis, School of Media and Journalism, Queensland University of Technology, Brisbane, 1997, 62.

41 Tedjabayu , 'Indonesia: The Net as a Weapon', which provides the details of this incident.

42 Ibid.

43 J.A. MacDougall, 'A Brief History of The Apakabar List', available online at <www.library.ohiou.edu/indopubs/briefhistory.html> (accessed 29 September 2003). The facilitator's initial welcome to the mailing list ('Talk To Your Facilitator!', posted 8 October 1990) is archived at <www.library.ohiou.edu/indopubs/1990/10/08/0001.html>, with MacDougall's final posting ('Over and Out' posted 8 February 2002) at <www.library.ohiou.edu/indopubs/2002/02/08/0012.htm> (both accessed 30 September 2003).

44 MacDougall, 'A Brief History of The Apakabar List'.

45 RM Roy Suryo, 'Kemana setelah 'apakabar' ditutup', *Media Indonesia*, 5 September 1996, p. 10.

46 Posting dated 1 February 1997, from Manneke Budiman <manneke@makara.cso.ui.ac.id>.

47 'Ini Milik MacDougall', *Gatra*, 2 December 1995, on <apakabar@clark.net>, 28 November 1995.

48 'Indonesia-L alias *apakabar*: Paduan fenomena politik dan Internet', *Republika Online*, 26 September 1996.

49 On ICMI, see D.E. Ramage, *Politics in Indonesia: Democracy, Islam and the Ideology of Tolerance*, Routledge, London and New York, 1995, pp. 75–121.

50 *Republika*, 29 July 1996, posted via *KdP* on <apakabar@clark.net> on 30 July 1996.

51 Information provided by John MacDougall via e-mail, 19 January 1997.

52 Tickle, 'Assessing the "Real Story" Behind Political Events in Indonesia', pp. 77–81, provides summaries of some of the key initial postings.

53 Posting headed 'Subject: KANTOR PDI DISERBU TENTARA … PAGI INI!!!' and dated Saturday 27 July 1996 (time: 11:16:50 +0700).

54 Posting titled 'IN: YLBHI – Tragedi Berdarah Penyerbuan Markas PDI', dated Saturday 27 July 1996 (time:17:45:07 +0000).

55 Posting headed 'To: Internet Users of Indonesia; Subject: Kronologi penyerbuan 27 Juli', on <apakabar@clark.net>, 29 July 1996.

56 Tickle, 'Assessing the "Real Story" Behind Political Events in Indonesia', p. 95. The comparison was with *Suara Merdeka*, *Kompas*, *The Australian*, and *The Courier-Mail.*

57 Ibid., p. 21. The fact that 28 July was also a Sunday meant that, even abroad, press coverage was lower than might have been the case on a weekday because Sunday editions are often prepared well in advance, with an emphasis on 'lifestyle' rather than 'news'.

58 Ibid., p. 86.

59 MacDougall, 'A Brief History of The Apakabar List'.

60 P. Eng, 'On-line Activists Step Up Fight', *Bangkok Post*, 29 April 1998, available online at <www.geocities.com/absdf_au/articles/article2.html> (accessed 17 September 2003).

61 Ibid., quotes John MacDougall.

62 Suryo, 'Kemana setelah 'apakabar' ditutup', p. 10.

63 J. Winters, 'Dampak Politis dari Sumber dan Teknologi Informasi Baru di Indonesia', in D.N. Hidayat, E. Gazali, H. Suwardi and S.K. Ishadi (eds), *Pers dalam 'Revolusi Mei' Runtuhnya Sebuah Hegemoni*, Gramedia Pustaka Utama, Jakarta, 2000, pp. 259–74: p. 270.

64 Statistics provided by KdPnet in personal e-mail communication, 28 January 1997.

65 According to the PRD's website at <www.xs4all.nl/~peace/pubeng/mov/movto/massorg.html> (accessed 25 September 2003), the following 'mass organisations' were affiliated to the party: the Indonesian Centre for Labour Struggles (PPBI – Pusat Perjuangan Buruh Indonesia); Students in Solidarity with Democracy in Indonesia (SMID – Solidaritas Mahasiswa Indonesia untuk Demokrasi); the National Peasants' Union (STN – Serikat Tani Nasional); People's Art Network (JAKER – Jaringan Kerja Kesenian Rakyat); the Jakarta People's Union (SRD – Sarekat Rakyat Djakarta) and the Solo People's Union (SRS – Sarekat Rakyat Solo); the Indonesian People's Solidarity Struggle with the Maubere People (SPRIM – Solidaritas Perjuangan Rakyat Indonesia untuk Maubere).

66 The Netherlands website was located at <www.xs4all.nl/~peace/pubeng/mov/mov.html> (accessed 25 September 2003), while the Australian site was at <www.prd.4-all.org>, which is now run by ASAP (Action in Solidarity with Asia and the Pacific), formerly ASIET (Action in Solidarity with Indonesia and East Timor).

67 Siar, 'Kasospol ABRI Kumpulkan 83 Ormas dan Orpol Untuk Menggolkan Keadaan SOB', on <Indonesia-L@userhome.com>, 23 February 1997.

68 A PCMCIA modem is a small, credit-card size modem which fits into a laptop computer slot and does not require its own external power.

69 Information on PRD use of the Internet during this period was provided by several party members during confidential interviews in Tebet, on 25 and 29 November 2001, from which the quotations are drawn.

70 One PRD member indicated that cadres used the Internet at *warnet* right across the archipelago, listing specifically Aceh, Medan, Binjai, Pekanbaru, Palembang, Jambi Lampung, Jakarta, Bogor, Bandung, Garut Bekasi, Cianjur, Tasikmalaya, Purwokerto, Yogyakarta, Pekolongan, Pemalang, Sidoarjo, Tuban, Solo, Semarang, Surabaya, Malang, Bali, Lombok, Manado, Makassar, Samarinda, Pontianak, Poso, Kendari, Gorontalo, Ambon and Manokwari (confidential interview, Jakarta, 29 November 2001).

71 On these bans, see D.T. Hill, *The Press in New Order Indonesia*, University of Western Australia Press/Asia Research Centre, Perth, 1994, pp. 41–4.

72 The Suharto government required all periodicals to obtain a government publication licence (SIUPP), without which they were regarded as illegal. Neither *Kabar dari PIJAR* nor *Independen* held, or would have been likely to be issued with, this permit. In addition, *Independen* was published by the Alliance of Independent Journalists (AJI), an independent rival to the government-backed Indonesian Journalists' Association (PWI), which all journalists were formally obliged to join.

73 *Suara Independen*, 'Tentang Tujuan Kami', available online at <www.gn.apc.org/independen/info.htm> (accessed 14 September 1999). Like many early webpages, this no longer exists, but the 1997 edition is archived at <http://web.archive.org/web/20010617204310/www.gn.apc.org/independen/edisi/10/index.htm> (accessed 16 October 2003).

74 The Association for Progressive Communications (APC) describes itself as 'an international network of civil society organisations dedicated to empowering and supporting groups and individuals working for peace, human rights, development and protection of the environment, through the strategic use of information and communication technologies (ICTs), including the Internet'. See 'About APC', available online at <www.apc.org/english/about/index.shtml> (accessed 16 October 2003).

75 V. Menayang, B. Nugroho and D. Listiorini, 'Pers Bawah Tanah: Media Sebagai Pergerakan Sosial', in Hidayat *et al.* (eds), *Pers dalam 'Revolusi Mei'*, pp. 275–97: p. 288.

76 'Matebean' refers to a mountain in eastern East Timor. 'MeunaSAH' refers to the small mosque or prayer house found in Acehnese villages which serves as the informal meeting place for citizens: see <http://groups.yahoo.com/group/indonesia/message/2573>, 1 August 1998 (accessed 24 September 2003). 'Mamberamo' refers to the largest river in the Indonesian province of West Papua (formerly Irian Jaya).

77 Tickle, 'Assessing the "Real Story" Behind Political Events in Indonesia', pp. 62 and 175–6, lists many of these.

78 van Dijk, *A Country in Despair*, p. 162.

79 Craddock and Lintner, 'Indonesia's Net War'.

80 Marcus, 'Indonesia Revolt was Net Driven', p. 73.

81 Ibid., p. 74. This observation also appears in Baskoro, 'Peranan Internet dalam Reformasi Indonesia', which appears to draw heavily on the Marcus article.

82 Craddock and Lintner, 'Indonesia's Net War'.

83 'ASEAN setuju memblokir Internet', *Kompas*, 7 September 1996, p. 3; D. Watts, 'Net Users' Free Speech Curbed', *The West Australian* (Perth), 21 January 1997, p. 22; and Rodan, *Information Technology and Political Control in Singapore.*

84 A. Harsono, 'Indonesia: From Mainstream to Alternative Media', *First Monday*, 1996, available online at <www.firstmonday.dk/issues/issue3/harsono> (accessed 30 August 2003).

85 Ibid.

86 Undang Undang Penyiaran, Bab X, Pasal 62 (Broadcast Act, Chapter X, Clause 62).

87 Quotation from Harsono, 'Indonesia: From Mainstream to Alternative Media'.

88 Dr Alwi Dahlan quoted in 'Information "key to restoring Indonesia's credibility"', *Straits Times*, at <www.asia1.com.sg/straitstimes/pages/stsea4.html>, 1 May 1998.

89 'Perangi Info Sampah ABRI Masuk Internet', *Republika*, 20 October 1995, and posted that day on <apakabar@clark.net>. As noted on <apakabar@clark.net> (19 January1996), an identical military homepage, HANKAM/ABRInet, could be found at both <www.abri.mil.id> and <www.hankam.go.id>.

90 A.H. Mulyanto, 'Cyberspace: ABRI dan "Perang Informasi"', *Republika Online*, 17 October 1996 (posted on INDONESIA-L).

91 Suharto is quoted in 'Indonesia's Information Highway is too Fast for Suharto: Strongman Seeks Net Roadblocks', *Chicago Tribute*, 17 May 1997, downloaded from <www.hartford-hwp.com/archives/54b/037.html> (accessed 17 September 2003).

92 Quotation from 'Indonesia asked to free Internet user', letter from Human Rights Watch/Asia Executive Director Sidney Jones, to M. Arifin Siregar, Indonesian Ambassador to the United States of America, 14 August 1996, included as Appendix 1, available online at <www.firstmonday.dk/issues/issue3/harsono> (accessed 30 August 2003).

93 M. Lim, 'The Internet, Social Networks, and Reform in Indonesia', in N. Couldry and J. Curran (eds), *Contesting Media Power: Alternative Media in a Networked World*, Rowman & Littlefield, Lanham, 2003, pp. 273–88, particularly p. 281.

94 Ibid., p. 282.

95 See B. Anderson, *Java in a Time of Revolution*, Cornell University Press, Ithaca, 1972.

96 The quotation is of Diana Lady Dougan, Chairperson of International Communications Studies at the Brookings Institution, Washington, quoted in Marcus, 'Indonesia Revolt was Net Driven', p. 75.

97 On this point, see also Winters, 'Dampak Politis', p. 273.

98 See advertisement for Sistelindo (p. 13) and information on INDOSATnet outlined in 'Didukung Citra, SDM dan Peralatan Canggih' (p. 76) in *Infokomputer*, special issue on the Internet [September 1996].

4 Mapping the Internet in Indonesia

1 The inequity in worldwide Internet access is indicated by 1997 figures on Internet users per 10,000 people, with Finland (653.61), Norway (474.63), USA (442.11), New Zealand (424.34) and Australia (382.44) ranked very highly, by contrast to Angola, Benin, Tanzania and Tunisia

with 0.02; Algeria, Burundi, Libya, Rwanda, Togo, Uganda and Cambodia with 0.01; and Bangladesh, Chad, Democratic Republic of Congo, Eritrea, Ethiopia, Gabon, Gambia, Guinea, Haiti, Iran, Iraq, North Korea, Laos, Malawi, Mauritania, Myanmar, Nigeria, Oman, Sierra Leone, Sudan, Tajikistan, Turkmenistan and Yemen, where the number of users was too low to even register (0.00) (C.J.P. Moschovitis, H. Poole, T. Schuyler and T.M. Senft, *History of the Internet: A Chronology, 1843 to the Present*, ABC-CLIO, Santa Barbara, 1999, pp. 274–5, cite World Development Indicators, 1998). By 2002, virtually all of these countries listed had some level of Internet usage: see 'Information Technology' statistics on <www.itu.int/ITU-D/ict/statistics/at_glance/internet02.pdf> (accessed 6 August 2003).

2 See, for instance, T. Locke, 'Participation, Inclusion, Exclusion and Netactivism: How the Internet Invents New Forms of Democratic Activity', in B.N. Hague and B.D. Loader (eds), *Digital Democracy: Discourse and Decision Making in the Information Age*, Routledge, London and New York, 1999, pp. 211–21.

3 The first English-language academic journal article we have identified concerning the Internet in Indonesia was in October 1996, namely Jesse Randall, 'Of Cracks and Crackdowns: Five Translations of Recent Internet Postings', *Indonesia*, 62, pp. 37–52, with our initial discussion of the arrival of the Internet in Indonesia appearing in D.T. Hill and K. Sen, 'Wiring the Warung to Global Gateways: The Internet in Indonesia', *Indonesia*, 63, April 1997, pp. 67–89.

4 D.T. Hill, *The Press in New Order Indonesia*, University of Western Australia Press/Murdoch Asia Research Centre, Perth, 1994, p. 14.

5 <www.itu.int/ITU-D/ict/statistics/at_glance/internet02.pdf> (accessed 6 August 2003).

6 For an overview of Asia, see T. Beal, 'The State of Internet Use in Asia', in K.C. Ho, R. Kluver and K.C.C. Yang (eds), *Asia.com: Asia Encounters the Internet*, RoutledgeCurzon, London, 2003, pp. 23–43.

7 A label for the New Order government first used by political scientist Herbert Feith in 1970s, and quickly accepted as a good working description of that regime.

8 'HP World '96: Joop Ave: Kebutuhan Instalasi Jaringan Komputer di Indonesia masih tinggi', *InfoKomputer*, September 1996, p. 119.

9 CyberAtlas, 'The Emerging 20 Nations', available online at <http://cyberatlas.Internet.com/big_pictur ... graphics/print/0,1323,5911_150661,00.html> (accessed 5 September 1999).

10 APJII (Asosiasi Penyedia Jasa Internet Indonesia), I2BC (Indonesia Internet Business Community) and Accenture, *Indonesia Cyber Industry & Market*, PT Elex Media Komputindo, Jakarta, 2001, p. 10, gives the Indonesian Telkom connections, but gives a different level of 'teledensity' (2.9 per cent) on p. x.

11 Pusat Pengkajian dan Penerapan Teknologi Informasi dan Elektronika (P3TIE), *Indikator Teknologi Informasi dan Komunikasi Tahun 2002*, Badan Pengkajian dan Penerapan Teknologi, Pusat Pengkajian dan Penerapan Teknologi Informasi dan Elektronika (P3TIE), Jakarta, 2002, available online at <www.apjii.or.id/dokumentasi/arsip/indikator/siti2002.pdf> (accessed 28 July 2003), p. viii.

12 CastleAsia, 2002, 'SMEs and E-Commerce', a report prepared for the Asia Foundation, January, available online at <www.asiafoundation.org/pdf/ID-SME-ecommerce-study–6–02.pdf> (accessed 30 September 2002), p. 22.

13 M. Minges, *Kretek Internet: Indonesia Case Study*, International Telecommunication Union, Geneva, Switzerland, March 2002, p. 26, available online at <www.itu.int/ITU-D/ict/cs/indonesia/material/IDN%20CS.pdf> (accessed 1 August 2003).

14 Estimate totalled from figures in R.M. Samik-Ibrahim, 'Indonesia–102: The Internet Service Providers', available online at <www.tjt.or.id/rms46/imho-eisp.html> (accessed 17 May 1997).

15 H. Hill, 'Introduction', in H. Hill and Thee Kian Wie (eds), *Indonesia's Technological Challenge*, Institute of Southeast Asian Studies, Singapore, 1998, pp. 1–54: quotation from p. 6.

16 <www.insan.co.id/internet-stats.html> (accessed 4 June 2004).

17 APJII, I2BC and Accenture, *Indonesia Cyber Industry & Market*, p. 14.

18 Ibid., p. xi.

19 The initial projections for 2001 were provided as estimates on the APJII website (accessed on15 November 2000, but no longer accessible).

20 B. Rahardjo, 'Indonesian Internet Statistics', claims that in October 2001, there were 600,000 'dial-up' subscribers and a total of two million users when those entering from company, university or other public-access points were included. In November 2001, Heru Nugroho, APJII Chairperson, gave the current figure as 700,000 subscribers (in D. Hendaru, Rusdianto Erawan, Edi Simon Siahaan and Achmad Adhito Hatanto (2001), 'Warnet pun Disikat', *Warta Ekonomi*, No. 44, Yr XIII, 5 November, pp. 38–43).

21 The ISP figures are given in M. Ihsan, F. Adrianto, S. Shahab and A.A. Hatanto, 'Akan Beraksi pada Tahun ini', *Warta Ekonomi*, 22:12, 4 June 2001, pp. 20–1, which compares with APJII, I2BC and Accenture, *Indonesia Cyber Industry & Market*, p. xi.

22 ISP licence holders are not required to be members of APJII. However, they would be likely to join if their business was operational since they would require APJII support, such as the allocation of an IP address and connection to the Indonesia Internet eXchange (IIX), which provides Indonesian ISPs with interconnection without having to go through international providers. 2003 statistics from <www.apjii.or.id/dokumentasi/statistik.php?lang=ind&PHPSESSID=d3b14b2a30c5ab04aab0941e716d1fd3>, updated 30 June 2003 (accessed 5 August 2003).

23 APJII, I2BC and Accenture, *Indonesia Cyber Industry & Market*, p. xi.

24 The latest list of '.id' domain names (by sub-domains) can be found at <http://tukang.the.net.id/domain> (accessed 30 September 2003).

25 APJII, I2BC and Accenture, *Indonesia Cyber Industry & Market*, p. xi.

26 G. Polla, B. Rahardjo, I.K. Hartono, S. Suyanto, Adi K. and S. Hengky, *Riset Domain CO.ID: Laporan Teknis Analisis tingkat kepuasan dan keamanan konsumen dalam upaya peningkatan penggunaan domain CO.ID*, Tim ccTLD-ID & APJII, Jakarta, 2002, p. 8, available online at <www.apjii.or.id/dokumentasi> (accessed 28 July 2003).

27 According to International Telecommunication Union (ITU) 2002 statistics, the estimate of the number of personal computers per 100 inhabitants in Indonesia was 1.10, compared to the world average of 9.22. Indonesia is considerably lower than Singapore (50.83), Malaysia (12.61), Brunei (7.31), Thailand (2.78) and the Philippines (2.17), though higher than Vietnam (0.98), Laos (0.33), Cambodia (0.15) and Myanmar (0.11): <www.itu.int/ITU-D/ict/statistics/at_glance/internet02.pdf> (accessed 6 August 2003), p. 2.

28 While the number of Indonesian provinces was increased to 33 in restructuring after the fall of President Suharto, the BPS still provides data according to the earlier division into 26 provinces. According to BPS data (cited in *Warta Ekonomi*, 40:13, 8 October 2001, p. 81), the 'provinces' of Bengkulu, Nusa Tenggara Barat, Sulawesi Tenggara and Maluku had per capita Gross Regional Domestic Product of less than three million rupiah (based on 1999 prices), the price of the cheapest personal computer at that time.

29 According to ITU statistics, there were only 2.3 million PCs but 4 million Internet users (or 1.10 PCs compared with 1.91 Internet users per 100 inhabitants): <www.itu.int/ITU-D/ict/statistics/at_glance/internet02.pdf> (accessed 6 August 2003), p. 2.

30 N. Idris and M.D. Ibrahim, 'Communication Scene of Indonesia', in A. Goonasekera and D. Holaday (eds), *Asian Communication Handbook*, Asian Mass Communication Research and Information Centre, Singapore, 1993, pp. 59–86.

31 For example, in Bandung the 40 *wartel* in 1990 had tripled to 120 by 1997 according to 'Tentang Wartelnet', available online at <http://wartelnet.melsa.net.id/tentang.htm> (accessed 21 August 1999), quoting an unnamed article from *Pikiran Rakyat* newspaper, 5 April 1997. The statistics for 2000–01 are from P3TIE, *Indikator Teknologi Informasi dan Komunikasi Tahun 2002*, p. viii.

32 J.D. Barker provides a thoughtful discussion of the development of telephony in 'Telephony at the limits of state control: "Discourse Networks" in Indonesia', in C.J.W.-L. Lee (ed.), *Local Cultures and the 'New Asia': The State, Culture and Capitalism in Southeast Asia*, ISEAS, Singapore, 2002, pp. 158–83.

33 P3TIE, *Indikator Teknologi Informasi dan Komunikasi Tahun 2002*, p. ix.

34 B.U. Donny, *Fakta dan Kondisi e-Government di Indonesia* (March 2004), available online at <www.ictwatch.com/data/index.htm> (accessed 27 March 2004).

35 M. Lim, 'The Internet, Social Networks, and Reform in Indonesia', in N. Couldry and J. Curran

(eds), *Contesting Media Power: Alternative Media in a Networked World*, Rowman & Littlefield, Lanham, 2003, pp. 273–88: p. 279.

36 APJII, I2BC and Accenture, *Indonesia Cyber Industry & Market*, p. xi.

37 S.E. Baskoro, 'Peranan Internet dalam Reformasi Indonesia', *Info Komputer Online*, June 1998, available online at <www.infokomputer.com/100798-l.shtml> (accessed 19 December 1998).

38 APJII, I2BC and Accenture, *Indonesia Cyber Industry & Market*, p. 16.

39 D. Hendaru, R. Erawan, E.S. Siahaan and A.A. Hatanto, 'Warnet pun Disikat', p. 39.

40 P3TIE, *Indikator Teknologi Informasi dan Komunikasi Tahun 2002*, p. ix.

41 APJII, I2BC and Accenture, *Indonesia Cyber Industry & Market*, pp. 58–9.

42 Though the average number of computer screens per *warnet* was not given, our observations in November 2001 in the Cikini area of Central Jakarta suggest an average of about 15 screens is likely, which would give a Jakarta ratio of one *warnet* screen per 1,300 people.

43 APJII, I2BC and Accenture, *Indonesia Cyber Industry & Market*, pp. 58–9.

44 P3TIE, *Indikator Teknologi Informasi dan Komunikasi Tahun 2002*, p. 19. The P3TIE estimate that, by 2002, there were about 261,000 *warnet* nationally would seem hard to substantiate.

45 P.W. Harvey, 'Bisnis Warung Internet di Malang dan Blitar', unpublished Field-study Report, Australian Consortium for 'In-Country' Indonesian Studies, Perth, [2000], pp. 12–15. We thank the author for permitting access to this unpublished document. Harvey counts a total of 339 *warnet* computers in Malang and 24 in Blitar. He uses different population figures to those given in this paragraph. On the basis of the population figures given in this paragraph, the ratio would be slightly lower with one *warnet* computer per 2,065 people in Malang and per 5,130 in Blitar.

46 *Kompas*, 31 August 2001.

47 H. Thimbleby, 'Personal Boundaries/Global Stage', *First Monday* [online], 3:3, 1998, <www.firstmonday.dk/issues/index.html>, cited in C. Mann and F. Stewart, *Internet Communication and Qualitative Research: A Handbook for Researching Online*, Sage, London, 2000, p. 31.

48 Joop Ave and Djakaria Purawidjaja are quoted in 'Internet: Larangan Buat Konglomerat', *Gatra*, 13:2, 10 February 1996, at <http://web.archive.org/web/19970717143928/http:www.gatra.com/II/13/14.html>, sighted 3 October 2003.

49 See 'Internet Business: Cyber war in a growing market': posted on 16 July 1997, now located at <www.library.ohiou.edu/indopubs/1997/07/16/0012.html> (accessed 29 September 2003); and V. Elisawati , 'Perang Internet', *SWA*: posted on <www.library.ohiou.edu/indopubs/1997/06/14/0002.html> on 14 June 1997 (accessed 30 September 2003). Henry Pribadi, a business associate of President Suharto's second son, Bambang Trihatmodjo, headed the Napan Group, which had extensive interests in petrochemicals, property and automotive parts manufacturing, and was regarded as an off-shoot of Liem Sioe Liong's Salim Group. Lippo was a large banking group, headed by Mochtar Riady. For an analysis of Lippo's misfortunes in e-business, under the stewardship of Mochtar's son, James Riady, see B. Putranto, 'Victim of Cyber Fever', *Indonesian Business*, October 2001, posted at <www.library.ohiou.edu/indopubs/2001/10/18/0071.html> on 18 October 2001 (accessed 29 September 2003).

50 It appears that, by November 2001 at least, 40 per cent of Wasantara-net was owned by the Bakrie Group, an indigenous business conglomerate. See Minges, *Kretek Internet: Indonesia Case Study*, p. 14.

51 Ibid.

52 On Wasantara.net, see the 'Profile' on <www.wasantara.net.id> (accessed 26 November 2003).

53 P3TIE, *Indikator Teknologi Informasi dan Komunikasi Tahun 2002*, p. 14.

54 Interview with Rudy Rusdiah, Chairperson of AWARI (Indonesian Internet Café Association), in 'Warnet, Bisnis Milik UKM', *Warta Ekonomi*, 44:13, 5 November 2001, pp. 42–3.

55 Information on *warnet* in Malang and Blitar is based on Harvey, 'Bisnis Warung Internet di Malang dan Blitar'.

56 Interview with Sariyono Setyabudi, unit head of Wasantara Yogyakarta, 5 December 1996, who believed that nationally Wasantara had about 2,000 subscribers at that time.

57 Harvey, 'Bisnis Warung Internet di Malang dan Blitar', pp. ix–xi.

58 Ibid. p. xii.

59 <www.id.mweb.com/corporate_profile.php> (accessed 6 September 2002).

60 <www.id.mweb.com/milestones.php> (accessed 6 September 2002).

61 Information on M-Web's *warnet* activities is based on F. Adrianto, A.A. Hatanto, S. Shahab, E.S. Siahaan and F. Lamak, 'Terus Menangguk Rupiah di Saat yang Lain Susah' (pp.10–16), and F. Adrianto, S. Shahab, M. Ihsan and E.S. Siahaan, 'Menit-menit yang Menghasilkan Duit' (pp. 17–19), *Warta Ekonomi*, 22:12, 4 June 2001.

62 In November 2001, a Jakarta taxi driver with whom we spoke knew the prices and levels of efficiency of a string of *warnet* around the city, and strongly recommended the UI W-Web centre as the best by far. He used it regularly to e-mail his family in North Sumatra.

63 <www.id.mweb.com/business_units.php> (accessed 6 September 2002).

64 See T. Arvianh and S. Widodo, 'M-Web PHK 40 Orang Karyawan', *detik.com*, 5 July 2002, available online at <www.detikinet.com/berita/2002/07/05/20020705–110802.shtml> (accessed 28 July 2003).

65 <http://imt.co.id/tmp/_ol0425,03,0918,49liq.html> (accessed 28 July 2003, by which date all reference to the Indonesian operations had been removed from the MIH website, and the M-Web Indonesian website address was defaulting to their Zambian operations). M-Web Indonesia's former President Director and COO, David Burke, headed up the new IMT company as their President Director and CEO.

66 Adrianto *et al.*, 'Menit-menit yang Menghasilkan Duit', p. 19.

67 Ibid. The AWARI mailing list can be found at <http://groups.yahoo.com/group/asosiasi-warnet/messages>.

68 Hendaru *et al.*, 'Warnet pun Disikat'.

69 Adrianto *et al.*, 'Terus Menangguk Rupiah di Saat yang Lain Susah', p. 10.

70 Adrianto *et al.*, 'Menit-menit yang Menghasilkan Duit'.

71 On the Warintek 9000 project, see 'Menggelar Warung Penjaja Informasi', *Kompas*, 21 October 2001, available online at <www.kompas.com/kompas-cetak/0110/21/iptek/meng22.htm> (accessed 12 September 2002); 'Fenomena Dotcom Masih Koma', *Kompas*, 6 March 2001, available online at <www.kompas.com/kompas-cetak/0103/06/iptek/feno37.htm> (accessed 12 September 2002); and 'Titik Terang Waralaba Myoh.com', *Majalah SWA*, 2–22 August 2001, available online at <www.warintek.net> (accessed 13 September 2002).

72 Quotation from 'Titik Terang Waralaba Myoh.com'.

73 <http://portal.unesco.org/ci/ev.php?URL_ID=5343&URL_DO=DO_TOPIC&URL_SECTION=201&reload=1034749574> (accessed 31 July 2003).

74 'Menggelar Warung Penjaja Informasi', *Kompas*, 21 October 2001, available online at <www.kompas.com/kompas-cetak/0110/21/iptek/meng22.htm> (accessed 12 September 2002). For further details, see also links from the *Warintek* homepage: <www.warintek.net> (accessed 13 September 2002).

75 'Myohdotcom terpaksa hentikan proyek warintek', posted on 21 January 2003 at <http://groups.yahoo.com/group/warnet2000/message/4941> (accessed 31 July 2003).

76 'Pemerintah kembangkan 4.000 warintek', posted on 6 January 2003 at <http://groups.yahoo.com/group/warnet2000/message/4903> (accessed 31 July 2003).

77 'Warintek bangun 500 outlet di Papua', posted on 25 April 2002 at <http://groups.yahoo.com/group/warnet2000/message/4229> (accessed 31 July 2003).

78 Centre for ICT Studies-ICT Watch with Pegasus and USAID, *Kondisi Industri Warnet di Indonesia*, downloadable from <http://www.ictwatch.com/data/index.htm>, sighted 3 April 2005.

79 D.T. Hill and K. Sen, 'Wiring the Warung to Global Gateways: The Internet in Indonesia'; and quotation from M. Lim, 'The Internet, Social Networks, and Reform in Indonesia', p. 284.

80 L. Aurora, 'Employees, Students Boost Internet Use Total to 8 Million', *The Jakarta Post*, 3 February 2004, available online at <www.thejakartapost.com> (accessed 3 February 2004).

81 B. Guerin, 'Indonesia faces long wait for a cyber-economy', *Asia Times Online*, <www.atimes.com/se-asia>, 15 February 2001.

82 'Sekitar 44 Juta Anak Belum Terjangkau Layanan Pendidikan', *Kompas*, 15 April 2004, available online at <www.kompas.co.id/kompas-cetak/0404/15/humaniora/971198.htm>.

83 See, for instance, a very representative collection of essays on cyberspace and cultural change:

D. Bell and B. Kennedy (eds), *The Cybercultures Reader*, Routledge, London and New York, 2000. All of the essays are in one way or another engaged in understanding global cultural shifts. The essays that look at people's actual engagement with the technology are exclusively about small web and Internet groups, not placed within the massive numbers of diverse users who make up the whole of the Internet.

84 P3TIE, *Indikator Teknologi Informasi dan Komunikasi Tahun 2002*, p. 16.

85 The research methodology and sampling details are provided in APJII, I2BC and Accenture, *Indonesia Cyber Industry & Market*, pp. 17–24. The cities were: Jakarta, Surabaya, Medan, Bandung, Semarang, Denpasar, Makassar, Balikpapan, Yogyakarta and Batam.

86 Pacific Rekanprima Research Team, 'Portrait of Internet Users in Indonesia – Findings of Quantitative Research of the Internet', in APJII, I2BC and Accenture, *Indonesia Cyber Industry & Market*, pp. 159–67, which cites P. Kotler, *Marketing Management*, Prentice Hall, New Jersey, 2000, as the source for this approach. The following discussion of the technographic segmentation is drawn from the Pacific Rekanprima analysis.

87 Ibid., p. 165.

88 Quotation from Foreword to APJII, I2BC and Accenture, *Indonesia Cyber Industry & Market*, p. iii, by APJII Executive Director, Pandji S. Choesin.

89 APJII, I2BC and Accenture, *Indonesia Cyber Industry & Market*, pp. 19–20 and p. x.

90 Harvey, 'Bisnis Warung Internet di Malang dan Blitar', outlines his research methodology on p. 7. His calculations regarding pornographic sites are based on the 'history' files (that is, the sites accessed over the previous 2–3 days) of a sample of 40 computers from ten *warnet* in Malang, and five computers from two *warnet* in Blitar.

91 Ibid., p. 53.

92 Ibid., p. xv.

93 Ibid., p. 49.

94 Adi Nugroho's data for 20–27 January 2002 cited in O.W. Purbo, 'An Experience in Empowering a Bottom-Up Indonesian Internet Infrastructure', unpublished paper delivered at the 'Mediating Human Rights and Democracy' Conference, Curtin University of Technology, Perth, February 2002, p. 16.

95 Ibid. provides a preliminary analysis, while a more developed argument appears in O.W. Purbo, 'Kekuatan Komunitas Indonesia di Dunia Maya', *Pantau*, 022:2, February 2002, pp. 14–19, available online at <www.pantau.or.id/txt/ss/08.html> (and subsequent pages) (accessed 23 May 2002). There are slight variations in the statistics provided in these two sources.

96 Purbo, 'An Experience in Empowering a Bottom-Up Indonesian Internet Infrastructure', p. 20.

97 All statistics from Purbo, 'Kekuatan Komunitas Indonesia di Dunia Maya' (file 08c.html).

98 Quotation translated from Ibid. Purbo includes in these informal national leaders of the IT community, such figures as Michael Sunggiardi, Hidayat Tjokro, Mas Wigrantoro, Heru Nugroho, Yohanes Sumaryo, Andi, H.P. Gatot and Roy Suryo, and notes local leaders including Umar Tjokroaminoto (Medan), Adi Nugroho (Makassar), Penjor (Yogyakarta), Didin (Malang), and Sanjaya Kosasih (Samarinda).

99 Ibid.

100 M. Castells, 'Epilogue: Informationalism and the Network Society', in P. Himanen, *The Hacker Ethic and the Spirit of the Information Age*, Secker & Warburg, London, 2001, pp. 155–78.

5 Communication technology for a new democracy

1 For example, R. Robison and V.R. Hadiz, *Reorganising Power in Indonesia: The Politics of Oligarchy in an Age of Markets*, RoutledgeCurzon, London, 2004.

2 For example, H. Antlöv, 'Introduction', in H. Antlöv and S. Cederroth, *Elections in Indonesia: The New Order and Beyond*, RoutledgeCurzon, London, 2004, pp. 1–17: quotation from p. 1.

3 For example, K. Ward, *The 1971 Election in Indonesia: An East Java Case Study*, Monash Centre for Southeast Asian Studies, Clayton, 1974; L. Suryadinata, *Political Parties and the*

1982 General Election in Indonesia, Institute of Southeast Asian Studies, Singapore, 1982; A. Gaffar, *Javanese Votes: A Case Study of Election under a Hegemonic Party System*, Gadjah Mada University Press, Yogyakarta, 1992.

4 J. McBeth, D. Murphy and M. Cohen, 'Free at Last', *Far Eastern Economic Review*, 17 June 1999, reprinted in Indonesian General Election Commission, *Analyzing Indonesian Election 1999* [sic], Komisi Pemilihan Umum, Jakarta, 2001, pp. 161–9, quotation from p. 162.

5 McBeth *et al.*, 'Free at Last', pp. 167–8.

6 M. Stevensen and A.-B. Albrectsen (eds), *Transition to Democracy: Report on the UNDP Technical Assistance Programme for the 1999 Indonesian General Elections*, United National Development Programme, Jakarta, 1999, available online at <www.un.or.id/ge/report.htm> (accessed 27 August 2002), Annex 1–2.

7 D.Y. King, 'The 1999 Electoral Reforms in Indonesia: Debate, Design and Implementation', *Southeast Asian Journal of Social Science*, 28:2, 2000, pp. 89–110, who (on p. 105) attributes the observation to John McBeth writing in the *Far Eastern Economic Review*, 17 September 1998.

8 The 1999 laws, numbered 2, 3 and 4, cancelled previous legislation (respectively Law No. 3, 1975; Law No. 15, 1969, and Law No. 1, 1985; and Law No. 16, 1969, and Law No. 5, 1995). See Appendix 2 'Undang-undang tentang Parlemen 1918–2000', in Yayasan API, *Panduan Parlemen Indonesia*, Yayasan API, Jakarta, 2001, p. 1312. Copies of the new legislation can be found in Yayasan API, *Almanak Parpol Indonesia Pemilu '99*, Yayasan API, Jakarta, 1999, pp. 647–87. The Indonesian parliament has two 'houses': the *Dewan Perwakilan Rakyat* [DPR] or People's Representative Council, and the larger *Majelis Permusyawaratan Rakyat* [MPR], the People's Consultative Assembly. Under the 1999 Law No. 4, the DPR had 500 members, with 462 elected in the June poll, plus 38 seats allocated to the police and Armed Forces (who are not eligible to vote). The MPR consisted of the DPR plus 135 representatives of the regions (nominated by regional parliaments, DPRD) and 65 representatives of other social groups selected by the KPU (see Yayasan API, *Panduan Parlemen Indonesia*, p. 359). King, 'The 1999 Electoral Reforms in Indonesia: Debate, Design and Implementation', provides a detailed comparison of the 1999 elections with previous ones and discusses the determination, and implementation of various post-Suharto electoral reforms.

9 King, 'The 1999 Electoral Reforms in Indonesia: Debate, Design and Implementation', p. 91.

10 Stevensen and Albrectsen, *Transition to Democracy: Report on the UNDP Technical Assistance Programme for the 1999 Indonesian General Elections*, p. 3.

11 For the details of the new media regulations for 1997 elections, see A.A. Ariwibowo, A. Jauhari, B. Setiawanto, H. Prihatna, R. Moechtar, S.H. Purnomojoyo and S. Muryono, *Pemilu 1997: Antara Fenomena Kampanye Dialogis & Mega-Bintang*, PT Penakencana, Jakarta, 1997, pp. 45–52.

12 Information on the parties' use of websites in the 1997 election is largely drawn from A. Andoko, 'Internet: Ajang baru kampanye para OPP', *Kompas*, 2 May 1997.

13 Aribowo *et al.*, *Pemilu 1997: Antara Fenomena Kampanye Dialogis & Mega-Bintang*, p. 107.

14 M.M.I. Ahyani, 'Internet fails to woo most political parties', *The Jakarta Post*, 29 May 1999, on <www.TheJakartaPost.com> (accessed 21 August 1999).

15 Yayasan API, *Almanak Parpol Indonesia Pemilu '99*.

16 Interview with Alvin Lee, PAN Member of Parliament, Jakarta, 11 February 2001.

17 Y.A. Pareanom, I. Setiawan and D. Arjanto, 'Menjual Partai di Dunia Maya', *Tempo*, 22 March 1999, p. 54. None of the URLs listed in this section are any longer official party sites. Some now appear to be general portals on Indonesian commerce and culture, while other domain names are currently for sale. One of the best ways to link into the party websites is through the National Library of Australia's Indonesian Internet Sites page at <www.nla.gov.au/asian/indo/indsites.html#gov>, which lists all current pages of the political parties discussed in this section.

18 Interview with Ida Sudoyo, Director of Ida Sudoyo and Associates Public Relations Consultants, Jakarta, 5 February 2001.

19 Ida Sudoyo & Associates and PT Narada Komunikatama, 'Golkar Website', unpublished report, prepared by Ida Sudoyo & Associates and PT Narada Komunikatama, Jakarta, 12 June 1999, pp. 7–8, which gives the figures of 6,081 visitors (approx. 209 per day) from 23 countries.

20 Ibid.; e-mail from <gunawan@indosat.net.id>, dated 5 June 1999.

21 Figures taken from the KPU site at <www.kpu.go.id/Sejarah/pemilu1999.shtml> (accessed 23 August 2002). The PRD's poor showing may be due to the continuing detention of the leadership until only a few months before the election.

22 The question listed: TV advertisement; TV news report or opinion of journalist; radio advertisement; radio news report/opinion of journalist; newspaper advertisement; newspaper article/ opinion of newspaper journalist; magazine article/opinion of magazine journalist; party brochure or handout; personal contact with party representative or candidate; public meeting with candidate or party representative; opinion of friend; opinion of family members; opinion of local official; other; don't know/no response. Internet may be considered part of the 'other' category that was noted by 5 per cent of respondents. See S. Wagner, 'Survey of the Indonesian Electorate following the June 1999 Elections', International Foundation for Election Systems (IFES), unpublished 'final amended report', Jakarta, n.d., Question 93.

23 Ahyani, 'Internet Fails to Woo most Political Parties'.

24 S. Eklöf, 'The 1997 General Election in Indonesia', *Asian Survey*, 37:12, December 1997, pp. 1181–96: quotation from p. 1192.

25 Ibid.

26 Information on KPU and Siskohat computer systems provided by Dhana Dharsono, interview, Jakarta, 29 November 2001.

27 Ibid.

28 Stevensen and Albrectsen, *Transition to Democracy: Report on the UNDP Technical Assistance Programme for the 1999 Indonesian General Elections*, p. 3.

29 'Indonesia holds its breath', *The Economist*, 10 June 1999, reprinted in Indonesian General Election Commission, *Analyzing Indonesian Election 1999*, pp. 77–81: quotation from pp. 77–8.

30 'Terjamin, Pengamanan Data pada Sistem Jaringan Komputer Pemilu', *Kompas*, 21 June 1999, p. 29.

31 Ibid. Although this source quotes 'Hendra Darsono', this was in fact Dhana Dharsono (whose given name is actually 'Hendra').

32 Ibid.

33 'Indonesian election – web sites', *Reuters*, available online at <http://asia.internet.com/Reuters/1999/05/3103-news.html> (accessed 5 September 1999).

34 On SPRED, see Stevensen and Albrectsen, *Transition to Democracy: Report on the UNDP Technical Assistance Programme for the 1999 Indonesian General Elections*, p. 34. The KPU results could be accessed by phone for 1,000 rupiah per minute compared to special Internet access for 150 rupiah per minute ($US1 was approximately 10,000 rupiah) ('Waspadai Manipulasi Penghitungan Suara', *Kompas*, 7 June 1999, p. 1; and 'Kilasan Peristiwa: Pulsa untuk yang 'Ngebet' Data', *Kompas*, 13 June 1999, p. 10).

35 Personal e-mail communication with Dhana Dharsono, 26 August 2002.

36 NDI (National Democratic Institute for International Affairs), 'The Prospects for Democratic Elections in Indonesia: Pre-Election Report', unpublished report, National Democratic Institute for International Affairs, Jakarta, 28 May 1999, p. 30. The Australian Electoral Commission, under Director of Operations Ross MacKay, assisted with the setting up of, and staff training for, the JOMC tally room: see <www.un.or.id/GE/newletters/vol1–7/newsletter1.htm> (accessed 25 August 2002). For flow-charts indicating the processes of vote calculation and transmission for the KPU and JOMC, see KPU, 'Laporan: Tim Verifikasi System Komputer KPU (Tim 4)', unpublished report, KPU, Jakarta, 25 July 1999, Appendix 3; and Stevensen and Albrectsen, *Transition to Democracy: Report on the UNDP Technical Assistance Programme for the 1999 Indonesian General Elections*, p. 35. Both JOMC and UNFREL relied on faxes rather than internet/e-mail for the communication of poll statistics from outlying regions.

37 Stevensen and Albrectsen, *Transition to Democracy: Report on the UNDP Technical Assistance Programme for the 1999 Indonesian General Elections*, p. 37.

38 See KPU, 'Laporan: Tim Verifikasi System Komputer KPU (Tim 4)'.

39 Antlöv, 'Introduction', p. 10.

40 Stevensen and Albrectsen, *Transition to Democracy: Report on the UNDP Technical Assistance Programme for the 1999 Indonesian General Elections*, p. 64.

41 The National Citizens' Movement for Free Elections (NAMFREL) website at <www.namfrel.org/Html/aboutus.html> (accessed 22 August 2002) describes the organisation as a 'non-partisan, nationwide organization of individual citizens and civic, religious, professional, business, labor, educational, youth and non-government organizations, voluntarily working for the cause of free, orderly and honest elections'. Although NAMFREL was formalised in October 1983, precursor organisations had existed since 1957.

42 Fifty organisations are listed in Yayasan API, *Almanak Parpol Indonesia Pemilu '99*, pp. 690–2, as being either election monitoring institutes or institutions with election education programmes. The names of thirteen indicate that they were explicitly local or regional organisations. For additional information on the major domestic and international monitoring organisations, see NDI, 'The Prospects for Democratic Elections in Indonesia: Pre-Election Report', pp. 27–9.

43 Stevensen and Albrectsen, *Transition to Democracy: Report on the UNDP Technical Assistance Programme for the 1999 Indonesian General Elections*, p. 65.

44 Ibid., p. 70.

45 By August 2002, the UNFREL and the Rectors' Forum websites had apparently ceased to exist. Examples of each, however, can be obtained from the Web Archives at <http://web.archive.org/web/20000410103614/http://forumrektor.itb.ac.id> and <http://web.archive.org/web/20000819020808/http://www.unfrel.or.id> (both accessed 27 August 2002).

46 Stevensen and Albrectsen, *Transition to Democracy: Report on the UNDP Technical Assistance Programme for the 1999 Indonesian General Elections*, p. 20.

47 On PT Ericsson Indonesia's donation to UNDP, see <www.un.or.id/GE/newletters/vol1–7/newsletter2.htm> (accessed 25 August 2002).

48 Information provided by Smita Notosusanto, Executive Director, Centre for Electoral Reform (CETRO), and former coordinator for UNFREL. Interview, Jakarta, 30 November 2001.

49 See S. Ma'shun, *KPU dan Kontroversi Pemilu 1999*, Pustaka Indonesia Satu, Jakarta 2001, pp. 102–14.

50 KPU,'Tugas dan fungsi Sekretariat Umum Komisi Pemilihan Umum', unpublished report, Komisi Pemilihan Umum, Jakarta, April 2001.

51 Details of the process by which the President was empowered to intervene are given in 'Pemilu 1999' on the KPU website at <www.kpu.go.id/Sejarah/pemilu1999.shtml> (accessed 23 August 2002).

52 IFES, 'Public Opinion in Indonesia Following the June 1999 Elections', unpublished preliminary report, International Foundation for Election Systems, Washington, 1999. Fieldwork was conducted by PT Taylor Nelson Sofres, Jakarta, during the period 14–29 August 1999, with a sample of 1520. To the statement 'The count of the votes in the June 7th election was honest', 86 per cent somewhat/completely agreed; 12 per cent somewhat/completely disagreed; and 3 per cent did not know.

53 The officially appointed Central Committee of Election Inspectors (*Panwas Pemilu Pusat*) listed 4,290 complaints in their final report, none of which concerned the technology as such (Ma'shun, *KPU dan Kontroversi Pemilu 1999*, pp. 152–9).

54 KPU, 'Laporan: Tim Verifikasi System Komputer KPU (Tim 4)', point 5.2.

55 H. Cahyono, M. Nurhasim, S. Nuryani and S. Yanuarti, 'A Portrait of Violations in Indonesia's 1999 General Election: a summary of monitoring results from eight monitored regions', unpublished report, YIPIKA (Yayasan Penguatan Partisipasi, Inisiatif dan Kemitraan Masyarakat Indonesia, Indonesian Foundation to Strengthen Civil Society's Participation, Partnership and Initiatives), Jakarta, May 2000, p. 41.

56 <www.mpr.go.id> (accessed 10 April 2002).

57 By August 2002, the swara.net 'streaming video' had ceased. E-mail correspondence with <swaranet@jditeam.com> (26 August 2002) confirmed low bandwidth as the impediment.

58 When accessed on 22 August 2002, the DPR site indicated that it had had 2,492 visitors since 8 August. The e-mail addresses are given on <www.dpr.go.id/infolain/mail_add.htm>.

59 Accessed 22 August 2002.

60 E.F.Hastuti, 'I don't like people being dishonest' (interview with Alvin Lie), *The Jakarta Post*, 4 February 2001, available online at <www.library.ohiou.edu/indopubs/2001/02/03/0032.html> (accessed 29 September 2003).

61 Interview with Pramono Anung, MPR Building, Jakarta, 6 December 2001.

62 One example of the kind of collaboration that encourages civil society organisations to embrace Internet communications technology is a joint programme of the Asia Foundation and the American Association for the Advancement of Science (AAAS) to build a system that will capture and analyse information on human rights violations, and to develop a user-friendly, custom-designed human rights database for local partners in the Papua and Aceh provinces. See <www.asiafoundation.org/programs/prog-us-ICT.htm> (accessed 26 August 2002).

63 Interview with Alvin Lie of PAN, DPR, Jakarta, 11 December 2001.

64 Interview with Pramono Anung, MPR Building, Jakarta, 6 December 2001. That the public are increasingly using SMS to lobby their political representatives was also commented upon by Alvin Lie (interview 11 December 2001).

65 Lembaga Tertinggi dan Tinggi Negara, shortened to LTTN/LTN, is used in Indonesia official documents to refer to the Upper House of Parliament (MPR, which is the highest state institution) and other high state institutions (LTN), namely the President, Lower House of the Parliament (DPR), the Supreme Court, Auditor General, and the Supreme Advisory Council (DPA). See Yayasan API, *Panduan Parlemen Indonesia*, p. 438.

66 Instruksi Presiden Republik Indonesia, Nomor 3 Tahun 2003 tentang 'Kebijakan dan Strategi Natsional Pengembangan E-Government', available online at <www.detiknet,com/database/uu/inpres3–2003-egov/1.shtml> (accessed 28 October 2003).

67 Ibid., Lampiran 1 (Appendix 1).

68 The duty, functions and authority of the Ministry, in accordance with Presidential Decision No. 101, 2001, are outlined on <www.kominfo.go.id/Artikel.asp?cid=51> (accessed 7 August 2003).

69 Motto from the English-language site <www.kominfo.go.id/bantuan.asp?iLanguage=2>, while the Indonesian page <www.kominfo.go.id/bantuan.asp?iLanguage=1> banner is 'Meningkatkan kualitas dan arus kominfo secara transparan, beretika dan bertangungjawab untuk mencerdaskan bangsa' (both accessed 8 August 2003).

70 *Tinjauan Penyelenggaraan Situs Web Pemerintah Daerah*, Kementerian Komunikasi dan Informasi RI, [Jakarta], 2003, with Foreword by Syamsul Mu'arif , 5 August 2003, available online at <www.kominfo.go.id/kebijakan.asp?cid=90> (accessed 7 August 2003).

71 Interview with Minister Syamsul Mu'arif, Jakarta, 4 December 2001.

72 *Berita Kominfo*, available online at <www.kominfo.go.id/berita_detail.asp?id=236> (accessed 7 August 2003).

73 See, for instance, interview with the District Head (*Bupati*) of Takalar, South Sulawesi, in *eBizzAsia*, January 2003, at <www.ictwatch.com> (accessed March 2004).

74 D. Kingsbury, *The Politics of Indonesia*, Oxford University Press, Melbourne, 2002, pp. 145–7, discusses the key elements of the regional autonomy legislation.

75 <www.bontang.go.id> (accessed 07 June 2004).

76 <www.takalar.go.id/utama/index.php?mn=1> (accessed 7 June 2004).

77 'Kondisi Umum e-Gov Kabupaten Takalar dan Kabupaten Kutai Timur' in *eBizzAsia*, September 2003, available online at <www.ictwatch.com> (accessed April 2004).

78 Examples (viewed on 7 August 2003) included: <www.blitar.go.id>, <www.cirebon.go.id> and <www.garut.go.id>.

79 <www.blitar.go.id/myResults.php?voted=getResults> (accessed 7 August 2003).

80 <www.bantul.go.id> (accessed 11 August 2003). Of those surveyed, 8 per cent agreed, 35 per cent disagreed and 57 per cent strongly disagreed.

81 M. Hale, J. Musso and C. Weare, 'Developing Digital Democracy: Evidence from Californian Municipal Web Pages', in B.N. Hague and B.D. Loader (eds), *Digital Democracy: Discourse and Decision Making in the Information Age*, Routledge, London and New York, 1999, pp. 96–115.

82 B. Anderson, 'Old States, New Societies: Indonesia's New Order in Comparative Historical Perspective', *Journal of Asian Studies*, 42:3, May 1983, pp. 477–96.

83 'Isma', from Kweni village to the east of the Madukismo sugar factory, complained about the polluting ash it produced (26 June 2003), while 'Co_sedih' from Balakan Sumberagung village appealed to the authorities to repair a village road that had virtually turned into a river during years of deterioration (9 June 2003), and 'glorio djati pamungkas' complained about local

officials wanting illegal payments (6 June 2003). For details, see the 'buku tamu' at <www.bantul.go.id>. When contacted towards the end of August, none had received any response whatsoever from authorities to their e-mails (personal e-mail correspondence).

84 S. Kalathil and T.C. Boas, *Open Networks Closed Regimes: The Impact of the Internet on Authoritarian Rule*, Carnegie Endowment for International Peace, Washington, 2003, p. 100.

85 King, 'The 1999 Electoral Reforms in Indonesia: Debate, Design and Implementation', p. 106.

86 For example, while PAN claimed 3,000 visitors per day, it won only 7 per cent of the final vote, compared to Golkar's 22 per cent, despite a paltry 200 daily hits on its website.

6 East Timor

1 This chapter is a slightly revised version of D.T. Hill, 'East Timor and the Internet: Global Political everage in/on Indonesia', *Indonesia*, 73, April 2002, pp. 25–51. We would like to thank the late Herb Feith, John Waddingham and Charles Scheiner for valuable comments on drafts of the paper.

2 From 17 July 1976 to 20 October 1999, the disputed territory of East Timor was claimed by Indonesia as its 27th province. The United Nations (Decolonization Committee, Security Council or General Assembly) never recognised this annexation into Indonesia. Indonesia relinquished its claims after 78.5 per cent of the East Timorese effectively voted in favour of independence (by rejecting the Indonesian offer of autonomy) in a 'Popular Consultation', sponsored by the United Nations, on 30 August 1999, and after a period of UN administration it became the independent state of the 'Democratic Republic of Timor-Leste' on 20 May 2002. The name for the territory in the Tetun *lingua franca* (sometimes written 'Tetum') is Timor Loro Sa'e, but the more common English 'East Timor' is used throughout this chapter.

3 A brief bibliography of material related to East Timor appears on <www.ci.uc.pt/Timor/bibhtml.htm> (accessed on 10 August 2001). This does not include the numerous books published in Australia about East Timor since the 30 August 1999 referendum, several of which are cited later in this paper.

4 G.J. Lloyd, 'The Diplomacy on East Timor: Indonesia, the United Nations and the International Community', in J.J. Fox and D.B. Soares (eds), *Out of the Ashes: Destruction and Reconstruction of East Timor*, Crawford House Publishing, Adelaide, 2000, pp. 79–105, provides an overview of the diplomatic negotiations, but does not comment on the technologies employed. See also E. Ward and P. Carey, 'The East Timor Issue in the Context of EU–Indonesian Relations, 1975–99', *Indonesia and the Malay World*, 29:83, 2001, pp. 51–74.

5 W. Huntley and P. Hayes, 'East Timor and Asian Security', in R. Tanter, M. Selden and S.R. Shalom (eds), *Bitter Flowers, Sweet Flowers: East Timor, Indonesia, and the World Community*, Pluto Press, Sydney, 2001, pp. 173–88: quotation from p. 183.

6 See C.J.P. Moschovitis, H. Poole, T. Schuyler and T.M. Senft, *History of the Internet: A Chronology, 1843 to the Present*, ABC-CLIO, Santa Barbara, 1999, particularly Chapter 3.

7 A summary detailing Australian government knowledge of the attack on Balibo are given in *East Timor: Final Report of the Senate Foreign Affairs, Defence and Trade References Committee*, The Parliament of the Commonwealth of Australia, Canberra, December 2000, pp. 133–5. The most revealing analysis of this event is D. Ball and H. McDonald, *Death in Balibo, Lies in Canberra*, Allen & Unwin, St Leonards, 2000.

8 A chronology of events relating to East Timor for the years 1974–76 is given in W. May (ed.), *Documents on Australian Foreign Policy: Australia and the Indonesian Incorporation of Portuguese Timor, 1974–1976*, Department of Foreign Affairs and Trade and Melbourne University Press, Melbourne 2000, pp. xvii–xxix. The Australian Broadcasting Commission broadcast initial reports of the journalists 'missing in the region' on the morning of 17 October 1975; other outlets quickly took up the story, particularly TV Channels 7 and 9 for whom the personnel worked. In Indonesia, *Kompas* first reported the deaths on 20 October (see Ibid., pp. 479, 481 and 491). For a study of how the Australian media covered East Timor, see R. Tiffen, *Diplomatic Deceits: Government, Media and East Timor*, University of New South Wales Press, Sydney, 2001.

9 Ball *et al.*, *Death in Balibo*, pp. 44–5.
10 Ball *et al.*, *Death in Balibo*, pp. 55–64 provides details of Fretilin and Falintil communication methods and Indonesian interception of these during October 1975.
11 Personal communication with John Waddingham, co-founder/editor of Timor Information Service (Australia), (1975–84), by telephone, Perth, 12 March 2001.
12 Tiffen, *Diplomatic Deceits*, p. 27
13 Quoted in Ball *et al.*, *Death in Balibo*, p. 177.
14 This supply and maintenance of radio contact during 1975–78 is vividly described in D. Freney, *A Map of Days: Life on the Left*, William Heinemann Australia, Melbourne, 1991, pp. 354–73.
15 Ball *et al.*, *Death in Balibo*, pp. 177–80.
16 I would like to thank Pat Walsh, formerly of the Australian Council for Overseas Aid, for discussing the methods used by Australian supporters of an independent East Timor, 13 March 2001.
17 Konis Santana was Field Commander of Falintil, the military arm of the resistance movement, until his accidental death in late 1997. See J. Martinkus, *A Dirty Little War*, Random House Australia, Sydney, 2001, p. 244.
18 On the opening up of 1989–91, see H. Feith, 'East Timor: The Opening Up, the Crackdown and the Possibility of a Durable Settlement', in H. Crouch and H. Hill (eds), *Indonesia Assessment 1992: Political Perspectives on the 1990s*, Political and Social Change Monograph No. 17, ANU, Canberra, 1992, pp. 63–80.
19 Domm entered East Timor briefly in January 1989, very soon after the territory was opened up to visitors, and returned again in September 1990 to interview Gusmão for the Australian Broadcasting Corporation's 'Background Briefing' radio programme. See M. Aarons and R. Domm, *East Timor: A Western Made Tragedy*, New Left Book Club, Sydney, 1992; and Tiffen, *Diplomatic Deceits*, pp. 51–2.
20 A.J. Kennedy, *The Rough Guide to the Internet*, Rough Guides, London, 2000, p. 481.
21 TCP/IP refers to 'Transmission Control Protocol/Internet Protocol', which drives the Internet. See Ibid.
22 Moschovitis *et al.*, *History of the Internet*, pp. 109 and 126.
23 Charles Scheiner (personal communication, 7 September 2001), who was one of the founding sponsors of reg.easttimor.
24 Moschovitis *et al.*, *History of the Internet*, pp. 102–3.
25 HTTP (hyper-text transfer protocol) is for web text transfer, while HTML (hyper-text markup language) is used to make web documents, and URL (uniform resource locator) is the formal name for a web address.
26 Moschovitis *et al.*, *History of the Internet*, p. 127.
27 Ibid., p. 153.
28 For a graphic description of the underground in East Timor and its links with sympathisers abroad, see C. Pinto and M. Jardine, *East Timor's Unfinished Struggle: Inside the Timorese Resistance*, South End Press, Boston 1997, particularly pp. 92–134. On RENETIL, see Q. Mok, 'The Role of RENETIL: National Resistance of East Timorese Students', in East Timor Relief Association (ETRA), *It's Time to Lead the Way*, ETRA, Collingwood, 1996, pp. 106–8. For a more comprehensive list of underground resistance groups, see D. Gomes, 'Resistance: Twenty Years of Struggle Supported by Young East Timorese', in Ibid., pp. 115–20. Member organisations of the International Federation for East Timor (IFET) are listed at <http://etan.org/ifet/member.html>, while an updated 'List of East Timor Support and Solidarity Groups Worldwide' is at <http://etan.org/ifet/support.html> (both accessed 29 August 2001).
29 Amy Goodman and Allan Nairn escaped to Guam on the day of the massacre and did phone and other interviews with world media from there.
30 For examples of the e-mail protest bulletins against Xanana's capture, see <www.library.ohiou.edu/indopubs/1992/11/23/0001.html>, posted on the *apakabar* mailing list on 23 November 1992 (accessed 30 September 2003). For details of the trial, see International Commission of Jurists, *Report on the Trial of Xanana Gusmão in Dili, East Timor*, ICJ, Geneva, 1993.

31 We would like to thank Ms Kirsty Sword Gusmão (who, as a member of the underground, smuggled information between Xanana Gusmão, Ramos-Horta and others) for discussing use of the Internet by activists in these early years (Jakarta, 12 June 2001). See also her own memoir of the period, K.S. Gusmão (with R. Lennox), *A Woman of Independence: A Story of Love and the Birth of a New Nation*, Pan Macmillan Australia, Sydney, 2003, with references to her early e-mail (p. 55) and Xanana's mobile phone use (p. 125).

32 Moschovitis *et al.*, *History of the Internet*, pp. 171–3.

33 See <www.ci.uc.pt/Timor/netret.htm> (accessed 10 August 2001).

34 Details sourced from <www.ci.uc.pt/Timor/mlists.htm> (accessed 10 August 2001).

35 Charles Scheiner, 'Grassroots in the Field – Observing the East Timor Consultation', in Tanter *et al.* (eds), *Bitter Flowers, Sweet Flowers*, pp. 109–24: quotation from p. 110. Scheiner was the national coordinator of ETAN/US until August 2001.

36 Renamed <east-timor@igc.topica.com>, this newsgroup continues to operate with several hundred subscribers around the world (Scheiner, personal communication, 7 September 2001).

37 Personal communication from Charles Scheiner, who published *Documents on East Timor* (7 September 2001).

38 Scheiner, 'Grassroots in the Field', p. 111.

39 My thanks to John Waddingham for making this point (personal e-mail, 5 September 2001).

40 Tiffen, *Diplomatic Deceits*, p. 42.

41 For a discussion of Indonesian support groups, see G.J. Aditjondro, *Menyongsong Matahari Terbit di Puncak Ramelau: Dampak Pendudukan Timor Lorosa'e dan Munculnya Gerakan Pro-Timor Lorosa'e di Indonesia*, Yayasan HAK & Fortilos, Jakarta, 2000, pp. 249–60. An earlier English version can be found at <www.asiet.org.au/reports/gja_pet1.htm> (accessed 3 September 2001).

42 From the early 1980s, underground Timorese student organisations in Java and Bali (such as RENETIL) found that they had easier access to resources and greater freedom for political discussion and action than their counterparts inside East Timor, who were subject to far greater surveillance and scrutiny. See C. Pinto, 'The Student Movement and the Independence Struggle in East Timor: An Interview', in Tanter *et al.* (eds), *Bitter Flowers, Sweet Flowers*, pp. 31–41, particularly pp. 33 and 38.

43 A. Harsono, 'Journalists' Use of the Internet Bubbled up from Underground', *Nieman Reports*, 54:4, winter 2000, pp. 74–6, available online at <http://global.umi.com/pqdweb> (accessed 8 March 2001). Harsono provides a valuable insider's view of the use of the Internet by Indonesian journalists both before and after the fall of Soeharto. I would like to thank Charles Scheiner, National Coordinator, East Timor Action Network/US, for background information on this aspect (personal e-mail communication, 27 March 2001).

44 R. Tanter, M. Selden and S.R. Shalom, 'East Timor Faces the Future', in Tanter *et al.*, *Bitter Flowers, Sweet Flowers*, pp. 243–72: quotation from p. 246.

45 We would like to thank Charles Scheiner for pointing this out, and suggesting Jose Antonio Belo as a well-known case in point.

46 Martinkus, *A Dirty Little War*, p. 43, describes the intimidating atmosphere in the Telkom office during his visit in 1997.

47 I. Cristalis, *Bitter Dawn: East Timor, a People's Story*, Zed Press, London, 2002, p. 51.

48 D. Greenlees and R. Garran, *Deliverance: The Inside Story of East Timor's Fight for Freedom*, Allen & Unwin, Sydney, 2002, pp. 124 and 355. The 5 April statement can be found at <www.etan.org/et99/april/3–10/5cnrtxa.htm> (accessed 11 June 2004). For Kirsty Sword Gusmão's description of the circumstances, see *A Woman of Independence*, pp. 226–8.

49 J. Ramos-Horta, 'Site Seeing', *Guardian*, 11 January 1999, p. 12, cited in C. Mann and F. Stewart, *Internet Communication and Qualitative Research: A Handbook for Researching Online*, Sage Publications, London, 2000, p. 18.

50 Martinkus, *A Dirty Little War*, p. 247. Taur Matan Ruak had become commander after the death of Konis Santana.

51 Cristalis, *Bitter Dawn: East Timor, a People's Story*, p. 198, describes Taur picking upon Internet stories (translated by his interpreter); and Greenlees and Garran, *Deliverance: The Inside Story of East Timor's Fight for Freedom*, p. 230, describe Taur's satellite television.

52 'A Digital Domain for East Timor', *The Irish Times on the Web*, 17 November 1997, available online at <http://scripts.ireland.com/search/higlig … =/newspaper/computimes/1997/1117/cmp4.htm> (accessed on 9 March 2001).

53 The East Timor Top Level Internet Domain (.tp), located at <www.nic.tp/etrules.htm> (accessed 9 March 2001).

54 S. Hayes, 'Push to Give Timor Control over Domain', *The Australian*, 13 February 2001, p. 42. The e-mail address for the administrator was apparently <xanana@minihub.org> (conversation with Kirsty Sword Gusmão, Jakarta, 12 June 2001).

55 W. Hederman, 'Internet Recognition for East Timor', *The Irish Times*, 6 December 1997, located on <www.freedom.tp/struggle.htm> (accessed 7 September 1999). The registration of the domain name may have been important symbolically but it had attracted only one host by January 1999. See Moschovitis *et al.*, *History of the Internet*, p. 280, which provides a table of 'Top-Level Domain names by Host Country'. East Timor's low host numbers for '.tp' contrast starkly with the commercially attractive domain name for the largely unknown South Pacific island state of Niue, with 1,608 hosts. This popularity was primarily due to Niue's memorable domain tag, '.nu', which means 'now' in Norwegian, Danish, Swedish and Dutch. For details, see 'A Digital Domain for East Timor', *The Irish Times on the Web*, 17 November 1997, available online at <http://scripts.ireland.com/search/higlig … =/newspaper/computimes/1997/1117/cmp4.htm> (accessed 9 March 2001).

56 Hederman, 'Internet Recognition for East Timor'.

57 'Internet Undermines E Timor Security Situation', *Antara*, 15 August 1997, located via a search of <http://global.umi.com> (accessed 8 March 2001).

58 'MP Suggests Opening up E Timor to European Mass Media', *Antara*, 10 September 1997, located via a search of <http://global.umi.com> (accessed 8 March 2001).

59 A 'virus' is 'code designed to infect computers and replicate itself by using other programs or data, either for no meaningful reason (a prank) or with malicious intent', while a 'worm' is a self-replicating programme that can spread from computer to computer within a network without requiring users to activate it (Moschovitis *et al.*, *History of the Internet*, pp. 136 and 294).

60 D.E. Denning, 'Activism, Hacktivism, and Cyberterrorism: The Internet as a Tool for Influencing Foreign Policy', Georgetown University, Washington DC, 2000, available online at <www.nautilus.org/info-policy/workshop/papers/denning.html> (accessed 15 March 2001).

61 The term 'hacker' was originally coined in the early 1960s by computer programmers at the Massachusetts Institute of Technology to connote positively programmers who were passionately dedicated to the belief that 'information-sharing is a powerful positive good', and who shared their computer expertise 'by writing free software and facilitating access to information and to computing resources wherever possible.' In the mid-1980s, the media popularised the term as a pejorative for computer criminals such as virus writers. This led hackers to coin the uncomplimentary term 'cracker' to differentiate those imbued with the 'hacker ethic' from 'criminal hackers': see P. Himanen, *The Hacker Ethic and the Spirit of the Information Age*, Secker & Warburg, London, 2001, esp. pp. vi–vii, which cites *The Jargon File* at <www.tuxedo.org/~esr/jargon>. This book uses 'hacker' in its original sense.

62 J. Grant, 'Guerilla Hackers take on Military', *South China Morning Post*, 3 May 1997, available online at <www.infowar.com/hacker/hackza.html-ssi> (accessed 15 March 2001).

63 'Looking Back … ', *Computing Canada*, 12 June 2000, p. 6, sourced through <http://web2.infotrac.galegroup.com> (accessed 9 March 2001). The Indonesian Government sites were apparently hit repeatedly on 19 January, 10 February, 24 April, 30 June and 22 November, while the other sites were only attacked once: NASA (March 5), UK Conservative Party (27 April) and Spice Girls (14 November).

64 The hacked page can be viewed at <www.kaotik.org/98/hankam1.html> (accessed 15 March 2001).

65 Details of the 45 servers hacked are given on <www.kaotik.org/98> (accessed 15 March 2001).

66 Quoted in A. Harmon, 'Hacktivists of All Persuasions Take their Struggle to the Web', <www.kaotik.org/98/nytimes1.html> (accessed 15 March 2001).

67 <www.uc.pt/scripts/timornet/sirius.exe/etmp?index.html> (accessed 23 May, 2005).

68 C. Torremendez, 'Situasi perhackingan indonesia [sic]', available online at <www.k-elektronik.org/ezine/situasi.htm> (accessed 27 March 2001).

69 Maguire is quoted by C. O'Doherty, *The Examiner Front Page*, 23 January 1999, located on the East Timor Ireland Solidarity Campaign site (article provided to me by John Waddingham).

70 Information on the Connect Ireland attack is given in 'Hackers Rob East Timor of Cyberspace Independence', at <http://asia.internet.com/Reuters/1999/01/2801-news.html>, B. McWilliams, 'Irish Provider Blames Failure on Other ISPs' at <www.internetnews.com/isp-news/print/0,1089,8_63651,00.html> (both accessed 5 September 1999), and 'Press Release – from Connect Ireland Communications Ltd' at <www.freedom.tp/press.htm> (accessed 7 September 1999).

71 Information from Martin Maguire, e-mail communication, 13 March 2001.

72 See Parliament of the Commonwealth of Australia, *East Timor: Final Report*, p. 178.

73 The initial date of the 'popular consultation' was to be 8 August, but it was postponed to 30 August.

74 The Parliament of the Commonwealth of Australia, *East Timor: Final Report*, p. 89.

75 There were, for example, 57 people killed in Liquiça on 6 April with a dozen more murdered in Dili on 17 April (see Parliament of the Commonwealth of Australia, *East Timor: Final Report*, p. 179). Martinkus, *A Dirty Little War*, pp. 116–262, describes this period graphically.

76 The 3 January 1996 e-mail is quoted in full in a CNRM Media Release 'IN/NET:Death Threats on the Net', posted 7 January 1996, and archived at <www.library.ohiou.edu/indopubs/1996/01/07/0019.html> (accessed 29 September 2003).

77 L. Murdoch, 'Computer Chaos Threat to Jakarta', *Sydney Morning Herald*, 18 August 1999, p. 9. This source was used by D. Legard, 'Cyberwar Threatens Indonesia', *The Standard*, 19 August 1999, available online at <www.thestandard.com/article/article_print/0,1153,5962,00.html> (accessed 29 March 2001).

78 L. Murdoch, 'Fury Over Computer Threat', *Sydney Morning Herald*, 20 August 1999, p. 8. This source was used by N. Weil, 'Indonesia Answers Hacker Threats', *The Standard*, 19 August 1999, available online at <www.thestandard.com/article/display/0,1151,5978,00.html> (accessed 29 March 2001).

79 'Press Release – from Connect-Ireland Communications Ltd', 19 August 1999, available online at <www.freedom.tp/press.htm> (accessed 7 September 1999).

80 'East Timor Cyberwar On New Global Battlefield: The Internet', *The Jakarta Post*, 30 August 1999, located at <http://www.infowar.com/mill_c4i/99/mil_c4I_083099b_j.shtml>, sighted on 13 March 2001.

81 The intense strain between the 4 September declaration of poll results and the 13 September acceptance by President Habibie of a UN peacekeeping force, as Ramos-Horta lobbied relentlessly for international intervention, is documented in Tom Zubrycki's film *The Diplomat* (produced by Sally Browning for Film Australia, Lindfield, 2000). The Ramos-Horta quotation is from T. Parkinson, 'Ramos Horta: The Inside Story', *The Age*, 28 August 2000, available online at <http://etan.org/et2000c/august/27–31/28ramos.htm> (accessed 28 August 2001).

82 Denning, 'Activism, Hacktivism, and Cyberterrorism'.

83 See [Indonesia-l] 'KIPER – Sulitnya Telekomunikasi di Timor Timur', dated 30 August 1999, available online at <www.indopubs.com/archives/0627.html> (accessed 3 September 1999).

84 'IFJ launches safety office for journalists in ET', 7 August 1999, available online at <http://etan.org/et99b/august/1–7/5ifj.htm> (accessed 10 March 2001).

85 Solahudin *et al.*, *Ganasnya Satgas, Kejamnya Milisi Timtim: Laporan Kekerasan terhadap Jurnalis dan Media Massa Mei 1999-April 2000 [The Ferociousness of Satgas, The Cruelty of East Timor Militia – A Report on Violence towards Journalists and Mass Media May 1999 – April 2000]*, AJI Indonesia, Jakarta, 2000, pp. 14–15.

86 Cristalis, *Bitter Dawn: East Timor, a People's Story*, notes the ease with which Xanana was able communicate by mobile phone during his last years in Cipinang prison and the prison house to which he was moved in the lead-up to the referendum (pp. 106 and 122).

87 See, for example, Martinkus *A Dirty Little War*, p. 106.

88 T. Fischer, *Seven Days in East Timor: Ballot and Bullets*, Allen & Unwin, Sydney, 2000, p. 46.

89 Ibid., p. 36. Fischer provides several examples of how communication by mobile phone enabled

the media (and the Australian government) to get direct reports from East Timor during the Popular Consultation (for example, pp. 69, 76, 94).

90 Initial figures are estimates provided by the UN's humanitarian coordinator for East Timor, Ross Mountain, on 19 September (cited in J.G. Taylor, *East Timor: The Price of Freedom*, Zed Books London & Pluto Press Australia, Annandale, 1999, p. 229, which provides a detailed chronology of the main events in East Timor since 1974, on pp. 200–30). The figure of 250,000 comes from a later Amnesty International 'Annual Report 2000: Indonesia and East Timor' at <www.web. amnesty. org/web/ar2000web.nsf/countries/a8b2dcbe3c6cac35802568f200552930?OpenDocument> (accessed 24 September 2001).

91 Martinkus, *A Dirty Little War*, pp. 321 and 324.

92 Indonesian journalists were routinely harassed and beaten up. A reporter with Indonesia's largest daily newspaper, *Kompas*, only survived being shot by five bullets on 26 August because of his bullet-proof jacket. A month later, his compatriot Agus Mulyawan (working for the Japanese agency, Asia Press International) was murdered at close range after identifying himself as an Indonesian journalist at a militia ambush on the Los Palos–Leuteum road. A survey of atrocities against journalists – East Timorese, Indonesian and others – is given in the bilingual publication Solahudin *et al.*, *Ganasnya Satgas, Kejamnya Milisi Timtim*, particularly pp. 13–28.

93 See [Indonesia-l] 'KMP – Di Timtim telepon pun akan dikuasai militer', datelined 8 September 1999, and quoted here from <www.indopubs.com/archives/0796.html> (accessed 8 September 1999).

94 For details on Radio 68H, see <www.radio68h.or.id> and J. Carstensen, 'Internet Radio', *Whole Earth*, spring 2000, p. 89, available online at <http://web2.infotrac.galegroup.com/itw> (accessed 9 March 2001).

95 Quoted in Taylor, *East Timor*, pp. 228–9.

97 <www.thejakartapost.com:8890/iscp_render?menu_name=frontpage> (accessed 13 September 1999).

97 B. Connole, 'Irony in the Pacific for Long-distance Diplomat', *The Australian*, 26 June 2000, available online at <http://etan.org/et2000b/june/25–30/26irony.htm> (accessed 10 March 2001).

98 Quotes in Parkinson, 'Ramos Horta: The Inside Story'.

99 Ramos-Horta's position is noted in M. Chipperfield,'Keeping the Issue Alive', in L. Taudevin and J. Lee (eds), *East Timor: Making Amends? Analysing Australia's Role in Reconstructing East Timor*, Otford Press, Sydney, 2000, pp. 145–7: quotation from p. 147.

100 B. Murray, 'US Peacekeepers Use Net to Access Classified Network', *Government Computer News*, 19:11, 15 May 2000, p. 40, available online at <http://web2.infotrac.galegroup.com/itw> (accessed 9 March 2001).

101 Moschovitis *et al.*, *History of the Internet*, p. 206 gives details of Operation Home Front. A. Ryan, *'Primary Responsibilities and Primary Risks': Australian Defence Force Participation in the International Force East Timor*, Land Warfare Studies Centre Study Paper No. 304, Duntroon, 2000, includes a photograph of the InterFET Internet café on pp. 66–7.

102 C. Brady and G. Rowell, 'Email to Dili – You Have Got to Be Joking!', at <www.caa.org.au/groups/IT/dili> (accessed 13 March 2001).

103 E. Ellis, 'Asia Buzz: Making a Difference Connecting Nuns in East Timor to the Internet', *Time Asia*, 4 January 2001, available online at <http://etan.org/et2001a/january/01–06/04conn.htm> (accessed 10 March 2001), describes helping the name of the Carmelite Convent in Comoro, outside Dili, download e-mails using a Darwin ISP. He says, of their enthusiasm, that '[w]ithin 30 minutes, the nuns had 50 new sites in their 'favourites' list and were busy sending e-mails around the world.'

104 Quoted from <www.etan.org/lh> (accessed 14 August 2001).

105 'Horta Sees Internet Future for East Timor' (visited 20 February 2000), at <www.cnn.com/2000/ASIANOW/southeast/02/13/timor.internet.reut/index.html>, cited in J. Yap, 'The Internet and the Knowledge Economy: Charting a Course in Cyberspace', unpublished paper, Harvard Project for Asian and International Relations Conference, Beijing, August 2000.

106 Ramos-Horta is quoted in C. Johnson, 'Interview: Horta sees Internet future for E.Timor [sic]', 13 February 2000, and available online at <http://etan.org/et2000a/february/13–19/13interv. htm> (accessed 10 March 2001).

107 Quotations in the paragraph are from East Timor Transitional Administration, 'Criteria for Operation as an Internet Service Provider in East Timor', last updated 6 August 2001, available online at <www.gov.east-timor.org/itpt/isp_criteria.php> (accessed 13 August 2001).

108 Charles Scheiner, personal e-mail communication, 19 and 25 May 2004. Timor Telecom, which commenced activity on 1 March 2003, is part of the Portugal Telecom Group, which holds 38.15 per cent of the share capital of the company. It has a 15-year concession, renewable for 10 years: see <www.telecom.pt/InternetResource/PTSite/UK/Canais/SobreaPT/mercado_internacional/timor_telecom.htm> (accessed 25 May 2004).

109 Charles Scheiner, personal communication, 19 May 2004. We are grateful for his various e-mails updating us on the use of Internet in Timor in 2004, as we finish writing this book.

110 Greenlees and Garran, *Deliverance: The Inside Story of East Timor's Fight for Freedom*, p. 333.

111 B. Meeks, 'No Justice, No Peace', *Association for Computing Machinery. Communications of the ACM*, 41:2, February 1998, pp. 17–19, located via a search of <http://global.umi.com> (accessed 8 March 2001).

112 C.M. Fukuda, 'Peace through Nonviolent Action: The East Timorese Resistance Movement's Strategy for Engagement', *Pacifica Review*, 12:1, February 2000, pp. 17–31. Quotation from p. 19.

113 Fukuda, 'Peace through Nonviolent Action', p. 25.

114 John Waddingham, co-founder/editor of *Timor Information Service* (1975–84), personal e-mail communication, 9 September 2001.

115 Huntley and Hayes, 'East Timor and Asian Security', p. 183.

116 B. Warf and J. Grimes, 'Counterhegemonic Discourses and the Internet', *Geographical Review*, 87:2, April 1997, pp. 259–74, located via a search of <http://global.umi.com> (accessed 8 March 2001).

7 Communal conflict

1 B. Bräuchler, 'Cyberidentities at War: Religion, Identity, and the Internet in the Moluccan Conflict', *Indonesia*, 75 (April), 2003, pp. 123–51.

2 Cyberethnography and cyberanthropology are terms that are now readily understood in both media studies and in anthropology. See the range of articles and discussions on <www.cyberanthropology.com> (accessed 5 May 2004).

3 In discussing messages and participants in electronic lists in the context of volatile communal conflict, we are mindful of ethical issues in online research. The selected list materials are freely available in public archives or websites, accessible to anyone who visits the sites. We do not quote contents restricted only to 'members' of a closed list. We generally refer to the participants by names or by the identity 'descriptors' they provide for themselves in the e-groups, although in some cases we have sought to follow through other avenues of participants' online lives to see where and how they were joining the battle for Maluku.

4 P. Spyer, 'Fire Without Smoke and Other Phantoms of Ambon's Violence: Media Effects, Agency, and the Work of Imagination', *Indonesia*, 74, October 2002, pp. 21–36, provides a detailed listing of the key writings about the Maluku conflict on p. 22, fn. 2.

5 M.C. Ricklefs, *A History of Modern Indonesia since c. 1200*, Palgrave, Houndmills, 2001, pp. 27–30, provides a succinct history of the early Portuguese arrival in Maluku, which took its name from the term used for it by Arab traders, Jazirat al-Muluk, the 'land of many kings'.

6 These statistics are taken from website of the Global IDP Project of the Norwegian Refugee Council, available online at <www.db.idpproject.org/Sites/IdpprojectDb/idpSurvey.nsf/SearchResults/62783AB4D4F1B9BEC1256959004FDF7D?OpenDocument> (accessed 7 November 2003). Excellent online maps of the region are available from <http://websitesrcg.com/ambon/maps.htm> (accessed 23 May 2005).

7 In this chapter we use the terms 'Maluku' and 'the Moluccas' to refer to the region spanning both these two new provinces: Maluku (which includes the former central and southeast Maluku districts) and North Maluku (which covers the ancient sultanates of Ternate, Tidore, Bacan and Jailolo).

8 These statistics are taken from website of the Global IDP Project of the Norwegian Refugee Council,

available online at <www.db.idpproject.org/Sites/IdpprojectDb/idpSurvey.nsf/SearchResults/62783AB4D4F1B9BEC1256959004FDF7D?OpenDocument> (accessed 7 November 2003).

9 For a summary of the RMS movement, see Ricklefs, *A History of Modern Indonesia since c. 1200*, p. 285. For a more detailed analysis, see R. Chauvel, *Nationalists, Soldiers and Separatists: The Ambonese Islands from Colonialism to Revolt, 1880–1950*, KITLV Press, Leiden, 1990, particularly pp. 347–92. On the expatriate community, see B. Allen and A. Loubert, 'History and Identity: Moluccans in the Netherlands', *The Hague Legal Capital*, 25 June 2003, available online at <www.geocities.com/lawamena_tabaos/junenews/hague25062003a.htm> (accessed 13 November 2003). During the current conflict in Maluku, some Muslim groups have accused Christians of reviving the RMS in order to separate from Indonesia. This has been denied by Christian spokespeople who have countered that in 1950 the RMS itself was supported by both Christian and Muslim Moluccans. For a photographic example displayed on a Christian website to illustrate Muslim support for the RMS, see <www.geocities.com/latoehalat/statisticsnf.htm> (accessed 5 November 2003). The figure of 12,000 Ambonese fleeing to Holland in 1950 is given in the Human Rights Watch, report *Indonesia: The Violence in Ambon* (HRW, March 1999), at <www.hrw.org.reports/1999/ambon/amron–02.htm>, endnote 17 (accessed 5 November 2003).

10 Figures from <www.websitercg.com/ambon/Malukupop.htm> (accessed 20 August 2000), which cites percentages based on 1997 Indonesian Bureau of Statistics figures.

11 In Indonesia, the term *Kristen* (Christian) refers exclusively to Protestants (who comprise about 11 per cent of the population) rather than Catholics (*Katolik*) (who account for about 4 per cent). In this chapter we use the term inclusively for both. Van Klinken observed: 'In the main, the Maluku wars involved conflicts between Muslims and Protestants.' (G. van Klinken, 'The Maluku Wars: Bringing Society Back In', *Indonesia*, 71 (April 2001), pp. 1–26: quotation from p. 3.)

12 For a discussion of how these figures are calculated, see G.J. Aditjondro, 'Guns, Pamphlets and Handie-Talkies: How the Military Exploited Local Ethno-religious Tensions in Maluku to Preserve their Political and Economic Privileges', in I. Wessel and G. Wimhöfer (eds), *Violence in Indonesia*, Abera-Verl., Hamburg, 2001, pp. 100–28: specifically p. 100. M.A. Tunny, 'Megawati Orders the Weeding out of RMS', *The Jakarta Post*, 23 May 2004, states that more than 6,000 had died by February 2002.

13 Van Klinken,'The Maluku Wars: Bringing Society Back In': quotation from p. 3. Van Klinken provides slightly different figures, however, to those in Aditjondro, 'Guns, Pamphlets and Handie-Talkies', p. 100.

14 International Crisis Group, *Indonesia: The Search for Peace in Maluku*, ICG, Jakarta/Brussels, p. ii, dated 8 February 2002, available online at <www.intl-crisis-group.org/projects/asia/indonesia/reports/A400544_08022002.pdf> (accessed 3 November 2003).

15 Van Klinken, 'The Maluku Wars: Bringing Society Back In', provides an excellent analysis of the conflict, arguing, because of the multiplicity of violent incidents, for the use of the plural 'wars', grouped into 'Ambon-related fighting in the south of Maluku province from January 1999 onwards, and North Maluku fighting following the establishment of a new province there in the second half of 1999' (p. 2).

16 N. Bubandt, 'Malukan Apocalypse: Themes in the Dynamics of Violence in Eastern Indonesia', in Wessel and Wimhöfer (eds), *Violence in Indonesia*, pp. 228–53: quotation from p. 237.

17 This summary is based mainly on the Human Rights Watch report (1999) *Indonesia: The Violence in Ambon* and van Klinken, 'The Maluku Wars: Bringing Society Back In', p. 3.

18 As an example of the difficulty in determining the accuracy of conflicting reports of such incidents, Human Rights Watch notes that 'even for the most thoroughly covered and analysed incident in Ambon, the fight on January 19 that ignited it all, there are two very difficult accounts', which it then proceeds to lay out in considerable detail. See Human Rights Watch, *Indonesia: The Violence in Ambon*.

19 Van Klinken, 'The Maluku Wars: Bringing Society Back In', p. 4.

20 A photo of the Silo church engulfed by flames appears on Ambon Berdarah On-Line: <www.geocities.com/latoehalat/links.htm> (accessed 15 November 2003).

21 Van Klinken, 'The Maluku Wars: Bringing Society Back In', p. 7.

22 International Crisis Group, *Indonesia's Maluku Crisis: The Issues*, ICG Indonesia Briefing, Jakarta/Brussels, 19 July 2000, p. 3, available online at <www.crisisweb.org//library/documents/report_archive/A400113_19072000.pdf> (accessed 11 November 2003). On Laskar Jihad, see N. Hasan, 'Faith and Politics: The Rise of the Laskar Jihad in the Era of Transition in Indonesia', *Indonesia*, 73, April 2002, pp. 145–69; K.E. Schulze, 'Laskar Jihad and the Conflict in Ambon', *The Brown Journal of World Affairs*, spring 2002, 9:1, pp. 57–69, available online at <www.watsoninstitute.org/bjwa/archive/9.1/Indonesia/Schulze.pdf> (accessed 18 November 2003); and S. Mulyadi, 'Violence under the Banner of Religion: The Case of Laskar Jihad and Laskar Kristus', *Studia Islamika*, 10:2, 2003, pp. 75–109.

23 'Civil emergency' is the 'lowest of three levels of emergency provided under the 1959 State of Emergency law' (International Crisis Group, *Indonesia: The Search for Peace in Maluku*, pp. 3 and 8).

24 International Crisis Group, *Indonesia: The Search for Peace in Maluku*, p. 11.

25 Ibid., p. 17.

26 Human Rights Watch, *Moluccan Islands: Communal Violence in Indonesia: Recommendations*, <www.hrw.org/press/2000/06/indo-back0629.htm> (accessed 5 November 2003).

27 These incidents are described in International Crisis Group, *Indonesia: The Search for Peace in Maluku*, pp. 12–13.

28 Ibid.

29 The website announcement of the disbanding (<www.laskarjihad.or.id>, accessed 16 October 2002) is translated in Mulyadi, 'Violence under the Banner of Religion: The Case of Laskar Jihad and Laskar Kristus', p. 90. Though the original site appears to have closed down, a press release (16 October 2002) providing details is archived at <http://web.archive.org/web/20021127175942/http://laskarjihad.or.id> (accessed 25 November 2003).

30 'Peaceful, Safe Celebrations Mark Idul Fitri across Country', *The Jakarta Post*, 27 November 2003 <www.thejakartapost.com/detailnational.asp?fileid=20031127.D01&irec=0>, sighted 29 November 2003.

31 On BakuBae, see 'Mayoritas Masyarakat Maluku Mendukung Pendekatan Penyelesaian Konflik "Dari Bawah"', available online at <www.preventconflict.org/portal/main/research/TafsirJajakPendapatDiMaluku2002.pdf> (accessed 12 November 2003).

32 For example, Aditjondro, 'Guns, Pamphlets and Handie-Talkies', pp. 112–22.

33 Van Klinken, 'The Maluku Wars: Bringing Society Back In', pp. 7–9.

34 Eriyanto, *Media dan Konflik Ambon Media, Berita, dan Kerusuhan Komunal di Ambon 1999–2002*, Kantor Berita Radio 68H, Jakarta, 2003. A seven-page English-language 'Executive Summary' was circulated as part of the promotion of the publication by 68H Director Santoso, dated 10 March 2003, from which some of the following information is drawn. For a profile of Radio 68H, see <http://adlog.radio68h.com/profile.php> (accessed 13 November 2003). Details of print media in North Maluku can be found in Stanley, 'Penerbitan di Maluku Utara', unpublished typescript produced for the Office of Transitional Initiatives, United States Agency for International Development (USAID), Jakarta, 7 September 2001.

35 On the *Jawa Pos* group, <www.jawapos.co.id/group> (accessed 13 November 2003); and K. Sen and D.T. Hill, *Media, Culture and Politics in Indonesia*, Oxford University Press, Melbourne, 2000, pp. 58–9.

36 Eriyanto, *Media dan Konflik Ambon*, p. 31.

37 Ibid., p. 34.

38 Ibid., pp. 38–9, for tables.

39 Spyer, 'Fire Without Smoke and Other Phantoms of Ambon's Violence', p. 33. Eriyanto, *Media and Konflik Ambon*, pp. 21–2, details several of these VCDs, made with hand-held video cameras and sold in Ambon markets and through organisations such as Laskar Jihad in places such as Jalan Malioboro in Yogyakarta.

40 'Executive Summary' (circulated with publication of Eriyanto 2003), p. 5. The agreement is often referred to as 'Malino II', since the previous month a similar accord ('Malino I') was signed there by parties involved in inter-communal conflict in Poso, Sulawesi.

41 International Crisis Group, *Indonesia's Maluku Crisis: The Issues*, p. 5.

42 Eriyanto, *Media dan Konflik Ambon*, p. 145.

43 International Crisis Group, *Indonesia: The Search for Peace in Maluku*, p. 13.

44 'Executive Summary' (circulated with publication of Eriyanto, *Media dan Konflik Ambon*), p. 7.

45 For details of particular cases, see Eriyanto, *Media dan Konflik Ambon*, pp. 182–4.

46 Bräuchler, 'Cyberidentities at War', p. 126.

47 Ibid., p. 127, notes also Howard Rheingold's creation of the term 'virtual community' in *The Virtual Community: Homesteading on the Electronic Frontier* (electronic edition, 1993), available online at <www.rheingold.com/vc/book> (accessed 22 August 2001).

48 Links to such sites may be found at <www.maluku2000.org/subdomain/weblinks/weblinks.html> (accessed 5 November 2003). See, for example, the International Crisis Group <www.crisisweb.org>, Human Rights Watch <www.hrw.org/campaigns/indonesia/moluccas.htm> and the Harvard Program on Humanitarian Policy and Conflict Resolution <www.preventconflict.org/portal/main> .

49 Author's details are given on the homepage <http://websitercg.com/ambon/about.htm> (accessed 5 November 2003).

50 See <http://websitercg.com/ambon/documents/laskar-jihad–010502.htm> and <http://websitercg.com/ambon/documents/Mailino-II-agreement.htm> (both accessed 5 November 2003).

51 This, at least, was the assessment of Eriyanto, *Media dan Konflik Ambon*, p. 17.

52 <www.domini.org/openbook/home.htm> (accessed 3 August 2000 and 13 November 2003).

53 <www.christianportal.com> (accessed 3 August 2000). When re-visited on 13 November 2003, the site appeared not to have been updated since the previous March. The ChristianPortal.com webmaster appears to be a Rev. Joe Jenkins, who, readers are informed, was 'selected to run in the 2003 Mendip District Council elections for the Conservative party in the UK'.

54 <www.petra.ac.id> (accessed 3 August 2000). When we re-visited the site on 13 November 2003, there were no longer any references to the Maluku conflict.

55 Bubandt, 'Malukan Apocalypse', p. 240, notes this influence. The original quotation is: 'Latar belakang konflik massa di Tobelo diawali dari beredarnya isu natal berdarah dan berita dari Internet tentang programme Jihad'. Yayasan SAGU (1999), 'Maluku Report 18: Peristiwa Kerusuhan di Tobelo dan Galela Desember 1999'.

56 Bubandt 'Malukan Apocalypse', p. 242.

57 <www.dlm.org/en/eng/htm> (accessed 3 August 2000). When re-visited on 13 November 2003, the original English-language pages were no longer accessible, with the homepage defaulting to a Dutch-language site <www.dlm.org/nl/ned.htm>. The links page had also moved to <www.dlm.org/nl/links/entree.htm>. The new site included a 'chat room' which, at the time we visited, had 11 participants, using a *patois* of Dutch, and Indonesian with Moluccan inflections. The 'Forum' site was being actively used with the 'news and media' sub-forum listing about one posting a day through November. The 'Politics' sub-forum, which was the most popular of the six sub-forums, had 32 messages and responses in the first 14 days of November 2003.

58 The site was originally at <www.geocities.com/alifuru67/noframe/index.htm> or <www.go.to/ambon> when accessed on 3 August 2000, but had moved to <www.geocities.com/latoehalat/index.htm> when accessed on 14 November 2003.

59 The mirror sites include: <www.fortunecity.com/tatooine/leiber/275/latoehalat/index.htm>, and <http://go.to/alifuru67> when accessed 14 November 2003, but it appears to have previously used alifuru67 ambon67, naulu67 and maluku67 as alternative sites.

60 Statistical breakdown compiled from <www.TheCounter.com> for Ambon Berdarah On-Line, for the period 10 November 1999 until 4 April 2000, provided on <www.geocities.com/ambon67/noframe/visitor_stats.htm> (accessed 5 November 2003). Other sizeable top-domains were networks (.net) 10 per cent, commercial (.com) 8 per cent and Australia (.au) 4 per cent. Both .net and .com are dominated by American entities. The figure of over 40,000 Moluccan expatriates in Holland is given in Human Rights Watch, *Indonesia: The Violence in Ambon*, endnote 17.

61 Bräuchler, 'Cyberidentities at War', p. 127, fn. 18.

62 S. Tekwani, 'The Tamil Diaspora, Tamil Militancy, and the Internet', in K.C. Ho, R. Kluver and K.C.C. Yang (eds), *Asia.com: Asia Encounters the Internet*, RoutledgeCurzon, London, 2003, pp. 175–92: quotation from p. 177.

63 <www3.cybercities.com/l/laskarjihad/mainframe.htm> (accessed 1 August 2000). This site no longer existed when we attempted to visit in November 2003.

64 Suara Ambon Online's photo collection of the unrest in Ambon was at: <wysiwyg://main.thepage.100/http://www.geocities.com/Paris/Gallery/1199/koleksi.html> (accessed 1 August 2000).

65 The CCDA's regular reports are downloadable from <www.malra.org/posko/archief2.php3> (accessed 15 November 2003). The Masariku e-mailing list at <http://groups.yahoo.com/group/masariku> (accessed 15 November 2003) was established on 18 August 1999 and was still operating in November 2003, with a membership of 204. The official e-mailing list of the FKAWJ's Laskar Jihad was <http://groups.yahoo.com/group/laskarjihad>, which operated only between 17 May 2000 and 21 December 2001 (accessed 15 November 2003), but appears to have had the largest membership of the three with 1,259 when it ceased.

66 Bräuchler, 'Cyberidentities at War', p. 129.

67 Bubandt 'Malukan Apocalypse', p. 242.

68 Ibid.

69 These were the settings when the site was visited on 17 November 2003.

70 Based on a 'keyword' search for 'Maluku' and 'Ambon' (21 May 2004).

71 Apart from the main 'laskarjihad' site (begun 17 May 2000), there was also the similarly named 'LashkarJihad' (founded 23 August 2001), which was described as the 'official mailing list of the Laskar Jihad Ahlus Sunnah wal Jamaah'. In addition, 'laskar_jihad' (established 29 May 2001) purported to be a 'Mailing list of Laskar Jihad news in Maluku', but its total of seven postings between 4 June 2001 and 19 October 2003 included only one message about Maluku, with the other six being either test messages, information about Muslims in India or requests for 'pen-friends' from a medical student in Pakistan! In addition, Yahoo! also hosted the mock 'laskyar-jihad' (with 16 members, but only three postings in total) established on 1 June 2001 as an attack on Laskar Jihad, made evident by the group's description: 'The Laskar Jihad are bloody thieves, murderers and rapists of the Maluku people, expel this bloody Javanese mailing list from the soil of Maluku.'

72 Figures as of 21 May 2004.

73 The e-group was originally at <www.egroups.com/group/ambon> when accessed on 3 August 2000, but had migrated to <http://groups.yahoo.com/group/ambon> when accessed on 15 November 2003, presumably because eGroups merged with Yahoo! in August 2000 (see <http://groups.yahoo.com/local/news.html>, accessed 17 November 2003). The list administrator announced the change in a posting on 1 September 2000. The homepage of the e-group gives the formal name as 'ambon.COM' but, to post, one sends to <ambon@yahoogroups.com>. For consistency, we refer to it simply as the 'ambon' e-group.

74 For details of the IID, see their homepage <www.iidnet.org>. The IID's Information and Communication Coordinator, Victor Sapar, was the dominant poster.

75 The 1999 figure is given in <http://groups.yahoo.com/group/ambon/message/2373> (accessed 20 November 2003), while that month we noted the August 2000 figure.

76 It was not possible to read all of the group's more than 32,771 messages (as of 21 May 2004), so we have both skimmed through various months each year as well as looked in more depth at selected weeks, so as to survey the general trend of the list and examine its specific content at key times.

77 Wattimena's personal details are from <www.tagnet.org/kadnet/kadnet/redaksi/wattimena_pc.html> (accessed 19 November 2003).

78 Ambon Berdarah On-Line includes a cross on the top left of the screen as an indication of its religious persuasion.

79 Elya Geeraldy Muskitta's homepage is at: <www.geocities.com/SouthBeach/5586> (accessed 19 November 2003). He appears also to have been involved in the 'Maluku Outreach Foundation' in Los Angeles in 2000: see <www.indonesiamedia.com/rubrik/localnews/localnews00june-pendukung.htm> (accessed 19 November 2003). By May 2003, he appears to be back in Jakarta as Product Director of PT Sigma Cipta Caraka.

80 Federalism was an issue of considerable concern in outer islands of Indonesia such as Maluku, where that model was thought by many to be more suitable for a multi-ethnic, multi-religious state.

81 'tali_hulaleng', 'Tragedi Ketapang', 30 December 1998, available online at <www.egroups.com/message/ambon/123> (accessed 15 August 2000).

82 P.C. Wattimena, 'Natal dan Halal Bi Halal', 12 December 1998, available online at <www.egroups.com/message/ambon/112> (accessed 15 August 2000).

83 In July 2000, Mickey Soukotta also signed a 'Joint Human Rights Statement: Protect All People's Lives In Maluku', on behalf of the 'Moluccan Community USA' (available from the Web Archive: <http://web.archive.org/web/20020827102859/http://www.esib.org/pipermail/members/2000-July/000112.html>, accessed 19 November 2003).

84 In this context, 'bangsa' could be translated as 'nation, people, race'. See J.M. Echols and H. Shadily, *Kamus Indonesia-Inggris: An Indonesian–English Dictionary*, Gramedia, Jakarta, 1990, p. 49.

85 Mickey Soukotta, 'Salam Bakudapa', 1 January 1999, available online at <www.egroups.com/message/ambon/131> (accessed 15 August 2000).

86 The homepage of AMBONnet (<www.egroups.com/group/ambon>, accessed 3 August 2000) claims 194 messages for January 1999, but a counting of the actual messages in the archive (from no. 129 to no. 320) totals only 192.

87 Noes Souisa's homepage is <www.xs4all.nl/~noes/index.html> (accessed 19 November 2003).

88 'Mujizat', from UPT-Komputer UNPATTI, 29 January 1999 on <www.egroups.com/message/ambon/303>.

89 For example, <http://groups.yahoo.com/group/ambon/message/622> (accessed 19 November 2003).

90 See <http://groups.yahoo.com/group/ambon/message/363> (accessed 19 November 2003).

91 For details,See see postings in late May 1999, including <http://groups.yahoo.com/group/ambon/message/679> and <http://groups.yahoo.com/group/ambon/message/738> (both accessed 19 November 2003).

92 The original 3 June 1999 posting is: 'Saya baru saja join di milis ini, karena merasa tertarik dan merasa "part of the Ambon family". Tapi sangat terkejut menerima e-mail berikut ini. Apa yang sedang terjadi? Mengapa harus ada caci maki, amarah dan permusuhan? Bukankah kita semua adalah saudara (satu gandong)? Mohon penjelasan.' <http://groups.yahoo.com/group/ambon/message/806> (accessed 20 November 2003).

93 For Noce Wattimena's calming response of 2 June 1999 (which included tracers on Andarinyo's e-mail address), see <http://groups.yahoo.com/group/ambon/message/785> (accessed 19 November 2003).

94 <http://groups.yahoo.com/group/ambon/message/898>, dated 6 June 1999 (accessed 20 November 2003).

95 Statistics and information on the AMBONnet/Ambon.COM site were given initially on <www.egroups.com/group/ambon> (accessed 3 August 2000) and updated at <http://groups.yahoo.com/group/ambon> (accessed 24 May 2004).

96 See, for example, protest from 'aprilmorn' that the media did not cover the Church Legal Team's 27 May 1999 report on the clashes in Maluku during the early months of the year: see <http://groups.yahoo.com/group/ambon/message/1041>, posted 10 June 1999 (accessed 20 November 2003).

97 For example, <http://groups.yahoo.com/group/ambon/message/2058>, dated 28 July 1999 (accessed 20 November 2003), was one of the earliest personal postings on the strife, while <http://groups.yahoo.com/group/ambon/message/2083> forwards an on-site report from <harry@ambon.wasantara.net.id>.

98 See <http://groups.yahoo.com/group/ambon/message/2433>, dated 26 August 1999 (accessed 20 November 2003) and <http://groups.yahoo.com/group/ambon/message/2449>, posted 29 August (accessed 10 July 2004).

99 The 'Muslim Netters Association International', which appears to be the same organisation as the one referred to by 'zUlFaN K' was also involved in setting up the site <http://listen.to/Rustam-Kastor>, which sold online books by controversial Islamic militant Rustam Kastor (accessed 24 November 2003).

100 Translation from *Ambon Berdarah Babak III: Praktek Keji "The Moslem Cleansing" di Ambon* <http://groups.yahoo.com/group/ambon/message/4026>, dated 6 January 2000 (accessed 20 November 2003).

101 The original exchange was on FICA-net but was cross-posted to <http://groups.yahoo.com/group/ambon/message/238> (accessed 19 November 2003) by 'Samuel'.

102 Quotations from <http://groups.yahoo.com/group/ambon/message/514> (accessed 19 November 2003).

103 In these general comments, our method of determining whether a participant is either 'Christian' or 'Muslim' is an imprecise one. In some cases the content of the posting makes it evident; in the case of less active participants it may be gleaned from a 'name': for example, 'Peter' is assumed to be Christian, while 'Abdurrahman Al-Mujury' is assumed to be Muslim. While the 'ambon' archive indicates that there were 416 messages for 1–7 July 2000, we identified only 404 postings, four of which had 'no author'. Our percentages are based on the remaining 400.

104 According to a biographical entry on website of *Two Lines*, an annual print-based journal publishing original English translations of international literature, Chaumont Devin had published some translations in their spring 1995 edition. Devin 'was born aboard the U.S.S. "Chaumont", on March 15, 1942, after several narrow escapes from the advancing Japanese. His parents were missionaries to the Moluccan Islands, in what is now eastern Indonesia': <www.twolines.com/bios/devin.html> (accessed 17 November 2003). In addition, Chaumont Devin, <devil@lava.net>, has developed a 'theory of natural language and knowledge representation' he refers to a 'Panlingua'. The manuscript, described as 'mainly a synthesis of work in semantic networks and linguistics', appears on <www.strout.net/info/science/ai/panlingua/intro.html> (accessed 17 November 2003).

105 'devil' was actively soliciting funds on 'ambon' e-group to purchase weapons for the Christian forces in Maluku. Providing his actual name (Chaumont Devin) and his Honolulu postal address, he urged readers to send US$10 a month to support the cause, 'so that if we have weapons, we can finish off all the Muslims who are in Ambon so we can begin afresh with a new Maluku based on justice'. See 'Apa Tempo Hitu Rata?' on <www.egroups.com/message/ambon/8434> (accessed 19 August 2000).

106 'Moluccan "Christians" in California', posted by 'devil' on 1 July 2000, at <www.egroups.com/message/ambon/8417> (accessed 16 August 2000).

107 Original: 'Apakah server mereka tidak akan macet? Mau coba ka seeng? Ayo, jangan satu yang coba sendiri, tapi tunggu dulu sampai ada persetujuan umum baru katorang samua hantam satu kali dan jangan kasi banapas sampai puluh2 hari. Mau ka seeng?'

108 Septiaji Eko Nugroho ('adjie') posted 'Re:[Ambon] Su Pastiu Dusta2 Eslam ka Baloong?' on 3 July 2000, at <www.egroups.com/message/ambon/8563> (accessed 17 August 2000).

109 The two contrasting accounts of the Lebaran 1999 Muslim–Christian clashes in Ambon are given in K. van Dijk, *A Country in Despair: Indonesia between 1997 and 2000*, KITLV Press, Jakarta, 2001, pp. 385–6.

110 See <http://groups.yahoo.com/group/ambon/message/9069>, 13 July 2000> (accessed 20 November 2003).

111 See <http://groups.yahoo.com/group/ambon/message/9090>, 13 July 2000 (accessed 21 November 2003).

112 'zUlFaN K', for example, rails against 'rioters from the Christian RMS' in his posting on 2 July 2000, at <www.egroups.com/message/ambon/8466> (accessed 17 August 2000).

113 'Re: [Ambon] Seruan', posted from 'anandadesa' on 1 July 2000, at <www.egroups.com/message/ambon/8418> (accessed 17 August 2000). This is a reply to a call that same day from (Christian) Agnes Patti urging 'moluccan women [to] maintain the struggle and give the spirit of Moluccan nationalism to husbands and children'.

114 'Surat dari Medan perang Ambon', posted by 'anandadesa', 1 July 2000, at <www.egroups.com/message/ambon/8413> (accessed 17 August 2000).

115 The initial posting can be found at <www.egroups.com/message/ambon/8423> (accessed 17 August 2000) with the response from 'elha' at <www.egroups.com/message/ambon/8425> (accessed 19 August 2000).

116 Spyer, 'Fire Without Smoke and Other Phantoms of Ambon's Violence', p. 35.

117 Van Klinken, 'The Maluku Wars: Bringing Society Back In', p. 14.

118 See <http://groups.yahoo.com/group/ambon/message/13784>, 4 December 2000 (accessed 20 November 2003).

119 For example, his administrator's notice dated 27 November 2000 at <http://groups.yahoo.com/group/ambon/message/13665> (accessed 21 November 2003).

120 See, for example, Elya Muskitta's attack dated 4 December 2000, at <http://groups.yahoo.com/group/ambon/message/13772>, and the response the same day from 'anandadesa' (Helmi Wattimena), at <http://groups.yahoo.com/group/ambon/message/13785 (both accessed 21 November 2003).

121 Tekwani, 'The Tamil Diaspora, Tamil Militancy, and the Internet', p. 182.

122 The Indonesian name was 'Kawanua Advent se-Dunia'. Details are available at <www.tagnet.org/kadnet/kadnet/kadnet.html> (accessed 19 November 2003).

123 Helmi Wattimena also appears to use the formal given name 'Wilhelm'. (See 'Maluku' group postings number 591 (27 October 2001) and 592 (28 October 2001).

124 See <http://groups.yahoo.com/group/maluku/message/591> (accessed 17 November 2003). The document is a 13 May 2001 press release from the FKM-USA.

125 See <www.nunusaku.net/index.htm> (accessed 17 November 2003).

126 See e-mails from 'Dr. Usman F. Aminu' of the 'Accounts Department of Petroleum (Special) Trust Fund (PTF)' of Nigeria offering the recipient 30 per cent of an illicit $US30.3! (<http://groups.yahoo.com/group/maluku/message/626>, accessed 17 November 2003).

127 Our sample included postings from Nos. 19470 to 19495, accessed 21 November 2003.

128 See <http://groups.yahoo.com/group/ambon/message/19607>, 22 January 2002 (accessed 21 November 2003). The posting that triggered this response was <http://groups.yahoo.com/group/ambon/message/19592>, 21 January 2002 (accessed 21 November 2003).

129 In English in the original; syntax and spelling are unchanged: <http://groups.yahoo.com/group/ambon/message/19906>, 14 February 2002 (accessed 21 November 2003).

130 The 'subject' of the posting was: 'The FKM rejects the Javanese satanic conspiracy in Malino for Maluku' ('FKM Tolak Konspirasi Iblis Jawa di Malino untuk Maluku'), 2 March 2002, <http://groups.yahoo.com/group/ambon/message/20145> (accessed 21 November 2003).

131 See, for example, Ambon's postings from Nos. 19945 to 19959, all dated 15 February 2002.

132 *Areopagus* is Greek for 'hill of Ares', with Ares being the god of war. According to Greek mythology Ares' trial (and acquittal) for murder at Areopagus was regarded as the first judicial gathering ever: see <www.areopagus.net/areopagus.htm> (accessed 24 November 2003). Though the homepage indicated 64 postings for July 2003, details are given for only 63.

133 For example, <http://groups.yahoo.com/group/ambon/message/27748>, 30 July 2003 (accessed 24 November 2003).

134 For example, <http://groups.yahoo.com/group/ambon/message/27717>, 18 July 2003 (accessed 24 November 2003).

135 For example, 'Penjara Lowokwaru [Lowokwaru Jail] 1965/1966', at <http://groups.yahoo.com/group/ambon/message/27703>, 11 July 2003 (accessed 24 November 2003).

136 For example, a news report on Imam Samudra, one of the 'Bali bombers', was tagged 'Muslim Cockroach Can't Handle the "Truth"': <http://groups.yahoo.com/group/ambon/message/27703>, 9 July 2003 (accessed 24 November 2003).

137 For example, <http://groups.yahoo.com/group/ambon/message/27695>, 5 July 2003 (accessed 24 November 2003).

138 For example, <http://groups.yahoo.com/group/ambon/message/27745>, 30 July 2003 (accessed 24 November 2003). In addition, two members posted one message each: one a positive response to the Umar Said's posting of the memoir of a 1965 detainee, and the other a BBC report on the death of Saddam Hussein's sons.

139 B. Loader, 'The Governance of Cyberspace: Politics, Technology and Global Restructuring', in B. Loader (ed.), *The Governance of Cyberspace: Politics, Technology and Global Restructuring*, Routledge, London, 1997, pp. 1–19 . Quotation from p. 2 where Loader cites D. Haraway (1985) 'A Manifesto for Cyborgs: Science, Technology, and Socialist Feminism in the 1980s', *Socialist Review*, 80, pp. 65–107.

8 Conclusions and more questions

1 K. Sen and D.T. Hill, *Media, Culture and Politics in Indonesia*, Oxford University Press, Melbourne, 2000.
2 R. Williams, *Television: Technology and Cultural Form*, Fontana, London, 1974, p. 119.
3 Ibid., p. 119.
4 D. Murray, *Knowledge Machines: Language and Information in a Technological Society*, Longman, London and New York, 1995, p. 161, quoted in C. Mann and F. Stewart, *Internet Communication and Qualitative Research: A Handbook for Researching Online*, Sage, London, 2000, p. 39.
5 See, for instance, S. Gan, J. Gomez and U. Johannen (eds), *Asian Cyberactivism: Freedom of Expression and Media Censorship*, Friedrich Naumann Foundation, Bangkok, 2004, in which cyberactivists from Asia reflect on their own work, several intensely aware of the threat of government regulation.
6 See, for instance, Chia Siow Yue and J.J. Lim (eds), *Information Technology in Asia: New Development Paradigms*, Institute of Southeast Asian Studies, Singapore, 2002.
7 I. Kleden, 'Our Democratic Tug-of-war', *The Jakarta Post*, 9 August 2001, available online at <www.thejakartapost.com/detaileditorial.asp> (accessed 9 August, 2001).
8 J.T. Sidel, 'It Takes a Madrasah: Habermas Meets Bourdieu in Indonesia', *South East Asia Research*, 9:1, 2001, p. 114.
9 M. Castells, *The Power of Identity* (Vol. 2 of *The Information Age: Economy, Society and Culture*, Blackwell, Oxford, 1997), p. 352, quoted in B. Warf and J. Grimes, 'Counterhegemonic Discourses and the Internet', *Geographical Review*, 87:2, April 1997, pp. 259–74: located via a search of <http://global.umi.com> (accessed 8 March 2001).

Select bibliography

Indonesian names: Indonesians may be known by single (Sukarno, for example) or multiple names (for example, Onno W. Purbo). The final (or sole) common name has been used for bibliographical purposes (although the individual may not ordinarily be known by that name in Indonesia).

Aarons, M. and R. Domm, *East Timor: A Western Made Tragedy*, New Left Book Club, Sydney, 1992.

Adam, A.B., *The Vernacular Press and the Emergence of Modern Indonesian Consciousness (1855–1913)*, Southeast Asia Program, Cornell University, Ithaca, 1995.

Aditjondro, G.J., *Menyongsong Matahari Terbit di Puncak Ramelau: Dampak Pendudukan Timor Lorosa'e dan Munculnya Gerakan Pro-Timor Lorosa'e di Indonesia*, Yayasan HAK & Fortilos, Jakarta, 2000.

——, 'Guns, Pamphlets and Handie-Talkies: How the Military Exploited Local Ethno-religious Tensions in Maluku to Preserve their Political and Economic Privileges', in I. Wessel and G. Wimhöfer (eds), *Violence in Indonesia*, Abera-Verlag, Hamburg, 2001, pp. 100–28.

Adrianto, F., A.A. Hatanto, S. Shahab, E.S. Siahaan and F. Lamak, 'Terus Menangguk Rupiah di Saat yang Lain Susah', *Warta Ekonomi*, 22:12, 4 June 2001, pp. 10–16.

—— , S. Shahab, M. Ihsan and E.S. Siahaan, 'Menit-menit yang Menghasilkan Duit', *Warta Ekonomi*, 22:12, 4 June 2001, pp. 17–19.

Agustine, H., 'Internet Replaces Bamboo Spears in Fight for Freedom', *The Jakarta Post*, 8 June 1998, p. 7.

Ahyani, M.M.I, 'Internet Fails to Woo Most Political Parties', *The Jakarta Post*, 29 May 1999, available online at <www.TheJakartaPost.com> (accessed 21 August 1999).

Allen, B., and A. Loubert, 'History and Identity: Moluccans in the Netherlands', *The Hague Legal Capital*, 25 June 2003, available online at <www.geocities.com/lawamena_tabaos/junenews/hague25062003a.htm> (accessed 13 November 2003).

Amnesty International, 'Annual Report 2000: Indonesia and East Timor', available online at <www.web.amnesty.org/web/ar2000web.nsf/countries/a8b2dcbe3c6cac35802568f200552930?OpenDocument> (accessed 24 September 2001).

Anderson, B., *Java in a Time of Revolution*, Cornell University Press, Ithaca, 1972.

Anderson, B.R., 'Old States, New Societies: Indonesia's New Order in Comparative Historical Perspective', *Journal of Asian Studies*, 42:3, May 1983, pp. 477–96.

——, *Imagined Communities: Reflections on the Origin and Spread of Nationalism*, Verso, London and New York, 1991.

Andoko, A., 'Tempat bertemunya pedagang dan pembeli', *Kompas*, 17 August 1996, p. 21.

——, 'Internet: Ajang baru kampanye para OPP', *Kompas*, 2 May 1997.

Ang, I., *Watching Dallas: Soap Opera and the Melodramatic Imagination*, Methuen, London and New York, 1985.

Antlöv, H., 'Not Enough Politics! Power, Participation and the New Democratic Polity in Indonesia', in E. Aspinall and G. Fealy (eds), *Local Power and Politics in Indonesia: Decentralisation & Democratisation*, ISEAS, Singapore, 2003, pp. 72–86.

——, 'Introduction', in H. Antlöv and S. Cederroth, *Elections in Indonesia: The New Order and Beyond*, RoutledgeCurzon, London, 2004, pp. 1–17.

Antlöv, H. and S. Cederroth, *Elections in Indonesia: The New Order and Beyond*, RoutledgeCurzon, London, 2004.

Appadurai, A., 'Disjuncture and Difference in the Global Cultural Economy', *Public Culture*, 2, 1990, pp. 1–24.

APJII (Asosiasi Penyedia Jasa Internet Indonesia), 'D. Profile', available online at <www/apjii.or.id'> (accessed 17 May 1997).

——, I2BC (Indonesia Internet Business Community) and Accenture, *Indonesia Cyber Industry & Market*, PT Elex Media Komputindo, Jakarta, 2001.

Ariwibowo, A.A., A. Jauhari, B. Setiawanto, H. Prihatna, R. Moechtar, S.H. Purnomojoyo and S. Muryono, *Pemilu 1997: Antara Fenomena Kampanye Dialogis & Mega-Bintang*, PT Penakencana, Jakarta, 1997.

Arvianh, T. and S. Widodo, 'M-Web PHK 40 Orang Karyawan', *detik.com*, 5 July 2002, available online at <www.detikinet.com/berita/2002/07/05/20020705–110802.shtml> (accessed 28 July 2003).

Aspinall, E., 'Opposition and Elite Conflict in the Fall of Soeharto', in G. Forrester and R.J. May (eds), *The Fall of Soeharto*, Crawford House Publishing, Bathurst, 1998, pp. 130–53.

Aspinall, E. and G. Fealy (eds) *Local Power and Politics in Indonesia: Decentralisation & Democratisation*, ISEAS, Singapore, 2003.

Aspinall, E., G. van Klinken and H. Feith (eds), *The Last Days of President Suharto*, Monash Asia Institute, Clayton, 1999.

Atkins, W., *Satellite Television and State Power in Southeast Asia: New Issues in Discourse and Control*, Centre for Asian Communication, Media and Cultural Studies, Edith Cowan University, Perth, 1995.

Atmakusumah, *Kebebasan Pers dan Arus Informasi di Indonesia*, Lembaga Studi Pembangunan, Jakarta, 1981.

Aurora, L., 'Employees, Students Boost Internet Use Total to 8 Million', *The Jakarta Post*, 3 February 2004, available online at <www.thejakartapost.com> (accessed 3 February 2004).

Bachir, S., 'Bisnis Pers di Tengah Arus Globalisasi', *Kompas*, 10 February 1992.

Ball, D. and H. McDonald, *Death in Balibo, Lies in Canberra*, Allen & Unwin, St Leonards, 2000.

Barker, J.D., 'Telephony at the Limits of State Control: "Discourse Networks" in Indonesia', in C.J.W.-L. Lee (ed.), *Local Cultures and the 'New Asia': The State, Culture and Capitalism in Southeast Asia*, ISEAS, Singapore, 2002, pp. 158–83.

Baskoro, S.E., 'Peranan internet dalam Reformasi Indonesia', *Info Komputer Online*, June 1998, available online at <www.infokomputer.com/100798-l.shtml> (accessed 19 December 1998).

Basral, A.N., 'Ini Milik MacDougall', *Gatra*, 2 December 1995 (circulated on 28 November 1995).

Beal, T., 'The State of Internet Use in Asia', in K.C. Ho, R. Kluver and K.C.C. Yang (eds), *Asia.com: Asia Encounters the Internet*, RoutledgeCurzon, London, 2003, pp. 23–43.

Bell, D. and B. Kennedy (eds), *The Cybercultures Reader*, Routledge, London and New York, 2000.

Bhakti, I.N., 'Chronology of Events Leading to the Fall of President Soeharto', in G. Forrester and R.J. May (eds), *The Fall of Soeharto*, Crawford House Publishing, Bathurst, 1998, pp. 239–45.

Bourchier, D. and V. Hadiz (eds), *Indonesian Politics And Society: A Reader*, Routledge, London, 2003.

Brady, C. and G. Rowell, 'Email to Dili – You Have Got to Be Joking!', available online at <www.caa.org.au/groups/IT/dili> (accessed 13 March 2001).

Bräuchler, B., 'Cyberidentities at War: Religion, Identity, and the Internet in the Moluccan Conflict', *Indonesia*, 75 (April), 2003, pp. 123–51.

Bubandt, N., 'Malukan Apocalypse: Themes in the Dynamics of Violence in Eastern Indonesia', in I. Wessel and G. Wimhöfer (eds), *Violence in Indonesia*, Abera-Verlag, Hamburg, 2001, pp. 228–53.

Budiman, A., B. Hatley and D. Kingsbury, 'Introduction', in A.Budiman, B. Hatley and D. Kingsbury (eds), *Reformasi: Crisis and Change in Indonesia*, Monash Asia Institute, Clayton, 1999, pp. i–viii.

Cahyono, H., M. Nurhasim, S. Nuryani and S. Yanuarti, 'A Portrait of Violations in Indonesia's 1999 General Election: A Summary of Monitoring Results from Eight Monitored Regions', unpublished report, YIPIKA (Yayasan Penguatan Partisipasi, Inisiatif dan Kemitraan Masyarakat Indonesia, Indonesian Foundation to Strengthen Civil Society's Participation, Partnership and Initiatives), Jakarta, May 2000.

Carstensen, J., 'Internet Radio', *Whole Earth*, spring 2000, p. 89, located via <http://web2.infotrac.galegroup.com/itw> (accessed 9 March 2001).

Castells, M., *The Rise of the Network Society*, Blackwell, Oxford, 1997.

——, 'Epilogue: Informationalism and the Network Society' (pp. 155–78), in P. Himanen, *The Hacker Ethic and the Spirit of the Information Age*, Secker & Warburg, London, 2001.

CastleAsia, 'SMEs and E-Commerce', Report prepared for the Asia Foundation, January 2002, available online at <www.asiafoundation.org/pdf/ID-SME-ecommerce-study–6–02.pdf> (accessed 30 September 2002).

Centre for ICT Studies – ICT Watch with Pegasus and USAID, *Kondisi Industri Warnet di Indonesia*, September 2003, available online at <www.indopubs.com/inco.html>.

Chauvel, R., *Nationalists, Soldiers and Separatists: The Ambonese Islands from Colonialism to Revolt, 1880–1950*, KITLV Press, Leiden, 1990.

Chia Siow Yue and J.J. Lim (eds), *Information Technology in Asia: New Development Paradigms*, Institute of Southeast Asian Studies, Singapore, 2002.

Chipperfield, M., 'Keeping the Issue Alive', in L. Taudevin and J. Lee (eds), *East Timor: Making Amends? Analysing Australia's Role in Reconstructing East Timor*, Otford Press, Sydney, 2000, pp. 145–7.

Connole, B., 'Irony in the Pacific for Long-distance Diplomat', *The Australian*, 26 June 2000, available online at <http://etan.org/et2000b/june/25–30/26irony.htm> (accessed 10 March 2001).

Couldry, N. and J. Curran (eds), *Contesting Media Power: Alternative Media in a Networked World*, Rowman & Littlefield, Lanham, 2003.

Craddock, A. and B. Lintner, 'Indonesia's Net War', *Wired News*, dated 29 May 1998, available online at <www.wired.com/news/politics/0,1283,12609,00.html> (accessed 17 September 2003).

Cribb, R., 'Problems in the Historiography of the Killings in Indonesia', in R. Cribb (ed.), *The Indonesian Killings, 1965–1966: Studies from Java and Bali*, Centre of Southeast Asian Studies, Monash University, Melbourne, 1990.

—— , *Historical Dictionary of Indonesia*, The Scarecrow Press, Metuchen & London, 1992.

Cristalis, I., *Bitter Dawn: East Timor, a People's Story*, Zed Press, London, 2002.

Crouch, H.,'Political Update 2002: Megawati's Holding Operation', in E. Aspinall and G. Fealy (eds), *Local Power and Politics in Indonesia: Decentralisation & Democratisation*, ISEAS, Singapore, 2003, pp. 15–34.

Crouch, H. and H. Hill (eds), *Indonesia Assessment 1992: Political Perspectives on the 1990s*, Political and Social Change Monograph No. 17, ANU, Canberra, 1992.

CyberAtlas, 'The Emerging 20 Nations' available online at <http://cyberatlas.Internet.com/ big_pictur ... graphics/print/0,1323,5911_150661,00.html> (accessed 5 September 1999).

D'Costa, A.P., 'Catching Up and Falling Behind: Inequality, IT, and the Asian Diaspora', in K.C. Ho, R. Kluver and K.C.C. Yang (eds), *Asia.com: Asia Encounters the Internet*, RoutledgeCurzon, London, 2003, pp. 44–66.

Denning, D.E., 'Activism, Hacktivism, and Cyberterrorism: The Internet as a Tool for Influencing Foreign Policy', Georgetown University, Washington DC, 2000, available online at <www.nautilus.org/info-policy/workshop/papers/denning.html> (accessed 15 March 2001).

Dhakidae, D., 'The State, the Rise of Capital and the Fall of Political Journalism: Political Economy of the Indonesian News Industry', unpublished doctoral dissertation, Cornell University, Ithaca, 1991.

Djiwandono, J.S., 'The Rupiah – One Year After Its Float', in G. Forrester (ed.), *Post-Soeharto Indonesia: Renewal or Chaos?*, Crawford House Publishing, Bathurst, 1999, pp. 144–52.

Donny, B.U., *Fakta dan Kondisi e-Government di Indonesia* (March 2004), available online at <www.ictwatch.com/data/index.htm> (accessed 27 March 2004).

Echols, J.M. and H. Shadily, *Kamus Indonesia-Inggris: An Indonesian–English Dictionary*, Gramedia, Jakarta, 1990.

Eklöf, S., 'The 1997 General Election in Indonesia', *Asian Survey*, 37:12, December 1997, pp. 1181–96.

—— , *Indonesian Politics in Crisis: The Long Fall of Suharto 1996–98*, NIAS, Copenhagen, 1999.

Eldridge, P.J., *The Politics of Human Rights in Southeast Asia*, Routledge, London, 2002.

Elisawati, V., 'Perang internet', *SWA* (posted on <www.library.ohiou.edu/indopubs/1997/ 06/14/0002.html> on 14 June 1997; accessed 30 September 2003).

Ellis, A. and E. Yudhini, *Law on the General Election of the President and Vice-President passed by the DPR on 8 July 2003: A Short Guide*, National Democratic Institute for International Affairs (NDI), [Jakarta?], 2003, available online at <www.accessdemocracy.org/ library/1622_id_presidentialelectionPDF.pdf> (accessed 27 November 2003).

Ellis, A. and E. Yudhini, *Law on the Structure and Composition of the MPR, DPR, DPD, and DPRDs (Susduk Law): A Short Guide*, National Democratic Institute for International Affairs (NDI), [Jakarta?], 2003, available online at <www.accessdemocracy.org/ library/1621_id_lawstructurePDF.pdf> (accessed 27 November 2003).

Ellis, E., 'Asia Buzz: Making a Difference Connecting Nuns in East Timor to the Internet', *Time Asia*, 4 January 2001, available online at <http://etan.org/et2001a/january/01–06/ 04conn.htm> (accessed 10 March 2001).

Elson, R.E., *Suharto: A Political Biography*, Cambridge University Press, Cambridge, 2001.

Embassy of the United States of America, 'Indonesia Economic Trends 1999 – Signs of Life', available online at <www.usembassyjakarta.org/econ/trends99–2.html> (accessed 2 September 1999).

Eng, P., 'On-line Activists Step up Fight', *Bangkok Post*, 29 April 1998, available online at <www.geocities.com/absdf_au/articles/article2.html> (accessed 17 September 2003).

Eriyanto, *Media dan Konflik Ambon: Media, Berita, dan Kerusuhan Komunal di Ambon 1999–2002*, Kantor Berita Radio 68H, Jakarta, 2003.

Evans, K., 'Economic Update', in G. Forrester (ed.), *Post-Soeharto Indonesia: Renewal or Chaos?*, Crawford House Publishing, Bathurst, 1999, pp. 105–27.

Feith, H., 'East Timor: The Opening up, the Crackdown and the Possibility of a Durable Settlement', in H. Crouch and H. Hill (eds), *Indonesia Assessment 1992: Political Perspectives on the 1990s*, Political and Social Change Monograph No. 17, ANU, Canberra, 1992, pp. 63–80.

Ferdinand, P. (ed.), *The Internet, Democracy and Democratization*, Frank Cass, London, 2000.

Fischer, T., *Seven Days in East Timor: Ballot and Bullets*, Allen & Unwin, Sydney 2000.

Forrester, G. (ed.), *Post-Soeharto Indonesia: Renewal or Chaos?*, Crawford House Publishing, Bathurst, 1999.

Forrester, G. and R.J. May (eds), *The Fall of Soeharto*, Crawford House Publishing, Bathurst, 1998.

Fox, J.J. and D.B. Soares (eds), *Out of the Ashes: Destruction and Reconstruction of East Timor*, Crawford House Publishing, Adelaide, 2000.

Freney, D., *A Map of Days: Life on the Left*, William Heinemann Australia, Melbourne 1991.

Friedland, L.A., 'Electronic Democracy and the New Citizenship', *Media, Culture and Society*, 18:2, April 1996, pp. 185–212.

Fukuda, C.M., 'Peace through Nonviolent Action: The East Timorese Resistance Movement's Strategy for Engagement', *Pacifica Review*, 12:1, February 2000, pp. 17–31.

Gaffar, A., *Javanese Votes: A Case Study of Election under a Hegemonic Party System*, Gadjah Mada University Press, Yogyakarta, 1992.

Gan, S., J. Gomez and U. Johannen (eds), *Asian Cyberactivism: Freedom of Expression and Media Censorship*, Friedrich Naumann Foundation, Bangkok, 2004.

Gandy, O., *The Panoptic Society*, Westview Press, Boulder, 1994.

Gomes, D., 'Resistance: Twenty Years of Struggle Supported by Young East Timorese', in ETRA, *It's Time to Lead the Way*, ETRA, Collingwood, 1996, pp. 115–20.

Goonasekera, A. and D. Holaday (eds), *Asian Communication Handbook*, Asian Mass Communication Research and Information Centre, Singapore, 1993.

Grant, J., 'Guerilla Hackers take on Military,' *South China Morning Post*, 3 May 1997, available online at <www.infowar.com/hacker/hackza.html-ssi> (accessed 15 March 2001).

Greenlees, D. and R. Garran, *Deliverance: The Inside Story of East Timor's Fight for Freedom*, Allen & Unwin, Sydney, 2002.

Guerin, B., 'Indonesia Faces Long Wait for a Cyber-economy', *Asia Times Online*, <www.atimes.com/se-asia> (accessed 15 February 2001).

Gunawan, T.S., 'Internet Mania Hits Indonesia', *The Jakarta Post*, 12 July 1995, p. 1.

Gusmão, K.S. (with R. Lennox), *A Woman of Independence: A Story of Love and the Birth of a New Nation*, Pan Macmillan Australia, Sydney, 2003.

Habermas, J., *The Structural Transformation of the Public Sphere*, Polity, Cambridge, 1989.

Hadiz, V.R., 'Reorganizing Political Power in Indonesia: A Reconsideration of So-called "Democratic Transitions"', *The Pacific Review*, 16:4, 2003, pp. 591–611.

Hague, B.N. and B.D. Loader (eds), *Digital Democracy: Discourse and Decision Making in the Information Age*, Routledge, London and New York, 1999.

Hale, M., J. Musso and C. Weare, 'Developing Digital Democracy: Evidence from Californian Municipal Web Pages', in B.N. Hague and B.D. Loader (eds), *Digital Democracy: Discourse and Decision Making in the Information Age*, Routledge, London and New York, 1999, pp. 96–115.

Hall, S., 'Coding and Decoding in the Television Discourse', in S. Hall *et al.* (eds), *Culture, Media, Language*, Hutchinson, London, 1980.

Hanazaki, Y., *Pers Terjebak*, Institut Studi Arus Informasi, Jakarta, 1998 (Indonesian translation by Danang Kukuh Wardoyo and Tim Cipinang of 'The Indonesian Press in the Era of Keterbukaan: A Force for Democratization', doctoral dissertation, Monash University, 1996).

Harmon, A., 'Hacktivists of All Persuasions Take their Struggle to the Web', available online at <www.kaotik.org/98/nytimes1.html> (accessed 15 March 2001).

Harsono, A., 'Indonesia: From Mainstream to Alternative Media', *First Monday*, 1996, available online at <www.firstmonday.dk/issues/issue3/harsono> (accessed 30 August 2003).

—— , 'Journalists' Use of the Internet Bubbled up from Underground', *Nieman Reports*, 54:4, winter 2000, pp. 74–6.

Harvey, P.W., 'Bisnis Warung Internet di Malang dan Blitar', unpublished field-study report, Australian Consortium for 'In-Country' Indonesian Studies (ACICIS), Perth, [2000].

Hasan, N.,'Faith and Politics: The Rise of the Laskar Jihad in the Era of Transition in Indonesia', *Indonesia*, 73, April 2002, pp. 145–69.

Hayes, S., 'Push to Give Timor Control over Domain', *The Australian*, 13 February 2001, p. 42.

Haywood, T., 'Global Networks and the Myth of Equality: Trickle Down or Trickle Away', in B. Loader (ed.), *Cyberspace Divide: Equality, Agency and Policy in the Information Society*, Routledge, London and New York, 1998, pp. 19–34.

Hederman, W., 'Internet Recognition for East Timor', *The Irish Times*, 6 December 1997, available online at <www.freedom.tp/struggle.htm> (accessed 7 September 1999).

Hendaru, D., R. Erawan, E.S. Siahaan and A.A. Hatanto, 'Warnet pun Disikat', *Warta Ekonomi*, 44:13, 5 November 2001, pp. 38–43.

Hewison, K. and G. Rodan, 'The Decline of the Left in Southeast Asia', in R. Miliband and L. Panitch (eds), *Socialist Register*, Merlin Press, London, 1994, pp. 235–40.

Hidayat, D.N., E. Gazali, H. Suwardi and S.K. Ishadi (eds), *Pers dalam 'Revolusi Mei' Runtuhnya Sebuah Hegemoni*, Gramedia Pustaka Utama, Jakarta, 2000.

Hill, D.T., *The Press in New Order Indonesia*, University of Western Australia Press/ Murdoch Asia Research Centre, Perth, 1994.

—— , 'East Timor and the Internet: Global Political Leverage in/on Indonesia', *Indonesia*, 73, April 2002, pp. 25–51.

—— and K. Sen, 'Wiring the Warung to Global Gateways: The Internet in Indonesia', *Indonesia*, 63, April 1997, pp. 67–89.

Hill, H., 'Introduction', in H. Hill and Thee Kian Wie (eds), *Indonesia's Technological Challenge*, Institute of Southeast Asian Studies, Singapore, 1998, pp. 1–54.

—— , 'The Indonesian Economy: The Strange and Sudden Death of a Tiger', in G. Forrester and R.J. May (eds), *The Fall of Soeharto*, Crawford House Publishing, Bathurst, 1998, pp. 93–103.

Hill, H. and Thee Kian Wie (eds), *Indonesia's Technological Challenge*, Institute of Southeast Asian Studies, Singapore, 1998.

Himanen, P., *The Hacker Ethic and the Spirit of the Information Age*, Secker & Warburg, London, 2001.

Ho, K.C., R. Kluver and K.C.C. Yang (eds), *Asia.com: Asia Encounters the Internet*, RoutledgeCurzon, London, 2003.

Human Rights Watch, *Indonesia: The Violence in Ambon* (March 1999) available online at <www.hrw.org.reports/1999/ambon/amron–02.htm> (accessed 5 November 2003).

——, *Moluccan Islands: Communal Violence in Indonesia: Recommendations*, available online at <www.hrw.org/press/2000/06/indo-back0629.htm> (accessed 5 November 2003).

Huntley, W. and P. Hayes, 'East Timor and Asian Security', in R. Tanter, M. Selden and S. R. Shalom (eds), *Bitter Flowers, Sweet Flowers: East Timor, Indonesia, and the World Community*, Pluto Press, Sydney, 2001, pp. 173–88.

Ida Sudoyo and Associates and PT Narada Komunikatama,'Golkar Website' unpublished report, prepared by Ida Sudoyo & Associates and PT Narada Komunikatama, Jakarta, 12 June 1999.

Idris, N. and M.D. Ibrahim, 'Communication Scene of Indonesia', in A. Goonasekera and D. Holaday (eds), *Asian Communication Handbook*, Asian Mass Communication Research and Information Centre, Singapore, 1993.

Ihsan, M., F. Adrianto, S. Shahab and A.A. Hatanto, 'Akan Beraksi pada Tahun ini', *Warta Ekonomi*, 22:12, 4 June 2001, pp. 20–1.

Ikawati, Y., 'Dr Joseph FP Luhukay: Perintis internet di Indonesia', *Kompas*, 30 December 1995, p. 20.

Indonesian General Election Commission, *Analyzing Indonesian Election 1999* [sic], [Komisi Pemilihan Umum, Jakarta], 2001.

International Commission of Jurists, *Report on the Trial of Xanana Gusmão in Dili, East Timor*, ICJ, Geneva, 1993.

International Crisis Group, *Indonesia's Maluku Crisis: The Issues*, ICG Indonesia Briefing, Jakarta/Brussels, 19 July 2000, available online at <www.crisisweb.org//library/documents/report_archive/A400113_19072000.pdf> (accessed 11 November 2003).

International Crisis Group, *Indonesia: The Search for Peace in Maluku*, ICG, Jakarta/Brussels, 8 February 2002, <www.intl-crisis-group.org/projects/asia/indonesia/reports/A400544_08022002.pdf> (accessed 3 November 2003).

Jensen, K.B., 'Conclusion', in K.B. Jensen (ed.), *News of the World: World Cultures Look at Television News*, Routledge, London, 1998.

Johnson, C., 'Interview: Horta Sees Internet Future for E.Timor [sic]', 13 February 2000, available online at <http://etan.org/et2000a/february/13–19/13interv.htm> (accessed 10 March 2001).

Jones, G. (ed.), *Australia in its Asian Context*, Academy of the Social Sciences in Australia Canberra, Occasional Paper No. 1, 1996.

Kalathil, S. and T.C. Boas, *Open Networks, Closed Regimes: The Impact of the Internet on Authoritarian Rule*, Carnegie Endowment for International Peace, Washington, 2003.

Kennedy, A.J., *The Rough Guide to the Internet*, Rough Guides, London, 2000.

King, D.Y., 'The 1999 Electoral Reforms in Indonesia: Debate, Design and Implementation', *Southeast Asian Journal of Social Science*, 28:2, 2000, pp. 89–110.

Kingsbury, D., *The Politics of Indonesia*, Oxford University Press, Melbourne, 2002.

Kitley, P., *Television, Nation and Culture in Indonesia*, Ohio University Press, Athens, 2000.

Kleden, I., 'Our Democratic Tug-of-war', *The Jakarta Post*, 9 August 2001, available online at <www.thejakartapost.com/detaileditorial .asp> (accessed 9 August 2001).

Kotler, P., *Marketing Management*, Prentice Hall, Englewood Cliffs, 2000.

KPU, 'Laporan: Tim Verifikasi System Komputer KPU (Tim 4)', unpublished report, KPU, Jakarta, 25 July 1999.

——, 'Tugas dan fungsi Sekretariat Umum Komisi Pemilihan Umum', unpublished report, Komisi Pemilihan Umum, Jakarta, April 2001.

Kuncoro, J., 'Internet: Demi Teknologi Atau Informasi?' *Media Indonesia*, 25 July 1996, p. 14.

Lee, C.J.W.-L. (ed.), *Local Cultures and the 'New Asia': The State, Culture and Capitalism in Southeast Asia*, ISEAS, Singapore, 2002.

Legard, D., 'Cyberwar Threatens Indonesia', *The Standard*, 19 August 1999, available online at <www.thestandard.com/article/article_print/0,1153,5962,00.html> (accessed 29 March 2001).

Leibes, T. and E. Katz, *The Export of Meaning: Cross-cultural Readings of Dallas*, Oxford University Press, New York, 1990.

Lev, D.S. and R. McVey (eds), *Making Indonesia: Essays on Modern Indonesia in Honor of George McT. Kahin*, Studies on Southeast Asia, Ithaca, 1996.

Lim, M., 'The Internet, Social Networks, and Reform in Indonesia', in N. Couldry and J. Curran (eds), *Contesting Media Power: Alternative Media in a Networked World*, Rowman & Littlefield, Lanham, 2003, pp. 273–88.

Lindsay, J., 'Making Waves: Private Radio and Local Identities in Indonesia', *Indonesia*, 64, October 1997, pp. 105–23.

Locke, T., 'Participation, Inclusion, Exclusion and Netactivism: How the Internet Invents New Forms of Democratic Activity', in B.N. Hague and B.D. Loader (eds), *Digital Democracy: Discourse and Decision Making in the Information Age*, Routledge, London and New York, 1999, pp. 211–21.

Lloyd, G.J., 'The Diplomacy on East Timor: Indonesia, the United Nations and the International Community', in J.J. Fox and D.B. Soares (eds), *Out of the Ashes: Destruction and Reconstruction of East Timor*, Crawford House Publishing, Adelaide, 2000.

Mann, C. and F. Stewart, *Internet Communication and Qualitative Research: A Handbook for Researching Online*, Sage, London, 2000.

Marcus, D.L., 'Indonesia Revolt was Net driven', *Boston Globe*, 23 May 1998, reproduced in E. Aspinall, G. van Klinken and H. Feith (eds), *The Last Days of President Suharto*, Monash Asia Institute, Clayton, 1999, pp. 73–5.

Martinkus, J., *A Dirty Little War*, Random House Australia, Sydney, 2001.

Ma'shun, S., *KPU dan Kontroversi Pemilu 1999*, Pustaka Indonesia Satu, Jakarta 2001.

May, W. (ed.), *Documents on Australian Foreign Policy: Australia and the Indonesian Incorporation of Portuguese Timor, 1974–1976*, Department of Foreign Affairs and Trade & Melbourne University Press, Melbourne, 2000.

McBeth, J., D. Murphy and M. Cohen, 'Free at last', *Far Eastern Economic Review*, 17 June 1999, reprinted in Indonesian General Election Commission, *Analyzing Indonesian Election 1999* [sic], [Jakarta: Komisi Pemilihan Umum], 2001, pp. 161–9.

McCargo, D., *Media and Politics in Pacific Asia*, RoutledgeCurzon, London, 2003.

McChesney, R.W., *Rich Media, Poor Democracy: Communication Policy in Dubious Times*, University of Illinois Press, Urbana, 1999.

McDaniel, D.O., *Broadcasting in the Malay World: Radio, Television, and Video in Brunei, Indonesia, Malaysia, and Singapore*, Ablex, Norwood, 1994.

MacDougall, J.A., 'A Brief History of The Apakabar List', available online at <www.library.ohiou.edu/indopubs/briefhistory.html> (accessed 29 September 2003).

McWilliams, B., 'Irish Provider Blames Failure on Other ISPs', available online at <www.internetnews.com/isp-news/print/0,1089,8_63651,00.html> (accessed 5 September 1999).

Meeks, B., 'No Justice, No Peace', *Association for Computing Machinery. Communications of the ACM*, 41:2, February 1998, pp. 17–19, located via a search of <http://global.umi.com> (accessed 8 March 2001).

Menayang, V., B. Nugroho and D. Listiorini, 'Pers Bawah Tanah: Media Sebagai Pergerakan Sosial', in Hidayat *et al.* (eds), *Pers dalam 'Revolusi Mei'*, pp. 275–97.

Miliband, R. and L. Panitch (eds), *Socialist Register*, Merlin Press, London, 1994.

Minges, M., *Kretek Internet: Indonesia Case Study*, International Telecommunication Union, Geneva, Switzerland, March 2002, p. 26, available online at <www.itu.int/ITU-D/ict/cs/indonesia/material/IDN%20CS.pdf> (accessed 1 August 2003).

Mok, Q., 'The Role of RENETIL: National Resistance of East Timorese Students', in East Timor Relief Association (ETRA), *It's Time to Lead the Way*, ETRA, Collingwood, 1996, pp. 106–8.

Moschovitis, C.J.P., H. Poole, T. Schuyler and T.M. Senft, *History of the Internet: A Chronology, 1843 to the Present*, ABC-CLIO, Santa Barbara, 1999.

Mulyadi, S., 'Violence under the Banner of Religion: The Case of Laskar Jihad and Laskar Kristus', *Studia Islamika*, 10:2, 2003, pp. 75–109.

Mulyanto, A.H., 'Cyberspace: ABRI dan "Perang Informasi"', *Republika Online*, 17 October 1996 (posted on INDONESIA-L).

Murdoch, L., 'Computer Chaos Threat to Jakarta', *Sydney Morning Herald*, 18 August 1999, p. 9.

——, 'Fury Over Computer Threat', *Sydney Morning Herald*, 20 August 1999, p. 8.

Murray, B., 'US Peacekeepers Use Net to Access Classified Network', *Government Computer News*, 19:11, 15 May 2000, p. 40, available online at <http://web2.infotrac.galegroup.com/itw> (accessed 9 March 2001).

Murray, D., *Knowledge Machines: Language and Information in a Technological Society*, Longman, London and New York, 1995.

NDI (National Democratic Institute), 'The Prospects for Democratic Elections in Indonesia: Pre-Election Report', unpublished report, National Democratic Institute for International Affairs, Jakarta, 28 May 1999.

Nugroho, L.E., 'Internet dan peranan komputer masa depan', *Kompas*, 3 April 1996, p. 17.

Oey Hong Lee, *Indonesian Government and Press During Guided Democracy*, Centre for Southeast Asian Studies, University of Hull/Inter Documentation Co, Zug, 1971.

O'Rourke, K., *Reformasi: The Struggle for Power in Post-Soeharto Indonesia*, Allen & Unwin, Sydney, 2002.

Pacific Rekanprima Research Team, 'Portrait of Internet Users in Indonesia – Findings of Quantitative Research of the Internet', in APJII, I2BC and Accenture, *Indonesia Cyber Industry & Market*, PT Elex Media Komputindo, Jakarta, 2001, pp. 159–67.

Pareanom, Y.A., I. Setiawan and D. Arjanto, 'Menjual Partai di Dunia Maya', *Tempo*, 22 March 1999, p. 54.

Parkinson, T., 'Ramos Horta: The Inside Story', *The Age*, 28 August 2000, available online at <http://etan.org/et2000c/august/27–31/28ramos.htm> (accessed 28 August 2001).

Parliament of the Commonwealth of Australia, *East Timor: Final Report of the Senate Foreign Affairs, Defence and Trade References Committee*, the Parliament of the Commonwealth of Australia, Canberra, December 2000.

Pattiradjawane, R.L., 'Demonstrasi di Jaringan Internet', *Kompas*, 7 February 1996, p. 16.

Perritt, H.H.,'Cyberspace and State Sovereignty', in *Journal of International Legal Studies*, summer 1997, available online at <www.kentlaw.edu/perritt/publications/3_J._INT%27L_L._STUD._155.htm> (accessed 21 November 2003).

Pinto, C., 'The Student Movement and the Independence Struggle in East Timor: An Interview', in R. Tanter, M. Selden and S.R. Shalom (eds), *Bitter Flowers, Sweet Flowers: East Timor, Indonesia, and the World Community*, Pluto Press, Sydney, 2001, pp. 31–41.

Pinto, C. and M. Jardine, *East Timor's Unfinished Struggle: Inside the Timorese Resistance*, South End Press, Boston, 1997.

Polla, G., B. Rahardjo, I.K. Hartono, S. Suyanto, K. Adi and S. Hengky, *Riset Domain CO.ID: Laporan Teknis Analisis tingkat kepuasan dan keamanan konsumen dalam upaya peningkatan penggunaan domain CO.ID*, Tim ccTLD-ID & APJII, Jakarta, 2002, available online at <www.apjii.or.id/dokumentasi> (accessed 28 July 2003).

Poster, M., *The Second Media Age*, Polity Press, Cambridge, 1995.

PRSSNI, *Kumpulan Peraturan tentang Radio Siaran Swasta di Indonesia: Tahun 1970 s/d 1992*, Sekretariat Pengurus Pusat, Persatuan Radio Siaran Swasta Nasional Indonesia [PRSSNI], [Jakarta], 1992.

——, *Petunjuk Radio Siaran Swasta Nasional '95*, Pengurus Pusat PRSSNI, Jakarta, 1995.

Purbo, O.W., 'Ceramah Ilmiah: Komunikasi internet dan Dunia Pendidikan', in *Duta Wacana menyongsong Budaya Teknologi*, Dies Natalis ke34, Duta Wacana Christian University, Yogyakarta, 31 October 1996, pp. 43–7.

——, 'An Experience in Empowering a Bottom-Up Indonesian Internet Infrastructure', unpublished paper delivered at the 'Mediating Human Rights and Democracy' Conference, Curtin University of Technology, Perth, February 2002.

——, 'Kekuatan Komunitas Indonesia di Dunia Maya', *Pantau*, 022:2, February 2002, pp. 14–19, available online at <www.pantau.or.id/txt/ss/08.html> (and subsequent pages) (accessed 23 May 2002).

——, *Digital Review of Indonesia*, electronic document (indonesia-digital-review–11–2002.zip) November 2002, located at <www.bogor.net/idkf>.

Pusat Pengkajian dan Penerapan Teknologi Informasi dan Elektronika (P3TIE), *Indikator Teknologi Informasi dan Komunikasi Tahun 2002*, Badan Pengkajian dan Penerapan Teknologi, Pusat Pengkajian dan Penerapan Teknologi Informasi dan Elektronika (P3TIE), Jakarta, 2002, available online at <www.apjii.or.id/dokumentasi/arsip/indikator/siti2002.pdf> (accessed 28 July 2003).

Putranto, B., 'Victim of Cyber Fever', *Indonesian Business*, October 2001, posted at <www.library.ohiou.edu/indopubs/2001/10/18/0071.html> on 18 October 2001, (accessed 29 September 2003).

Rahardjo, B., *Buku Pegangan Sistem Unix dan internet*, Open Pathways, Bellingham WA, 1994.

——, 'Indonesian Internet Statistics', unpublished report, PT INDOCISC & PT Insan Infonesia, version 1.7, 2001, available online at <www.insan.co.id/indonesia-internet-statistics.pdf> (accessed 3 September 2002).

Rai, A.S., 'India On-line: Electronic Bulletin Boards and the Construction of a Diasporic Hindu Identity', *Diaspora*, 4:1, 1995, pp. 31–57.

Ramage, D.E., *Politics in Indonesia: Democracy, Islam and the Ideology of Tolerance*, Routledge, London and New York, 1995.

Ramos-Horta, J., 'Site seeing', *Guardian*, 11 January 1999.

Randall, J., 'Of Cracks and Crackdowns: Five Translations of Recent Internet Postings', *Indonesia*, 62, October 1996, pp. 37–52.

Rao, M. (ed.), *News Media and New Media: The Asia-Pacific Internet Handbook*, Eastern Universities Press, London and Singapore, 2003.

Reporters without Borders, 'The Internet Under Surveillance', 2004 Report, available online at <www.rsf.org> (accessed 24 June 2004).

Rheingold, H., *The Virtual Community: Homesteading on the Electronic Frontier*, William Patrick, Reading, Massachusetts, 1993.

Ricklefs, M.C., *A History of Modern Indonesia since c. 1200*, Palgrave, Houndmills, 2001.

Ridwan, S.B., 'From TEMPO to TEMPO *Interaktif*: An Indonesian Media Scene Case Study', paper presented at Third Australian World Wide Web Conference, 5–9 July 1997, Southern Cross University, Lismore, Australia, <http://ausweb.scu.edu.au/aw97/papers/ridwan/paper.htm> (accessed 26 March 2004).

Robison, R., *Indonesia: The Rise of Capital*, Allen & Unwin, Sydney, 1986.

Robison, R. and V.R. Hadiz, *Reorganising Power in Indonesia: The Politics of Oligarchy in an Age of Markets*, RoutledgeCurzon, London, 2004.

Rodan, G., *Information Technology and Political Control in Singapore*, Working Paper No. 26, Japan Policy Research Institute, Cardiff, November 1996.

——, *Transparency and Authoritarian Rule in Southeast Asia: Singapore and Malaysia*, RoutledgeCurzon, London, 2004.

Rushkoff, D., *Media Virus: Hidden Agendas in Popular Culture*, Random House Australia, Sydney, 1994.

Ryan, A., *'Primary Responsibilities and Primary Risks': Australian Defence Force Participation in the International Force East Timor*, Land Warfare Studies Centre, Study Paper No. 304, Duntroon, 2000.

Samik-Ibrahim, R.M., 'Indonesia–102: The Internet Service Providers', <www.tjt.or.id/rms46/imho-eisp.html> (accessed 17 May 1997).

Scheiner, C., 'Grassroots in the Field – Observing the East Timor Consultation', in R. Tanter, M. Selden and S.R. Shalom (eds), *Bitter Flowers, Sweet Flowers: East Timor, Indonesia, and the World Community*, Pluto Press, Sydney, 2001, pp. 109–24.

Schiller, H.I., *Culture Inc.: The Corporate Takeover of Public Expression*, Oxford University Press, New York, 1989.

——, *Information Inequality*, Routledge, New York, 1996.

Schulze, K.E., 'Laskar Jihad and the Conflict in Ambon', *The Brown Journal of World Affairs*, spring 2002, 9:1, pp. 57–69, available online at <www.watsoninstitute.org/bjwa/archive/9.1/Indonesia/Schulze.pdf> (accessed 18 November 2003).

Sen, K., 'Australia, Asia and the Media', in G. Jones (ed.), *Australia in its Asian Context*, Academy of the Social Sciences in Australia, Canberra, Occasional Paper No. 1, 1996, pp. 44–9.

——, 'Indonesia: Media and the End of Authoritarian Rule', in M.E. Price, B. Rozumilowicz and S.G. Verhulst (eds), *Media Reform: Democratizing the Media, Democratizing the State*, Routledge, London and New York, 2002.

——, 'Radio Days: Media-politics in Indonesia', *The Pacific Review*, 16:4, 2003, pp. 573–89.

Sen, K. and D.T. Hill, *Media, Culture and Politics in Indonesia*, Oxford University Press, Melbourne, 2000.

Shiraishi, T., 'Rewiring the Indonesian State', in D.S. Lev and R. McVey (eds), *Making Indonesia: Essays on Modern Indonesia in Honor of George McT. Kahin*, Studies on Southeast Asia, Ithaca, 1996, pp. 164–179.

Sidel, J.T., 'It takes a Madrasah: Habermas meets Bourdieu in Indonesia', *South East Asia Research*, 9:1, 2001, pp. 109–22.

Smith, E.C., 'A History of Newspaper Suppression in Indonesia 1949–1965', doctoral dissertation, University of Iowa, 1969.

Solahudin *et al.*, *Ganasnya Satgas, Kejamnya Milisi Timtim: Laporan Kekerasan terhadap Jurnalis dan Media Massa Mei 1999-April 2000 [The Ferociousness of Satgas, The Cruelty of East Timor Militia – A Report on Violence towards Journalists and Mass Media May 1999 – April 2000]*, AJI Indonesia, Jakarta, 2000.

Spyer, P., 'Fire Without Smoke and Other Phantoms of Ambon's Violence: Media Effects, Agency, and the Work of Imagination', *Indonesia*, 74, October 2002, pp. 21–36.

Sreberny-Mohammadi, A., with K. Nordenstreng, R. Stevenson and F. Uboajha (eds), *Foreign News in the Media: International Reporting in 29 countries*, UNESCO, Paris, 1985.

Stanley, 'Penerbitan di Maluku Utara', unpublished typescript produced for the Office of Transitional Initiatives, United States Agency for International Development (USAID), Jakarta, dated 7 September 2001.

Stevensen, M. and A.-B. Albrectsen (eds), *Transition to Democracy: Report on the UNDP Technical Assistance Programme for the 1999 Indonesian General Elections*, United National Development Programme, Jakarta, 1999, available online at <www.un.or.id/ge/report.htm> (accessed 27 August 2002).

Subakti, B. and E. Katoppo (eds), *Media Scene 1995–1996 Indonesia: The Official Guide to Advertising Media in Indonesia*, PPPI, Jakarta, 1996.

Suryadinata, L., *Political Parties and the 1982 General Election in Indonesia*, Institute of Southeast Asian Studies, Singapore, 1982.

Suryo, R.M.R., 'Kemana setelah "apakabar" ditutup', *Media Indonesia*, 5 September 1996, p. 10.

Susanto, A., 'The Mass Communications System in Indonesia', in K.D. Jackson and L.W. Pye (eds), *Political Power and Communications in Indonesia*, University of California Press, Berkeley, 1978, pp. 229–58.

Tanter, R., M. Selden and S.R. Shalom, 'East Timor Faces the Future', in R. Tanter, M. Selden and S.R. Shalom (eds), *Bitter Flowers, Sweet Flowers: East Timor, Indonesia, and the World Community*, Pluto Press Australia, Sydney, 2001, pp. 243–72.

Tanter, R., M. Selden and S.R. Shalom (eds), *Bitter Flowers, Sweet Flowers: East Timor, Indonesia, and the World Community*, Pluto Press Australia, Sydney, 2001.

Taylor, J.G., *East Timor: The Price of Freedom*, Zed Books London and Pluto Press Australia, Annandale, 1999.

Tedjabayu, 'Indonesia: The Net as a Weapon', *Cybersociology*, 5, 1999, available online at <www.socio.demon.co.uk/magazine/5/5indonesia.html> (accessed 23 September 2003).

Tekwani, S., 'The Tamil Diaspora, Tamil Militancy, and the Internet', in K.C. Ho, R. Kluver and K.C.C. Yang (eds), *Asia.com: Asia Encounters the Internet*, RoutledgeCurzon, London, 2003, pp. 175–92.

Thee Kian Wie, 'Determinants of Indonesia's Industrial Technology Development', in H. Hill and Thee Kian Wie (eds), *Indonesia's Technological Challenge*, ISEAS, Singapore, 1998, pp. 117–35.

Thimbleby, H., 'Personal Boundaries/Global Stage', *First Monday* [online], 3:3, 1998, available online at <www.firstmonday.dk/issues/index.html>.

Tickle, S., 'Assessing the "Real Story" Behind Political Events in Indonesia: Email Discussion List Indonesia-L's News Coverage of the 27 July 1996 Jakarta Riots', unpublished Master of Arts thesis, School of Media & Journalism, Queensland University of Technology, Brisbane, 1997.

Tiffen, R., *Diplomatic Deceits: Government, Media and East Timor*, University of New South Wales Press, Sydney, 2001.

Torremendez, C., 'Situasi perhackingan indonesia [sic]', available online at <www.k-elektronik.org/ezine/situasi.htm> (accessed 27 March 2001).

Tunny, M.A. 'Megawati orders the weeding out of RMS', *The Jakarta Post*, 23 May 2004.

Turner, M., and O. Podger (with M. Sumardjono and W.K. Tirthayasa), *Decentralisation in Indonesia: Redesigning the State*, Asia Pacific Press at the Australian National University, Canberra, 2003.

van Dijk, K., *A Country in Despair: Indonesia between 1997 and 2000*, KITLV Press, Jakarta, 2001.

van Klinken, G., 'The Maluku Wars: Bringing Society Back In', *Indonesia*, 71 (April 2001), pp. 1–26.

Wagner, S., 'Survey of the Indonesian Electorate following the June 1999 Elections', International Foundation for Election Systems (IFES), unpublished 'final amended report', Jakarta, no date.

Ward, E. and Peter Carey, 'The East Timor Issue in the Context of EU–Indonesian Relations, 1975–99', *Indonesia and the Malay World*, 29:83, 2001, pp. 51–74.

Ward, K., *The 1971 Election in Indonesia: An East Java Case Study*, Monash Centre for Southeast Asian Studies, Clayton, 1974.

Warf, B. and J. Grimes, 'Counterhegemonic Discourses and the Internet', *Geographical Review*, 87:2, April 1997, pp. 259–74, located via a search of <http://global.umi.com> (accessed 8 March 2001).

Watts, D., 'Net users' free speech curbed', *The West Australian* (Perth), 21 January 1997, p. 22.

Weil, N., 'Indonesia Answers Hacker Threats', *The Standard*, 19 August 1999, available online at <www.thestandard.com/article/display/0,1151,5978,00.html> (accessed 29 March 2001).

Wessel, I. and G. Wimhöfer (eds), *Violence in Indonesia*, Abera-Verlag, Hamburg, 2001.

Williams, R., *Television: Technology and Cultural Form*, Fontana, London, 1974.

Winarno, P.M., 'Peran internet di tengah krisis', *Info Komputer Online*, 13 April 1998, available online at <www.infokomputer.com/analisa/130498–1.shtml> (accessed 19 December 1998).

Winters, J., 'Dampak Politis dari Sumber dan Teknologi Informasi Baru di Indonesia', in D.N. Hidayat, E. Gazali, H. Suwardi and S.K. Ishadi (eds), *Pers dalam 'Revolusi Mei' Runtuhnya Sebuah Hegemoni*, Gramedia Pustaka Utama, Jakarta, 2000, pp. 259–74.

Yap, J., 'The Internet and the Knowledge Economy: Charting a Course in Cyberspace', unpublished paper, Harvard Project for Asian and International Relations Conference, Beijing, August 2000.

Yayasan API, *Almanak Parpol Indonesia Pemilu '99*, Yayasan API, Jakarta, 1999.

——, *Panduan Parlemen Indonesia*, Yayasan API, Jakarta, 2001.

Yayasan SAGU, 'Maluku Report 18: Peristiwa Kerusuhan di Tobelo dan Galela Desember 1999', Yayasan SAGU (Solidaritas Anak Negeri Maluku), 31 December 1999, available online at <www.malra.org/posko/malra.php4?oid=229794> (accessed 18 November 2003).

Young, I.M., *Inclusion and Democracy*, Oxford University Press, Oxford, 2000.

Zubrycki, T., *The Diplomat* (film), produced by Sally Browning, Film Australia, Lindfield, 2000.

Index

Page numbers in *italics* indicate tables.

For Product Safety Concerns and Information please contact our EU representative GPSR@taylorandfrancis.com
Taylor & Francis Verlag GmbH, Kaufingerstraße 24, 80331 München, Germany

www.ingramcontent.com/pod-product-compliance
Ingram Content Group UK Ltd.
Pitfield, Milton Keynes, MK11 3LW, UK
UKHW020202200926
475702UK00004B/568
9780415285643